DATE DUE

NO 12 99		
DE 3'99		
DE 20'00		
DE 17'04		
FE 10 05		
MY 12 05		

DEMCO 38-296

AFRICAN-AMERICAN RELIGION::

::AFRICAN-AMERICAN RELIGION

INTERPRETIVE ESSAYS
IN HISTORY AND CULTURE

::EDITED BY

TIMOTHY E. FULOP AND
ALBERT J. RABOTEAU

Routledge
New York & London

Published in 1997 by

Routledge
29 West 35th Street
New York, NY 10001

Routledge
11 New Fetter Lane
London EC4P 4EE

Library of Congress Cataloging-in-Publication Data is
available from the Library of Congress.

CONTENTS::

ACKNOWLEDGMENTS::

We would like to thank Judith Weisenfeld, A. G. Miller, Bill Hutchinson, Yvonne Chireau, Ian Straker, Randall Burkett, David Hall, Evelyn Brooks Higginbotham, Preston Williams, David Wills, and John F. Wilson for their comments and reflections on this project. Thanks from Timothy to my wife, Jacklyn, and our children, Evan, Grace, Emma, and Lily for their love and laughter. Finally, we are grateful to the editors and staff at Routledge, and to all of our colleagues working in the field of African-American Religion.

In the preface to his *Souls of Black Folk*, W. E. B. Du Bois made the modest claim that his purpose was "to sketch, in vague, uncertain outline, the spiritual world in which ten thousand thousand Americans live and strive."[1] In reality, *The Souls of Black Folk*, in the words of Du Bois biographer David Levering Lewis, "was one of those events epochally dividing history into a before and after."[2] Until the publication of this book in 1903, the religious experiences of African Americans had found little expression outside of denominational publications and spirituals, but now the souls of black folk were finally to be given their long deserved due in a scholarly treatment designed for a broad audience. The pioneering work of Du Bois, however, stood practically alone until the publication of Carter G. Woodson's *History of the Negro Church* in 1921. In subsequent decades, the field of African-American religious history slowly expanded. Notable works included Benjamin E. Mays's and Joseph W. Nicholson's *The Negro's Church* (1933), Arthur H. Fauset's *Black Gods of the Metropolis* (1944), Ruby F. Johnston's *The Development of Negro Religion* (1954), Leonard L. Haynes's *The Negro Community within American Protestantism, 1619–1844* (1953), and Willis D. Weatherford's *American Churches and the Negro: An Historical Study from Early Slave Days to the Present* (1957).[3]

It was not until the last third of the twentieth century that the study of the religious experience of African Americans began to blossom and gain its rightful place in American scholarship. Propelled by the Civil Rights and Black Consciousness movements, the 1960s and 1970s—an arguably "golden era"— saw a vast increase in the visibility of African Americans in American history, especially American religious history, through the creation and growth of Black Studies programs, conferences, and study groups such as the Afro-American Religious History Group. Scholarly monographs and articles in African-American religious history began to proliferate. Studies by Clifton H. Johnson, John Blassingame, Sterling Stuckey, Albert J. Raboteau, Lawrence Levine, and Eugene Genovese demonstrated that the earlier presumed "invisibility" of slave religion was more a result of scholarly neglect than the paucity of slave sources.[4] Black church studies were revisited in E. Franklin Frazier's *The Negro Church* (1963), Joseph R. Washington, Jr.'s *Black Religion* (1964), and the anthology by Nelsen, Yokley, and Nelsen entitled *The Black Church in America* (1971).[5] This productive period also saw groundbreaking work on Black preaching, the Black Muslims, the sociology of African-American religion and the appearance of the first—and still only—bibliography, Ethel L. Williams and Clifton E. Brown's *Afro-American Religious Studies: A Comprehensive Bibliography with Locations in American Libraries* (1979).[6] The decade-by-decade expansion of contributions to the field has continued into the 1980s and 1990s with notable explorations into newer and more diverse areas of inquiry.[7]

Although the number of fine monographic studies in African-American religious history has been increasing, the field has yet to see a synoptic history. As David W. Wills, a noted historian of African-American religion at Amherst College, states, "The study of African-American religious history still lacks an obvious entry point for persons seeking an initial orientation to the field."[8] A fine collection of essays, C. Eric Lincoln's *The Black Experience in Religion*,[9] appeared over twenty years ago, but the field of African-American religion has expanded and evolved since that time. It is the hope of the editors that this collection of some of the finest and most salient essays in the field will fill a gap and help facilitate the study of this important and burgeoning area of interest.

The essays that follow are broadly organized chronologically while allowing for a focus on particular themes within and across time periods. This anthology seeks to be as inclusive as possible so that the reader will leave with a broad understanding of the religious experience of African Americans and its historical development. The selections cover a wide rage of topics, demonstrating the diversity of the field, and have been organized under the rubric of "Models for Studying African-American Religion," "Slave Religion," "The Black Church North of Slavery," "Emancipation, Mission, and Black Destiny," "Urbanization, New Religious Movements, and Social Activism," and "African-American Religious Culture." Subjects include the early cultural contact of Africans and Europeans, the relationship between slavery and an emerging Black Christianity, the mission of Black churches after emancipation, the place of Africa in African-American religious consciousness, women and ministry, the emergence of new religious movements and resurgence of traditional African religions. A brief bibliography follows each essay to assist the reader desiring to undertake further research. Although synoptic and comprehensive histories of African-American religion still need to be written, this anthology may serve scholars and students alike as a convenient and up-to-date entry point into the field.

In giving voice to recent work in this dynamic and evolving field, another intention of this collection is to point to new avenues of investigation and new interpretive directions. The areas of African-American Catholicism, the Black ecumenical experience, Sunni Islam among African Americans, historical study of Black churches and institutions, and the influence of African-American religion on European-American religion, especially Evangelicalism, are beginning to be addressed, but more work needs to be done.[10] Important interpretive issues that deserve attention include the relationship between social activism and scholarship, and whether one can even speak of *the* African-American religious experience in light of the diversity of African-American communities and religions, and the socially constructed nature of categories such as race, gender, and class. Such questions and the current scholarly ferment suggest that the scholarly examination of the religious experiences of African Americans will continue to flourish in the future.

NOTES

1. W. E. B. Du Bois, *The Souls of Black Folk* (Chicago: A.C. McClurg, 1903), v.
2. David Levering Lewis, *W. E. B. Du Bois: Biography of a Race, 1868–1919* (New York: Henry Holt, 1993), 277.
3. Carter G. Woodson, *History of the Negro Church* (Washington: Associated Publishers, 1921); Benjamin E. Mays and Joseph W. Nicholson, *The Negro's Church* (New York: Institute of Social and Religious Research, 1933); Arthur H. Fauset, *Black Gods of the Metropolis* (Philadelphia: University of Pennsylvania Press, 1944); Ruby F. Johnston, *The Development of Negro Religion* (New York: Philosophical Library, 1954); Leonard L. Haynes, *The Negro Community within American Protestantism, 1619–1844* (North Quincy, MA: Christopher Publishing House, 1953); and Willis D. Weatherford, *American Churches and the Negro: An Historical Study from Early Slave Days to the Present* (North Quincy, MA: Christopher Publishing House, 1957).
4. Clifton H. Johnson, ed., *God Struck Me Dead: Religious Conversion Experiences and Autobiographies of Ex-Slaves* (Philadelphia: Pilgrim Press, 1960); John Blassingame, *The Slave Community: Plantation Life in the Antebellum South* (New York: Oxford University Press, 1972); Sterling Stuckey, "Through the Prism of Folklore: The Black Ethos in Slavery," in *Black and White in American Culture*, edited by Jules Chametzky and Sidney Kaplan (New York: Viking Press, 1971), 172–91; Albert J. Raboteau, *Slave Religion: The "Invisible Institution" in the Antebellum South* (New York: Oxford University Press, 1978); Lawrence W. Levine, *Black Culture and Black Consciousness* (New York: Oxford University Press, 1977); and Eugene D. Genovese, *Roll, Jordan, Roll: The World the Slaves Made* (New York: Pantheon Books, 1974).
5. E. Franklin Frazier, *The Negro Church* (New York: Shocken Books, 1963); Joseph R. Washington, Jr., *Black Religion* (Boston: Beacon Press, 1964); and Hart M. Nelsen, Raytha L. Yokley and Anne K. Nelsen, eds., *The Black Church in America* (New York: Basic Books, 1971).

6. C. Eric Lincoln, *The Black Muslims in America* (Boston: Beacon Press, 1961); E.U. Essien-Udom, *Black Nationalism: A Search for an Identity in America* (Chicago: University of Chicago Press, 1963); and Ethel L. Williams and Clifton E. Brown, *Afro-American Religious Studies: A Comprehensive Bibliography with Locations in American Libraries* (Metuchen, NJ: Scarecrow Press, 1979).

7. For the decade of the 1980s, see Michael W. Harris, "African American Religious History in the 1980s: A Critical Review," *Religious Studies Review* 20:4 (October 1994): 263–75.

8. David W. Wills, "Bibliographical Essay: African-American Religious History," *Evangelical Studies Bulletin* 11, no. 1 (Spring 1994): 6.

9. C. Eric Lincoln, ed., *The Black Experience in Religion* (Garden City, NY: Doubleday, 1974).

10. See Cyprian Davis, *The History of Black Catholics in the United States* (New York: Crossroad, 1990); Stephen J. Ochs, *Desegregating the Altar: The Josephites and the Struggle for Black Priests, 1871–1960* (Baton Rouge: Louisiana State University Press, 1990); Mary R. Sawyer, *Black Ecumenism: Implementing the Demands of Justice* (Valley Forge, PA: Trinity Press International, 1994); Aminah Beverly McCloud, *African American Islam* (New York: Routledge, 1995); Albert J. Raboteau and David W. Wills, "Retelling Carter Woodson's Story: Archival Sources for Afro-American Church History," *Journal of American History* 77 (1990): 183–99; and John Edward Philips, "The African Heritage of White America," in *Africanisms in American Culture*, edited by Joseph E. Holloway (Bloomington: Indiana University Press, 1990), 225–39.

MODELS FOR STUDYING AFRICAN-AMERICAN RELIGION

I ::

David W. Wills

I ::

:: A common question posed of American religion concerns its distinctiveness, and a common response found in discussions of American religious history is that pluralism and toleration have been in dialectical tension with Puritanism, communitarianism, and collective purpose throughout that history. David Wills makes a thoughtful and suggestive argument that the painful and often ignored encounter of black and white is a third theme that distinguishes the story of American religion from those of other countries. ::

:: I THE CENTRAL THEMES

OF AMERICAN

RELIGIOUS HISTORY

Pluralism, Puritanism, and the
Encounter of Black and White

David W. Wills

:: **W**hat is the religious history of the United States *about*? One answer, of course, is that it is about the same things as the history of religion everywhere—the human quest for the sacred, perhaps, and its expression in doctrine, practice, and community. The question as it is asked here, however, aims at what is distinctive or at least characteristic about the story of religion in America. It is a question about the central themes that do or should provide the plot lines for American religious history. The answer to this question, if one is to judge from most of the existing literature, is that there are two such themes—(1) pluralism and toleration and (2) Puritanism and collective purpose. The contention of this essay is that there is a third: the encounter of black and white.

PLURALISM AND TOLERATION VS. PURITANISM AND COLLECTIVE PURPOSE

The most common way of telling the tale of the United States' religious past is to center it on the theme of pluralism and toleration—the existence of religious variety in America and the degree to which it has (or has not) been tolerated and even affirmed. Typically, this version of our religious past tends toward some kind of American triumphalism: the United States has successfully solved the problem of religious diversity, a problem that elsewhere in the world has occasioned persistent repression and/or enduring intercommunal violence. This emphasis on success in the area of religion is often linked, moreover, with a generally triumphalist view of American institutions. The liberalism that has guided our practice of religious liberty is seen to have expressed itself in our political and social life as well.

Not all pluralism and toleration versions of our religious past are identical, however, nor equally upbeat in their assessment of the American experiment. They in fact vary considerably, mostly depending on the point at which genuine pluralism and toleration are seen to have been institutionalized in American life. According to the popular culture's cult of Thanksgiving and some of the older more filiopietistic histories of the colonial period, religious liberty was established at the center of our religious life as soon as the Pilgrims landed at Plymouth Rock. Those who know anything of the history of religious establishments in the thirteen colonies, most especially in New England, know that this is a fantasy. More commonly, therefore, it is the adoption of the Constitution, above all the passage of the First Amendment, which is seen as the crucial landmark in the emergence of a normative religious pluralism in America. In this account, the colonial period was a time of struggle against repressive old-world establishmentarianism, but in our moment of birth as a nation we broke free of that past into an era when diversity was embraced and liberty made the religious law of the land.

Still other versions of the pluralism and toleration tale, however, suggest that the constitutional separation of church and state was merely a stage on the way to a genuine pluralism that had not yet arrived in the early national period. After all, religious establishments were still possible at the state level and they endured, in however attenuated form, in Connecticut until 1818 and in Massachusetts until 1833. Elsewhere, moreover, legal barriers sometimes remained to Catholic and to Jewish participation in political office-holding and everywhere a kind of normative WASPness prevailed. On this account, it was only in the late nineteenth and early twentieth centuries, as wave after wave of immigration eroded the Protestant predominance, that true religious diversity emerged as both fact and norm in American life. Writing of the post-World War I era, surveyors of American religious history who follow this line typically speak of "a post-Protestant America" or a new "age of religious pluralism."

Others, however, are persuaded that not even the twenties saw the real triumph of pluralism and toleration in the United States. The unhappy fate of Catholic Al Smith's 1928 presidential campaign is, according to this view, a vivid symbol of the persistence of exclusionary religious prejudice—and power. Only in the 1960s, it is sometimes proposed, was the full promise of our constitutional religious liberty realized. A Catholic at last occupied the White House, and in a decade of profound cultural upheaval, the hard crust of a repressive Protestantism was broken through and a thousand flowers of religion, both Eastern and Western, were allowed to bloom. Even this version, however, is prematurely celebratory for some. They suggest that while America in the 1960s may for a moment have repented of its past sins of intolerance, there has been a good deal of backsliding since. We are therefore still pilgrims on the path to the pluralist promised land. But perhaps it is just around the next cultural corner.

If those who stress the pluralism and toleration theme may be said to vary primarily in their optimism about when the American experiment in religious liberty was—or will be—fully realized, interpreters of our past who emphasize Puritanism may be classified according to their degree of pessimism about when the Puritan legacy either was—or will be—fully dissipated. Generally they agree that in its origins the American experiment was not so much an experiment in religious liberty as an attempt at a holy commonwealth. Whatever their sins of oppression against religious dissenters, this account suggests, the Puritans had an admirable sense of common purpose that stands in favorable contrast to the prevailing privatism and individualism of much of our subsequent history—including our religious history. Before they had even set foot in Massachusetts, the Puritans were advised by Governor John Winthrop that if they wished to succeed in building their "city upon a hill," they "must be knit together in this work as one man . . . as members of the same body." Puritanism, however, together with its strong sense of collective purpose, was destined to go downhill in America from this promising beginning. According to the gloomiest accounts, Puritanism scarcely outlived the generation that brought it to the New World. The settlers' children and their children's children went from Puritan to Yankee, as crass commercialism dissolved religious bonds and individual material goals supplanted common spiritual purpose.

Not all such accounts, however, are this pessimistic. Some contend that the Puritan legacy endured through the eighteenth century, decisively shaping the public-spirited patriotic zeal of the revolutionary years, the constitutional era's quest for "a more perfect union," and the new nation's sense of its historic mission. Only in the early nineteenth century, these interpreters suggest, was the Puritan legacy at last dissipated, as an orgy of revivalist religion, political democracy, and economic and geographical expansion set the country on its incurably individualist way. Still others, moreover, claim that even these accounts underestimate Puritanism's durability in American religion, especially in shaping our most deeply shared views of national destiny. Did not the Civil War, they ask, especially on the northern side, involve a great renewal of a broadly Puritan sense of collective purpose, enunciated with unsurpassed eloquence by Lincoln? Only later, they suggest, with the collapse of Calvinist orthodoxy as an intellectually respectable tradition and the more or less complete immersion of the country in the "great barbecue" of postwar economic development and the nascent culture of consumption, did the Puritan era in American culture finally come to a close.

It is a curious feature of the history of American Puritanism, however, that its demise seems to be announced afresh in every generation. For some, it was only the antibourgeois cultural revolt of the 1920s that at last broke the iron grip of Puritanism on the American spirit. Others, however, found in the extraordinary revival of scholarly interest in and appreciation for Puritanism in the 1930s the neo-Puritan spirit of much Protestant neo-orthodoxy and in the corporatist ethos of the New Deal signs that the Puritan impulse was not yet played out. Some thought the end came only in the 1960s. Sydney Ahlstrom, for example, at the conclusion of his massive *Religious History of the American People* (New Haven: Yale University Press, 1972), suggested that the Puritan Age in Anglo-American religious history lasted from the reign of Queen Elizabeth I to the decade that began with the election of John F. Kennedy. Others think the end is still not yet upon us, though presumably, sometime in the aftermath of the Reagan era, we can expect to hear again that the Puritan era in American cultural and religious history is, at long last, over.

For all their differences of tone and emphasis, the pluralism and toleration version of our religious past and the Puritanism and collective purpose way of telling the story have much in common. Indeed, it is relatively easy to combine them by seeing them as two sides of the same story: Puritanism's loss is pluralism and toleration's gain. The purpose of this essay, however, is not to resolve the question of which of these two interpretations is more adequate or how they might be combined. It is rather to suggest that whether together or alone these two ways of understanding our religious past are inadequate to one of the central realities of our history—the encounter of black and white.

THE SOUTHERN THEME: THE ENCOUNTER OF BLACK AND WHITE

One of the easiest and most vivid ways to see what is left out by the two prevailing accounts of our religious past is to ask—literally—where in the colonial era they begin their stories. New England is clearly the primary locus of early American Puritanism, and Puritan-centered stories of American religious history characteristically spend a great deal of time on the founding and initial development of the Massachusetts and Connecticut colonies. The religious and political ideas of such Puritan leaders as John Winthrop, John Cotton, Thomas Hooker, and Thomas Shepard are traced out in meticulous detail and the workings of the Puritan family, church, and polity analyzed with great care. In this sometimes stony New England soil, it is suggested, lie our deepest religious and cultural roots.

The pluralism and toleration story, however, more characteristically begins in the middle colonies of New York, New Jersey, and Pennsylvania. Granted, there is an important chapter of this story which also occurs in New England— the chapter centering on Roger Williams and Anne Hutchinson. But the pluralistic and tolerant Rhode Island colony clearly lies at the margin of the New England story, whereas the normative diversity of Pennsylvania (and West Jersey) and the moral *de facto* pluralism of New York (and East Jersey) constitute the very center of the religious history of the middle colonies. The contrast is further reinforced if one compares the remarkable ethnic homogeneity of colonial New England to the English, Scottish, Scotch-Irish, Dutch, and German mixture of the Middle Atlantic area. For those to whom the story of American religion centers on the positive embracing of diversity, that story is best seen to begin in the middle colonies.

What, then, about the Southern colonies? Where do they fit in either of the prevailing stories? Attempts have been made to win the interpretive game, as it were, two-to-one, by assimilating the southern story into that of one of the other two sections. It has sometimes been suggested, for example, that the dominant ethos of both early southern Anglicanism and southern dissent was, in the broadest sense, Puritan, and that the religious history of these colonies may therefore be subsumed rather easily under the New England story. Since colonial southern Protestantism is generally regarded as a less potent cultural force than the northern version, it can be argued that it makes sense to study Puritanism primarily in its intense New England form rather than in its somewhat diffuse southern version. Knowing, for example, that the son of Boston's John Cotton went to Charles Town, South Carolina, to serve as a Congregationalist pastor, helps us to be aware of the Puritan presence in the South, but it is still the father and not the son who is of primary interest to us.

Attempts have also been made, however, to interpret the early religious history of the South as essentially another phase in the history of pluralism and toleration. Indeed, on occasion it has been proposed that the South itself is the real heartland for this theme. In such accounts, the middle colonies tend to disappear altogether, and a cosmopolitan, tolerant, Jeffersonian South is contrasted to a parochial, intolerant, Puritan North. That Virginia and Virginians should have played such an important role in the institutionalization of religious liberty in the constitutional era (e.g., through the state's adoption of the separationist Statute on Religious Liberty in 1785 and James Madison's shaping of the First Amendment a few years later) is here presented as the predictable flowering of a southern sensibility that has made its peace with religious diversity in a way that the northern conscience had not. America, it is suggested, began in Virginia.

If this is true, however, it seems odd to leave entirely out of account in defining the central themes of America's religious history the extraordinary black presence in Virginia and elsewhere in the South. Once the slave labor system had become established in the late seventeenth century, there was a rapid increase in the southern colonies' black population, so much so that in the eighteenth century parts of the Chesapeake area and all of the Carolina low country were characterized by a black majority. Under these circumstances, it seems highly questionable to characterize colonial southern religion solely on the basis of the religion of white Southerners—or to see as its central theme either the presence of diluted Puritanism or the triumph of a benign pluralism.

Is it not more plausible to see as the central theme of religion in the colonial South the encounter of black and white? This is, in a sense, a negative theme. It is the story of a distance, a gap. The Puritan colonies contained many dissenters and even more of what might be called the lukewarm. In the middle colonies, English and German Protestants sometimes had trouble understanding one another—literally—and there were in this region numerous other frontiers of religious difference and misunderstanding as well. But nowhere in colonial America was there a cultural or religious chasm comparable to that which separated black and white southerners. In part, of course, it was simply a matter of sheer cultural difference. Most of the Africans who were brought to the English colonies had not been Christians in their homeland and did not become such in the New World. Numerically significant Christianization of the slave population only began after 1760 and did not really come to full tide until after 1830, by which time most American blacks were native born. While some blacks at the time of their capture and enslavement were Muslims, the vast majority were adherents of some form of African traditional religion—and it is presumably as such that they lived and died in America. For the most part, then, they did not speak the same religious language as white Southerners.

The distance between black and white in the colonial South was, however, far more than just a difference in religious or cultural tradition, and therefore not a gap that could have been closed, had the attempt been made, simply by acknowl-edging and accepting diversity. Since the encounter of black and white occurred within the context of a slave system that broadly and consistently subordinated blacks to whites, the previously existing cultural gap was transformed into a gap that involved power as well as meaning—and above all the relationship between the two. The world that had to be made sense of, by African Americans and European Americans alike, was a world that included the brutal reality of racial slavery. Given the vast difference in religious standpoint and the utter disparity in power with which their encounter began, it is scarcely surprising that black and white then and now have found it difficult to tell a shared, religiously meaningful story about their common fate.

It is this problematic encounter of black and white—which tests the limits of all our views of pluralism and undermines every attempt to formulate a sense of collective purpose—that is the Southern theme in American religious history. This is not to say, of course, that it is only a Southern theme. Just as one can see the footprints of the Puritans in both the Middle Atlantic region and in the South and can hear the voice of toleration throughout the colonies, so one can also find the encounter of black and white in New England and the middle colonies. But just as the Puritan theme in our religious history initially comes to sharpest focus in New England, and the story of pluralism and toleration first takes center stage in the middle colonies, so the encounter of black and white is rooted most deeply in the colonial South. And just as we have to learn that black history is not to be thought of as only "black history" while white history is considered "American history," so we must come to see that southern history is no less "American histo-ry" than the history of New England or of the Mid-Atlantic states. The Southern theme in our religious history is equally as important as the other two and it is only by taking these three themes together, in all their complex interaction, that we can begin to move toward an adequate understanding of our religious past—and present.

BLACK AND WHITE FROM THE EVANGELICAL AWAKENING TO THE PRESENT

If the encounter of black and white is one of the main themes of our religious history, what are the main stages in the development of this theme? If pluralism and toleration seem almost continuously to be on the increase in our history and Puritanism seems ever to be in decline, what is to be said of the encounter of black and white? Simply put, it is the story of a persisting and seemingly in-tractable gap or distance. Recurrent and sometimes heroic efforts have been made to overcome this gap, but in the end it seems always to endure. The story of these efforts—and their failure—can be sketched here only in its broadest outline, concentrating on the eighteenth- and nineteenth-century encounter of blacks and whites in the context of evangelical Protestantism and their twentieth-century meeting in a religious milieu importantly shaped by ecumenical Protestantism and by cultural pluralism. The full story, of course, is as rich and complicated—and as subject to various interpretations—as the stories of Puritanism or pluralism and toleration.

It was Protestant evangelicalism that in part of the eighteenth and most of the nineteenth century played a central role both in defining the acceptable limits of pluralism and in mediating the legacy of Puritanism in American religious life. It was also in the context of evangelicalism that blacks and whites were for the first time drawn together religiously in significant numbers. No doubt before the evangelical wakenings of the mid-eighteenth century, blacks and whites in the South (and elsewhere) had begun to exchange folk beliefs and practices of a religious or quasi-religious sort, an important phenomenon that historians are only beginning to take sufficiently seriously. But it was only with the rise of evangelicalism that a biracial religious movement appeared in organized, public form. Particularly among the Baptists and the Methodists, who became the numerically preponderant Protestants during the evangelical era, there was a very considerable number of black converts; in some places they outnumbered white Baptists and Methodists. Testifying publicly about their conversions, taking part in church discipline, serving as exhorters and sometimes as pastors—even, on occasion, of predominantly white congregations—black Baptists and Methodists participated in the evangelical movement in a way they had participated in no previous colonial religious movement. Full mutuality and equality had scarcely been achieved, but the gap between black and white did seem to be narrowing.

Soon, however, the gap reappeared, this time in the very heart of evangelicalism itself. Early evangelicalism had attracted blacks in part because of its antislavery tendency, most marked among the Methodists. With the end of the social ferment of the revolutionary period, however, and the rapid movement of evangelicalism from the margins to the very center of Southern society, white evangelicals reconsidered the meaning of American slavery and for the most part came to accept it. Meanwhile black evangelicals, eager for autonomy in administering their own affairs, discovered that when it came to questions of the exercise of leadership or control over property, white power was the almost invariable rule of ecclesiastical as well as civil order. The result of these developments—which undermined the sharing of both meaning and power—was racial schism.

Black Methodists, under the leadership of such men as Richard Allen and James Varick, withdrew in large numbers to form their own independent denominations, most importantly the African Methodist Episcopal Church (1816) and the African Methodist Episcopal Zion Church (1821). (Black Baptists in 1840 organized the American Baptist Missionary Convention, the first in a series of black Baptist conventions that culminated decades later—in 1895—with the formation of the largest of all the black churches, the National Baptists Convention, U.S.A.) In the South, in a violation of religious liberty that tellers of the pluralism and toleration tale frequently overlook, slaves were often prevented by law from either joining these Northern-based denominations or forming comparable institutions of their own. But through song and story and informal networks, they maintained an Afro-American evangelical tradition sharply at odds with the slavery-affirming religion of their masters.

With the coming of the Civil War and more especially the era of Reconstruction, it momentarily seemed once again that the distance between black and white might be narrowed. Crucial here, of course, was the end of slavery—and the reinterpretation of what the meaning of American slavery had all along been. Among black evangelicals, slavery had long been regarded as an offense against God, a great wickedness for which all whites—North and South alike—could one day expect to feel the wrath of a just God. Some even speculated that God might both work that judgment and set the captives free by sowing violent conflict among the whites, a prophecy that the events of the Civil War years seemed to vindicate. It was essentially this interpretation of slavery and its end that Lincoln advanced in his second inaugural address, a speech that went further than any previous presidential statement toward creating a community of interpretation between black and white Americans. In the ensuing Reconstruction era, moreover, it initially seemed that this retelling of the nation's racial past might be matched with new opportunities for black participation—and the exercise of power—in the church and state alike. Unprecedented biracial efforts were made, often within the framework of evangelical Protestant ideas and institutions, both to foster religious collaboration and create a racially inclusive polity.

Soon, however, it became clear that the gap between black and white would not be closed, even in this the very heyday of evangelical influence. Southern white evangelicals proved unable to respond positively to emancipation and their northern counterparts had trouble overcoming paternalism, or sustaining long-term interest in the black struggle. The freedmen themselves, eager to take full control of their own religious lives, for the most part broke their ties to the evangelical churches of white Southerners and either joined the existing Afro-

American denominations or helped launch such new black churches as the Colored Methodist Episcopal Church (1870). Their collaboration with Northern white evangelicals, especially in the field of education, was in some cases more enduring, but even here there was mounting stress, often centering on the question of black versus white control. By the end of the century, when blacks experienced increased disenfranchisement, segregation, and economic oppression, white evangelicals—whether Northern or Southern—made little protest. The distance between blacks and whites seemed as wide as it had ever been.

In the twentieth century, the main moment in which the gap between black and white in American religious life seemed to be closing was no doubt the Civil Rights era of the 1950s and 60s. The crumbing of the Southern system of segregation, under the combined onslaught of popular protest and federal power, seemed to represent the collapse of the great dividing wall between the races and, with blacks and whites marching together behind Martin Luther King, Jr., and even President Johnson declaring, "We Shall Overcome," an unprecedented day of biracial mutuality and understanding seemed at hand. This moment, though importantly shaped by the tradition of black evangelicalism, was primarily the product of religious and cultural forces other than evangelicalism. Among these two may be singled out ecumenical Protestantism and cultural pluralism.

Much of the prestige and social influence enjoyed by evangelicalism in the nineteenth century was assumed by ecumenical Protestantism in the twentieth. When it first took organizational form as the Federal Council of Churches in 1908, ecumenical Protestantism showed little interest in the gap between blacks and whites. Gradually, however, in part in response to the pressures from blacks within its own ranks, ecumenical Protestantism became increasingly concerned with race relations. In 1946, the Federal Council of Churches endorsed "a non-segregated church and a non-segregated society" and thereafter ecumenical Protestantism moved slowly but steadily along the path that led eventually to its active support of the Civil Rights movement of the 1960s.

Ecumenical Protestantism was scarcely capable on its own, however, of shaping the twentieth century encounter of black and white, even in its religious dimension. The term "cultural pluralism," which became current only during this period, does not refer simply to the empirical fact of cultural and religious variety, but rather to a movement to take from these facts a norm; to contend that America should understand itself precisely as a multicultural nation, a nation where people could have particular and varying cultural identities without forfeiting their status as full Americans. Normative pluralism, however, is never without its boundaries, and as the idea of cultural pluralism was applied to

American religion, it came to mean that a religiously respectable American could be a Protestant, a Catholic, or a Jew—a formulation brilliantly analyzed by Will Herberg, in his mid-1950s classic, *Protestant-Catholic-Jew*. Ecumenical Protestantism, then, came to function as a kind of senior partner in a triple religious establishment with Catholicism and Judaism. By the time of the Civil Rights movement, Catholics and Jews were important and necessary allies for ecumenical Protestantism in its efforts to close the gap between blacks and whites.

At the height of the Civil Rights movement, to many that gap seemed ready to close. Soon, however, as the Civil Rights movement turned into the black power movement and a white backlash against black progress eclipsed white support for it, the gap seemed once again to widen, even within the world of the "triple establishment" itself. Ecumenical Protestantism's own black leaders proved surprisingly receptive to the newly emergent and highly polemical "black theology," as well as to militant demands that the churches both pay sizable "reparation" for their historic complicity in American racism and make room for a new degree of autonomous black power in the running of their own affairs. Black Catholics—a group that had grown steadily since the 1930s—became more insistent that the Roman Catholic church show greater respect for Afro-American patterns of piety, and make more room for black leadership. How could their church be truly catholic, some asked, if it insisted on canceling out their blackness rather than embracing it? Blacks and Jews meanwhile became involved in bitter recriminations over allegations of "Jewish racism" and "black anti-Semitism." What had gone wrong?

Both the prevailing sense of collective purpose and the dominant view of pluralism, it might be said, had been tested against the realities of the encounter of black and white and found wanting. Ecumenical Protestant supporters of the Civil Rights movement, bearers in many ways of the Puritan vision of the American "city on a hill," often wanted to believe that racial injustice in America consisted mostly in Southern racial segregation, and that a federally legislated end to that evil represented the final triumph of collective religious and moral purpose over recalcitrant regional wickedness. But in the light of the burning ghettoes, it became clear that it would take a good deal more than civil rights legislation to provide a happy ending for the story of American race relations. Meanwhile, religious pluralists who saw support for civil rights as an unproblematic extension of interfaith goodwill among Protestants, Catholics, and Jews discovered to their surprise that black America could not so easily be fitted into the prevailing—and rather comfortable—framework of religious pluralism and tolerations. The Nation of Islam was a homegrown religion that diverged in many ways from patterns of belief and practice common among Muslims in most parts of the world. But the pressure within black religious life of a powerful movement preaching Allah's imminent judgment on a Satanic America and calling for a "return" to the pure teachings of Islam made clear the limitations of the "Protestant-Catholic-Jew" definition of American pluralism.

Since the late 1960s, there has been a clear retreat from a direct facing of the gap between black and white as it was then so strikingly revealed. Laments for the loss of community in America and calls for a renewal of collective purpose are once more issued and debated with little or no mention of the realities of race. Religious pluralism in the United States is analyzed and celebrated with little acknowledgement that the polarities of race in our history are not quite the same thing as the varieties of our religion. Acknowledged or not, however, the gap between the races—a gap involving both the interpretation of the American experience and the degree of empowerment within it—remains one of the foundational realities of our national religious life. And however much members of both races might sometimes wish it were otherwise, the painful encounter of black and white is likely to remain in the future what it has been in the past—one of the crucial, central themes in the religious history of the United States.

SELECTED BIBLIOGRAPHY FOR FURTHER READING

Harris, Michael W. "African American Religious History in the 1980s: A Critical Review." *Religious Studies Review* 20:4 (October 1994): 263–75.

Lincoln, C. Eric. *Race, Religion, and the Continuing American Dilemma.* New York: Hill & Wang, 1984.

Raboteau, Albert J. and David W. Wills. "Retelling Carter Woodson's Story: Archival Sources for Afro-American Church History." *Journal of American History* 77 (1990): 183–99.

Sernett, Milton C., ed. *Afro-American Religious History: A Documentary Witness.* Durham, NC: Duke University Press, 1985.

Wilmore, Gayraud S., ed. *African American Religious Studies: An Interdisciplinary Anthology.* Durham, NC: Duke University Press, 1989.

PERSPECTIVES FOR A STUDY OF AFRICAN-AMERICAN RELIGION IN THE UNITED STATES

Charles H. Long

::Charles Long argues in this 1971 article that the study of African-American religion has traditionally limited itself to either the methodology of the social sciences or the confessional perspective of an explicit theological tradition. A historian of religion, Long calls for a broader interpretation of African-American religion that gives serious attention to deeper symbolic images and interpretive principles such as the historical reality and religious images of Africa, the involuntary presence of Africans in America, and the images of God as experienced by African Americans.::

:: 2

PERSPECTIVES FOR A STUDY OF AFRICAN-AMERICAN RELIGION IN THE UNITED STATES

Charles H. Long

∴ Americans of African descent have for some time been the subject of countless studies and research projects—projects extending from the physical through the social sciences. The religion of this culture has not been overlooked.[1]

Most of the studies of religion have employed the methodology of the social sciences; hardly any of the studies have come to terms with the specifically religious elements in the religion of black Americans. We have not yet seen anything on the order of Pierre Verger's[2] study of African religion in South America or of Alfred Metraux's[3] study of the same phenomenon in the Atlantic islands.

On the contemporary scene, a group of younger blacks are about the task of writing a distinctively "black theology." I refer here to the works of Joseph Washington (*Black Religion* [Boston, 1961], James Cone (*Black Theology and Black Power* [New York, 1969]), and to Albert Cleage's sermons (*The Black Messiah* [New York, 1968]). In this enterprise these men place themselves in the religious tradition of David Walker, Henry Garnett, Martin Delaney, and W. E. B. Du Bois. They are essentially apologetic theologians working implicitly and explicitly from the Christian theological tradition.

What we have in fact are two kinds of studies: those arising from the social sciences, and an explicitly theological apologetic tradition. This limitation of methodological perspectives has led to a narrowness of understanding and the failure to perceive certain creative possibilities in the black community in America.

One of the most telling examples of this limitation of perspectives in the study of black religion is to be found in Joseph Washington's work cited above. Washington has correctly seen that black religion is not to be understood as a black imitation of the religion of the majority population. His religious norm is Christianity, and the internal norm for Christianity is faith expressing itself in theology. From his analysis he concludes that black religion is not Christian, thus does not embody faith, and therefore has produced no theology. Black religion has, in his view, been more concerned with civil rights and protest, and hardly, if ever, concerned with genuine Christian faith.

I do not wish to take issue with Washington regarding his understanding of Christian faith and theology, for this lies outside the scope of our concerns in this paper. However, a word or two must be said in passing. Washington seems to conceive of Christianity and theology in static terms unrelated to historical experience. He seems to be unaware of the historical situations which were correlative to European and American theology, and he seems equally unaware of the fact that Americans have produced few theologians of the variety that would meet his norm. In short, his critique of black religion from the stance of Christian theology is blunted by the lack of his historical understanding of theology.

But now, to the point which is most relevant for our discussion: the distinctive nature of black religion. Washington's insights here are very accurate, for he shows in his work how folkloric materials, social protest, and Negro fraternalism, along with biblical imagery, are all aspects of black religion. He experiences a difficulty here, for he is unable to deal with religion outside of the normative framework of Christian theology. But even if one is to have a theology, it must arise from religion, something which is prior to theology.

I have felt the need for some time to present a systematic study of black religion—a kind of initial ordering of the religious experiences and expressions of the black communities in America. Such a study should not be equated with Christianity, or any other religion for that matter. It is rather an attempt to see what kind of images and meanings lie behind the religious experiences of the black communities in America. While recognizing the uniqueness of this community, I am also working as a historian of religions, and thus the context for my interpretation is the variety of the religious traditions of mankind.

I should like in this paper to present three interrelated perspectives for a study of black religion from the point of view of a historian of religion. These perspectives constitute symbolic images as well as methodological principles.

They are:

    A. Africa as historical reality and religious image.

    B. The involuntary presence of the black community in America.

    C. The experience and symbol of God in the religious experience of blacks.

A. AFRICA AS HISTORICAL REALITY AND RELIGIOUS IMAGE

It is a historical fact that the existence of the black communities in America is due to the slave trade of numerous European countries from the seventeenth to the nineteenth centuries (slaves were still being illegally smuggled into the United States as late as the 1880s). The issue of the persistence of African elements in the black community is a hotly debated issue. On the one hand, we have the positions of E. Franklin Frazier and W. E. B. Du Bois,[4] emphasizing the lack of any significant persisting elements of Africanism in America. Melville Herskovitz held this same position but reversed his position in the *Myth of the Negro Past* (Boston, 1958), where he places a greater emphasis on the persistence of African elements among the descendants of the slaves in North America. One of the issues in this discussion had to do with the comparative level of the studies. Invariably, the norm for comparison was the black communities in the Atlantic islands and in South America. In the latter the African elements are very distinctive, and, in the case of Brazil, Africans have gone back and forth between Africa and Brazil.[5] African languages are still spoken by blacks in Brazil. Indeed, Pierre Verger first became interested in Yoruba religion when he saw it being practiced in South America!

It is obvious that nothing of this sort has existed in the United States. The slave system of the United States systematically broke down the linguistic and cultural pattern of the slaves, but even a protagonist for the loss of all African-isms, such as E. Franklin Frazier, acknowledges the persistence of "shout songs," African rhythm, and dance in American culture. Frazier, and in this matter, Du Bois, while acknowledging such elements did not see these elements of ultimate significance, for they could not see these forms playing an important role in the social cohesion of the black community. Without resolving this discussion, another issue needs to be raised. The persistence of elements of what some anthropologists have called "soft culture" means that given even the systematic breakdown of African cultural forms in the history of North America slavery, the slaves did not confront America with a religious *tabula rasa*. If not the content of culture, a characteristic mode of orienting and perceiving reality has probably persisted. We know, for example, that a great majority of the slaves came from West Africa, and we also know from the studies of Daryll Forde that West Africa is a cultural as well as a geographical unit.[6] Underlying the empirical diversity of languages, religions, and social form, there is, according to Forde, a structural unity discernible in language and religious forms.[7] With the breakdown of the empirical forms of language and religion as determinants for the social group, this persisting structural mode and the common situation as slaves in America may be the basis for the persistence of an African style among the descendants of the Africans.

In addition to this, in the accounts of the slaves and their owners we read of "meetings" which took place secretly in the woods. It is obvious that these "meetings" were not the practice of the masters' religion. They were related to what the slaves themselves called "conjuring," and the connotation reminds one of Voodoo rites in Haiti.

Added to this is the precise manner in which, by being a slave and a black man, one was isolated from any self-determined legitimacy in the society of which one was a part and was recognized by one's physiological characteristics. This constituted a complexity of experience revolving around the relationship between one's physical being and one's origins. So even if he had no conscious memory of Africa, the image of Africa played an enormous part in the religion of the black man. The image of Africa, an image related to historical beginnings, has been one of the primordial religious images of great significance. It constitutes the religious revalorization of the land, a place where the natural and ordinary gestures of the black man were and could be authenticated. In this connection, one can trace almost every nationalistic movement among the blacks and find Africa to be the dominating and guiding image. Even among religious groups not strongly nationalistic the image of Africa or Ethiopia still has relevance.[8] This is present in such diverse figures as Richard Allen, who organized the African Methodist Episcopal church in the early nineteenth century, through Martin Delaney in the late nineteenth century, and then again in Marcus Garvey's[9] "back to Africa movement" of the immediate post-World War I period, and finally the taking up of this issue again among black leaders of our own time.

The image of Africa as it appears in black religion is unique, for the black community in America is a landless people. Unlike the American Indian, the land was not taken from him, and unlike the black Africans in South Africa or Rhodesia, his land is not occupied by groups whom he considers aliens. His image of the land points to the religious meaning of land even in the absence of these forms of authentication. It thus emerges as an image which is always invested with historical and religious possibilities.

B. THE INVOLUNTARY PRESENCE OF THE BLACK COMMUNITY IN AMERICA

Implied in the discussion concerning the land and the physiological characteristics of the black is the significance attributed to his meaning in America. His stance has, on the one hand, been necessitated by historical conditions, and on the other hand, been grasped as creative possibility. From the very beginning, he was brought to America in chains, and this country has attempted to keep him in this condition in one way or another. His very presence as a *human being* in the United States has always constituted a threat to the majority population. From the point of view of the majority population, he has been simply and purely a legal person, first as a slave defined in terms of property, and then, after the abolition of chattel property, as a citizen who had to seek legal redress before he could use the common facilities of the country—water fountains, public accommodations, restaurants, schools, etc. There is no need to repeat this history; it is too well known, and the point I wish to make is more subtle than these specific issues, important as they may be.

In addition to the image and historical reality of Africa one must add, as another persisting datum, the involuntary presence and orientation as a religious meaning. I have stated elsewhere the importance of the involuntary structure of the religious consciousness in the terms of oppugnancy.[10] In the case of the slaves America presented a bizarre reality, not simply because of the novelty of a radical change of status and culture, but equally because their presence as slaves pointed to a radical contradiction within the dominant culture itself. The impact of America was a discovery, but one had little ability to move from the bizarre reality of discovery to the level of general social rules of conduct, which happens in the case of other communities presented with an ultimate discovery. In addition to this, to normalize the condition of slavery would be to deny his existence as a human being.

The slave had to come to terms with the opaqueness of his condition and at the same time oppose it. He had to experience the truth of his negativity and at the same time transform and create *an-other* reality. Given the limitations imposed upon him, he created on the level of his religious consciousness. Not only did this transformation produce new cultural forms, but its significance must be understood from the point of view of the creativity of the transforming process itself.

Three short illustrations of this phenomenon must suffice at this point. Listen to this spiritual:

> He's so high, you can't get over him
> He's so low, you can't get under him
> So round, you can't get around him
> You got to go right through the door

or this poem by a black poet:

> Yet do I marvel at this curious thing
> To make a poet black and bid him sing

or a folk aphorism:

> What do you mean I gotta do that
> Ain't but two things I got to do—Be black and die.

The musical phenomenon, the blues, is another expression of the same consciousness. What is portrayed here is a religious consciousness that has experienced the "hardness" of life, whether the form of that reality be the slave system, God, or simply life itself. It is from such a consciousness that the power to resist and yet maintain one's humanity has emerged. Though the worship and religious life of blacks have often been referred to as forms of escapism, one must always remember that there has always been an integral relationship between the "hardness" of life and the ecstasy of religious worship. It is, in my opinion, an example of what Gaston Bachelard described in Hegelian language as the lithic imagination. Bachelard had reference to the imaginary structure of consciousness that arises in relationship to the natural form of the stone and the manner in which the volitional character of human consciousness is related to this imaginary form.[11] The black community in America has confronted the reality of the historical situation as immutable, impenetrable, but this experience has not produced passivity; it has, rather, found expression as forms of the involuntary and transformative nature of the religious consciousness. In connection with this point, let me illustrate by returning to the meaning of the image and historical reality of Africa.

Over and over again this image has ebbed and flowed in the religious consciousness. It has found expression in music, dance, and political theorizing. There has been an equally persistent war against this image in the religion of black folk. This war against the image of Africa and blackness can be seen in the political and social movements connected with the stratagems of segregation and integration. Even more telling is the history of the names by which this community has chosen to call itself. From African to colored, Negro, Afro-American, and, presently, black. The history of these designations can be seen as a religious history through which this community was coming to terms with a primary symbol of opacity.

Recall the words of G. van der Leeuw. In speaking of religious experience, he said, "Religious experience, in other terms, is concerned with a 'somewhat.' But this assertion often means no more than this 'Somewhat' is merely a vague 'something,' and in order that man may be able to make more significant statements about this 'Somewhat,' it must force itself upon him, oppose it to him as being Something Other. Thus the first statement we can make about religion is that it is a highly exceptional and extremely impressive 'Other.'"[12] From the point of view of religious history, one could say that this community in its own self-interpretation has moved from a vague "somewhat" to the religious experience of a highly exceptional and *extremely impressive* "Other." The contemporary expressions of black power attest to this fact, and the universalizing of this notion in terms of pan-Africanism, negritude, or neo-Marxian and Christian conceptions must equally be noted.

The meaning of the involuntary structure or the opacity of the religious symbol has within this community held together eschatological hopes and the archaic religious consciousness. In both secular and religious groups, new expressions such as Moorish Temple, Black Jews, Black Muslims retain an archaic structure in their religious consciousness, and this structure is never quite settled for; it is there as a datum to be deciphered in the context of their present experience.

C. THE EXPERIENCE AND SYMBOL OF GOD

The sources for my interpretation of the experience of the holy in this community are from the folkloric tradition. By this, I mean an oral tradition which exists in its integrity as an oral tradition, the writing down of which is a concession to scholarship.

These sources are slave narratives, sermons, the words and music of spirituals and the blues, the cycle of Brer Rabbit, and High John the Conqueror stories. These materials reveal a range of religious meanings extending from trickster-transformer hero to High Gods.

To be sure, the imagery of the Bible plays a large role in the symbolic presentations, but to move from this fact to any simplistic notion of blacks as slaves or former slaves converted to Christianity would, I think, miss several important religious meanings.

The biblical imagery was used because it was at hand; it was adapted to and invested with the experience of the slave. Strangely enough, it was the slave who gave a religious meaning to the notions of freedom and land. The deliverance of the children of Israel from the Egyptians became an archetype which enabled him to live with promise.

God for this community appears as an all-powerful and moral deity, though one hardly ever knows why he has willed this or that. God is never, or hardly ever, blamed for the situation of man, for somehow in an inscrutable manner there is a reason for all this. By and large a fundamental distinction is made between God and Jesus Christ. To the extent that the language of Christianity is used, black Americans have held to the trinitarian distinction, but adherence to this distinction has been for experiential rather than dogmatic reasons. Historians of religion have known for a long time that the Supreme Being appears in differing forms. To be sure, God, the first person of the trinity, is a powerful creator deity.

It is not so much the dogma of the trinity as it is the modalities of experience of the trinity that are most important. The experience of God is thus placed within the context of the other images and experiences of black religion. God, as first person of the trinity, is, of course, a powerful Creator Supreme deity. Though biblical language is used to speak of his historical presence and intervention in history, we neither have a clear Hebraic nor what has become a Christian interpretation of history. I am not implying that the deity is a *deus otiosus* for there is an acceptance of historical reality, but neither in its Hebraic nor traditional Christian mode. We must remember that the historicity of these two traditions was related to the possession of a land, and this has not been the case for blacks in America. In one sense, it is possible to say that their history in America has always presented to them a situation of crisis. The intervention of the deity into their community has not been synonymous with the confirmation of the reality of their being within the structures of America. God has been more often a transformer of their consciousness, the basis for a resource which enabled them to maintain the human image without completely acquiescing to the norms of the majority population. He provided a norm of self-criticism which was not derivative from those who enslaved them. I cite two examples as illustrations:

> When I was very small my people thought I was going to die. Mama used to tell my sister that I was puny and that she didn't think that she would be able to raise me. I used to dream nearly all the time and see all kinds of wild-looking animals. I would nearly always get scared and nervous.
>
> Some time later I got heavy one day and began to die. For days I couldn't eat, I couldn't sleep; even the water I drank seemed to swell in my mouth. A

voice said to me one day, "Nora you haven't done what you promised." And
again it said, "You saw the sun rise, but you shall die before it goes down." I
began to pray. I was making up my bed. A light seemed to come down from
heaven, and it looked like it just split me open from my head to my foot. A
voice said to me, "Ye are freed and free indeed. My son set you free. Behold,
I give you everlasting life."

During all this time I was just dumb. I couldn't speak or move. I heard a
moaning sound, and a voice said, "Follow me, my little one, and I will show
you the marvelous works of God." I got up, it seems, and started to traveling. I
was not my natural self but a little angel. We went and came to a sea of glass,
and it was mingled with fire. I opened my mouth and began to pray, "Lord, I
will perish in there." Then I saw a path that led through the fire, I journeyed in
this path and came to a green pasture where there were a lot of sheep. They
were all of the same size and bleated in a mournful tone. A voice spoke to me,
and it sounded like a roar of thunder: "Ye are my workmanship and the creation of my hand. I will drive all fears away. Go, and I go with you. You have a
deed to your name, and you shall never perish."[13]

Everybody seemed to be getting along well but poor me. I told him so. I said,
"Lord, it looks like you come to everybody's house but mine. I never bother
my neighbors or cause any disturbance. I have lived as it is becoming a poor
widow woman to live and yet, Lord, it looks like I have a harder time than anybody." When I said this, something told me to turn around and look. I put my
bundle down and looked towards the east part of the world. A voice spoke to
me as plain as day, but it was inward and said, "I am a time-God working after
the counsel of my own will. In due time I will bring all things to you.
Remember and cause your heat to sing."

When God struck me dead with his power I was living on Fourteenth
Avenue. It was the year of the Centennial. I was in my house alone, and I declare unto you, when his power struck me I died. I fell out on the floor flat on
my back. I could neither speak nor move, for my tongue stuck to the roof of
my mouth; my jaws were locked and my limbs were stiff.[14]

These two narratives are illustrative of the inner dynamics of the conversion
experience. The narratives combine and interweave the ordinary events with the
transformation of the religious consciousness. It is not merely a case of God acting in history, for the historical events are not the locus of the activity, but then
neither do we have a complete lack of concern for historical events in favor of a

mystification of the consciousness. It is the combination of these two structures that is distinctive in these narratives; clues such as these might help us to understand the specific nature of the black religious consciousness.

But this structure of the deity is present in non-Christian movements among the blacks; the transforming power of the deity may be seen among the Black Muslims and the Black Jews. This quality of the presence of the deity has enabled blacks to affirm the historical mode by seeing it more in terms of an initiatory structure than in terms of a progressivistic or evolutionary understanding of temporality.

Continuing with the Christian language of the trinity, Jesus has been experienced more in the form of a dema-deity[15] than as conquering hero. One could make the case that this understanding of Jesus Christ has always been present in the history of the Western church, but it is clear that this image of the Christ has not been experienced as a symbol of the total Western culture since the seventeenth century. Christ as fellow sufferer, as the little child, as the companion, as the man who understands—these symbols of Christ have been dominant. For example, the spirituals:

I told Jesus it would be all right if he changed my name
Jesus told me that the world would hate me if he changed my name

or

Poor little Jesus boy, made him to be born in a manger.
World treated him so mean
Treats me mean too. . . .

But there is more than the biblical imagery as a datum. In the folklore we see what appears as the trickster, transformer hero. More than often he appears in the Brer Rabbit cycle of stories, which seem related to similar West Africa stories of Ananse, the Spider.

This is one of the cycles of the Brer Rabbit stories:[16] Brer Rabbit, Brer Fox, and Brer Wolf were experiencing a season of drought. They met to decide the proper action to take. It was decided that they should dig a well so that they would have a plenteous supply of water. Brer Rabbit said that he thought this was a very good plan, although he did not wish to participate in the digging of the well because he said that he arose early in the morning and drank the dew from the grass, and thus did not wish to participate in the arduous task of digging. Brer Fox and Brer Wolf proceeded with their task and completed the digging of the deep well. After the well was dug, Brer Rabbit arose early each morning and went to the well and drank his fill, pretending all the time that he was drinking the morning dew. After a while, Brer Fox and Brer Wolf became suspicious of Brer Rabbit and set about to spy upon him. Sure enough, they caught him one morning drinking from their well. They subjected him to some punishment, which we need not go into for the point of the story has been made.

Brer Rabbit is not simply lazy and clever; it is clear that he feels that he has something else to do—that life cannot be dealt with in purely conventional terms and committee meetings. In many respects the preacher in the black community exhibits many of the traits of Brer Rabbit, and it was often the preacher who kept alive the possibility for another life, or who protested and affirmed by doing nothing.

One other instance should be mentioned: High John, the Conqueror. Now it is stated explicitly in the folklore that High John came dancing over the waves from Africa, or that he was in the hold of the slave ship. High John is a flamboyant character. He possesses great physical strength and conquers more by an audacious display of his power than through any subtlety or cunning. He is the folkloric side of a conquering Christ, though with less definite goals.

The essential elements in the expression and experience of God is his transforming ability. This is true in the case of God as absolute moral ruler as well as in Brer Rabbit or High John the Conqueror. Insofar as society at large was not an agent of transformation, the inner resources of consciousness and the internal structures of his own history and community became not simply the locus for new symbols but the basis for a new consciousness for the black.

It is therefore the religious consciousness of the black in America which is the repository of who he is, where he has been, and where he is going. A purely existential analysis cannot do justice to this religious experience. Probably a new interpretation of American religion would come about if careful attention is given to the religious history of this strange American.

NOTES

1. W.E.B. Du Bois, ed., *The Negro Church* (Atlanta, Ga.: Atlanta University Press, 1903); Carter G. Woodson, *The History of the Negro Church* (Washington, D.C.: Associated Publishers, 1921); Benjamin E. Mays and Joseph Nicholson, *The Negro Church* (New York: Russell & Russell, 1969); Arthur Fauset, *Black Gods of the Metropolis* (Philadelphia: University of Pennsylvania Press, 1944; London: Oxford University Press, 1944; E. Franklin Frazier, *The Negro Church in America* (New York: Schocken Books, 1962); Howard M. Brotz, *The Black Jews of Harlem* (New York:

Schocken Books, 1970); C. Eric Lincoln, *The Black Muslims in America* (New York: Beacon Press, 1961); and E. U. Essien-Udom, *Black Nationalism: A Search for an Identity in America* (Chicago: University of Chicago Press, 1962).

2. Pierre Verger, *Notes sur le culte des Orisa et Vodum à Bahia la Baie de tous les saints au Bresil et à l'ancienne Côtes des esclaves en Afrique* (Dakar, 1957).

3. Alfred Metraux, *Le Vaudou haitien* (Paris, 1958).

4. See W. E. B. Du Bois, *The Souls of Black Folk* (Chicago, 1903).

5. See Verger.

6. Daryll Forde, "The Cultural Map of West Africa: Successive Adaptations to Tropical Forests and Grassland," in *Cultures and Societies of Africa*, ed. S. and P. Ottenborg (New York, 1960).

7. Joseph Greenberg makes a similar argument for the structural similarity of West African languages in his *Studies in African Linguistic Classification* (New Haven, Conn., 1955).

8. See especially Edward W. Blyden's *Christianity, Islam and the Negro Race* (London, 1887). Blyden, though born in the Virgin Islands and ordained as a Presbyterian minister, was one of the early leaders in pan-Africanism. It is interesting to note that he set the problem within a religious context. The publication of his work is directly related to the problems created in the 1840s by the passage of the Fugitive Slave Law and the Dred Scott decision of the United States Supreme Court.

9. See Edmund D. Cronon, *Black Moses* (Madison: University of Wisconsin Press, 1962).

10. See Charles H. Long, "Prolegomenon to a Religious Hermeneutic," *History of Religions*, 6, no. 3, (February 1967): 254–64.

11. See Gaston Bachelard, *La Terre et les reveries de la volonte* (Paris, 1948).

12. G. van der Leeuw, *Religion in Essence and Manifestation*, trans. J. E. Turner (London, 1933), p. 23.

13. Clifton H. Johnson, ed., *God Struck Me Dead*, Religious Conversion Experiences and Autobiographies of Ex-Slaves, with a forward by Paul Radin (Philadelphia: Pilgrim Press, 1969), pp. 62–63.

14. Ibid., pp. 58–59.

15. Adolf E. Jensen defined this religious structure as a result of his researches in Ceram. See his *Hainuwele* (Frank-furt, 1939) and *Myth and Cult among Primitive People* (Chicago, 1963). I do not wish to say that Jesus Christ is understood in any religious structure that one should begin the deciphering of the meaning of Jesus. Essential to this structure is the notion of the deity as companion and creator, a deity related more to the human condition than deities of the sky, and the subjection of this deity to death at the hands of men.

16. See T. F. Crane, "Plantation Folklore," in *The Negro and His Folklore* (Austin, Tex., 1967), pp. 157–67.

SELECTED BIBLIOGRAPHY FOR FURTHER READING

Asante, Molefi K. *The Afrocentric Idea*. Philadelphia: Temple University Press, 1987.

Long, Charles H. *Significations: Signs, Symbols, and Images in the Interpretation of Religion*. Philadelphia: Fortress, 1986.

Marks, Morton. "Uncovering Ritual Structures in Afro-American Music" in *Religious Movements in Contemporary America*. ed. Irving I. Zaretsky and Mark P. Leone. Princeton: Princeton University Press, 1974.

Smith, Theophus H. *Conjuring Culture: Biblical Formations of Black Culture*. New York: Oxford University Press, 1994.

Thompson, Robert Farris. *Flash of the Spirit: African & Afro-American Art & Philosophy*. New York: Vintage, 1983.

::In the middle of the twentieth century, a debate raged concerning the question of whether traditional African beliefs and patterns of worship survived in the United States, especially in light of their apparent continuation in Caribbean and South American societies. Two conflicting answers were proposed: one associated with the sociologist E. Franklin Frazier is that African retentions in the United States were negligible because Africans were almost totally stripped of their culture by the brutal nature of enslavement; and the other, advocated foremost by the anthropologist Melville Herskovits, argued that the slave system did not destroy the slaves' African culture and a considerable number of "Africanisms" continue to define African-American culture in the United States. Sidney Mintz and Richard Price responded in 1976 that a flatly "for" or "against" position in regard to African cultural retentions assumed a rigid understanding of culture and proposed instead a more flexible model of encounter that places the emphasis on the creative choices of slaves in forging a unique African-American culture.::

:: 3

THE BIRTH OF AFRICAN-AMERICAN CULTURE

Sidney W. Mintz and *Richard Price*

:: **D**iscussions of the origins and growth of African-American societies in the New World have usually involved a model, implicit or explicit, of the ways in which encounters between Africans and Europeans occurred and the consequences of these encounters. Usually, this model posits the existence of two "cultures," one African and one European, which are brought into contact in the New World by white colonists and black slaves. Such a model, because of its rather misleading simplicity, then requires that the researcher choose between two neat but questionable "explanations" of the African side of the equation. In order to think of an "African" culture coming into contact with a European culture, scholars have been compelled either (1) to posit the existence of a generalized West African cultural "heritage," which Africans of diverse backgrounds brought to a given colony; or (2) to argue that the bulk of Africans in that colony came from some particular "tribe" or cultural group. We shall suggest that, in either version, this model needs considerable rethinking. The concept of some kind of common West African heritage requires additional refinement, in our view, even though this will inevitably increase the difficulties it poses for the historically minded Afro-Americanist. Similarly, we shall inquire as to the factual basis for attributing relative ethnic homogeneity to the Africans introduced into any New World colony.

We have already suggested a fundamental contrast between the Europeans and Africans who arrived in a particular colony, arguing that the former were relatively homogeneous culturally, while the latter were drawn from diverse cultures and societies and spoke different and often mutually unintelligible languages. The European colonists in particular settlements—English Jamaica, French Sant-Dominguo, Spanish Cuba, etc.—commonly came from the same national homeland, even though their regional origins and their class statuses often varied. Moreover, in colonies in which Europeans from several different countries were found, they often maintained ethnic separation from one another.[1] In contrast, it was not usual for culture-specific groups of Africans to have been able to travel together or to settle together in substantial numbers in the New World. This is one reason why we feel that the Africans who were brought to any specific New World colony could not be said to have had a single collective culture to transport. If we define "culture" as a body of beliefs and values, socially acquired and patterned, that serve an organized group (a "society") as guides of and for behavior, then the term cannot be applied without some distortion to the manifold endowments of those masses of enslaved individuals, separated from their respective political and domestic settings, who were transported, in more or less heterogeneous cargoes, to the New World.[2]

It has often been pointed out that the cultures and societies of the slaving area of Africa were (and are) in many regards *similar* and/or related to one another, due to common ultimate origins, in many cases, or to centuries or even millennia of intermittent but often intense contact and mutual influence. They are said to form, in certain ways, a "culture area," when contrasted with other parts of the African continent. The late Melville J. Herskovits is the best-known proponent of the model we are discussing and we may take his formulation as exemplary. Though Herskovits's conception of the cultural unity of West Africa was not highly systematic, most of the common elements in terms of which he described it were of a single type—overt or explicit social and cultural forms such as "patrilocality," "hoe agriculture," "corporate ownership of land," and so forth.[3] Increasing knowledge of West African cultural complexity suggests that many of these allegedly widespread or universal West African cultural "elements," "traits," or "complexes" are not at all so widespread as Herskovits supposed. In fact, it seems fair to say that many Africanists would be more inclined to stress intercultural variation on this level of cultural form and to argue that a generalized heritage of the sort Herskovits postulated for African-Americans probably does not exist.[4] Yet we believe that it is less the *unity* of West (and Central) Africa as a broad culture area that is called into question by our criticism than the *levels* at which one would have to seek confirmation of this postulated unity.

An African cultural heritage, widely shared by the people imported into any new colony, will have to be defined in less concrete terms, by focusing more on values, and less on sociocultural forms, and even by attempting to identify unconscious "grammatical" principles, which may underlie and shape behavioral response. To begin with, we would call for an examination of what Foster has called "cognitive orientations,"[5] on the one hand, basic assumptions about social relations (what values motivate individuals, how one deal with others in social situations, and matters of interpersonal style), and, on the other, basic assumptions and expectations about the way the world functions phenomenologically (for instance, beliefs about causality, and how particular causes are revealed). We would argue that certain common orientations to reality may tend to focus the attention of individuals from West and Central African cultures upon similar kinds of events, even though the ways for handling these events may seem quite diverse in formal terms. For example, the Yoruba "deify" their twins, enveloping their lives and deaths in complex ritual,[6] while the nearby Igbo summarily destroy twins at birth.[7] But both peoples appear to be responding to the same set of widespread underlying principles having to do with the supernatural significance of unusual births.

Similarly, the comparative study of people's attitudes and expectations about sociocultural change (e.g., orientations toward "additivity" in relation to foreign elements, or expectations about the degree of internal dynamism in their own culture) might reveal interesting underlying consistencies. More generally, for almost any aspect of culture one could probably identify abstract principles which are widespread in the region. For example, though "witchcraft" may figure importantly in the social life of one group and be absent from that of its neighbor, both peoples may still subscribe to the widely held African principle that social conflict can produce illness or misfortune (by means of mechanisms which Westerners class as "supernatural," and of which witchcraft is only one variant). We are aware that, in many aspects of life, the underlying principles will prove difficult to uncover. However, scholars have begun seriously to attempt to define the perceived similarities in African (and African-American) song style, graphic art, motor habits and so forth.[8]

On the basis of such research, it seems reasonable to assume that, if the perceived similarities are real, there must exist underlying principles (which will often be unconscious) that are amenable to identification, description, and confirmation. In considering African-American cultural continuities, it may well be that the more formal elements stressed by Herskovits exerted less influence on the nascent institutions for newly enslaved and transported Africans than did their common basic assumptions about social relations or the workings of the universe.

In theory at least, Herskovits himself approved of this approach. On occasion, he explicitly suggested an analogy between the "similarities in the grammar of language over the entire West African region . . . [and] what may be termed the grammar of culture."[9] Elsewhere, discussing Afro-American research strategies, he noted that "much of socially sanctioned behavior lodges on a psychological plane that lies *below the level of consciousness*," and he suggested, therefore, that more attention be paid to the study of "motor habits," "aesthetic patterns," "value systems," and so forth.[10] Likewise Simpson, writing programmatically, showed an awareness that "in the acculturative situation . . . philosophical principles and psychological attitudes are frequently more persistent and tenacious [than cultural forms] because they [may] exist below the level of consciousness."[11] Yet in spite of these pronouncements, neither Herskovits nor his students were able to advance very far beyond the level of overt forms or explicit beliefs when they actually tried to enumerate the shared characteristics of the peoples of Africa.

In commenting on the New World situation, Dalby has written:

> It is obvious that black Americans were prevented from maintaining in North America the large number of African cultural institutions and traditional customs which have survived in the Caribbean and South America. It has been less obvious to outside observers however, that black Americans have succeeded in preserving a high degree of their African "character" at the much deeper and more fundamental level of interpersonal relationships and expressive behavior.[12]

We are faced, then, with a growing awareness of the need to define and describe these deeper-level aspects of the African heritage even if we still remain quite remote from this objective. Recent ethnographic work in Africa holds promise for an eventual understanding of the kinds of principles on which such a model will have to be built, though we will need to exercise great caution in projecting current findings backward through time.

An obvious difficulty with our proposal is that anthropologists have given relatively little attention to such matters as cognitive orientations or interpersonal style, and, when they have, they have rarely done it well. But we believe that this neglect has less to do with the importance such concepts ought to have in cultural description (ethnography) than with the poverty of our conceptual tools. Our lack of the intimate knowledge of a society needed to describe a people's concepts of determinism or aesthetics, for instance, contrasts sharply with our ability to analyze an anthropologically more conventional subject, such as their patterns of residence. If there has been a tendency, then, to define the similarities among West African cultures and societies in terms of less abstract elements, we feel that this has been very much a function of the nature of traditional anthropological concerns.

We do not propose to deal with the intellectual history of American anthropology, but perhaps it is fair to note that Herskovits, the distinguished pioneer anthropologist of Afro-America in the United States, was trained in North American historical anthropology. This school placed heavy—and justifiable—emphasis upon the retrieval of the past, particularly among North American Indian peoples. Such scholarship subscribed enthusiastically to the development of techniques for the classification of aspects of culture, and the geographical description of similarities and differences among "culture areas."[13] Early studies of the indigenous peoples of North America, for example, paid much attention to food-getting techniques and principal foods, and divided up the continent into food and environmental regions. Herskovits's initial studies of Africa were devoted to defining and describing its "culture areas," in particular the so-called "East African cattle area."[14] In later work he gave careful attention to the utility of classifying culture in terms of elements, complexes, areas, etc.[15] It is neither our intention to ignore the importance of such research, nor to claim that scholars such as Herskovits and Kroeber were unaware of the limitations of their methodology. But it seems to us that it was inevitable that such work might lead to a somewhat mechanical view of culture and deemphasize processes of change and diversification. Herskovits himself often discussed these processes in a general fashion and was one of the leading figures in the development of a theory of acculturation intended to account for the nature of change.[16] But the classifactory tendency repeatedly reasserted itself in his programmatic papers,[17] and the task of combining a theory of change with a system of culture classification for Afro-America still remains to be carried out.

However one may choose to define a generalized African "heritage" shared by the slaves transported to any New World colony, we have already indicated our reservations about treating it as "a culture." We conceive of culture as being closely tied to the institutional forms which articulate it. In contrast, the notion of a shared African heritage takes on meaning only in a comparative context, when one asks what, if any, features the various cultural systems of West and Central Africa may have had in common. From a transatlantic perspective, those deep-level cultural principles, assumptions, and understandings which were shared by the Africans in any New World colony—usually, an ethnically hetero-

geneous aggregate of individuals—would have been a limited though crucial resource. For they could have served as a catalyst in the processes by which individuals from diverse societies forged new institutions, and could have provided certain frameworks within which new forms could have developed. We shall argue
later, however, that the probable importance of such generalized principles
notwithstanding, the Africans in any New World colony in fact became a *community* and began to share a *culture* only insofar as, and as fast as, they themselves
created them.

We have already suggested that there is a second shorthand way of dealing with
the ethnic heterogeneity of Africans, within the same bipartite model of culture
contact. It postulates a connection between some particular African people and
some New World colony or society and argues that the bulk of the African content
of the New World culture in question is traceable to that specific African society:
Suriname or Jamaica to the Ashanti, Haiti to the Dahomeans, and so forth. All too
often, however, the historical connections are simply inferred from a small number of formal similarities, with lexical items, for example, playing a major role in
"documenting" alleged relationships. The dangers of comparing the cultures of
contemporary Jamaica and contemporary Ashanti should be fairly obvious; so are
the difficulties in comparing what is known of the culture of the slaves in colonial
Jamaica with what can be retrieved historically concerning the Ashanti peoples of
the eighteenth century.

It seems self-evident that such comparative studies no longer can ignore the
need to demonstrate historical connection (in the sense that historians and historically minded ethnologists would use the term). Certainly the presence of
some item of behavior among both contemporary Jamaicans and contemporary
Ghanaians cannot be taken as proof of such connection. In this regard, it does not
surprise us that recent studies which begin with slave provenience and demography (rather than with historical connections inferred from cultural similarities)
tend to suggest that the slaves transported to any given colony were more ethnically heterogeneous than had previously been believed. In Haiti, for example,
there are now quantitative indications that slaves from Central Africa may actually have outnumbered those from Dahomey.[18] In *The Atlantic Slave Trade: A Census*,
Curtin, depending heavily upon Debien, concludes that almost half of the total
slave imports to Saint-Domingue in the eighteenth century came from Angola,
and only much smaller percentages from other regions.[19] Girod, also relying on
Debien, comes to the following conclusions: in the period 1756 to 1767, one-
third of the slaves in the trade to Saint-Domingue were "Congos," one-fourth
"Aradas," one-fifth "Bambaras and Senegalese," and one-sixth "Nagos and Ibos."

Between 1780 and 1792, he continues, one-sixth were "Congos," while another one-sixth consisted of slaves from the Slave Coast, Nigeria, and Dahomey.[20] Fouchard questions the tendency to reason backward to Dahomey from an analysis of *vodoun* as follows:

> The hypothesis is attractive, but it does not stand up. It is contradicted among other things by the details, for the plantation inventories attest on the one hand to numerical predominance of Congolese among runaways and, on the other, give no evidence in the peopling of Sant-Domingue—and in no period—of substantial importations of Dahomeans, but rather of Aradas in general, far from being limited to Dahomey, which was, by the way, rather hostile to the trade.[21]

Likewise, in Suriname, research over the last two decades has revealed that there was far greater ethnic heterogeneity and a very different ethnic balance than had previously been assumed. It had been customary in studies of the African heritage in Suriname to stress Guinea Coast (and particularly Gold Coast) proveniences almost to the exclusion of the Bantu-speaking region. Our quantitative data suggest, however, that slaves from Loango/Angola predominated over those from the Gold Coast at almost every period of the slave trade. In the case of Suriname, as in that of Haiti, such findings qualify long-cherished historical beliefs, which were based on large part on inference from perceived cultural similarities.[22]

We would note one final problem with the model that posits a single African culture as the source for a particular New World tradition. The holistic concept of culture implied in it has the effect of masking the processes implicit in both the continuities and discontinuities between Africa and the Americas. To assume that the slaves in any colony were somehow committed culturally to one or another path of development both evades the empirical question of what really happened and masks the central theoretical issue of how cultures change. For example, to attribute the form of *vodoun* initiation rites to Dahomey[23] might be justified, on a provisional level. But on another more interesting level, we still face the question of which elements of the ritual were faithfully transmitted, which lost, which modified, and by what processes, so that the Haitian rite of today may be understood for what it is: a truly Haitian innovation, constructed in particular ways and under particular circumstances by particular enslaved Africans, and perpetuated by succeeding generations—doubtless, in ever-changing form—for more than two centuries.

The tendency to assume initial cultural homogeneity among the enslaved in a particular colony nevertheless persists. Here are examples: G. Hall writes, "The West African brought with him complex ideas about property. In Dahomey, *which had the greatest cultural influence in St. Domingue*, everything belonged, in theory, to the king" (emphasis added).[24] Hurbon goes further:

> But Africa is still so evident in America that one could speak of the existence of three Americas, one white, one Indian and, finally, black America. In North America, for instance, one can find in the Gullah Islands and in Virginia, the predominance of Fanti-Ashanti cultures; in New Orleans, Dahomean and Bantu culture; in Central America, Yoruba culture; and in Haiti and Northern Brazil, that of Dahomean (Fon) culture; in Jamaica, and the Barbadian Islands [sic] and Saint Lucia, that of the Kromonti of the Gold Coast; in French and Dutch Guiana, that of Fanti-Ashanti.[25]

Maps tracing alleged lines of cultural influence from particular African regions to particular New World colonies are still popular among Afro-Americanists,[26] though it seems increasingly clear that they involve risky oversimplifications.

We have suggested that much of the problem with the traditional model of early African-American culture history lies in its view of culture as some sort of undifferentiated whole. Given the social setting of early New World colonies, the encounters between Africans from a score or more different societies with each other, and with their European overlords, cannot be interpreted in terms of two (or even many different) "bodies" of belief and value, each coherent, functioning, and intact. The Africans who reached the New World did not compose, at the outset, *groups*. In fact, in most cases, it might even be more accurate to view them as *crowds*, and very heterogeneous crowds at that. Without diminishing the probable importance of some core of common values, and the occurrence of situations where a number of slaves of common origin might indeed have been aggregated, the fact is that these were not *communities* of people at first, and they could only become communities by processes of cultural exchange. What the slaves undeniably shared at the outset was their enslavement; all—or nearly all—else had to be *created by them*. In order for slave communities to take shape, normative patterns of behavior had to be established, and these patterns could be created only on the basis of particular forms of social interaction.

While immense quantities of knowledge, information, and belief must have been transported in the minds of the enslaved, they were not able to transfer the human complement of their traditional institutions to the New World. Members of ethnic groups of differing status, yes; but different status systems, no. Priests and priestesses, yes; but priesthoods and temples, no. Princes and princesses, yes; but courts and monarchies, no. In short, the personnel responsible for the orderly perpetuation of the specific institutions of African societies were not (in any instance known to us) transferred intact to the new settings. (We repeat that the same problem was faced, though in most cases to a different degree, by the European migrants as well.) Thus the organizational task of enslaved Africans in the New World was that of creating institutions—institutions that would prove responsive to the needs of everyday life under the limiting conditions that slavery imposed upon them.

It is in delineating the difference between such institutions and the cultural materials of African origin that could form part of African-American life that the distinction between what is "social" and what is "cultural" becomes relevant. For some years now, the importance of this distinction to the study of African-American culture history has been sporadically pointed out on a programmatic level. Herskovits, for instance, noted that in acculturation studies "it must always be borne in mind that the carriers [of culture] themselves are the crucial elements." M. G. Smith discusses more fully the fact that "social structure is embodied in cultural process . . . [and] vice versa," adding that "the study of African heritage [in the New World] in purely cultural terms is not adequately conceived and cannot by itself reveal the processes and conditions of acculturation. Thus, if acculturation, rather than the simple identification of elements as African or other, is the aim of such study, we must study the relevant social conditions equally and simultaneously." We do not believe, however, that enough researchers have taken full advantage of these insights in their substantive studies.[27]

We might illustrate the difference between these terms by an example. The Africans who were imported into the New World came from groups speaking many different languages and had no single common language to employ among themselves. Some or many may have been bilingual or even trilingual, and some undoubtedly found in the new setting a few others with whom they could converse in a familiar language. Yet we can assume with confidence that the *initial* aggregates of slaves in particular New World enterprises usually did not constitute speech communities. Often, the languages in which slaves and masters communicated were "pidgin" or trade languages, that is, languages with reduced grammars and lexicons, used for specialized activities (such as trade) involving groups with no language in common. There is no consensus as to whether such languages were created in the New World or based ultimately on pidgins spoken in West Africa.[28] Nonetheless, it is clear that the first language of communication between masters and slaves would have been a specialized language of this kind. This same language would commonly become what the slaves spoke among themselves in the same setting, whether or not some of them had spoken this same pidgin or a different one in Africa, and whether or not it was learned before or during enslavement.

Soon after the slave settlements had begun to grow in the New World, the various African languages spoken by their inhabitants would, in the absence of a continuing speech community, begin to fall into disuse (except in special ritual settings), to be supplanted by a pidgin. Children born to slave mothers would learn the pidgin spoken by their parents as their first or native language, and in the process the pidgin would expand lexically to serve the new expressive functions of a language no longer narrowly specialized. At this stage, once the language has become the native idiom of a speaking group, it is no longer a pidgin but a "creole." The distinction we employ here is based on a sociological, not a linguistic, criterion, though linguistic criteria also may be utilized to clarify the difference.

We feel it important to stress this distinction between a language's "social" (or social-relational) and "cultural" dimensions. True, these are simply different ways of looking at the same phenomenon. But these different perspectives call into question different problems. The content and structure of a creole language, its syntax, phonology, lexicon, and morphology, as well as the history of its various features, constitute the subject matter of one set of research questions. The ways in which the language is used, by whom, and under what circumstances raise a quite different set. By no means do we suppose that all problems connected with the study of such a language can be grouped neatly under a "cultural" or "social-relational" rubric. But the failure to employ these different perspectives may conceal a number of issues that lend themselves to analysis only if the distinction is taken into account. We want to know not only how a particular language, as language, assumed a systematic and distinctive shape, in terms of its linguistic character, but also by what social processes such a language became standardized, was taught to newly imported slaves, could be enriched by new experiences, invested with new symbolic meanings, and attached to status differences. We would suggest, in fact, that the first set of questions cannot really be entirely resolved without reference to the second, because language as such does not take on its characteristic shape without reference to such sociological features as the number of speakers involved, the context in which communication occurs (or does not occur), the purposes to which such communication is put, and the like.[29] Treating culture as a list of traits or objects or words is to miss the manner in which social relations are carried on through it—and thus to ignore the most important way in which it can change or be changed.

We have sought here to propose an approach to the study of African-American societies and cultures which refines—rather than discards or disproves—earlier approaches. Our central thesis is simple: that continuities between the Old World and the New must be established upon an understanding of the basic conditions under which the migrations of enslaved Africans occurred. To support this thesis, we have employed both documentary materials and speculation to describe those conditions and to suggest some of the social processes at work in the early confrontations between Europeans and Africans.

We are not prepared to analyze these processes, neither by assuming that the African societies which contributed peoples and cultural heritages to the building of Afro-America were homogeneous, nor by assuming that any New World colony was peopled primarily by migrants from some single African social-relational and cultural perspective in understanding what really happened, since we understand the proliferation of new social institutions under slavery to be the precondition and basis for continuities in culture. Our view of the free and slave sectors as deeply divided from each other, yet profoundly interdependent, is critical to our understanding of how such institution-building took place. As we have contended, some of these institutions were rooted in the relationships between the two sectors; others, even more important to our argument here, developed largely within the slave sector, though always subject to outer limits of variability imposed by the society at large. Thus, when seen from the vantage point of daily social interaction, slave institutions do appear to assume in some fashion a concentric order, extending from the immediate interpersonal links between two persons, through the domestic and familial ties of larger groupings, and outward to the religious, economic, and other institutions that bound slave communities together. The institutions linking enslaved and free people constitute a different order, or dimension, of social action, since the linkages inevitably crossed the chasm between the sectors. But as we have sought to stress, these are not different orders or dimensions in the sense that they were totally separate; such separation was more apparent than real, so far as day-to-day life was concerned.

African-American social and cultural forms were forged in the fires of enslavement, but these forms could not, and cannot, be defined by confining them to those peoples or societies whose physical origins were African any more than Euro-American social and cultural forms are limited to those whose physical origins were European. The eminent historian of the American South, C. Vann Woodward, is close to the truth when he asserts that "so far as their culture is concerned, all Americans are part Negro."[30] Some would prefer to say "part

African" and others "part black"; in any case, we stand with Herskovits: "whether Negroes borrowed from whites or whites from Negroes, in this or any other aspect of culture, it must always be remembered that the borrowing was never achieved without resultant change in whatever was borrowed, and, in addition, without incorporating elements which originated in the new habits that, as much as anything else, give the new form its distinctive quality."[31] As we have sought to suggest, "borrowing" may not best express the reality at all—"creating" or "remodeling" may be more precise.

We regard few of our contentions as proved or even certain. The test of their validity, in fact, should rest more with the tasks of serious historical and anthropological research, and far less with their persuasiveness on logical, ideological, or sentimental grounds. Indeed we suspect that our arguments can be pressed into service for quite different *partis-pris*, much as occurred with the positions taken by our predecessors in the study of Afro-America. The inescapable fact in the study of Afro-America is the humanity of the oppressed, and the inhumanity of the systems that oppressed them. But not all slavery systems oppressed all slaves equally, and not all slaves dealt with their oppression in the same ways. We have attempted here to suggest certain research directions that might prove fruitful in the examination of contemporary African-American societies by ethnographic procedures, and the histories of such societies, through the use of documents, historical records, and the recollections of living people. It is our concern to support our contention that the people in African-American societies, in which oppression was pervasive, quite literally built their life-ways to meet their daily needs.

The general theoretical position we take in this essay is that the past must be viewed as the conditioning circumstance of the present. We do not believe that the present can be "understood"—in the sense of explaining the relationships among different contemporary institutional forms—without reference to the past. We suppose this to be the case, whether our interest be in the European peoples who conquered the world they called "new," the Indian peoples they destroyed and subjugated with it, or the African—and, later, Asian—peoples they dragged into it. New World it is, for those who became its peoples remade it, and in the process, they remade themselves.

NOTES

1. H. Hoetink, *The Two Variants in Caribbean Race Relations* (London: Oxford University Press, 1967):111 *et seq.*

2. The relative cultural homogeneity of African peoples in their ancestral homeland, as compared with that of the Europeans, is not at issue here. What we would stress is that enslaved Africans were usually randomized (or in some cases even deliberately heterogenized) by enslavement, transportation, and seasoning so as to make their initial New World experience very different from that of the Europeans.

3. Melville J. Herskovits, *The Myth of the Negro Past* (1941; reprint, Boston: Beacon Press, 1990), 81–85.

4. See, for example, P.C. Lloyd, *Africa in Social Change* (Baltimore: Penguin, 1972): 25–27, and T. O. Ranger, "Recent developments in the study of African religious and cultural history and their relevance for the historiography of the Diaspora," *Ufahamu* 4(2)(1973):17–34. M. G. Smith offers one of the more extreme statements of this position: "[T]he types of ambiguity which lurk within the unitary concept of an african inheritance are great indeed . . . [It presupposes a uniformity and uniqueness of African cultures which ethnography does not support . . . [There are] marked cultural dissimilarities within the West African regions from which the bulk of Caribbean Negroes trace descent. Even when the influence of Islam in this area is excluded, there remain sufficiently important differences of culture for reference to or definition of a cultural pattern as characteristic of this area to remain highly suspect." M. G. Smith, "The African heritage in the Caribbean," in *Caribbean Studies: A Symposium*, ed. V. Rubin (Seattle: University of Washington Press, 1957): 36, 39–40.

5. George M. Foster, "Peasant society and the image of limited good," *American Anthropologist* 67(1965):293.

6. Robert F. Thompson, *Black Gods and Kings*, Occasional Papers of the Museum and Laboratories of Ethnic Arts and Technology (Los Angeles: University of California, 1971), ch. 13, 1–5.

7. Victor C. Uchendu, *The Igbo of Southeast Nigeria* (New York: Holt, Rinehart and Winston, 1965):58.

8. See, for example, Alan Lomax, "The homogeneity of African-Afro-American musical style," in *Afro-American Anthropology*, ed. N. Whitten and J. Szwed (New York: Free Press, 1970):181–201; Alan P. Merriam, "African music," in *Continuity and Change in African Cultures*, ed. William R. Bascom and Melville J. Herskovits (Chicago: University of Chicago Press, 1969): 49–86; J. H. Kwabena Nketia, "African music," in *Peoples and Cultures of Africa*, ed. E. P. Skinner (Garden City: Natural History Press, 173); 580–99; Robert P. Armstrong, *The Affecting Presence* (Urbana: University of Illinois Press, 1971); Robert F. Thompson, "An esthetic of the cool: West African dance," *African Forum* 2(2) (1966): 85–102; and Roger D. Abrahams, "The shaping of folklore traditions in the British West Indies," *Journal of Inter-American Studies* 9(1967):456–80.

9. Herskovits, *Myth of the Negro Past*: 81.

10. Melville J. Herskovits, "Some psychological implications of Afroamerican studies,"

in *Acculturation in the Americas*, ed. Sol Tax (Chicago: University of Chicago Press, 1952): 153 (his italics); 153–55.

11. George E. Simpson, "Afro-American religions and religious behavior," *Caribbean Studies* 12(2) (1972):12.

12. David Dalby, "The African element in American English," in *Rappin' and Stylin' Out: Communication in Urban Black America*, ed. T. Kochman (Urbana: University of Illinois Press, 1972): 173.

13. See, for instance, Alfred L. Kroeber, *Cultural and Natural Areas of Native North America*, University of California Publications in American Archeology and Ethnology 38 (Berkeley: University of California Press, 1939).

14. Melville J. Herskovits, "A preliminary consideration of the culture areas of Africa," *American Anthropologist* 26(1924):50–63.

15. See, for instance, Melville J. Herskovits, *Man and His Works* (New York: Knopf, 1948).

16. Melville J. Herskovits, *Acculturation: The Study of Culture Contact* (New York: J. J. Augustin, 1938); Herskovits, "Introduction," in Tax, ed., *Acculturation in the Americas* 48–63; Robert Redfield, Ralph Linton, and Melville J. Herskovits, "Memorandum for the study of acculturation," *American Anthropologist* 38 (1936):149–52.

17. See, for example, Melville J. Herskovits, "Problem, method and theory in Afroamerican studies," *Afroamérica* 1 (1945):5–24.

18. See Dieudonné Rinchon, *Le trafic négrier* (Brussels: Atlas, 1938); Gabriel Debien, "Les origines des esclaves des Antilles," *Bulletin de l'Institut Français d'Afrique Noire* 23, sér. B., nos. 3–4 (1961):363–87; *idem*, "Les origines des esclaves des Antilles," *Bulletin de l'Institut Français d'Afrique Noire* 27, sér. B., nos. 3–4 (1965):755–99; *idem*, "Les origines des esclaves aux Antilles," *Bulletin de l'Institut Français d'Afrique Noire* 24, sér. B., nos. 3–4 (1967):536–58; M. Delafosse and G. Debien, "Les origines des esclaves aux Antilles," *Bulletin de l'Institut Français d'Afrique Noire* 27, sér. B., nos. 1–2 (1965):319–69; J. Houdaille, "Les origines des esclaves des Antilles," *Bulletin de l'Institut Français d'Afrique Noire* 26, sér. B., nos. 3–4 (1964):601–75; and J. Houdaille, R. Massio, and G. Debien, "Les origines des esclaves des Antilles," *Bulletin de l'Institut Français d'Afrique Noire* 25, sér. B., nos. 3–4 (1963):215–65.

19. Philip Curtin, *The Atlantic Slave Trade: A Census* (Madison: University of Wisconsin Press, 1969).

20. Francois Girod, *De la socélé créole: Saint-Domingue au 18e siècle* (Paris: Hachette, 1972):123.

21. Jean Fouchard, *Les marrons de la liberté* (Paris: Editions de l'Ecole, 1972): 183–89.

22. For details, see Richard Price, "KiKoongo and Saramaccan: A reappraisal," *Bijdragen tot de Taal-, Land-, en Volkenkunde* 131 (1975): 461–78; *idem, The Guiana Maroons, A Historical and Bibliographical Introduction* (Baltimore and London: The Johns Hopkins University Press, 1976). We do not mean to contend that absolute numbers were the only, or necessarily the most important, determinant of the particular forms

cultural development would take in these situations. In fact, our contention is more to the contrary: quite apart from much more careful research on the precise composition of migrant groups in particular locales at particular points in time, we need to examine very carefully whatever is available concerning the specific social contexts within which cultural innovation and perpetuation could occur. We recognize—as we shall later make clear—that even single individuals might make a disproportionately large contribution to the evolution of specific forms.

23. Angelina Pollak-Eltz, *Afro-Amerikaanse godsdiensten en culten* (Roermond: J. J. Romen en Zonen, 1970): 142.

24. Gwendolyn M. Hall, *Social Control in Slave Plantation Societies* (Baltimore: Johns Hopkins University Press, 1971):66.

25. Laënnee Hurbon, *Dieu dans le vaudou haïtien* (Paris: Payot, 1972): 73.

26. See, for instance, Roger Bastide, *Les Amériques noires* (Paris: Payot, 1967): 17–19; Pollak-Eltz, *Afro-Amerikaanse godsdiensten*: 68.

27. Herskovits, *Myth of the Negro Past*: 86–87; M. G. Smith, "African heritage": 35.

28. See Mervyn C. Alleyne, "Acculturation and the cultural matrix of creolization," in *Pidginization and Creolization of Languages*, ed. Dell Hymes (Cambridge: Cambridge University Press, 1971): 169–86; David DeCamp, "Introduction: The study of pidgin and creole languages," in Hymes, *Pidginization*: 13–39; Sidney W. Mintz, "The socio-historical background of pidginization and creolization," in Hymes, *Pidginization*: 153–68.

29. Dell Hymes, *Foundations in Sociolinguistics: An Ethnographic Approach* (Philadelphia: University of Pennsylvania Press, 1974); William Labov, *Sociolinguistic Patterns* (Philadelphia: University of Pennsylvania Press, 1972).

30. C. Vann Woodward, "Clio with soul," *Journal of American History* 56(1969):17.

31. Herskovits, *Myth of the Negro Past*: 225.

SELECTED BIBLIOGRAPHY FOR FURTHER READING

Herskovits, Melville J. *The Myth of the Negro Past*. Boston: Beacon, 1990.

Holloway, Joseph E., ed. *Africanisms in American Culture*. Bloomington: Indiana University Press, 1990.

Sobel, Mechal. *The World They Made Together: Black and White Values in Eighteenth-Century Virginia*. Princeton: Princeton University Press, 1987.

Stuckey, Sterling. *Slave Culture: Nationalist Theory and the Foundations of Black America*. New York: Oxford University Press, 1987.

Thornton, John. *Africa and Africans in the Making of the Atlantic World, 1400–1680*. Cambridge: Cambridge University Press, 1992.

SLAVE RELIGION   II::

Lawrence W. Levine

4 ::

::Black religion under slavery has been termed "the invisible institution" because independent religious meetings led by African-Americans were illegal and had to be conducted in secret. Because of the secrecy involved and the fact that most participants were illiterate, slave religion was considered invisible to historians until the 1970s when several scholars demonstrated that there were indeed ample sources deriving from the slaves themselves in the forms of grave art, folklore, slave narratives, and autobiographies. An influential example of this fresh approach was the following 1971 article by Lawrence W. Levine that explored the songs of slaves.::

:: 4

SLAVE SONGS AND
SLAVE CONSCIOUSNESS

An Exploration in
Neglected Sources

Lawrence W. Levine

:: Negroes in the United States, both during and after slavery, were anything but inarticulate. They sang songs, told stories, played verbal games, listened and responded to sermons, and expressed their aspirations, fears, and values through the medium of an oral tradition that had characterized the West African cultures from which their ancestors had come. By largely ignoring this tradition, much of which has been preserved, historians have rendered an articulate people historically inarticulate, and have allowed the record of their consciousness to go unexplored.

Having worked my way carefully through thousands of Negro songs, folk-tales, jokes, and games, I am painfully aware of the problems inherent in the use of such materials. They are difficult, often impossible, to date with any precision. Their geographical distribution is usually unclear. They were collected elatedly, most frequently by men and women who had little understanding of the culture from which they sprang, and little scruple about altering or suppressing them. Such major collectors as John Lomax, Howard Odum, and Newman White all admitted openly that many of the songs they collected were "unprintable" by the moral standards which guided them and presumably their readers. But historians have overcome imperfect records before. They have learned how to deal with altered documents, with consciously or unconsciously biased first hand accounts, with manuscript collections that were deposited in archives only after being filtered through the overprotective hands of fearful relatives, and with the comparative lack of contemporary sources and the need to use their materials retrospectively. The challenge presented by the materials of folk and popular culture is neither totally unique nor insurmountable.

In this essay I want to illustrate the possible use of materials of this kind by discussing the contribution that an understanding of Negro songs can make to the recent debate over slave personality. In the process I will discuss several aspects of the literature and problems related to the use of slave songs.

The subject of Negro music in slavery has produced a large and varied literature, little of which has been devoted to questions of meaning and function. The one major exception is Miles Mark Fisher's 1953 study, *Negro Slave Songs in the United States*, which attempts to get at the essence of slave life through an analysis of slave songs. Unfortunately, Fisher's rich insights are too often marred by his rather loose scholarly standards, and despite its continuing value his study is in many respects an example of how *not* to use Negro songs. Asserting, correctly, that the words of slave songs "show both accidental and intentional errors of transmission," Fisher changes the words almost at will to fit his own image of their pristine form. Arguing persuasively that "transplanted Negroes continued to promote their own culture by music," Fisher makes their songs part of an "African cult" which he simply wills into existence. Maintaining (again, I think, correctly), that "slave songs preserved in joyful strains the adjustment which Negroes made to their living conditions within the United States," Fisher traces the major patterns of that adjustment by arbitrarily dating these songs, apparently unperturbed by the almost total lack of evidence pertaining to the origin and introduction of individual slave songs.[1]

Fisher aside, most other major studies of slave music have focused almost entirely upon musical structure and origin. This latter question especially has given rise to a long and heated debate.[2] The earliest collectors and students of slave music were impressed by how different that music was from anything familiar to them. Following a visit to the Sea Islands in 1862, Lucy McKim despaired of being able "to express the entire character of these negro ballads by mere musical notes and signs. The odd turns made in the throat; and that curious rhythmic effect produced by single voices chiming in at different irregular intervals, seem almost as impossible to place on score, as the singing of birds, or the tones of an Aeolian Harp."[3] Although some of these early collectors maintained, as did W.F. Allen in 1865, that much of the slave's music "might no doubt be traced to tunes which they have heard from the whites, and transformed to their own use,

. . . their music . . . is rather European than African in its character,"[4] they more often stressed the distinctiveness of the Negro's music and attributed it to racial characteristics, African origins, and indigenous developments resulting from the slave's unique experience in the New World.

This tradition, which has had many influential twentieth-century adherents,[5] was increasingly challenged in the early decades of the century. Such scholars as Newman White, Guy Johnson, and George Pullen Jackson argued that the earlier school lacked a comparative grounding in Anglo-American folk song. Comparing Negro spirituals with Methodist and Baptist evangelical religious music of the late eighteenth and early nineteenth centuries, White, Johnson, and Jackson found similarities in words, subject matter, tunes, and musical structure.[6] Although they tended to exaggerate both qualitatively and quantitatively the degrees of similarity, their comparisons were often a persuasive and important corrective to the work of their predecessors. But their studies were inevitably weakened by their ethnocentric assumption that similarities alone settled the argument over origins. Never could they contemplate the possibility that the direction of cultural diffusion might have been from black to white as well as the other way. In fact, insofar as white evangelical music departed from traditional Protestant hymnology and embodied or approached the complex rhythmic structure, the percussive qualities, the polymeter, the syncopation, the emphasis on overlapping call and response patterns that characterized Negro music both in West Africa and the New World, the possibility that it was influenced by slaves who attended and joined in the singing at religious meetings is quite high.

These scholars tended to use the similarities between black and white religious music to deny the significance of slave songs in still another way. Newman White, for example, argued that since white evangelical hymns also used such expressions as "freedom," the "Promised Land," and the "Egyptian Bondage," "without thought of other than spiritual meaning," these images when they occurred in Negro spirituals could not have been symbolic "of the Negro's longing for physical freedom."[7] The familiar process by which different cultural groups can derive varied meanings from identical images is enough to cast doubt on the logic of White's argument.[8] In the case of white and black religious music, however, the problem may be much less complex, since it is quite possible that the similar images in the songs of both groups in fact served similar purposes. Many of those whites who flocked to the camp meetings of the Methodists and Baptists were themselves on the social and economic margins of their society, and had psychic and emotional needs which, qualitatively, may not have been vastly different from those of black slaves. Interestingly, George Pullen Jackson, in his attempt to prove the white origin of Negro spirituals, makes exactly this point: "I may mention in closing the chief remaining argument of the die-hards for the Negro source of the Negro spirituals. . . . How could any, the argument runs, but a natively musical and sorely oppressed race create such beautiful things as 'Swing Low,' 'Steal Away,' and 'Deep River'? . . . But were not the whites of the mountains and the hard-scrabble hill country also 'musical and oppressed'? . . . Yes, these whites were musical, and oppressed too. If their condition was any more tolerable than that of the Negroes, one certainly does not get that impression from any of their songs of release and escape."[9] If this is true, the presence of similar images in white music would merely heighten rather than detract from the significance of these images in Negro songs. Clearly, the function and meaning of white religious music during the late eighteenth and early nineteenth centuries demands far more attention than it has received. In the interim, we must be wary of allowing the mere fact of similarities to deter us from attempting to comprehend the cultural dynamics of slave music.

Contemporary scholars, tending to transcend the more simplistic lines of the old debate, have focused upon the process of syncretism to explain the development of Negro music in the United States. The rich West African musical tradition common to almost all of the specific cultures from which Negro slaves came, the comparative cultural isolation in which large numbers of slaves lived, the tolerance and even encouragement which their white masters accorded to their musical activities, and the fact that, for all its differences, nothing in the European musical tradition with which they came into contact in America was totally alien to their own traditions—all these were conducive to a situation which allowed the slaves to retain a good deal of the integrity of their own musical heritage while fusing to it compatible elements of Anglo-American music. Slaves often took over entire white hymns and folks songs, as White and Jackson maintained, but altered them significantly in terms of words, musical structure, and especially performance before making them their own. The result was a hybrid with a strong African base.[10]

One of the more interesting aspects of this debate over origins is that no one engaged in it, not even advocates of the white derivation theory, denied that the slaves possessed their own distinctive music. Newman White took particular pains to point out again and again that the notion that Negro song is purely an imitation of the white man's music "is fully as unjust and inaccurate, in the final analysis, as the Negro's assumption that his folk-song is entirely original." He observed that in the slaves' separate religious meetings they were free to do as they would with the music they first learned from the whites, with the result that their spirituals became "the greatest single outlet for the expression of the Negro folk-mind."[11] Similarly, George Pullen Jackson, after admitting that he could find no white parallels for over two-thirds of the existing Negro spirituals, reasoned that these were produced by Negro singers in true folk fashion "by endless singing of heard tunes and by endless, inevitable and concomitant singing differentiation." Going even further, Jackson asserted that the lack of deep roots in Anglo-American culture left the black man "even freer than the white man to make songs over unconsciously as he sang . . . the free play has resulted in the very large number of songs which, though formed primarily in the white man's moulds, have lost all recognizable relationship to known individual white-sung melodic entities."[12] This debate over origins indicates clearly that a belief in the direct continuity of African musical traditions or in the process of syncretism is not a necessary prerequisite to the conclusion that the Negro slaves' music was their own, regardless of where they received the components out of which it was fashioned, a conclusion which is crucial to any attempt to utilize these songs as an aid in reconstructing the slaves' consciousness.

Equally important is the process by which slave songs were created and transmitted. When James McKim asked a freedman on the Sea Islands during the Civil War where the slaves got their songs, the answer was eloquently simple: "Dey make em, sah."[13] Precisely *how* they made them worried and fascinated Thomas Wentworth Higginson, who became familiar with slave music through the singing of the black Union soldiers in his Civil War regiment. Were their songs, he wondered, a "conscious and definite" product of "some leading mind," or did they grow "by gradual accretion, in an almost unconscious way"? A freedman rowing Higginson and some of his troops between the Sea Islands helped to resolve the problem when he described a spiritual which he had a hand in creating:

> Once we boys went for some rice and de nigger-driver he keep a'callin' on us; and I say, "O de ole nigger-driver!" Den anudder said, "Fust ting my mammy tole me was, notin' so bad as nigger-driver." Den I made a sing, just puttin' a word, and den anudder word.

He then began to sing his song:

> O, de ole nigger-driver!
> O, gwine away!
> Fust ting my mammy tell me,
> O, gwine away!

> Tell me 'bout de nigger-driver,
> O, gwine away!
> Nigger-driver second devil,
> O, gwine away!

Higginson's black soldiers, after a moment's hesitation, joined in the singing of a song they had never heard before as if they had long been familiar with it. "I saw," Higginson concluded, "how easily a new 'sing' took root among them."[14]

This spontaneity, this sense of almost instantaneous community which so impressed Higginson, constitutes a central element in every account of slave singing. The English musician Henry Russell, who lived in the United States in the 1830s, was forcibly struck by the ease with which a slave congregation in Vicksburg, Mississippi, took a "fine old psalm tune" and, by suddenly and spontaneously accelerating the tempo, transformed it "into a kind of negro melody."[15] "Us old heads," an ex-slave told Jeanette Robinson Murphy, "use ter make 'em up on de spurn of de moment. Notes is good enough for you people, but us likes a mixtery." Her account of the creation of a spiritual is typical and important:

> We'd all be at the "prayer house" de Lord's day, and de white preacher he'd splain de word and read whar Esekial done say—
>
> *Dry bones gwine ter lib ergin.*
>
> And, honey, de Lord would come a-shinin' thoo dem pages and revive dis ole nigger's heart, and I'd jump up dar and den and holler and shout and sing and pat, and dey would all cotch de words and I'd sing it to some ole shout song I'd heard 'em sing from Africa, and dey'd all take it up and keep at it, and keep a-addin' to it, and den it would be a spiritual.[16]

This "internal" account has been verified again and again by the descriptions of observers, many of whom were witnessing not slave services but religious meetings of rural southern Negroes long after emancipation. The essential continuity of the Negro folk process in the more isolated sections of the rural South through the early decades of the twentieth century makes these accounts relevant for the slave period as well. Natalie Curtis Burlin, whose collection of spirituals is musically the most accurate one we have, and who had a long and close acquaintance with Negro music, never lost her sense of awe at the process by which these songs were molded. On a hot July Sunday in rural Virginia, she sat in a Negro meeting house listening to the preacher deliver his prayer, interrupted now and then by an "O Lord!" or "Amen, Amen" from the congregation.

Minutes passed, long minutes of strange intensity. The mutterings, the ejaculations, grew louder, more dramatic, till suddenly I felt the creative thrill dart through the people like an electric vibration that same half-audible hum arose,—emotion was gathering atmospherically as clouds gather—and then, up from the depths of some "sinner's" remorse and imploring came a pitiful little plea, a real "moan," sobbed in musical cadence. From somewhere in that bowed gathering another voice improvised a response: the plea sounded again, louder this time and more impassioned; then other voices joined in the answer, shaping it into a musical phrase; and so, before our ears, as one might say, from this molten metal of music a new song was smithied out, composed then and there by no one in particular and by everyone in general.[17]

Clifton Furness has given us an even more graphic description. During a visit to an isolated South Carolina plantation in 1926, he attended a prayer meeting held in the old slave cabins. The preacher began his reading of the Scriptures slowly, then increased his tempo and emotional fervor, assuring his flock that "Gawd's lightnin' gwine strike! Gawd's thunder swaller de ert!"

Gradually moaning became audible in the shadowy corners where the women sat. Some patted their bundled babies in time to the flow of the words, and began swaying backward and forward. Several men moved their feet alternately, in strange syncopation. A rhythm was born, almost without reference to the words that were being spoken by the preacher. It seemed to take shape almost visibly, and grow. I was gripped with the feeling of a mass intelligence, a self-conscious entity, gradually informing the crowd and taking possession of every mind there, including my own.

In the midst of this increasing intensity, a black man sitting directly in front of Furness, his head bowed, his body swaying, his feet patting up and down, suddenly cried out: "Git right—sodger Git right—sodger! Git right—wit Gawd!"

Instantly the crowd took it up, moulding a melody out of half-formed familiar phrases based upon a spiritual tune, hummed here and there among the crowd. A distinct melodic outline became more and more prominent, shaping itself around the central theme of the words, "Git right, sodger!"

Scraps of other words and tunes were flung into the medley of sound by individual singers from time to time, but the general trend was carried on by a deep undercurrent, which appeared to be stronger than the mind of any individual present, for it bore the mass of improvised harmony and rhythms into the most effective climax of incremental repetition that I have ever heard.

I felt as if some conscious plan or purpose were carrying us along, call it mob-mind, communal composition, or what you will.[18]

Shortly after the Civil War, Elizabeth Kilham witnessed a similar scene among the freedmen, and described it in terms almost identical to those used by observers many years later. "A fog seemed to fill the church," she wrote, " . . . an invisible power seemed to hold us in its iron grasp; . . . A few moments more, and I think we should have shrieked in unison with the crowd."[19]

These accounts and others like them make it clear that spirituals both during and after slavery were the product of an improvisational communal consciousness. They were not, as some observers thought, totally new creations, but were forged out of many preexisting bits of old songs mixed together with snatches of new tunes and lyrics and fit into a fairly traditional but never wholly static metrical pattern. They were, to answer Higginson's question, *simultaneously* the result of individual and mass creativity. They were products of that folk process which has been called "communal re-creation," through which older songs are constantly recreated into essentially new entities.[20] Anyone who has read through large numbers of Negro songs is familiar with this process. Identical or slightly varied stanzas appear in song after song; identical tunes are made to accommodate completely different sets of lyrics; the same song appears in different collections in widely varied forms. In 1845 a traveler observed that the only permanent elements in Negro song were the music and the chorus. "The blacks themselves leave out old stanzas, and introduce new ones at pleasure. Travelling through the South, you may, in passing from Virginia to Louisiana, hear the same tune a hundred times, but seldom the same words accompanying it."[21] Another observer noted in 1870 that during a single religious meeting the freedmen would often sing the words of one spiritual to several different tunes, and then take a tune that particularly pleased them and fit the words of several different songs to it.[22] Slave songs, then, were never static; at no time did Negroes create a "final" version of any spiritual. Always the community felt free to alter and recreate them.

The two facts that I have attempted to establish thus far—that slave music, regardless of its origins, was a distinctive cultural form, and that it was created or constantly recreated through a communal process—are essential if one is to justify the use of these songs as keys to slave consciousness. But these facts in themselves say a good deal about the nature and quality of slave life and personality. That black slaves could create and continually recreate songs marked by the poetic beauty, the emotional intensity, the rich imagery which characterized the spirituals—songs which even one of the most devout proponents of the white man's origins school admits are "the most impressive religious folk songs in our language"[23]—should be enough to make us seriously question recent theories which conceive of slavery as a closed system which destroyed the vitality of the Negro and left him a dependent child. For all of its horrors, slavery was never so complete a system of psychic assault that it prevented the slaves from carving out independent cultural forms. It never pervaded all of the interstices of their minds and their culture, and in those gaps they were able to create an independent art form and a distinctive voice. If North American slavery eroded the African's linguistic and institutional life, if it prevented him from preserving and developing his rich heritage of graphic and plastic art, it nevertheless allowed him to continue and to develop the patterns of verbal art which were so central to his past culture. Historians have not yet come to terms with what the continuance of the oral tradition meant to blacks in slavery.

In Africa, songs, tales, proverbs, and verbal games served the dual function of not only preserving communal values and solidarity, but also of providing occasions for the individual to transcend, at least symbolically, the inevitable restrictions of his environment and his society by permitting him to express deeply held feelings which he ordinarily was not allowed to verbalize. Among the Ashanti and the Dahomeans, for example, periods were set aside when the inhabitants were encouraged to gather together and, through the medium of song, dance, and tales, to express openly their feelings about each other. The psychological release this afforded seems to have been well understood. "You know that everyone has a *sunsum* (soul) that may get hurt or knocked about or become sick, and so make the body ill," an Ashanti high priest explained to the English anthropologist R. S. Rattray:

> Very often . . . ill health is caused by the evil and the hate that another has in
> his head against you. Again, you too may have hatred in your head against an-
> other, because of something that person has done to you, and that, too, causes
> your *sunsum* to fret and become sick. Our forbears knew this to be the case,
> and so they ordained a time, once every year, when every man and woman,
> free man and slave, should have freedom to speak out just what was in their
> head, to tell their neighbours just what they thought of them, and of their ac-
> tions, and not only their neighbors, but also the king or chief. When a man has
> spoken freely thus, he will feel his *sunsum* cool and quieted, and the *sunsum* of
> the other person against whom he has now openly spoken will be quieted also.

Utilization of verbal art for this purpose was widespread throughout Africa, and was not confined to those ceremonial occasions when one could directly state one's feelings. Through innuendo, metaphor, and circumlocution, Africans could utilize their songs as outlets for individual release without disturbing communal solidarity.[24]

There is abundant internal evidence that the verbal art of the slaves in the United States served many of these traditional functions. Just as the process by which the spirituals were created allowed for simultaneous individual and communal creativity, so their very structure provided simultaneous outlets for individual and communal expression. The overriding antiphonal structure of the spirituals—the call and response pattern which Negroes brought with them from Africa and which was reinforced by the relatively similar white practice of "lining out" hymns—placed the individual in continual dialogue with his community, allowing him at one and the same time to preserve his voice as a distinct entity and to blend it with those of his fellows. Here again slave music confronts us with evidence which indicates that however seriously the slave system may have diminished the strong sense of community that had bound Africans together, it never totally destroyed it or left the individual atomized and emotionally and psychically defenseless before his white masters. In fact, the form and structure of slave music presented the slave with a potential outlet for his individual feelings even while it continually drew him back into the communal presence and permitted him the comfort of basking in the warmth of the shared assumptions of those around him.

Those "shared assumptions" can be further examined by an analysis of the content of slave songs. Our preoccupation in recent years with the degree to which the slaves actually resembled the "Sambo" image held by their white masters has obscured the fact that the slaves developed images of their own which must be consulted and studied before any discussion of slave personality can be meaningful. The image of the trickster, who through cunning and unscrupulousness prevails over his more powerful antagonists, pervades slave tales. The trickster figure is rarely encountered in the slave's religious songs, though its presence is sometimes felt in the slave's many allusions to his narrow escapes from the devil.

> The Devil's mad and I'm glad,
> He lost the soul he thought he had.[25]

> Ole Satan toss a ball at me.
> O me no weary yet . . .

> Him tink de ball would hit my soul.
> O me no weary yet . . .

De ball for hell and I for heaven.
O me no weary yet . . .[26]

Ole Satan thought he had a mighty aim;
He missed my soul and caught my sins.
Cry Amen, cry Amen, cry Amen to God!

He took my sins upon his back;
Went muttering and grumbling down to hell.
Cry Amen, cry Amen, cry Amen to God![27]

The single most persistent image the slave songs contain, however, is that of the chosen people. The vast majority of the spirituals identify the singers as "de people dat is born of God," "We are the people of God," "we are de people of de Lord," "I really do believe I'm a child of God," "I'm a child ob God, wid my soul sot free," "I'm born of God, I know I am." Nor is there ever any doubt that "To the promised land I'm bound to go," "I walk de heavenly road," "Heav'n shall-a be my home," "I gwine to meet my Saviour," "I seek my Lord and I find Him," "I'll hear the trumpet sound / In that morning."[28]

The force of this image cannot be diminished by the observation that similar images were present in the religious singing of white evangelical churches during the first half of the nineteenth century. White Americans could be expected to sing of triumph and salvation, given their longstanding heritage of the idea of a chosen people which was reinforced in this era by the belief in inevitable progress and manifest destiny, the spread-eagle oratory, the bombastic folklore, and, paradoxically, the deep insecurities concomitant with the tasks of taming a continent and developing an identity. But for this same message to be expressed by Negro slaves who were told endlessly that they were members of the lowliest of races *is* significant. It offers an insight into the kinds of barriers the slaves had available to them against the internalization of the stereotyped images their masters held and attempted consciously and unconsciously to foist upon them.

The question of the chosen people image leads directly into the larger problem of what role religion played in the songs of the slave. Writing in 1862, James McKim noted that the songs of the Sea Island freedmen "are all religious, barcaroles and all. I speak without exception. So far as I heard or was told of their singing, it was all religious." Others who worked with recently emancipated slaves recorded the same experience, and Colonel Higginson reported that he rarely heard his troops sing a profane or vulgar song. With a few exceptions, "all had a religious motive."[29] In spite of this testimony, there can be little doubt that the slaves sang nonreligious songs. In 1774, an English visitor to the United States, after his first encounter with slave music, wrote in his journal: "In their songs they generally relate the usage they have received from their Masters or Mistresses in a very satirical stile and manner."[30] Songs fitting this description can be found in the nineteenth-century narratives of fugitive slaves. Harriet Jacobs recorded that during the Christmas season the slaves would ridicule stingy whites by singing:

> Poor Masssa, so dey say;
> Down in de heel, so dey say;
> Got no money, so dey say;
> God A'mighty bress you, so dey say.[31]

"Once in a while among a mass of nonsense and wild frolic," Frederick Douglass noted, "A sharp hit was given to the meanness of slaveholders."

> We raise de wheat,
> Dey gib us de corn;
> We bake de bread,
> Dey gib us de crust;
> We sif de meal,
> Dey gib us de huss;
> We peal de meat,
> Dey gib us de skin;
> And dat's de way
> Dey take us in;
> We skim de pot,
> Dey gib us de liquor,
> And say dat's good enough for nigger.[32]

Both of these songs are in the African tradition of utilizing song to bypass both internal and external censors and give vent to feelings which could be expressed in no other form. Nonreligious songs were not limited to the slave's relations with his masters, however, as these rowing songs, collected by contemporary white observers, indicate:

> We are going down to Georgia, boys,
>   Aye, aye.
> To see the pretty girls, boys,
>   Yoe, Yoe.

We'll give 'em a pint of brandy, boys,
    Aye, aye.
And a hearty kiss, besides, boys,
    Yoe, yoe.[33]

Jenny shake her toe at me,
    Jenny gone away;
Jenny shake her toe at me,
    Jenny gone away.
Hurrah! Miss Susy, oh!
    Jenny gone away;
Hurrah! Miss Susy, oh!
    Jenny gone away.[34]

The variety of nonreligious songs in the slave's repertory was wide. There were songs of in-group and out-group satire, songs of nostalgia, nonsense songs, songs of play and work and love. Nevertheless, our total stock of these songs is very small. It is possible to add to these by incorporating such post-bellum secular songs which have an authentic slavery ring to them as "De Blue-Tail Fly," with its ill-concealed satisfaction at the death of a master, or the ubiquitous

My ole Mistiss promise me,
W'en she died, she'd set me free,
She lived so long dat 'er head got bal',
An' she give out'n de notion a dyin' at all.[35]

The number can be further expanded by following Constance Rourke's suggestion that we attempt to disentangle elements of Negro origin from those of white creation in the "Ethiopian melodies" of the white minstrel shows, many of which were similar to the songs I have just quoted.[36] Either of these possibilities, however, forces the historian to work with sources far more potentially spurious than those with which he normally is comfortable.

Spirituals, on the other hand, for all the problems associated with their being filtered through white hands before they were published, and despite the many errors in transcription that inevitably occurred, constitute a much more satisfactory source. They were collected by the hundreds directly from slaves and freedmen during the Civil War and the decades immediately following, and although they came from widely different geographical areas they share a common structure and content, which seems to have been characteristic of Negro music wherever slavery existed in the United States. It is possible that we have a greater number of religious than nonreligious songs because slaves were more willing to sing these ostensibly innocent songs to white collectors who in turn were more anxious to record them, since they fit easily with their positive and negative images of the Negro. But I would argue that the vast preponderance of spirituals over any other sort of slave music, rather than being merely the result of accident or error, is instead an accurate reflection of slave culture during the antebellum period. Whatever songs the slaves may have sung before their wholesale conversion to Christianity in the late eighteenth and early nineteenth centuries, by the latter century spirituals were quantitatively and qualitatively their most significant musical creation. In this form of expression slaves found a medium which resembled in many important ways the world view they had brought with them from Africa, and afforded them the possibility of both adapting to and transcending their situation.

It is significant that the most common form of slave music we know of is sacred song. I use the term "sacred" not in its present usage as something antithetical to the secular world; neither the slaves nor their African forebears ever drew modernity's clear line between the sacred and the secular. The uses to which spirituals were put are an unmistakable indication of this. They were not sung solely or even primarily in churches or praise houses, but were used as rowing songs, field songs, work songs, and social songs. On the Sea Islands during the Civil War, Lucy McKim heard the spiritual "Poor Rosy" sung in a wide variety of contexts and tempos.

> On the water, the oars dip "Poor Rosy" to an even andante; a stout boy and girl
> at the hominy-mill will make the same "Poor Rosy" fly, to keep up with the
> whirling stone; and in the evening, after the day's work is done, "Heab'n shall-
> a be my home" [the final line of each stanza] peals up slowly and mournfully
> from the distant quarters.[37]

For the slaves, then, songs of God and the mythic heroes of their religion were not confined to any specific time or place, but were appropriate to almost every situation. It is in this sense that I use the concept sacred—not to signify a rejection of the present world but to describe the process of incorporating within this world all the elements of the divine. The religious historian Mircea Eliade, whose definition of sacred has shaped my own, has maintained that for men in traditional societies religion is a means of extending the world spatially upward so that communication with the other world becomes ritually possible, and extending it temporally backward so that the paradigmatic acts of the gods and mythical ancestors can be continually reenacted and indefinitely recoverable. By creating sacred time and space, man can perpetually live in the presence of his gods, can hold on to the certainty that within one's own lifetime "rebirth" is continually possible, and can impose order on the chaos of the universe. "Life," as Eliade puts it, "is lived on a twofold plane; it takes its course as human existence and, at the same time, shares in a trans-human life, that of the cosmos or the gods."[38]

This notion of sacredness gets at the essence of the spirituals, and through them at the essence of the slave's world view. Denied the possibility of achieving an adjustment to the external world of the antebellum South which involved meaningful forms of personal integration, attainment of status, and feelings of individual worth that all human beings crave and need, the slaves created a new world by transcending the narrow confines of the one in which they were forced to live. They extended the boundaries of their restrictive universe backward until it fused with the world of the Old Testament, and upward until it became one with the world beyond. The spirituals are the record of a people who found the status, the harmony, the values, the order they needed to survive by internally creating an expanded universe, by literally willing themselves reborn. In this respect I agree with the anthropologist Paul Radin that

> The ante-bellum Negro was not converted to God. He converted God to himself. In the Christian God he found a fixed point and he needed a fixed point, for both within and outside of himself, he could see only vacillation and endless shifting. . . . There was no other safety for people faced on all sides by doubt and the threat of personal disintegration, by the thwarting of instincts and the annihilation of values.[39]

The confinement of much of the slave's new world to dreams and fantasies does not free us from the historical obligation of examining its contours, weighing its implications for the development of the slave's psychic and emotional structure, and eschewing the kind of facile reasoning that leads Professor Elkins to imply that, since the slaves had no alternatives open to them, their fantasy life was "limited to catfish and watermelons."[40] Their spirituals indicate clearly that there *were* alternatives open to them—alternatives which they themselves fashioned out of the fusion of their African heritage and their new religion—and that their fantasy life was so rich and so important to them that it demands understanding if we are even to begin to comprehend their inner world.

The God the slaves sang of was neither remote nor abstract, but as intimate, personal, and immediate as the gods of Africa had been. "O when I talk I talk wid

God," "Mass Jesus is my bosom friend," "I'm goin' to walk with [talk with, live with, see] King Jesus by myself, by myself," were refrains that echoed through the spirituals.[41]

> In de mornin' when I rise,
> Tell my Jesus huddy [howdy] oh,
> I wash my hands in de mornin' glory,
> Tell my Jesus huddy oh.[42]

> Gwine to argue wid de Father and chatter wid de son,
> The last trumpet shall sound, I'll be there.
> Gwine talk 'bout de bright world dey des' come from.
> The last trumpet shall sound, I'll be there.[43]

> Gwine to write to Massa Jesus,
> To send some Valiant soldier
> To turn back Pharaoh's army, Hallelu![44]

The heroes of the scriptures—"Sister Mary," "Brudder Jonah," "Brudder Moses," "Brudder Daniel"—were greeted with similar intimacy and immediacy. In the world of the spirituals, it was not the masters and mistresses, but God and Jesus and the entire pantheon of Old Testament figures who set the standards, established the precedents, and defined the values; who, in short, constituted the "significant others." The world described by the slave songs was a black world in which no reference was ever made to any white contemporaries. The slave's positive reference group was composed entirely of his own peers: his mother, father, sister, brother, uncles, aunts, preacher, fellow "sinners" and "mourners" of whom he sang endlessly, to whom he sent messages via the dying, and with whom he was reunited joyfully in the next world.

The same sense of sacred time and space which shaped the slave's portraits of his gods and heroes also made his visions of the past and future immediate and compelling. Descriptions of the Crucifixion communicate a sense of the actual presence of the singer: "Dey pierced Him in the side . . . Dey nail Him to de cross . . . Dey rivet His feet . . . Dey hanged him high . . . Dey stretch Him wide . . ."

> Oh sometimes it causes me to tremble,-tremble,-tremble,
> Were you there when they crucified my Lord?[45]

The Slave's "shout"—that counterclockwise, shuffling dance which frequently occurred after the religious service and lasted long into the night—often became a medium through which the ecstatic dancers were transformed into actual participants in historic actions: Joshua's army marching around the walls of Jericho, the children of Israel following Moses out of Egypt.[46]

The thin line between time dimensions is nowhere better illustrated than in the slave's visions of the future, which were, of course, a direct negation of his present. Among the most striking spirituals are those which pile detail upon detail in describing the Day of Judgment: "You'll see de world on fire . . . see de element a meltin', . . . see the stars a fallin' . . . see the moon a bleedin' . . . see the forked lightning. . . . Hear the rumblin' thunder . . . see the righteous marching, . . . see my Jesus coming . . . ," and the world to come where "Dere's no sun to burn you . . . no hard trials . . . no whips a crackin' . . . no stormy weather . . . no tribulation . . . no evil-doers . . . All is gladness in de Kingdom."[47] This vividness was matched by the slave's certainty that he would partake of the triumph of judgment and the joys of the new world:

> Dere's room enough, room enough, room enough in de heaven, my Lord
> Room enough, room enough, I can't stay behind.[48]

Continually, the slaves sang of reaching out beyond the world that confined them, of seeing Jesus "in de wilderness," of praying "in de lonesome valley," of breathing in the freedom of the mountain peaks:

> Did yo' ever
> Stan' on mountun,
> Wash you' han's
> In a cloud?[49]

Continually, they held out the possibility of imminent rebirth: "I look at de worl' an' de worl' look new, . . . I look at my hands an' they look so too . . . I looked at my feet, my feet was too."[50]

These possibilities, these certainties were not surprising. The religious revivals which swept large numbers of slaves into the Christian fold in the late eighteenth and early nineteenth centuries were based upon a *practical* (not necessarily theological) Armianism: God would save all who believed in Him; Salvation was there for all to take hold of if they would. The effects of this message upon the slaves who were exposed to and converted by it have been passed over too easily by historians. Those effects are illustrated graphically in the spirituals that were the products of these revivals and which continued to spread the evangelical word long after the revivals had passed into history.

The religious music of the slaves is almost devoid of feelings of depravity or unworthiness, but is rather, as I have tried to show, pervaded by a sense of change, transcendence, ultimate justice, and personal worth. The spirituals have been referred to as "sorrow songs," and in some respects they were. The slaves snag of "rollin' thro' an unfriendly world," of being "a-trouble in de mind," of living in a world which was a "howling wilderness," "a hell to me," of feeling like a "motherless child," "a po' little orphan chile in de worl'," a "homeless child," of fearing that "Trouble will bury me down.'"[51]

But these feelings were rarely pervasive or permanent; almost always they were overshadowed by a triumphant note of affirmation. Even so despairing a wail as "Nobody Knows the Trouble I've Had" could suddenly have its mood transformed by lines like: "One morning I was a-walking down, . . . Saw some berries a-hanging down, . . . I pick de berry and I suck de juice, . . . Just as sweet as de honey in de comb."[52] Similarly, amid the deep sorrow of "Sometimes I feel like a Motherless chile," sudden release could come with the lines: "Sometimes I feel like / A eagle in de air. . . . Spread my wings an' / Fly, fly, fly,"[53] Slaves spent little time singing of the horrors of hell or damnation. Their songs of the Devil, quoted earlier, pictured a harsh but almost semicomic figure (often, one suspects, a surrogate for the white man), over whom they triumphed with reassuring regularity. For all their inevitable sadness, slave songs were characterized more by a feeling of confidence than of despair. There was confidence that contemporary power relationships were not immutable: "Did not old Pharaoh get lost, get lost, get lost, . . . get lost in the Red Sea?"; confidence in the possibilities of instantaneous change: "Jesus make de dumb to speak. . . . Jesus make de cripple walk. . . . Jesus give de blind his sight. . . . Jesus do most anything"; confidence in the rewards of persistence: "Keep a' inching along like a poor inchworm, / Jesus will come by'nd bye"; confidence that nothing could stand in the way of the justice they would receive: "You kin hender me here, but you can't do it dah," "O no man, no man, no man can hinder me"; confidence in the prospects of the future: "We'll walk de golden streets / Of de New Jerusalem." Religion, the slaves sang, "is good for anything, . . . Religion make you happy, . . . Religion gib me patience . . . O member, get Religion . . . Religion is so sweet."[54]

The slaves often pursued the "sweetness" of their religion in the face of many obstacles. Becky Isley, who was 16 when she was emancipated, recalled many years later:

> 'Fo' de war when we'd have a meetin' at night, wuz mos' always 'way in de woods or de bushes some whar so de white folks couldn't hear, an' when dey'd sing a spiritual an' de spirit 'gin to shout some de elders would go 'mongst de folks an' put dey han' over dey mouf an' some times put a clof in day mouf an'

say "Spirit don talk so loud or de patterol break us up." You know dey had white patterols what went 'roun' at night to see de niggers didn't cut up no devilment, an' den de meetin' would break up an' some would go to one house an' some to er nudder an' dey would groan er w'ile, den go home.[55]

Elizabeth Ross Hite testified that although she and her fellow slaves on a Louisiana plantation were Catholics, "lots didn't like that 'ligion."

> We used to hide behind some bricks and hold church ourselves. You see, the Catholic preachers from France wouldn't let us shout, and the Lawd done said you gotta shout if you want to be saved. That's in the Bible.
>
> Sometimes we held church all night long, 'til way in the mornin'. We burned some grease in a can for the preacher to see the Bible by. . . . See, our master didn't like us to have much 'ligion, said it made us lag in our work. He jest wanted us to be Catholicses on Sundays and go to mass and not study 'bout nothin' like that on week days. He didn't want us shoutin' and moanin' all day' long, but you gotta shout and you gotta moan if you wants to be saved.[56]

The slaves clearly craved the affirmation and promise of their religion. It would be a mistake, however, to see this urge as exclusively otherworldly. When Thomas Wentworth Higginson observed that the spirituals exhibited "nothing but patience for this life,—nothing but triumph in the next," he, and later observers who elaborated upon this judgment, were indulging in hyperbole. Although Jesus was ubiquitous in the spirituals, it was not invariably the Jesus of the New Testament of whom the slaves sang, but frequently a Jesus transformed into an Old Testament warrior: "Mass' Jesus" who engaged in personal combat with the Devil; "King Jesus" seated on a milk-white horse with sword and shield in hand. "Ride on, King Jesus," "Ride on, conquering King," "The God I serve is a man of war," the slaves sang.[57] This transformation of Jesus is symptomatic of the slaves' selectivity in choosing those parts of the Bible which were to serve as the basis of their religious consciousness. Howard Thurman, a Negro minister who as a boy had the duty of reading the Bible to his grandmother, was perplexed by her refusal to allow him to read from the epistles of Paul:

> When at length I asked the reason, she told me that during the days of slavery, the minister (white) on the plantation was always preaching from the Pauline letters—"Slaves, be obedient to your masters," etc. "I vowed to myself," she said, "that if freedom ever came and I learned to read, I would never read that part of the Bible!"[58]

Nor, apparently, did this part of the Scriptures ever constitute a vital element in slave songs or sermons. The emphasis of the spirituals, as Higginson himself noted, was upon the Old Testament and the exploits of the Hebrew children.[59] It is important that Daniel and David and Joshua and Jonah and Moses and Noah, all of whom fill the lines of the spirituals, were delivered in *this* world and delivered in ways which struck the imagination of the slaves. Over and over their songs dwelt upon the spectacle of the Red Sea opening to allow the Hebrew slaves past before inundating the mighty armies of the Pharaoh. They lingered delightedly upon the image of little David humbling the great Goliath with a stone—a pretechnological victory which postbellum Negroes were to expand upon in their songs of John Henry. They retold in endless variation the stories of the blind and humbled Samson bringing down the mansions of his conquerors; of the ridiculed Noah patiently building the ark which would deliver him from the doom of a mocking world; of the timid Jonah attaining freedom from his confinement through faith. The similarity of these tales to the situation of the slaves was too clear for him not to see it; too clear for us to believe that the songs had no worldly content for the black man in bondage. "O my Lord delivered Daniel," the slaves observed, and responded logically: "O why not deliver me, too?"

> He delivered Daniel from de lion's den,
>   Jonah from de belly ob de whale,
> And de Hebrew children from de fiery furnace,
>   And why not every man?[60]

These lines state as clearly as anything can the manner in which the sacred world of the slaves was able to fuse the precedents of the past, the conditions of the present, and the promise of the future into one connected reality. In this respect there was always a latent and symbolic element of protest in the slave's religious songs which frequently became overt and explicit. Frederick Douglass asserted that for him and many of his fellow slaves the song, "O Canaan, sweet Canaan, / I am bound for the land of Canaan," symbolized "something more than a hope of reaching heaven. We meant to reach the *North*, and the North was our Canaan," and he wrote that the lines of another spiritual, "Run to Jesus, shun the danger, / I don't expect to stay much longer here," had a double meaning which first suggested to him the thought of escaping from slavery.[61] Similarly, when the black troops in Higginson's regiment sang:

> We'll soon be free, [three times]
> When de Lord will call us home.

a young drummer boy explained to him: "Dey think *de Lord* mean for say *de Yankees*."[62] Nor is there any reason to doubt that slaves could have used their songs as a means of secret communication. An ex-slave told Lydia Parrish that when he and his fellow slaves "suspicioned" that one of their number was telling tales to the driver, they would sing lines like the following while working in the field:

> O Judas he wuz a 'ceitful man
> He went an/ betray a mos' innocen' man.
> Fo' thirty pieces a silver dat it wuz done
> He went in de woods an' e' self he hung.[63]

And it is possible, as many writers have argued, that such spirituals as the commonly heard "Steal away, steal away, steal away to Jesus!" were used as explicit calls to secret meetings.

But it is not necessary to invest the spirituals with a secular function only at the price of divesting them of their religious content, as Miles Mark Fisher has done.[64] While we may make such clear-cut distinctions, I have tried to show that the slaves did not. For them religion never constituted a simple escape from this world, because their conception of the world was more expansive than modern man's. Nowhere is this better illustrated than during the Civil War itself. While the war gave rise to such new spirituals as "Before I'd be a slave / I'd be buried in my grave, / And go home to my Lord and be saved!" or the popular "Many thousand Go," with its jubilant rejection of all the facets of slave life—"No more peck o' corn for me, . . . No more driver's lash for me, . . . No more pint o' salt for me, . . . No more hundred lash for me, . . . No more mistress' call for me"[65]—the important thing was not that large numbers of slaves now could create new songs which openly expressed their views of slavery; that was to be expected. More significant was the case with which their old songs fit their new situation. With so much of their inspiration drawn from the events of the Old Testament and the Book of Revelation, the slaves had long sung of wars, of battles, of the Army of the Lord, of Soldiers of the Cross, of trumpets summoning the faithful, of vanquishing the hosts of evil. These songs especially were, as Higginson put it, "available for camp purposes with very little strain upon their symbolism." "We'll cross de mighty river," his troops sang while marching or rowing,

> We'll cross de danger water, . . .
> O Pharaoh's army drownded!
> My army cross over.

"O blow your trumpet, Gabriel," they sang,

> Blow your trumpet louder;
> And I want dat trumpet to blow me home
> To my new Jerusalem.

But they also found their less overtly militant songs quite as appropriate to warfare. Their most popular and effective marching song was:

> Jesus call you, Go in de wilderness,
>   Go in de wilderness, go in de wilderness,
> Jesus call you. Go in de wilderness
>   To wait upon de Lord.[66]

Black Union soldiers found it no more incongruous to accompany their fight for freedom with the sacred songs of their bondage than they had found it inappropriate as slaves to sing their spirituals while picking cotton or shucking corn. Their religious songs, like their religion itself, was of this world as well as the next.

Slave songs by themselves, of course, do not present us with a definitive key to the life and mind of the slave. They have to be seen within the context of the slave's situation and examined alongside such other cultural materials as folk tales. But slave songs do indicate the need to rethink a number of assumptions that have shaped recent interpretations of slavery, such as the assumption that because slavery eroded the linguistic and institutional side of African life it wiped out almost all the more fundamental aspects of African culture. Culture, certainly, is more than merely the sum total of institutions and language. It is also expressed by something less tangible, which the anthropologist Robert Redfield has called "Style of life." Peoples as different as the Lapp and the Bedouin, Redfield has argued, with diverse languages, religions, customs, and institutions, may still share an emphasis on certain virtues and ideals, certain manners of independence and hospitality, general ways of looking upon the world, which give them a similar life style.[67] This argument applies to the West African cultures from which the slaves came. Though they varied widely in language, institutions, gods, and familial patterns, they shared a fundamental outlook toward the past, present, and future and common means of cultural expression which could well have constituted the basis of a sense of community and identity capable of surviving the impact of slavery.

Slave songs present us with abundant evidence that in the structure of their music and dance, in the uses to which music was put, in the survival of the oral tradition, in the retention of such practices as spirit possession which often accompanied the creation of spirituals, and in the ways in which the slaves expressed their new religion, important elements of their shared African heritage remained alive not just as quaint cultural vestiges but as vitally creative elements of slave culture. This could never have happened if slavery was, as Professor Elkins maintains, a system which so completely closed in around the slave, so totally penetrated his personality structure as to infantalize him and reduce him to a kind of *tabula rasa* upon which the white man could write what he chose.[68]

Slave songs provide us with the beginnings of a very different kind of hypothesis: that the preliterate, premodern Africans, with their sacred world view, were so imperfectly acculturated into the secular American society into which they were thrust, were so completely denied access to the ideology and dreams which formed the core of the consciousness of other Americans, that they were forced to fall back upon the only cultural frames of reference that made any sense to them and gave them any feeling of security. I use the word "forced" advisedly. Even if the slaves had had the opportunity to enter fully into the life of the larger society, they might still have chosen to retain and perpetuate certain elements of their African heritage. But the point is that they really had no choice. True acculturation was denied to most slaves. The alternatives were either to remain in a state of cultural limbo, divested of the old cultural patterns but not allowed to adopt those of their new homeland—which in the long run is no alternative at all—or to cling to as many as possible of the old ways of thinking and acting. The slaves' oral tradition, their music, and their religious outlook served this latter function and constituted a cultural refuge at least potentially capable of protecting their personalities from some of the worst ravages of the slave system.

The argument of Professors Tannenbaum and Elkins that the Protestant churches in the United States did not act as a buffer between the slave and his master is persuasive enough, but it betrays a modern preoccupation with purely institutional arrangements.[69] Religion is more than an institution, and because Protestant churches failed to protect the slave's inner being from the incursions of the slave system, it does not follow that the spiritual message of Protestantism failed as well. Slave songs are a testament to the ways in which Christianity provided slaves with the precedents, heroes, and future promise that allowed them to transcend the purely temporal bonds of the Peculiar Institution.

Historians have frequently failed to perceive the full importance of this because they have not taken the slave's religiosity seriously enough. A people cannot create a music as forceful and striking as slave music out of a mere uninternalized anodyne. Those who have argued that Negroes did not oppose slavery in any meaningful way are writing from a modern, political context. What they really mean is that the slaves found no *political* means to oppose slavery. But slaves, to borrow Professor Hobsbawm's term, were prepolitical beings in a prepolitical situation.[70] Within their frame of reference there were other—and from the point of view of personality development, not necessarily less effective—means of escape and opposition. If mid-twentieth-century historians have difficulty perceiving the sacred universe created by slaves as a serious alternative to the societal system created by southern slaveholders, the problem may be the historians' and not the slaves'.

Above all, the study of slave songs forces the historian to move out of his own culture, in which music plays a peripheral role, and offers him the opportunity to understand the ways in which black slaves were able to perpetuate much of the centrality and functional importance that music had for their African ancestors. In the concluding lines of his perceptive study of primitive song, C. M. Bowra has written:

> Primitive song is indispensable to those who practice it. . . . they cannot do without song, which both formulates and answers their nagging questions, enables them to pursue action with zest and confidence, brings them into touch with gods and spirits, and makes them feel less strange in the natural world. . . . it gives to them a solid centre in what otherwise would be almost chaos, and a continuity in their being, which would too easily dissolve before the calls of the implacable present . . . through its words men, who might otherwise give in to the malice of circumstances, find their old powers revived or new powers stirring in them, and through these life itself is sustained and renewed and fulfilled.[71]

This, I think, sums up concisely the function of song for the slave. Without a general understanding of that function, without a specific understanding of the content and meaning of slave song, there can be no full comprehension of the effects of slavery upon the slave or the meaning of the society from which slaves emerged at emancipation.

NOTES

An earlier version of this essay was presented as a paper at the American Historical Association meetings on December 28, 1969. I am indebted to the two commentators on that occasion, Professors J. Saunders Redding and Mike Thelwell, and to my colleagues Nathan I. Huggins, Robert Middlekauff, and Kenneth M. Stampp for their penetrating criticisms and suggestions.

1. Miles Mark Fisher, *Negro Slave Songs in the United States* (New York, 1963, orig. pub. 1953), 14, 39, 132, and *passim*.

2. The contours of this debate are judiciously outlined in D. K. Wilgus, *Anglo-American Folksong Scholarship Since 1989* (New Brunswick, 1959), App. One, "The Negro-White Spirituals."

3. Lucy McKim, "Songs of the Port Royal Contrabands," *Dwight's Journal of Music,* XXII (November 8, 1862), 255.

4. W. F. Allen, "The Negro Dialect," *The Nation*, I (December 14, 1865), 744–45.

5. See, for instance, Henry Edward Krehbiel, *Afro-American Folksongs* (New York, 1963, orig. pub. 1914); James Wesley Work, *Folk Songs of the American Negro* (Nashville, 1915); James Weldon Johnson, *The Book of American Negro Spirituals* (New York, 1925), and *The Second Book of Negro Spirituals* (New York, 1926); Lydia Parrish, *Slave Songs of the Georgia Sea Islands* (Hatboro, Penna., 1965, orig. pub. 1942); LeRoi Jones, *Blues People* (New York, 1963).

6. Newman I. White, *American Negro Folk-Songs* (Hatboro, Penna., 1965, orig. pub. 1928); Guy B. Johnson, *Folk Culture on St. Helena Island, South Carolina* (Chapel Hill, 1930); George Pullen Jackson, *White and Negro Spirituals* (New York, 1943).

7. White, *American Negro Folk-Songs*, 11–13.

8. Professor John William Ward gives an excellent example of this process in his discussion of the different meanings which the newspapers of the United States, France, and India attributed to Charles Lindbergh's flight across the Atlantic in 1927. See "Lindbergh, Dos Passos, and History," in Ward, *Red, White, and Blue* (New York, 1969), 55.

9. George Pullen Jackson, "The Genesis of the Negro Spiritual," *The American Mercury* XVI (June 1932), 248.

10. Richard Alan Waterman, "African Influence on the Music of the Americas," in Sol Tax (ed.), *Acculturation in the Americas: Proceedings and Selected Papers of the XXIXth International Congress of Americanists* (Chicago, 1952), 207–18; Wilgus, *Anglo-American Folksong Scholarship Since 1898*, 363–64; Melville H. Herskovits, "Patterns of Negro Music" (pamphlet, no publisher, no date); Gilbert Chase, *America's Music* (New York, 1966), Chap. 12; Alan P. Merriam, "African Music," in William R. Bascom and Melville J. Herskovits (eds.), *Continuity and Change in African Cultures* (Chicago, 1959), 29, 55.

11. White, *American Negro Folk-Songs*, 29, 55.

12. Jackson, *White and Negro Spirituals*, 266–67.

13. James Miller McKim, "Negro Songs," *Dwight's Journal of Music*, XXI (August 9, 1862), 149.

14. Thomas Wentworth Higginson, *Army Life in a Black Regiment* (Beacon Press edition, Boston, 1962, orig. pub. 1869), 218–19.

15. Henry Russell, *Cheer! Boys, Cheer!*, 84–85, quoted in Chase, *America's Music*, 235–36.

16. Jeanette Robinson Murphy, "The Survival of African Music in America," *Popular Science Monthly* 55 (1899), 660–72, reprinted in Bruce Jackson (ed.), *The Negro and His Folklore in Nineteenth-Century Periodicals* (Austin, 1967), 328.

17. Natalie Curtis Burlin, "Negro Music at Birth," *Musical Quarterly*, V (January 1919), 88. For Mrs. Burlin's excellent reproductions of Negro folk songs and spirituals, see her *Negro Folk-Songs* (New York, 1918–1919), Vol. I-IV.

18. Clifton Joseph Furness, "Communal Music Among Arabians and Negroes," *Musical Quarterly* XVI (January 1930), 49–51.

19. Elizabeth Kilham, "Sketches in Color: IV," *Putnam's Monthly*, XV (March 1870), 304–11, reprinted in Jackson, *The Negro and His Folklore in Nineteenth-Century Periodicals*, 127–28.

20. Bruno Nettl, *Folk and Traditional Music of the Western Continents* (Englewood Cliffs, 1965), 4–6; Chase, *America's Music*, 241–43.

21. J. K., Jr., "Who Are Our National Poets?," *Knickerbocker Magazine*, 26 (October 1845), 336, quoted in Dena J. Epstein, "Slave Music in the United States Before 1860: A Survey of Sources (Part I)," *Music Library Association Notes*, XX (Spring 1963), 208.

22. Elizabeth Kilham, "Sketches in Color: IV," *Putnam's Monthly*, XV (March 1870), 304–11, reprinted in Jackson, *The Negro and His Folklore in Nineteenth-Century Periodicals*, 129.

23. White, *American Negro Folk-Songs*, 57.

24. Alan P. Merriam, "Music and the Dance," in Robert Lystad (ed.), *The African World: A Survey of Social Research* (New York, 1965), 452–68; William Bascom, "Folklore and Literature," in *Ibid.*, 469–88; R. S. Rattray, *Ashanti* (Oxford, 1923), Chap. XV; Melville Herskovits, "Freudian Mechanisms in Primitive Negro Psychology," in E. E. Evans-Pritchard *et al.* (eds.), *Essays Presented to C. G. Seligman* (London, 1934), 75–84; Alan P. Merriam, "African Music," in Bascom and Herskovitz, *Continuity and Change in African Cultures*, 49–86.

25. William Francis Allen, Charles Pickard Ware, and Lucy McKim Garrison, compilers, *Slave Songs of the United States* (New York, 1867, Oak Publications ed., 1965), 164–65.

26. *Ibid.*, 43.

27. Harriet Jacobs, *Incidents in the Life of a Slave Girl* (Boston, 1861), 109.

28. Lines like these could be quoted endlessly. For the specific ones cited, see the songs in the following collections: Higginson, *Army Life in a Black Regiment*, 160–61; Thomas P. Fenner, compiler, *Religious Folk Songs of the Negro as Sung on the Plantations* (Hampton, Virginia, 1909, orig. pub. 1874), 10–11, 48; J. B. T. Marsh, *The Story of the Jubilee Singers; With Their Songs* (Boston, 1880), 136, 167, 178.

29. McKim, "Negro Songs," 148; H. G. Spaulding, "Under the Palmetto," *Continental Monthly*, IV (1863), 188–203, reprinted in Jackson, *The Negro and his Folklore in*

Nineteenth-Century Periodicals, 72; Allen, "The Negro Dialect," 744–45; Higginson, *Army Life in a Black Regiment*, 220–21.

30. *Journal of Nicholas Cresswell, 1774–1777* (New York, 1934), 17–19, quoted in Epstein, *Music Library Association Notes*, XX (Spring 1963), 201.

31. Jacobs, *Incidents in the Life of a Slave Girl*, 180.

32. *Life and Times of Frederick Douglass* (rev. ed., 1892, Collier Books Edition, 1962), 146–47.

33. John Lambert, *Travels Through Canada and the United States of North America in the Years, 1806–1807 and 1808* (London, 1814), II, 253–54, quoted in Dena J. Epstein, "Slave Music in the United States Before 1860: A Survey of Sources (Part 2)," *Music Library Association Notes*, XX (Summer 1963), 377.

34. Frances Anne Kemble, *Journal of a Residence on a Georgian Plantation in 1838–1839* (New York, 1863), 128.

35. For versions of these songs, see Dorothy Scarborough, *On the Trail of Negro Folk-Songs* (Cambridge, 1925), 194, 201–203, 223–25, and Thomas W. Talley, *Negro Folk Rhymes* (New York, 1922), 25–26. Talley claims that the majority of the songs in his large and valuable collection "were sung by Negro fathers and mothers in the dark days of American slavery to their children who listened with eyes as large as saucers and drank them down with mouths wide open," but offers no clue as to why he feels that songs collected for the most part in the twentieth century were slave songs.

36. Constance Rourke, *The Roots of American Culture and Other Essays* (New York, 1942). Newman White, on the contrary, has argued that although the earliest minstrel songs were Negro derived, they soon went their own way and that less than ten percent of them were genuinely Negro. Nevertheless, these white songs "got back to the plantation, largely spurious as they were and were undoubtedly along those which the plantation-owners encouraged the Negroes to sing. They persist today in isolated stanzas and lies, along the songs handed down by plantation Negroes . . ." White, *American Negro Folk-Songs*, 7–10 and Appendix IV. There are probably valid elements in both theses. A similarly complex relationship between genuine Negro folk creations and their more commercialized partly white influenced imitations was to take place in the blues of the twentieth century.

37. McKim, "Songs of the Port Royal Contrabands," 255.

38. Mircea Eliade, *The Sacred and the Profane* (New York, 1961), Chaps. 2, 4, and *passim*. For the similarity of Eliade's concept to the world view of West Africa, see W. E. Abraham, *The Mind of Africa* (London, 1962), Chap. 2, and R. S. Rattray, *Religion and Art in Ashanti* (Oxford, 1927).

39. Paul Radin, "Status, Phantasy, and the Christian Dogma," in Social Science Institute, Fisk University, *God Struck Me Dead: Religious Conversion Experiences and Autobiographies of Negro Ex-Slaves* (Nashville, 1945, unpublished typescript).

40. Stanley Elkins, *Slavery* (Chicago, 1959), 136.

41. Allen *et al., Slave Songs of the United States*, 33–34, 105; William E. Barton, *Old Plantation Hymns: A Collection of Hitherto Unpublished Melodies of the Slave and the Freedmen* (Boston, 1899), 30.

42. Allen *et al., Slave Songs of the United States*, 47.

43. Barton, *Old Plantation Hymns,* 19.

44. Marsh, *The Story of the Jubilee Singers*, 132.

45. Fenner, *Religious Folk Songs of the Negro*, 162; E. A. McIlhenny, *Befo' De War Spirituals: Worlds and Melodies* (Boston, 1933), 39.

46. Barton, *Old Plantation Hymns*, 15; Howard W. Odum and Guy B. Johnson, *The Negro And His Songs* (Hatboro, Penn., 1964, orig. pub. 1925), 33–34; for a vivid description of the "shout" see *The Nation*, May 30, 1867, 432–33; see also Parrish, *Slave Songs of the Georgia Sea Islands*, Chap. III.

47. For examples of songs of this nature, see Fenner, *Religious Folk Songs of the Negro*, 8, 63–65; Marsh, *The Story of the Jubilee Singers*, 240–41; Higginson, *Army Life in a Black Regiment*, 205; Allen *et al., Slave Songs of the United Sates*, 91, 100; Burlin, *Negro Folk-Songs*, I, 37–42.

48. Allen *et al., Slave Songs of the United States*, 32–33.

49. *Ibid.*, 30–31; Burlin, *Negro Folk-Songs*, II, 8–9; Fenner, *Religious Folk Songs of the Negro*, 12.

50. Allen *et al., Slave Songs of the United States*, 128–29; Fenner, *Religious Folk Songs of the Negro*, 127; Barton, *Old Plantation Hymns*, 26.

51. Allen *et al., Slave Songs of the United States*, 70, 102–103, 147; Barton, *Old Plantation Hymns*, 9, 17–18, 24; Marsh, *The Story of the Jubilee Singers*, 133, 167; Odum and Johnson, *The Negro and his Songs*, 35.

52. Allen *et al., Slave Songs of the United States*, 102–103.

53. Mary Allen Grissom, compiler, *The Negro Sings a New Heaven* (Chapel Hill, 1930), 73.

54. Marsh, *The Story of the Jubilee Singers*, 179, 186; Allen *et al., Slave Songs of the United States*, 40–41, 44, 146; Barton, *Old Plantation Hymns*, 30.

55. McIlhenny, *Befo' De War Spirituals*, 31.

56. *Gumbo Ya-Ya: A Collection of Louisiana Folk Tales*, compiled by Lyle Saxon, Edward Dreyer, and Robert Tallant from materials gathered by workers of the WPA, Louisiana Writer's Project (Boston, 1945), 242.

57. For examples, see Allen *et al., Slave Songs of the United States*, 40–41, 82, 97, 106–108; Marsh, *The Story of the Jubilee Singers*, 168, 203; Burlin, *Negro Folk-Songs*, II, 8–9; Howard Thurman, *Deep River* (New York, 1945), 19–21.

58. Thurman, *Deep River*, 16–17.

59. Higginson, *Army Life in a Black Regiment*, 202–205. Many of those northerners who came to the South to "uplift" the freedmen were deeply disturbed at the Old Testament emphasis of their religion. H. G. Spaulding complained that the ex-slaves needed to be introduced to "the light and warmth of the Gospel," and reported that

a Union army officer told him: "Those poor people had enough of the Old Testament thrown at their heads under slavery. Now give them the glorious utterances and practical teachings of the Great Master." Spaulding, "Under the Palmetto," reprinted in Jackson, *The Negro and His Folklore in Nineteenth-Century Periodicals*, 66.

60. Allen *et al., Slave Songs of the United States* 148; Fenner, *Religious Folk Songs of the Negro*, 21; Marsh, *The Story of the Jubilee Singers*, 134–35; McIlhenny, *Befo' De War Spirituals*, 248–249.

61. *Life and Times of Frederick Douglass*, 159–60; Marsh, *The Story of the Jubilee Singers*, 188.

62. Higginson, *Army Life in a Black Regiment*, 217.

63. Parrish, *Slave Songs of the Georgia Sea Islands*, 247.

64. "Actually, not one spiritual in its primary form reflected interest in anything other than a full life here and now." Fisher, *Negro Slave Songs in the United States*, 157.

65. Barton, *Old Plantation Hymns*, 25; Allen *et al., Slave Songs of the United States*, 94; McKim, "Negro Songs," 149.

66. Higginson, *Army Life in a Black Regiment*, 201–202, 211–12.

67. Robert Redfield, *The Primitive World and Its Transformations* (Ithaca, 1953), 51–53.

68. Elkins, *Slavery*, Chap. III.

69. *Ibid.*, Chap. II; Frank Tannenbaum, *Slave and Citizen* (New York, 1946).

70. E. J. Hobsbawm, *Primitive Rebels* (New York, 1959), Chap. 1.

71. C. M. Bowra, *Primitive Song* (London, 1962), 285–86.

SELECTED BIBLIOGRAPHY FOR FURTHER READING

Epstein, Dena J. *Sinful Tunes and Spirituals: Black Folk Music to the Civil War*. Urbana: University of Illinois Press, 1977.

Genovese, Eugene. *Roll, Jordan, Roll: The World the Slaves Made*. New York: Vintage, 1972.

Levine, Lawrence W. *Black Culture and Black Consciousness: Afro-American Folk Thought From Slavery to Freedom*. New York: Oxford University Press, 1977.

Blassingame, John W. *The Slave Community*. New York: Oxford University Press, 1972.

White, John. "Veiled Testimony: Negro Spirituals and the Slave Experience." *Journal of American Studies* 17 (1983): 251–63.

Albert J. Raboteau

5 ::

::Many African Americans adopted evangelical Christianity during the revivals of the eighteenth and nineteenth centuries, and this has posed many troubling questions: How could blacks accept a religion that was used by many whites to justify slavery? How could Christianity be meaningful for African Americans if it were, as it seemed, a "white-man's religion?" How could the Christian God be loving and just while African Americans suffered under slavery? Such dilemmas have led many to dismiss black Christianity as an example of the oppressed internalizing the ideology of the oppressed. Black Christians and scholars of African-American religion led by Albert Raboteau, however, argue that African-American Christians developed a distinctive evangelical tradition that established an identity and meaning for African Americans and a challenge to American racism.::

5

THE BLACK EXPERIENCE
IN AMERICAN
EVANGELICALISM
The Meaning of Slavery

Albert J. Raboteau

God is no respecter of persons, but in every nation, he that feareth God and worketh righteousness is accepted of Him.

—ACTS 10:34–35.

There is neither Jew nor Greek, there is neither slave nor free, there is neither male nor female; for ye are all one in Christ Jesus.

—GALATIANS 3:28.

Princes shall come out of Egypt; Ethiopia shall soon stretch out her hands unto God.

—PSALMS 68:31.

:: L̲ate in the eighteenth century, black Americans, slave and free, Southern and Northern, began to convert to Christianity in larger numbers than ever before. The type of Christianity that they joined and continued to join in mounting numbers during the next century was experiential, revivalistic, and biblically oriented. That is, it placed heavy stress upon the necessity of an inward conversion experience for Christian salvation; it institutionalized the revival as a means of converting sinners, extending church membership, and reforming society; and finally, it read the Bible literally and interpreted the destiny of America accordingly.

Black Evangelicals, no less than whites, sought conversion, attended revivals, and viewed their lives in biblical terms. There was a fundamental difference between the two, however. American slavery and the doctrine of white supremacy, which rationalized and outlived it, not only segregated evangelical congregations along racial lines, but also differentiated the black experience of evangelical Christianity from that of whites. The existence of chattel slavery in a nation that claimed to be Christian, and the use of Christianity to justify enslavement, confronted black Evangelicals with a basic dilemma, which may be most clearly formulated in two questions: What meaning did Christianity, if it were a white man's religion, as it seemed, have for blacks; and, why did the Christian God, if he were just as claimed, permit blacks to suffer so? In struggling to answer these

questions, a significant number of Afro-Americans developed a distinctive evangelical tradition in which they established meaning and identity for themselves as
individuals and as a people. Simultaneously, they made an indispensable contribution to the development of American Evangelicalism. If evangelical
Protestantism has formed a major part of the cultural history of Afro-Americans,
from the beginning black Evangelicals have troubled the conscience of Christian
Americans.

A WHITE-MAN'S RELIGION?

The fires of revival that initially swept most of the British North American
colonies in the 1740s flared up intermittently during the 1780s and 1790s particularly in the Chesapeake region of the upper South, and broke out anew on the
Kentucky and Tennessee frontier around the turn of the century. These successive
"Awakenings" inaugurated a new religious movement in America. Whether
viewed as a renewed Puritanism, an extension of Continental Pietism, or as the
rise of popular denominations on the expanding frontier, Evangelicalism was by
the early decades of the nineteenth century the predominant voice on the
American religious scene. By the 1830s, revival had linked with reform to institute an energetic and influential evangelical front that intended nothing less than
the purification of the nation from sin in order to prepare for the coming millennium, which undoubtedly would begin in America. During these same decades,
1780–1830, Evangelicalism had been planted and had taken hold among enslaved Africans and their descendants, some free, but most of them slaves.

Initially, blacks had heard the message of evangelical Christianity from
whites, but rapidly a cadre of early black preachers, licensed and unlicensed,
took it upon themselves to convert and to pastor their own people. By 1830,
these "pioneers" had been succeeded by a second and more numerous generation
of black clergymen, so that blacks were no longer exclusively dependent upon
whites for the Christian gospel, though white missionaries might think so.
Separate black churches—mainly Baptist due to the congregational independence of that denomination—sprang up not only in the North, where emancipation gave blacks more leeway to organize institutionally, but also in the South,
where an increasingly entrenched slave system made any kind of black autonomy
seem subversive. In the North and upper South, two black evangelical denominations formed and chose bishops of their own to lead them. Already, black
American missionaries had established Baptist and Methodist congregations in

Nova Scotia, Jamaica, and Sierra Leone. In short, blacks showed no reluctance in taking a leading role in the spread of evangelical religion.

The opportunity for black religious separatism was due to the egalitarian character of evangelical Protestantism; its necessity was due, in part, to the racism of white Evangelicals. The egalitarian tendency of evangelical revivals to level the souls of all men before God had been one of the major attractions to black converts in the first place. Early white Evangelicals in the South, where the majority of blacks were, appeared to the Anglican establishment as a revolutionary rabble, a disorderly, "outlandish, misshapen sort of people," in the words of one Virginian.[1] They threatened the established order, both in ecclesiastical and civil terms. The lower sort made up their church membership, and the unlettered, even including servants, spoke at their meetings. Racial and social status was overturned in the close communion of Baptist conventicles and Methodist societies in the 1780s and 1790s. Runaway slave advertisements in Virginia and Maryland newspapers complained that blacks were being ruined by the "leveling" doctrinesof Baptist and Methodist sectarians. Not surprisingly, Anglican authorities in Virginia and North Carolina jailed evangelical preachers, and mobs frequently harassed or assaulted them. Some, but not all, eighteenth-century Methodists and Baptists concluded that holding slaves was sinful and encouraged converts either by legislation or admonition to emancipate their slaves.[2]

Blacks were impressed by this gospel of freedom; and after white Evangelicals retreated from the antislavery principles and became more respectable, they acknowledged that Christianity and slavery were contradictory. In the North, it was possible for blacks to criticize slaveholding Christianity publicly; in the South, the message had to be muted. Whether their critiques were open or secret, by 1800, black Evangelicals, slave and free, had already scored a significant victory in the war to assert their "manhood." By that date, the black church had begun.

Because they converted, churched, and pastored themselves, black Evangelicals were able to deny, in effect, that Christianity was a white religion. Even in the South, where whites were legally in control of black congregations, their control was nominal, since black exhorts and deacons functioned in reality as the pastors of their people. At times black evangelical congregations challenged white authorities, and in some cases succeeded in preserving their independence from white domination, as did the African Methodists of Mother Bethel in Philadelphia and the black Baptists of First African in Savannah. The astute leadership of men like Richard Allen and Andrew Marshall was tangible proof of black competence and skill in the affairs of men. Of even greater symbolic value was the power of black preachers in the affairs of God.[3]

Due to the emphasis on conversion, an awakened clergy was more important than a learned one, at least in the early days of American Evangelicalism. Blacks seized the opportunity afforded by the willingness of Methodists and Baptists to license them to "exercise their gift." Whites as well as blacks fell under the powerful preaching of eloquent "brethren in black." The sight of whites humbled in the dust by blacks was a spectacular, if rare, demonstration of the lesson that "God is no respecter of persons."

More common was the day-to-day presence of the black minister in his community, slave or free, preaching funerals, weddings, prayer meetings, Sabbath sermons, with a force that uplifted blacks and proved the ability of black men. The point was not lost on defenders of the slave system who saw the existence of black churches and the activity of black clergymen as dangerous anomalies. Racists in the North and South found it necessary to denigrate black churches and black preachers by ridicule and restriction in order to be consistent with the doctrine of white supremacy. The racial hierarchy was threatened by any independent exercise of black authority, even though spiritual in nature. While whites had tried to limit Christian egalitarianism to the spiritual realm, the wall between spiritual and temporal equality was too frequently breached (most conspicuously by Denmark Vesey and Nat Turner). Yet, despite the threat to slave control that black religious independence posed, the evangelical tradition insured that suppression could only go so far. To deny blacks the possibility of preaching or gathering for religious meetings would have violated the tradition of gospel freedom as understood by evangelical Protestants (in contrast to a hierarchical tradition, like Catholicism, which had no such problem). When legislators took this step, evangelical objections led to amendment or evasion of the law.[4]

Thus black churches functioned as much more than asylums from the "spirit of slavery and the spirit of caste." As Bishop Daniel Alexander Payne of the A.M.E. Church put it, in the African Methodist and Baptist churches they "found freedom of thought, freedom of speech, freedom of action, freedom for the development of a true Christian manhood." Significantly, Payne and other black clergymen linked "True Christian manhood" with the exercise of freedoms that sound suspiciously like civil and political rights. The ineluctable tendency of the black evangelical ethos was in the direction of asserting "manhood" rights, which were understood as a vital form of self-governance. In this sense, long before emancipation the black evangelical churches were political, though in the slave

South they could be only incipiently so. In the North, the free black churches clearly functioned as a political institution, not simply because they were the only institutions that blacks were allowed to control, but because black Evangelicals connected the concept of "Christian manhood" with the exercise of political rights.[5]

Though Southern black Evangelicals had already experienced self-governance in separate congregations, they had to wait until emancipation to make the connection between church and political life clear and, for a short time during Reconstruction, viable. When they swarmed out of white-controlled churches to form independent congregations or to affiliate with Northern-based black denominations, the freedmen found immediate and tangible evidence of their manhood rights. Long after emancipation, William Heard, a former slave in Georgia, recalled that he had first learned the meaning of manhood from the example of William White, a black Baptist preacher from Augusta, who traveled to Heard's country town to give apolitical speech shortly after slavery. The seventeen-year-old Heard was so impressed by White's address that he determined "from that night to be a MAN, and to fill an important place in life's arena." He was even more impressed when White, despite threats from local white democrats, went about his tasks as agent for the Freedman's Bureau, editor of the *Georgia Baptist*, and organizer for the Republican party, apparently without fear. He remained, according to Heard, "always outspoken for Orthodox Religion and for the Republican Party." White's example took, as Heard became a minister, a South Carolina state legislator, bishop in the A.M.E. Church, and minister to Liberia. The political activism of black evangelical preachers like Heard, Richard Cain, Henry McNeal Turner, James W. Hood, T.G. Campbell, Isaac S. Campbell, and others was not an aberration from the tradition of black Evangelicalism but its logical extension.[6]

BLACK JEREMIADS

American blacks made evangelical Christianity their own by assuming, whenever possible, leadership of their own religious life. By doing so they denied that Christianity was a white religion. But the assertion of institutional autonomy was not enough. History affords many examples of oppressed people internalizing and institutionalizing the ideology of their oppressors in their own social organizations. Some critics of the black church have accused it of precisely this failure; however, black Evangelicals went beyond institutional separatism: they denied the doctrinal basis of "slaveholding Christianity" by refusing to believe that God had made them inferior to whites. Though whites might appeal to scriptural texts, such as "Cursed be Canaan; a servant of servants shall he be until his brethren," or "Servants be obedient to them that are your masters," blacks rejected the notion that either the Bible or Christianity supported American slavery.

Among the first public protests by black "citizens" were pre-Revolutionary petitions from slaves in Massachusetts pointing out the contradictions between slavery and a "free and Christian land."[7] Over the next century, black condemnation of the sin of slavery ranged from the assignment of individual slaveholders to hell, to the castigation of American Christianity as hypocritical and false, to the prophecy that the nation itself was doomed to God's wrath unless it repented its crime.

By far the most affecting condemnation to emerge from the antebellum period was the pamphlet published by David Walker, a free black of Boston, in 1829. Known as Walker's *Appeal*, this amazing document has been read by some scholars as an early manifesto of black nationalism. Essentially it is a religious pamphlet, a black jeremiad urging the nation to turn from the sin of slavery before it was too late:

> Are . . . Americans innocent of the blood and groans of our fathers and us, their children? Every individual may plead innocence, if he pleases, but God will, before long, separate the innocent from the guilty unless something is speedily done—which I suppose will hardly be, so that their destruction may be sure. Oh Americans! let me tell you, in the name of the Lord, it will be good for you, if you listen to the voice of the Holy Ghost, but if you do not; you are ruined!!! Some of you are good men; but the will of my God must be done. Those avaricious and ungodly tyrants among you, I am awfully afraid will drag down the vengeance of God upon you. When God almighty commences his battle on the continent of America for [because of] the oppression of his people, tyrants will wish they never were born.[8]

Besides issuing apocalyptic warnings, Walker attacked the claims of whites to superiority. Summarizing the evils of Greek, Roman, British, and European societies (American civilization's fictive pedigree), he concluded that "whites have always been an unjust, jealous, unmerciful avaricious and blood-thirsty set of beings, always seeking after power and authority." He questioned whether whites, given the record of the past, "are *as good by nature* as we are or not." Walker then raised a topic that would be discussed by black theologians for at least another century after his death: "It is my solemn belief, that if ever the world becomes Christianized (which must certainly take place before long) it will be through the means, under God of the *Blacks*, who are now held in wretchedness, and degradation, by the white *Christians* of the world. . . ."[9]

Walker contemplated a revolution, albeit couched in religious terms. He leaves the effecting of the revolution to God's designs, but has no doubt that it will happen in this world, not the next. His God is the biblical God of nations and wars "who rules in the armies of heaven and among the inhabitants of the earth, and who dethrones one earthly king and sits [*sic*] up another." Unless Americans speedily abandon slavery and oppression of blacks, "God Almighty," Walker warned, "will tear up the very face of the earth" and "you and your *Country are gone*." Lest Walker's rhetoric make him seem like a religious eccentric, it should be remembered that the Psalms, prophets, and apocalyptic books of the Bible have fueled a long tradition of Christian protest against injustice. Walker's jeremiad was part of this tradition as well as an eloquent example of black American Christianity standing in prophetic judgment against the perversion of Christianity by whites.[10]

Though they could not declare it publicly, slaves in the South, like their Northern brethren, distinguished between true Christianity and false. They knew that holding a fellow Christian in bondage was a blatant violation of the fundamental spirit of Christianity and they saw that white Christians failed to understand this or else refused to acknowledge it. They scorned the doctrine of slavery's preachers, "don't steal, obey your masters," and held their own meetings when they wanted some "real preaching," even when it was forbidden. When their master's authority contradicted God's, some slaves risked severe punishment by choosing the latter. White claims of superiority and white norms of morality collapsed in the context of slavery. "They always tell us it am wrong to lie and steal," recalled Josephine Howard, "but why did the white folks steal my mammy and her mammy?" "That the sinfullest stealin' there is."[11]

Disdainful of the religious hypocrisy of whites, slaves protested in several ways. Some rejected Christianity outright as a sham. Others who were tired of the moralistic misuse of the gospel to make slaves better—that is, better slaves—focused on the experience of God's spirit in states of ecstatic possession as the essence of Christianity. When accused of immorality they defended their piety by denying that God was concerned about every little sin.

White (and Northern black) missionaries were shocked to find former slaves who valued the experience of God's power as the norm of Christian truth rather than the Bible. The Bible, for them, came *after* conversion. "They wanted to see their children and friends get religion as they did. They fell under the mighty power of God . . . after mourning many days, and then came out shouting, for an angel they said, told them their sins were forgiven. They said their masters and families were Bible Christians, and they did not want to be like them."[12] Undoubtedly the African heritage, which placed spirit possession at the center of religious worship, played a significant role in their interpretation of Christianity, but so did their reaction to the slaveowner's version of the Bible. At the other extreme, some slaves cherished obedience to a strict moral code, in part at least because it assured their moral superiority over whites.

Despite their condemnations of white Christianity, black Evangelicals acknowledge that there were some good whites and offered them the hand of fellowship. Northern Evangelicals, black and white, cooperated in the antislavery movement, though blacks were irked at the paternalism and prejudice of the best-intentioned whites. In the South some slaves took to heart the hard saying, "Forgive your enemies, do good to those who persecute and spitefully use you," and tried, incredibly, to put the lesson into practice. Human relationships being as complex as they are, there were occasions of religious fellowship between blacks and whites, no matter how fixed in law and custom race relations were supposed to be. Particularly in the first year of the evangelical movement in the South, during the emotional tumult of the revivals and protracted meetings, blacks and whites influenced one another in the liminal experience of conversion.

Even as both races shared many of the same doctrines, beliefs, and rituals, they differed fundamentally about God's will for black people and about the meaning of the black presence in America.

THE MEANING OF SLAVERY

Blacks could accept Christianity because they rejected the white version with its trappings of slavery and caste for a purer and more authentic gospel. They were certain that God did not condone slavery and that he would end it: the problem was how and when. While black Evangelicals believed that the issue was ultimately in God's hands, they also believed that God used instruments. What were black people to do to end slavery? Vesey and Turner had offered one option: since God is on our side, we strike for freedom, confident in his protection. The Reverend Henry Highland Garnet offered a similar solution: "To such degradation it is sinful in the extreme for you to make voluntary submission . . . Brethren arise, arise! Strike for your lives and liberties. Now is the day and the hour. . . . *Rather die freemen than live to be slaves.*"[13]

Most blacks, slave and free, realized that revolt, even with God on one's side, was doomed to failure. Garnet's address, though stirring, was rejected by the National Negro Convention before which it was given. Black Evangelicals believed that the relationship between God's sovereignty and human action was more mysterious than Vesey, Turner, or Garnet appreciated. Still, it was their duty to act. Three movements formed the arenas for black organization and activism in the North—anti-slavery, anticolonization, and moral reform. Stressing solidarity with their slave brothers, Northern black clergymen, many of them refugees from the South, organized antislavery societies; agitated from pulpit, press, and platform against slavery and oppression; fostered boycotts of slave-produced goods; formed networks to assist fugitive slaves; and strenuously opposed the American Colonization Society's plan to repatriate Afro-Americans in Africa.

While they generally favored voluntary emigration of American blacks to civilize and Christianize Africans, most black clergymen decried the American Colonization Society as a hypocritical organization bent on pressuring Congress into deporting all free blacks in order to insure the permanent security of slavery. In freedom-day celebrations and annual sermons, the American identity of blacks, their contributions to the nation, and their sacrifices in its wars, were increasingly stressed by black ministers and other spokesmen to counter the threat of forced emigration. That descendants of Africans, forced to America against their wills, were now fighting against a forced return to Africa seemed a particularly galling irony.

Black Evangelicals in the North also viewed moral reform, self-help, and education as part of the campaign against slavery. Ignorance, poverty, crime, and disease not only enslaved nominally free blacks, they were also excuses employed by racists to argue that blacks were incapable of the responsibilities of freedom and citizenship. Thus for black Evangelicals, doing good and avoiding evil were proofs of racial equality as well as signs of justification or sanctification. In this context, bourgeois values of honesty, thrift, temperance, and hard work took on a social significance for free black communities in the North that they did not have for slave communities in the South. For slaves, dishonesty, theft, and malingering were moral acts if directed against whites but not fellow blacks.

Moreover, for slave Evangelicals the essence of Christian life was not ethics, but liturgy. The ecstatic experience of God's powerful presence and the singing, dancing, and shouting that accompanied it were central, not rules, duties, and obligations. Although religious ecstasy was not absent from black evangelical churches in the North, increasing stress on education and moral reform (represented most firmly by men like Daniel Alexander Payne) led to discordance between the tone of black evangelical piety in the North and South. This discrepancy would become clear when Northern black missionaries, some originally from the South, began to work among the freedmen. Payne, for example, could not abide the former slaves' ring-shout, which he ridiculed as a "voodoo dance," heathenish, a disgrace to the race. He was shocked to find how resilient the custom was; the former slaves declared it to be "the essence of religion."[14]

Antislavery, anticolonization, and moral reform were three issues around which black Evangelicals organized in the North. In these causes they attempted to answer the question, "What must we do to end slavery?" Though they believed the final outcome was hidden in the providence of God, this belief did not lead them to fatalism or quietism but instead to activism.

In the South, slaves believed just as strongly that God would deliver them from bondage as he had the biblical children of Israel. Indeed, their situation seemed to be appropriately characterized in Moses' words to the Israelites at the Red Sea: "Stand still and see the salvation of God." According to testimony from former slaves, Christianity did foster quietism just as it fostered acts of resistance, sometimes claiming both in the same slave. External acts must be distinguished from internal attitudes, especially in a situation like American slavery where coercion and effective police power made rebellion futile in the majority of cases.

External accommodation did not necessarily entail internal acceptance, however. Oppression may easily force outward acquiescence, but internal dissent is virtually impossible to control. The inner world of slaves was the fundamental battleground and there evangelical Christianity served as an important weapon in the slave's defense of his psychological, emotional, and moral freedom from white domination. In a brutal system, Evangelicalism helped slaves resist brutalization.

In particular, conversion, a profound experience of personal acceptance and validation, reoriented the individual slave's view of himself and of the world. "The eyes of my mind were open, and I saw things as I never did before," recalled one, recounting his conversion experience. "Everything looked new," claimed another. The visionary experiences that occurred during the sometimes lengthy period of mourning and conversion moved the slave through a series of emotional transformations, from dread to security, from pressure to release, from depression to elation, from the danger of annihilation to the assurance of salvation. These "otherworldly" symbols clearly reflected "thisworldly" concerns.

In the *Narrative* of his life, Frederick Douglass articulated in romantic nature imagery that moment of internal transformation that convinced him that he was, though still enslaved, free. Many less famous former slaves described that same moment, but in the evangelical imagery of conversion. Contradicting a system that valued him like a beast for his labor, conversion *experientially* confirmed the slave's value as a human person, indeed attested to his ultimate worth as one of the chosen of God.

Like all "peak experiences" the intensity of conversion waned in the face of day-to-day drudgery and occasional brutality. Now and then the experience needed to be recaptured. Moreover, conversion was essentially an individualistic experience, though it certainly was influenced by and shared with others. It gave an invaluable sense of personal meaning and direction to the individual held captive in slavery, but it failed to explain why a just God allowed the innocent to be enslaved at all. In other words, evangelical conversion gave meaning *to* life in slavery; it did not explain the meaning *of* slavery. In the prayer meetings and worship services held in the quarters or the hush harbors of the plantation South, slaves sought a renewed vision of their worth and an answer to the riddle of slavery from the evangelical community.

Slaves did find tangible relief from the misery of slavery in the ecstatic worship of the praise meetings during which they literally "stood outside" their normal selves seized and refreshed by the spirit of God. One former slave vividly recreated the scene many years later: "They'd preach and pray and sing—shout too. I heard them git up with a powerful force of the spirit, clappin' they hands and walkin' round the place. They'd shout, 'I got the glory . . . in my soul.' I seen some powerful figurations of the spirit in them day."[15] The extemporaneous form of these meetings encouraged participants to include references to individual misfortunes and problems in their prayers and songs, so that they might be shared by all. This type of consolation, which has taken on the pejorative connotation of "compensatory," should be seen more positively as the answer to the crucial need of individuals for community.

The communal identity of slave Evangelicals was based upon the story of biblical Israel's enslavement and exodus from Egypt. Without doubt, the Exodus story was the most significant myth for American black identity, whether slave or free. White Americans had always thought of themselves as Israel, of course, but as Israelites in Canaan, the Promised Land. Black Americans were Israelites in Egypt. And even after emancipation they found that Canaan was still a far way off. Even so, they were a chosen people, destined for some special task under the direct protection of God. Identification with Israel intensified during the emotional climaxes of the prayer meetings. As Lawrence Levine has suggested, slaves dramatically reenacted the events of the Bible in their worship, with the result that time and distance collapsed into the sacred time of ritual as the congregation imaginatively became the biblical heroes whom they sang, danced, and preached about.[16]

So strong was their identification with Israel that the slaves thought of Jesus, according to one missionary, as "a second Moses who would eventually lead *them* out of their prison-house of bondage." Though the longing was there, and sometimes expressed, no historical figure emerged around whom the Moses-Messiah figure could coalesce. Freedmen sometimes referred to Lincoln, Grant, and other Union figures as deliverers and saviors like Moses and Jesus, but it seems to have been an analogy and not a literal or symbolic identification. Others were quite clear that it was God who had freed them and left little credit to any man at all.

Nor did the slaves develop millenarian expectations around the long-hoped-for emancipation. Certainly they envisaged it as a glorious event, the day of "Jubilo," but perhaps they were too realistic about the ambiguities of freedom in a land that they did not control to forecast emancipation as the beginning of a thousand-year reign of peace and justice. As one former slave put it, "De preachers would exhort us dat us was de chillen o' Israel in de wilderness an' de Lord done sent us to take dis land o' milk and honey. But how us gwine-a take land what's already been took?"[17]

By thinking of themselves as Israelites in Egypt, the slaves assured themselves that the God who had delivered his people once would do so again. Understanding their destiny as a repetition of Exodus, slaves found hope and purpose, but at the same time deferred the underlying question: Why does God allow the innocent to suffer slavery? Similarly, free blacks in the North were preoccupied with the God of Israel who would someday soon overthrow the wicked and raise up the just as he had done in the past. However, they also were engaged in arguing for abolition and black manhood rights, intellectual tasks that forced them to face difficult questions about the past, present, and future destiny of the black race.

Emancipation proved that God was faithful to his people, that their trust had been justified, but it also sharpened the problem. As freedom turned out to be less than complete, as Reconstruction was overthrown, as civil rights legislation was declared unconstitutional, as terrorism and Jim Crow legislation mounted, the questions became all the more urgent: What was God's purpose in permitting Africans to be enslaved? What is his purpose for the colored race now? In the decades of the 1880s and 1890s black theologians and clergymen would confront these problems head-on. They would persist for the rest of the century and beyond.

During the last three decades of the nineteenth century, black Evangelicals (and other black Christians) articulated more fully than before systematic answers to the vexed problem of the destiny of black folk. Frequently their discussions revolved around the ubiquitous topic, "the Negro problem." Perhaps the most acceptable answer to the greatest number of Evangelicals was that God had permitted but not condoned slavery, so that enslaved Africans might accept Christianity and civilization and then return one day to Africa to convert the fatherland. It was a disconcerting answer to some black Americans like T. Thomas Fortune, the radical editor of the New York *Age*, who dismissed the "talk about the black people being brought to this country to prepare themselves to evangelize Africa" as "so much religious nonsense boiled down to a sycophantic platitude." "The Lord, who is eminently just," insisted Fortune, "had no hand in their forcibly coming here, it was preeminently the work of the devil. Africa will have to be evangelized *from within*, not *from without*." Fortune's views did not convince many Evangelicals on this matter, but his voice—intellectual, rational, skeptical—did represent the development of a new force in black America with which Evangelicalism would have to cope.[18]

Some proponents of the evangelization of Africa linked it with the old theme of black manhood, most notably Henry McNeal Turner. For Turner and others, Africa was a challenge both to the missionary vocation of the black churches and to their full Christian manhood as formed by education and morality. Not all Afro-Americans would go to Africa, just as not all Israelites left Egypt, claimed Turner. However, it was clear in this schema that the colonization and evangelization of Africa was the destiny of Afro-Americans and the purpose of God in allowing slavery.[19]

Another not necessarily antithetical solution to the question of black destiny had been stated but not fully developed during the antebellum period. Actually, it had been implicit in all the critiques of white Christianity penned by blacks: American Christianity was corrupt and blacks would reform it (or replace it with a pure Christianity). As early as 1837, the American Moral Reform Society had employed a striking image to state just this belief: the descendants of Africa should multiply and increase in virtue in America so "that our visages may be as so many Bibles, that shall warn this guilty nation of her injustice . . . until righteousness, justice, and truth shall rise in their might and majesty . . . and without distinction of nation or complexion, she disseminates alike her blessings of freedom to all mankind." Blacks, in this view, are the leaven that will save Christian America, whose noble ideals have been sadly betrayed by whites.[20]

A more radical version of this notion, explicated most fully by black theologians James Theodore Holly and Theopilus G. Steward in the late nineteenth century, declared that Euro-American Christianity and civilization were corrupt, violent, materialistic, and nearly at an end. Black Christianity, new and vital, would succeed white Christianity and usher in an age when religion would be practiced, not just preached.[21]

Black Evangelicals supported all these theological opinions by appealing to Psalms 68:31, probably the most widely quoted verse in Afro-American religious history, "Princes shall come out of Egypt; Ethiopia shall soon stretch out her hands unto God." Whether interpreted as a divine commission to evangelize Africa, as a prophecy of the black Christian role in restoring Christianity, or as both of the above, it well represented the self-conscious identity of black Evangelicals as they struggled and suffered to build a separate tradition in search of the meaning of their distinct destiny in America. As the twentieth century approached, black Evangelicals, like their forerunners for a century, would look to revival, conversion, and the Bible for the strength to endure and to improve their lives.

NOTES

1. David Benedict, *Fifty Years Among the Baptists* (New York: Sheldon, 1860) 93–94.
2. Rhys Isaac, "Evangelical Revolt," *William and Mary Quarterly* 3d Ser. 31 (July 1974): 318–53; Robert B. Semple, *A History of the Rise and Progress of the Baptists in Virginia*, revised and extended by the Rev. George W. Beale (Philadelphia: Pitt and Dickinson, 1894) 30; Charles F. James, ed., *Documentary History of the Struggle for Religious Liberty in Virginia* (Lynchburg VA: J. P. Bell & Co., 1900) 84–85; Virginia Gazette (Purdie and Dixon) 1 October 1767; ibid., 27 February 1772; *The Maryland Journal and Baltimore Advertiser* 14 June 1793; *The Maryland Gazette* 3 January 1798; ibid., 4 September 1800; David Barrow, *Circular Letter*, 14 February 1798, 4–5; Wesley M. Gewehr, *The Great Awakening in Virginia, 1740–1790* (Durham NC: Duke University Press, 1930) 240–41; Nathan Bangs, *The Life of the Rev. Freeborn Garrettson* (New York: J. Emory & B. Waugh, 1832) 39; Donald G. Mathews, *Slavery and Methodism* (Princeton: Princeton University Press, 1965) 293–99.
3. Robert E. Park, "The Conflict and Fusion of Cultures with Special Reference to the Negro," *Journal of Negro History* 4 (April 1919): 120; James M. Simms, *The First Colored Baptist Church in North America* (Philadelphia: J. B. Lippincott Co., 1888) 36–39; Walter H. Brooks, "The Priority of the Silver Bluff Church and Its Promoters," *Journal of Negro History* 7 (April 1922): 172–75, 182–90; John Rippon, *The Baptists Annual Register, 1790–1793* (ca. 1794), 263, 332–35, 340–42, 540–41;

Simms, 46–78, 93–103; Rev. E. K. Love, *History of the First African Baptist Church* (Savannah GA: The Morning News Print, 1888) 10–24; Richard Allen, *The Life Experiences and Gospel Labors of the Rt. Rev. Richard Allen* (rpt. ed., New York and Nashville: Abingdon Press, 1959) 30–35.

4. Whitemarsh B. Seabrook, *An Essay on the Management of Slaves* (Charleston SC: The Society, 1834) 14–22; Lewis G. Jordan, *Negro Baptist History, U.S.A., 1750–1993* (Nashville: The Sunday School Publishing Board, n.d.) 103–104.

5. Daniel A. Payne, "Thought about the Past, the Present and the Future of the African M.E. Church," *A.M.E. Church Review* 1 (July 1884): 1–3.

6. William H. Heard, *From Slavery to the Bishopric in the A.M.E. Church* (Philadelphia: The A.M.E. Book Concern, 1924) 89–90.

7. *Collections of the Massachusetts Historical Society* 5th ser., no. 3 (1877) 423–33.

8. *Walker's Appeal, in Four Articles Together with a Preamble, to the Colored Citizens of the World . . .* (1830), in Sterling Stuckey, *The Ideological Origins of Black Nationalism* (Boston: Beacon Press, 1972) 83.

9. Ibid., 55–57.

10. Ibid., 76–77.

11. George P. Rawick, ed., *The American Slave: A Composite Autobiography*, 17 vols., (Westport CT: Greenwood Publishing Co., 1972) 8 *Arkansas*, 1:35; 7 *Mississippi*, 24; 17 *Florida*, 166; 4 *Texas*, 2:163.

12. *American Missionary* 12 (January 1868): 9; ibid., 14 (September 1870): 194, 221.

13. Henry Highland Garnet, *An Address to the Slaves of the United States of America* (1843), in Stuckey, 172.

14. Daniel Alexander Payne, *Recollections of Seventy Years* (1886) (rpt. 3d., New York: Arno Press, 1969) 253–56.

15. Rawick, 4 *Texas*, 2:170.

16. Lawrence Levine, "Slave Songs and Slave Consciousness: An Exploration in Nineteenth-Century Social History," in *Anonymous Americans*, ed. Tamara K. Hareven (Englewood Cliffs NJ: Prentice-Hall, 1971) 114–15; see also Lawrence W. Levine, *Black Culture and Black Consciousness* (New York: Oxford University Press, 1977).

17. W. G. Kiphant, Letter of 9 May 1864, Decatur AL, A.M.A. Archives, Amistad Research Center, Dillard University, New Orleans; Eugene D. Genovese, *Roll, Jordan, Roll: The World the Slaves Made* (New York: Pantheon Books, 1974) 273–79; Donald G. Matthews, *Religion in the Old South* (Chicago and London: University of Chicago Press, 1977) 222–25; Norman R. Yetman, ed., *Voices from Slavery* (New York: Holt, Rinehart & Winston, 1970) 75.

18. T. Thomas Fortune, *Black and White: Land, Labor, and Politics in the South* (1884) (rpt. Chicago: Johnson Publishing Co., 1970) 86–87.

19. H. M. Turner, "Essay: The American Negro and the Fatherland," in *Africa and the American Negro: Addresses and Proceedings of the Congress on Africa*, ed. J.W.E. Bowen (1896) (rpt., Miami: Mnemosyne Publication, Inc., 1969) 195–98; see also the col-

lection of Turner's writings and speeches in Edwin S. Redkey, ed., *Respect Black* (New York: Arno Press, 1971), passim. For the opinions of other black clergymen on this issue, see "What Should Be the Policy of the Colored American toward Africa," a symposium published in the *A.M.E. Church Review* 2(July 1995):68–74; Bishop W. J. Gaines, *The Negro and the White Man* (1887) (rpt., New York: Negro Universities Press, 1969) 19–21; Alexander Walters, *My Life and Work* (London and Edinburgh: Fleming H. Revell Co., 1917) 173.

20. *Minutes and Proceedings of the First Annual Meeting of the American Moral Reform Society* (1937) in *Early Negro Writing, 1760–1837,* ed. Dorothy Porter (Boston: Beacon Press, 1971) 203.

21. See James Theodore Holly, "The Divine Plan of Human Redemption, in Its Ethnological Development," *A.M.E. Church Review* 1 (October 1884):79–85.

SELECTED BIBLIOGRAPHY FOR FURTHER READING

Boles, John B., ed. *Masters and Slaves in the House of the Lord: Race and Religion in the American South, 1740–1870.* Lexington: University of Kentucky Press, 1988.

Creel, Margaret Washington. *"A Peculiar People": Slave Religion and Community-Culture Among the Gullahs.* New York: New York University Press, 1988.

Mathews, Donald. *Religion in the Old South.* Chicago: University of Chicago Press, 1977.

Raboteau, Albert J. *Slave Religion: The "Invisible Institution" in the Antebellum South.* New York: Oxford University Press, 1978.

Sernett, Milton C. *Black Religion and American Evangelicalism: White Protestants, Plantation Missions, and the Flowering of Negro Christianity, 1787–1865.* Metuchen, NJ: Scarecrow Press, 1975.

6 ::

Vincent Harding

:: Christianity was often experienced by African-Americans as a double-edged sword, one edge emphasizing obedience and accommodation to the status quo and the other inspiring rebellion against unjust structures. One illustration of this tension in the twentieth century are the contrasting figures of Malcolm X who argued that Christianity "deceived and brainwashed the so-called Negro to always turn the other cheek . . . and to look for his pie in the sky," and Martin Luther King, Jr. whose Christian beliefs inspired the civil rights movement. Likewise, Antebellum slave owners attempted to use religion as a mechanism for social control by giving preeminence to the Biblical passages of St. Paul that stress obedience, but as Vincent Harding demonstrates in the following seminal essay published in 1969, Christianity could also provide motivation and a foundation for black protest. ::

6

RELIGION AND RESISTANCE AMONG ANTEBELLUM SLAVES, 1800–1860

Vincent Harding

In these days of ecumenicism among the academic disciplines, it would likely be both fair and appropriate to describe the state of our historical understanding of Negro religion in America as a variety of cultural lag. This is clearly the case when we try to assess the role of black religion in the antebellum period of American history, and especially when an attempt is made to understand its relationship to acts of protest and resistance.

Stated in simplest terms, the situation may be described in this way: Thanks to the crucial work of Aptheker, the Bauers, Stampp, and others, we have moved beyond a naive and often distorted view of happy or indifferent Negro slaves whose docility was a sight to behold.[1] Indeed the movement towards the new theme of slave rebellion and resistance has often been so strong that the inevitable reconsiderations and revisions have already set in.[2] But it would appear unlikely that even such fascinating and worthy caveats as those raised by Elkins, Wade, and Genovese will drive us back to the old dominions—if for no other reason than the uneasiness our increasingly black-oriented age feels with such interpretations. So the new slaves seem to be a permanent fixture. On the other hand, we have not yet been released from the traditional views of black religion that supported the older generalizations concerning submissive and humble slaves. Here precisely is the lag.

Much of the current historical opinion about the role of religion among ante-

bellum southern Negroes still follows the classic lines set out in Benjamin Mays'
The Negro's God, which claimed that the Negroes' idea of God "kept them submissive, humble and obedient."[3] Repeatedly Mays referred to this religion as "other-worldly" and "compensatory," inclining its votaries "to do little or nothing to improve their status here. . . ."[4] Even so shrewd and perceptive a scholar as E.
Franklin Frazier later adumbrated the theme in his important work on *The Negro
Church*.[5] There the antebellum Negroes—especially in the South—were identified with a religion that "turned their minds from the sufferings and privations of
this world to a world after death where the weary would find rest and the victims
of injustice would be compensated."[6]

The views of Mays and Frazier are representative of most discussions of the
black religion that developed before the Civil War. In many ways these men
helped to set the theme. Their views, of course, represented an American adaptation of the classic statement by Karl Marx:

> Religion is the sign of the oppressed creature, the heart of the heartless
> world . . . the spirit of a spiritless situation. It is the *opium* of the people.[7]

In this essay what we question is not the applicability of such an understanding of religion to a majority of antebellum Negroes. Indeed, the traditional view
often has much support in the records. For instance, it was not accidental that a
slaveholder said in the 1830s, "The deeper the piety of the slave, the more valuable he is in every respect."[8] This was a widespread opinion. Nor was that eloquent refugee from slavery, William Wells Brown, wrong when in 1850 he
claimed that religious instruction for his fellow-bondsmen consisted "in teaching
the slave that he must never strike a white man, that God made him a slave; and
that when whipped he must find no fault. . . ."[9]

That was likely an accurate description of most instruction, and many slaves
seem to live by it. (Generally, of course, they had no other choice than to give at
least an impression that they did.) However the present dispute does not center
there. Rather this paper seeks to raise the issue of the ambiguity, the doubleness,
of black religions experience. It seeks not to deny the opiate quality of much
slave religion but to offer the suggestion that there were significant, identifiable
black responses to religion which often stormed beyond submissiveness to
defiance.

Perhaps Frederick Douglass best sets the scene for an understanding of this
ambiguous and two-edged Negro reaction to religions teaching. In one of his autobiographical writings, this most famous of fugitive slaves, recorded words
which scarcely covered his underlying scorn. He said,

> I have met, at the south, many good, religious colored people who were under
> the delusion that God required them to submit to slavery and to wear their
> chains with meekness and humility.

Then he added, "I could entertain no such nonsenses as this. . . ."[10] For
Douglass, as for countless others, the requirements of God pointed in other
directions, and black religion led them away from slavery. Often it led to protest,
resistance and death.

Recently a teacher of religion has tried to articulate this theme of the protest
role of Negro faith. In his *Black Religion*, Joseph Washington wrote, "the religion
of the Negro folk was chosen to bear roles of both protest and relief."[11] Indeed
Washington went on to suggest that "The uniqueness of black religion" since the
days of slavery was to be found in its constant and often risky search for "the elusive but ultimate goal of freedom and equality by means of protest and action."[12]
Like so much of Washington's work, those last phrases may be understatements,
but they help to balance the scales set by Frazier, Mays, and Marx.

Perhaps, then, this paper can be thought of as an attempt to suggest pathways
towards an historical documentation of Joseph Washington's intuitive thesis, at
least that part of it which seeks to appreciate the proper relationship of black religion to Negro protest and resistance. Without such an attempt we shall be in
danger of fruitlessly trying to apply the religion of Ulrich Phillips' Negroes to
the defiant men and women who often leap out of the pages of Aptheker and
Stampp. To quote Douglass slightly out of context, "we can entertain no such
nonsense as this. . . ." (Even Marxists came to realize that religious commitment
might produce revolutionary action.[13] Those who claim to be unhindered by the
fetters of ideology can do no less.)

II

It has seemed wise for the present to confine this statement to the period
1800–1860, and to focus on Negroes in the South. Therefore it may be significant
to note that it was in 1800 that South Carolina's legislature indicated a keen awareness of the possible connections between black rebellion and black religion, an
awareness that was apparently the property of many southern white persons.
In that year the legislature passed one of the first of those countless nineteenth-
century laws restricting black religious services. This one forbade Negroes

> even in company with white persons to meet together and assemble for the

purpose of . . . religious worship, either before the rising of the sun or after
the going down of the same.[14]

Magistrates were given the power to break up all such gatherings. Behind the legislation was obviously a fear that these religious meetings might lead to trouble,
especially if they were held at hours when they could not easily be monitored.

If the fear needed substantiation it was soon available. In Virginia's Henrico
county Tom Prosser's slave, Gabriel, and Gabriel's brother, Martin, were then
gathering slaves and free Negroes at strange hours and making strange uses of
"religious services." Gabriel was plotting insurrection, and building a force that
had evidently mounted into the thousands by 1800. At their religious services it
was said that both Martin and Gabriel—what fitting names!—regularly set forth

> an impassioned exposition of Scripture . . . The Israelites were glowingly
> portrayed as a type of successful resistance to tyranny; and it was argued, that
> now, as then, God would stretch forth his arm to save, and would strengthen a
> hundred to overthrow a thousand.[15]

The black men of Henrico county were the new Israelites. Gabriel was their
Moses. Would they follow?

It is not known how deeply this appeal from the Old Testament moved the
persons who gathered in those secret meetings, nor which of them joined the attempted rebellion in response to it. But the analogy to the Israelites was a traditional one in the black community, and it continued to have great force among
the slaves. Therefore it would not be too much to expect that some of the men
who set themselves on the path of rebellion in those Virginia meetings were responding to a profoundly religious call, as well as to the news from Santo
Domingo, or to the stirring cries of "Death or Liberty." Haiti was a good example, and the political motto was a moving cry, but it surely helped to believe as
well that the God of Israel would "stretch forth his arm" to intervene on behalf of
the blacks.[16]

When the insurrection was foiled by the sudden downpour of torrential
rains, the white residents of Virginia would, of course, have been justified in
thinking that divine intervention was indeed present—on their side.[17] But they
were likely caused to be suspicious about other religious matters as the trials of
the rebels revealed that Methodists and Quakers—as well as Frenchmen—were
to be spared the vengeful swords of Gabriel's band.[18] What could that mean?

Religion and its relationship to black rebellion continued to be a matter for
concern and for questions in Virginia, even before the coming of Nat Turner. For

instance, one Richard Byrd of that state wrote to his Governor in May, 1810, to express his conviction that "slave preachers used their religious meetings as veils for revolutionary schemes," and he cited a "General Peter" from Isle of Wight as an example of the danger.[19]

Six years later this kind of fear was given solid ground in the Old Dominion again, but it was a white preacher who now seemed to be using black religion for seditious purposes. George Boxley, proprietor of a county store, was a regular participant in the religious meetings held by the Negroes of Spottsylvania and Louisa counties. Soon he began telling them "that a little white bird had brought him a holy message to deliver his fellowmen from bondage. . . ."[20] Again the promise of divinely aided deliverance found active response, and Phillips says that Boxley "enlisted many blacks in his project" for messianic insurrection. Unfortunately for the black believers, as was so often the case, the plot was betrayed. Some Negro followers were hanged, others were sold out of the state, but Boxley escaped from jail.[21] Perhaps the message of deliverance had been meant only for him. After all, it was a white bird.

The pattern of religious connections to rebellious movements continued consistently into South Carolina in the same year—1816. There, in Camden, a plot had evidently been maturing, and when the almost inevitable betrayal and arrests finally came, a local newspaper offered its own version of the relationship between religion and resistance:

> It is a melancholy fact [the editor said] that those who were most active in the conspiracy occupied a respectable stand in one of the churches, several were professors [i.e., avowed Christians], and one a class leader.[22]

Camden was not the only place in South Carolina where black Christians and class leaders were making life difficult for the keepers of the established order. Charleston was having its difficulties with the darker variety of Methodists, trouble that would eventually lead into deep distress.[23]

The Negroes in the port city's Methodist congregations had long outnumbered their white brethren by ten to one. They had known a sense of significant independence through their own quarterly conference and as a result of the control they exercised over finances and the discipline of their members. In 1815 alleged "abuses" had led to the loss of these privileges as well as much of the independence that went with them. But black church leaders like Denmark Vesey, Peter Poyas and Jack Pritchard (Gullah Jack) had no intentions of accepting such debilitating penalties without offering direct and open response.

They led agitation among the Negro members, rounded up a thousand new members and sent two of their leaders up to Philadelphia to be ordained by the African Methodist Episcopal bishops there. Then in 1818 a dispute over their burial ground provided the occasion for more than 4,000 of the 6,000 black Methodists to withdraw their membership *en masse* from the white Charleston congregations. With ordained ministers of their own they now moved ahead to build a meeting house and establish an independent congregation called the African Church of Charleston.

It is in this context that we may speak more precisely of rebellion. Here the crucial issue is not the nature of what happened in 1822, not the matter of whether widely organized insurrection was being planned.[24] At this juncture it is of critical importance simply to see that organized rebellion on another level had already been built deeply into the structure of black church life in Charleston. The agitation from 1815 to 1818 and the concerted withdrawal from the white congregations in the latter year took significant courage for the slaves. The raising of an independent house of worship implied not only the gathering of financial resources, but it was clearly an act of defiance for the world to see. The municipal officials knew this and responded accordingly with harassments, arrests, banishments, and finally with the closing of the church in 1821.[25] It is, then, essential to note that the sense of black solidarity was imbedded in the organization of the Negro church. Attempts to dilute this or break it down met inevitably with resistance, resistance centered in that church's life.

Did the defiance include a wider plan for insurrection? It is not the purpose of this essay to enter into the argument that has been interestingly raised by Mr. Wade. However, my own examination of available evidence leads me to suspect that the plot was "more than loose talk by aggrieved and embittered men."[26] These men had already given evidence of impressive skill in organizing black discontent for action. They had followers in their defiance, and their leadership was evidently trusted. There was no reason for them to be content with "loose talk" by 1822.

Whatever the extent of the new action being planned, it seems clear that some continuing organizing was going on, that it was centered in the membership of the African Church and that the charismatic Denmark Vesey was at the heart of the affair.[27] Now, for our purposes it is necessary only to continue to deal with the role of religion as it participated in a movement that went beyond the defense of church-oriented prerogatives to new and likely bolder concerns. If, as seems probable, an insurrection was being planned, Vesey surely knew how to continue to use themes that had led the blacks to organize for independent church status.

His focus was regularly on religion. One witness testified that this leader's "general conversation . . . was about religion, which he would apply to slavery." Indeed, "all his religious remarks were mingled with slavery," according to the testimony.[28] Was this surprising? For the most part these were church members who were being addressed, and they were also slaves. What other focus was more natural? These were also persons whose extant religious records indicate that they were profoundly attracted to the analogy between their condition and the condition of the Hebrews in Egypt. As a class leader, Vesey surely knew all this very well. So one of the alleged conspirators was probably quite accurate when he said that Denmark Vesey "read to us from the Bible, how the *children of Israel were delivered out of Egypt from bondage.* . . ."[29] Nor did the persuasive exhorter stop there. It is said that he made it clear to the bondsmen that it was imperative to their faith that slaves "attempt their emancipation, 'however shocking and bloody might be the consequences.'" And on the strength of his magnificent authority as a class leader—and as a man—he declared that such efforts would be "pleasing to the Almighty," and that their success was thereby guaranteed.[30]

If, as we are suggesting, religion did play a critical role in the motivating of his followers, then Vesey chose wisely (or was fortunate, if he did not make the choice himself) when he gained an accomplice like Jack Pritchard, better known as Gullah Jack. This black man of Angolan background provided an excellent counterpoint to Vesey's Old Testament theme. For he was not only a member of the African Church but a conjurer, a medicine man in the African tradition. Therefore Vesey had the best of both religious worlds, and we are told that Gullah Jack exerted tremendous influence over the other members of his ancestral group.[31]

This, of course, does not mean that Vesey did not seek to rally his forces through the use of other issues as well. The tradition of Santo Domingo, the debate over Missouri, the general mistreatment of the Negroes by the city authorities and by some of their masters—these were all part of the strategy.[32] But it would be derelict to fail to note how crucial was the religious issue, especially in the light of the post–1814 church experiences. Was this not the significance of the note found in Peter Poyas' trunk after he was arrested: "Fear not, the Lord God that delivered Daniel is able to deliver us."[33]

Then in the summer of 1822, when deliverance appeared to have been aborted and the gallows were heavy with black bodies, it was fitting that the city should demolish the First African Church.[34] This was not only a rehearsal of more modern southern church treatment, but it was a testimony to the significant role the people of that congregation had played in carrying the contagion of rebellion. Nor was it surprising that an Episcopalian minister boasted that such things could never happen among black Episcopalians because their Negroes "were not allowed to exhort or expound scriptures in words of their own . . . and to utter . . . whatever nonsense might happen to their minds."[35]

Regardless of how we see such matters now, it was evidently clear to most Charlestonians of the time that "religious enthusiasm" had been one of the motivating forces in Vesey's action. So all preachers of the gospel to slaves—white and black—were suspect.[36] And a Charleston editor condemned the white Christian missionaries who,

> with the Sacred Volume of God in one hand scattered with the other the fire-brands of discord and destruction; and *secretly* dispensed among our Negro population, the seeds of discontent and sedition.[37]

Though he saw much, the editor did not see that the firebrands and the seeds were often in the same hand as "the Sacred Volume," but he surely must have known that the hands were often black.

At least this was the case with Nat Turner, who carried his own Volume, fire and seeds. Whatever doubts we may entertain about the authenticity of Vesey's rebellion, Turner leaves us with no choice. Even more important for our present concerns is the central theme of Turner's *Confession*—the theme of a black, avenged Messiah, urged into action by nothing less than the repeated calling of God.[38] Here was religion and resistance that would not be separated.

Based primarily on the *Confession*, the story develops. As a child he became convinced that he was "intended for some great purpose." Evidently he nurtured the search for his destiny through arduous prayer and fasting and the development of an austere personal life. Turner claimed to be directed many times by "the Spirit" as it spoke to him in his lonely vigils or as he worked in the fields. A major theme of that direction was "Seek ye the kingdom of Heaven and all things shall be added unto you." When asked later about this "Spirit," the 31-year-old prisoner made it clear that he stood self-consciously in the prophetic tradition, for he said that he had been visited by "The Spirit that spoke to the Prophets in former days."

Eventually the young mystic became fully confirmed in his sense of ordination to some "great purpose in the hands of the Almighty," and he went through his own Wilderness experience—thirty days in the forests of Virginia as a runaway slave. Then the Spirit drove him back for his great encounter with the future. In 1825 Turner saw his first major vision suggestively describing his ultimate calling. White and black spirits were battling in the air. Thunder rang out. The sun was darkened, and he watched in awe as blood flowed through the land. The same Spirit promised him the wisdom and strength needed for the task.

After a fascinating variety of other visions, the critical revelation came in May, 1828. According to Nat,

> I heard a loud noise in the heavens and the Spirit instantly appeared to me and said the Serpent was loosened, and Christ had laid down the Yoke he had borne for the sins of men, and that I should take it on and fight against the Serpent, for the time was fast approaching when the first should be last and the last should be first.

The Spirit also revealed to him that there would be adequate signs in nature to let him know when he should begin the messianic work for which he was ordained, when to "arise and prepare myself to slay my enemies with their own weapons." In an eclipse of the sun—that most ancient of signs—Nat Turner found his signal to begin. He ate a last supper with some of his followers and went forth to carry out his own version of the work of Christ, using the weapons of the Old Testament, drenching the ground with blood, for "neither age nor sex was to be spared." And when he was asked if he thought himself mistaken as he faced execution at the end, Turner's response came fittingly enough: "Was not Christ crucified?" To the charge of dastardly crime, his plea, of course, was "Not Guilty."

Obviously Nat Turner was one of those religious charismatics who arise in a variety of settings, from the walls of Münster to the fields of Southampton County.[39] He was not a "preacher" in any formal sense of the word, and evidently belonged to no structured church group. But he was an "exhorter," and he clearly convinced his fellow slaves by the power of his message and the strange sense of his presence that he was the anointed one of God for their deliverance— a deliverance for which slaves never ceased to yearn.

No other explanation will open the intricacies of Nat Turner. Thus when they were wounded and waiting to die, it was said of his companions that some of them "in the agonies [sic] of Death declared that they was going happy fore that God had a hand in what they had been doing. . . ."[40] They still believed that "Prophet Nat" was sent from God.

When all the dyings were over, after the fierce retaliations had taken place, the conviction and the legend lived on. Black people believed and remembered, and some acted. The religion of Nat Turner, the religion of black rebellion became part of their tradition.[41] Whites, on the other hand, believed variations of the black themes and acted in their own ways. Their response was well summed up by a writer in the Richmond *Enquirer* who said then

> The case of Nat Turner warns us. No black man ought to be permitted to turn a preacher through the country. The law must be enforced—or the tragedy of Southampton appeals to us in vain.[42]

In the minds of blacks and whites alike religion and rebellion had been welded into one terrifying—or exalting—reality through the black body of Nat Turner.

So the laws set off by fear swept through the states, forbidding Negroes to preach, in many places interdicting all meetings, attempting as it were to exorcise so troubling a religious spirit.[43] The Mississippi law of 1831 provided a good example when it ruled that "It is 'unlawful for any slave, free Negro, or mulatto to preach the gospel' under pain of receiving thirty-nine lashes upon the naked back of the . . . preacher."[44]

The laws did not stop the strange gospel of freedom from infiltrating into the ranks of the slaves—partly because it was already there. So an insurrectionary attempt came to light in Duplin County, North Carolina, in the fall of 1831, even before Turner had been captured. In the course of its account a newspaper article revealed that "a very intelligent negro preacher named David, was put on his trial . . . and clearly convicted . . ." as one of the ringleaders.[45] Elsewhere in that same year another newspaper correspondent says, "It is much to be regretted that [the apparent wave of insurrectionary attempts] are instigated by fierce, ignorant fanatics, assuming to be preachers." His comment closed with this prophecy: "I foresee that this land must one day or other, become a field of blood."[46] Thus in the mind of at least one man, black preachers of religion might well lead a people to bloody revolution. Strange opium.

In 1833 when Frederick Douglass, still a slave, tried to organize a Sabbath School class among the black young people of the eastern shore of Maryland, he found out that this white coreligionists had not yet disassociated themselves from earlier memories and convictions. Two Methodist class leaders led the mob that stormed Douglass' Sabbath School and Douglass said he was told by one Methodist that "I wanted to be another Nat Turner, and that, if I did not look out, I should get as many balls in me as Nat did into him."[47]

Two years later, during the slave insurrection scare in Mississippi, it was again said that "suspicion centered around the 'itinerant preachers'" and other troublemakers in the neighborhood.[48] In New Orleans the newspapers were complaining in 1839 about a Negro church which was "the greatest of all public nuisances and den for hatching plots against [the] masters."[49] Seven years later the same problem existed in the city as the police arrested twelve Negroes in "a makeshift church" and charged them with "the habit of repairing to this place for . . . singing hymns and cantiques which was followed by sermons the subject of which was the most inflammatory character."[50] Firebrands and sermons were continually being combined by black men whose religion had not yet made them "otherworldly" enough to suit the authorities.

It may be that the ambiguous nature of American religion, as it related to antebellum blacks, was best seen by a visitor to this land, one who had become a heroic figure among abolitionists by 1841. This was Joseph Cinquez, the African who had led a rebellion aboard the vessel *Amistad*, as it carried a load of slaves along the coast of Cuba in 1839.[51] In the course of the revolt the captain and the cook had been killed by the rebels, the ship was steered to American shores and Cinquez had been brought to New England with his fellow slaves. There they were exposed to American Christianity with all of its contradictory potentials.

Then, in 1841, just before leaving for his native continent Cinquez was given the rare opportunity to apply this nation's religion to his rebellion—after the fact. One of his fellow rebels said to a group of Christians, "We owe everything to God: he keeps us alive and makes us free." Filled with enthusiasm, another went on to claim that he would now pray for the captain and cook rather than kill them if the rebellion were to be done over again. We are told that "Cinquez, hearing this, smiled and shook his head. When asked if we would not pray for them, he said: 'Yes I would pray for 'em, an' kill 'em too.'"[52]

III

While the religion of some slaves could lead them to pray and kill, and though the Jesus of Southampton beckoned black men through streams of the masters' blood, there were other bondsmen who were evidently no less religiously motivated but who were led to seek different alternatives in their struggle. The Bauers have reminded us of the many levels of resistance to slavery that existed in the South, and they have indicated that some slaves who shed blood as an act of protest were known to draw their own or to take the lives of their children.[53] Death and self-mutilation were preferred to slavery, and one of the accounts of such death may offer some hint concerning the religions motivation involved here.

In Kentucky it was reported that "a father and mother, shut up in a slave baracoon and doomed to the southern market . . . did by mutual agreement send the souls of their children to Heaven rather than have them descend to the hell of slavery, and then both parents committed suicide."[54] No one may be sure that the theology of the contemporary writer was shared by the parents he described, but is it impossible to conceive that a religion that stressed the reality of heaven after death might strengthen slaves to leave their bondage for the freedom they had heard was ahead? If the "other world" was really so good, why allow children to suffer the agonies that parents had known?

In spite of the possible force of such reasoning, especially in extreme situations, it is certain that the action of the Kentucky parents was not typical. Perhaps a more common religious response to slavery was simply the act of refusing to believe the Christian teachings that justified the system of exploitation. A most striking instance of this alternative was found in Georgia shortly before 1830. In Liberty County a group of slaves were listening to a white minister hold forth on a staple topic—the escaped slave, Onesimus, and his return to his master. According to the report from Georgia, half of the Negro group walked out when the point of the sermon became clear, and "the other half stayed mostly for the purpose of telling [the preacher] that they were sure there was no such passage in the Bible."[55]

Because action could often be more costly than thoughts it is likely that many more slaves were involved in the kind of resistance to such religion that was identified by a former slave who said that Negroes simply refused to believe "a proslavery doctrine."[56] But Henry Bibb went on to point to what might have been an even more significant kind of defiance when he said that "This kind of preaching has driven thousands into infidelity."[57] Bibb's observations were supported by a southern Presbyterian minister who noted that many white ministers had assumed that Negroes "are an unsophisticated race" only to discover among them "deism, universalism, skepticism, and all the strong objections against the truth of God . . . which he may perhaps have considered peculiar only to the cultivated minds . . . of critics and philosophers."[58]

May we not suggest that the turn to "deism, universalism" and other unapproved forms of southern faith on the part of the slaves was in itself a profoundly religious act of protest against a system that seemed to be supported by all the correct lines of doctrine? Thus one may possibly speak of both protest and accommodation, if the accommodation were carried out under the new religiously protestant ground rules, rules that needed perforce to remain largely interior, but nonetheless real for that.

We are, however, concerning ourselves here with the more exterior, reportable, forms of resistance, and it is clear that one of the most obvious of these was the act of running away from slavery. It was not an act lightly taken up nor easily accomplished, and a sampling of fugitive slave narratives readily reveals the level of inner conviction and strength that was most often necessary for a slave to strike out for freedom. The difficulty of the path and the disobedience of the act provided good testing grounds for the nature of religious faith.

Frederick Douglass recalled his own struggle with the issue of escape as an older man continued to speak to him of the great things that he thought Douglass was meant to do in the world. Young Frederick responded: "I am a slave, and a slave for life, how can I do anything?" To this "Uncle Lawson" replied:

> The Lord can make you free, my dear; all things are possible with him . . . if you want liberty, ask the Lord for it in faith, and he will give it to you.[59]

From that point on Douglass began asking—in his own unorthodox way—and planning, until he felt he had freedom grasped securely in his hands. This was why the religion of chains and submission seemed like "nonsense" to him.

Samuel Ringgold Ward, another fugitive who became a brilliant abolitionist lecturer, lived the struggle through his mother. When he was a child this matriarch had to decide whether she would remain in Maryland and likely be sold further south or whether she would encourage her husband to lead them all to freedom. The will of God was discussed at that point, and the strong, single-minded black woman decided that they should leave. As Ward later described it,

> Submission to the will of God was one thing, she was prepared for that, but submission to the machinations of Satan was quite another thing: neither her womanhood nor her theology could be reconciled to the latter.[60]

In one of the most famous of the antebellum slave narratives William Wells Brown spoke of the same issue—the relationship of his mother's God to freedom. He told of how he confided in her his own plans for escape from slavery in St. Louis just as she was being sold into the deep South. Without any hesitation she urged him to go, and her last word may have expressed her theology of slave rebellion: "God be with you."[61]

There is only one woman whose journey from Southern slavery to freedom is readily available, and that story—half legend by now—is a religious pilgrimage in itself.[62] Harriet Tubman grew up on the stories of the Hebrew children, heard the whispered descriptions of Nat Turner, and sang the songs of impossible hope. Like Turner she saw visions and dreamed dreams of struggle and conflict and searching for freedom. Like him she prayed and talked with God and became fully convinced that her God willed freedom. Indeed, one of her more radical biographers said that by the time she escaped from her native Maryland in 1849 "she was ready to kill for freedom, if that was necessary, and defend the act as her religious right."[63]

The year after Harriet's arrival in the North her fellow black runaways were cast in a new light as a result of the Compromise of 1850 and its Fugitive Slave law. Therefore, while Douglass and Harriet Tubman gained most lasting fame as fugitives, it was a slave who arrived north in 1854—Anthony Burns—whose case became the *cause célebrè* of his time.[64] As a result of the notoriety resulting from the Boston abolitionist furor, Burns received a letter of rebuke and excommunication from the white Baptist church he had joined as a slave in Virginia. In his response we have one of the best statements of the religious apologia for resistance through flight.

Burns wrote,

> You charge me that, in escaping, I disobeyed God's law. No, indeed! That law which God wrote upon the table of my heart, inspiring the love of freedom, and impelling me to seek it at every hazard, I obeyed, and by the good hand of my God upon me, I walked out of the house of bondage.

Then, in response to the inevitable citation of Paul and Onesimus which had been in the church's letter, Burns said he would be glad to return if he had any reason to believe that he too would be received in the brotherly spirit that Paul had requested for Onesimus. But Burns said that he did not believe in such a possibility, and was staying North. Finally he stated his basic defense and comfort in the terms of his faith: "You have thrust me out of your church fellowship. So be it. You cannot exclude me from heaven. . . ."[65]

Such was the religion of the runaways. They were obviously a self-selective group, but an important and impressive one too. None of them was willing to wait for Frazier's "world after death" to find their rest or to gain compensation for their condition, and they had thousands of brothers in their impatience. (Even heaven-oriented Anthony Burns wanted to try out Boston before confirming his reservation in heavenly places.)

Indeed, persons like Brown, Ward, Douglass and Harriet Tubman (to say nothing of their Northern-born counterparts) seemed unwilling to accept rest anywhere. Their religion was a restless one while slavery existed in the South and segregation shamed the North. The extreme form of this eternally protesting religion was expressed, of course, by Harriet Tubman shortly after her arrival in Philadelphia. There, upon being asked to settle in the city, she was quoted as having said,

There are three million of my people on the plantations of the south. I must go down, like Moses into Egypt, to lead them out.[66]

Such a spirit breeds legends and makes history difficult to write, but Harriet Tubman did return and she delivered some small, but important fragment of the waiting people. She returned often enough to end up with rewards amounting to 40,000 dollars being offered for her. Just as her own escape from slavery was the Lord's doing in her mind, so too did a sense of divine obsession now drive Harriet Tubman to continue this strange and courageous work of deliverance.[67] She too knew how to exhort, sing spirituals and carry a gun.

If the sparse evidence available is any guide, Harriet Tubman's efforts were child's play compared to a plan that was already at work in the South when she was escaping. It was a plan that revived memories of Gabriel and Vesey and Prophet Nat, expanding them beyond imagination. According to the Reverend Moses Dickson, the founder of a post-Civil War Negro benevolent society, in 1846 he had been instrumental in forming a group of twelve young men who called themselves the twelve Knights of Tabor.[68] They vowed in that year to spend the next decade organizing an army of liberation throughout the South, and were preparing to strike for the freedom of the slaves sometime after 1856. The Old Testament name was self-consciously chosen, Dickson said, for it "gave the members courage."[69]

According to his story, they were encouraged because they knew that

God was with Israel, and gave the victory to the bondsmen, though they were opposed by twenty times their number. Our cause was just, and we believed in the justice of the God of Israel and the rights of man. Under the name of Tabor we resolved to make full preparation to strike the blow for liberty.[70]

With this sense of divine calling the members supposedly organized within ten years more than forty thousand recruits who were "well drilled, with ample arms and ammunition." They were located in all the slave states except Texas and Missouri. The larger group was dubbed Knights of Liberty.[71]

In 1857 they were prepared, by Dickson's account, to gather more followers and converge on Atlanta with 150,000 troops. They were to spare women and children, but "march, fight, and conquer was the command, or leave their bodies on the battle field." Their flag was to have a cross made up of twelve stars. Then when all was prepared, just before an unidentified "Chief" was about to give the command to march, Dickson says, "it was plainly demonstrated to [the leader] that a higher power was preparing to take part in the contest between the North and South . . ." So the group was told to hold off, and it disbanded when the Civil War came.[72]

If this account is true, America was on the verge of experiencing the work of a Holy Liberation Front. So far it has not proved possible to go beyond one or two documentary sources related to this movement. However it is important to note that if such a movement was indeed on foot, it was self-consciously arrayed in the train of Nat Turner. Event or legend, it testified to the fact that there was a strong tradition of religious rebellion among antebellum blacks.

While the Knights of Liberty failed to march, John Brown did not fail. His religious self-image is well known. Less known is the fact that many Negroes took John Brown's insurrectionary action and fitted it into their understanding of religion without any apparent difficulty.

For instance, Frances Ellen Watkins, a gifted writer who published constantly in the cause of Negro freedom, wrote these words to Brown as he awaited execution:

> The Cross becomes a glorious ensign when Calvary's . . . sufferer yields up his
> life upon it. And, if Universal Freedom is ever to be the dominant power of
> the land, your bodies may be only her first stepping stones to dominion.[73]

A writer representing "The Colored Women of Brooklyn" became even more explicit in setting the messianic theme as she wrote, "We . . . recognize in you a Saviour commissioned to redeem us, the American people, from the great National Sin of Slavery . . ."[74]

Harriet Tubman had meant to march with Brown, but became ill and was evidently on her way to meet him when the old man was captured. Out of the religious world in which she moved it was clear that she spoke honest words when she said after his death: "It was not John Brown that died at Charleston . . . It was Christ—it was the savior of our people."[75] The black cross had passed from Nat Turner to John Brown. Therefore it was fitting that a traditional Negro tune should be used to carry the words of "John Brown's Body."

IV

Though "John Brown's Body" is not a spiritual, its presence bears a reminder that it is impossible to conclude any discussion of black religion without at least a reference to those songs. They represent the most profound verbal expression of Afro-American religious experience. As W.E.B. Du Bois has said, they are "the siftings of centuries. . . ."[76]

In spite of their significance it will not be fitting to attempt any lengthy exposition of them here—neither time nor skill allows that. However, it should be noted that these songs have been subjected to much of the same difficulties that we encountered at the outset of this discussion of black religion. Frazier is found again speaking of them as "essentially religious in sentiment and . . . otherworldly in outlook," thereby suggesting that he had missed the point of much of the greatest religious sentiments of man.[77] (Perhaps he was not blessed to hear Paul Tillich's definition of religion.)

Mays also describes most of the spirituals as expressing "compensatory" and heaven-oriented attitudes, but he faces the texts and is willing to admit that some of them clearly bespeak real protest in the present world. Especially does he cite "Go Down Moses" and "Oh Freedom" in this vein.[78] But the author of one of the most carefully wrought attempts to set the spirituals in a historical context goes much further, and develops a theme concerning the spirituals quite similar to the one being suggested here for all of Negro religion.

Miles Mark Fisher sees black religion so closely allied to protest that he suggests that some of the spirituals were likely the creation of Nat Turner, Denmark Vesey, and Harriet Tubman.[79] Especially provocative is Fisher's suggestion that "Steal Away" emerged directly out of Nat Turner's vision of 1825, when the call of God came to him through convulsions in the elements, as he grew increasingly convinced that his great future task would lead him away from all that he had known before.[80] By this Fisher does not mean to deny that many persons have sung that haunting song with longings for a heavenly place, but he affirms that it may well have originated in a marvelously earthbound experience, an experience of affirmation and rebellion.

This recognition that the spirituals surely bore many possible meanings for many persons is strongly supported by Frederick Douglass, who sang so many of them while they were yet fresh in the air. As he later recalled his youth, Douglass pointed to two examples of the potential for profound ambiguity which rested at the center of the songs. There was one with the words

O Canaan, Sweet Canaan
I am bound for the land of Canaan.

In Douglass's experience, as he put it, "The North was our Canaan." There was no doubt about that. He says, too, that a song with the word "I don't expect to stay much longer here" (probably a variant of "Steal Away") was another favorite and had "a double meaning." He explained the duality in this way: "On the lips of some it meant the expectation of a speedy summons to a world of spirits, but on the lips of our company [of young men in Maryland] it simply meant a speedy pilgrimage to a free state, and deliverance from all the evils and dangers of slavery."[81]

It would then appear that even in the midst of so community-oriented an experience as the singing of spirituals, many men may have sung out of many varied visions. For some—perhaps for most—the visions took them beyond this earth entirely, and made the experiences of their surroundings fade in importance. For other black persons the music and the faith it expressed—and engendered—filled them with a sense of God's awesome calling for their present moment, and supplied new determination to struggle, build, and resist here.

This dual function of religion should not be surprising. Speaking of another oppressed people in another time, Reinhold Niebuhr lately reminded us that "The radical sectarians [of the Reformation period] appropriated Messianism to make of it an instrument of social revolt, while the more conservative religious forces used otherworldly hopes to beguile men from injustices in history."[82]

Unless we grasp that common historical truth and apply it to the black experience in America we shall not only be unprepared to meet those Negroes who break out of the pages of Aptheker and Stampp, but we shall certainly fail to understand so recent and lately controversial a phenomenon as Martin Luther King. He stands in a long tradition of black exhorters whose lives and whose religion can neither be spiritualized, captured, or denied. They can, however, be understood, and that is our task.[83]

NOTES

1. See especially Herbert Aptheket, *American Negro Slave Revolts*, (New York: International Publishers, 1963); Raymond A. Bauer and Alice H. Bauer, "Day to Day Resistance to Slavery," *Journal of Negro History*, xxvii, 4 (October, 1942), 388–419; Kenneth M. Stampp, *The Peculiar Institution*, (New York: Vintage Books, 1956), particularly Chap. 3.

2. Some of the most persuasive concerns are raised in Stanley M. Elkins, *Slavery*. Paperback edition (New York: Grosset and Dunlap, 1963); Richard C. Wade, *Slavery in the Cities* (New York: Oxford University, 1964); also Wade's "The Vesey Plot: A Reconsideration," *Journal of Negro History*, xxx, 2 (May, 1964), 143–61; Eugene D. Genovese, "The Legacy of Slavery and the Roots of Black Nationalism," *Studies on the Left*, vi. 6 (November-December, 1966), 3–26.

3. Benjamin E. Mays, *The Negro's God as Reflected in His Literature* (Boston: Chapman and Grimes, 1938), 26.

4. Ibid., 24.

5. *The Negro Church in America* (New York: Schocken Books, 1964).

6. Ibid., 45.

7. Karl Marx and Friedrich Engels, *On Religion* (New York: Schocken Books, 1964), 42; quoted from the "Introduction to Marx's Contribution to the Critique of Hegel's Philosophy of Right."

8. Quoted in Haven P. Perkins, "Religion for Slaves: Difficulties and Methods," *Church History,* x, 3 (September, 1941), 228–45.

9. *Narrative of the Life of William Wells Brown* (London: Charles Gilpin, 1850), 22–83.

10. *Life and Times,* Paperback edition (New York: Crowell-Collier, 1962), 85.

11. (Boston: Beacon Press, 1964), 33.

12. Ibid.

13. See Engels on "The Peasant War in Germany," in Marx and Engles, *On Religion,* 97–118; also Eduard Bernstein, *Cromwell and Communism* (New York: Schocken Books, 1963).

14. Quoted in W. E. B. Du Bois (ed.), *The Negro Church* (Atlanta: The Atlanta University press, 1903), 22.

15. Harvey Wish, "American Slave Insurrections Before 1861," *Journal of Negro History,* xxii, 3 (July, 1937); Thomas Wentworth Higginson, *Travellers and Outlaws* (Boston: Lee and Shepard, 1889), 1899; Aptheker, *Slave Revolts,* 220–24.

16. Ibid., 220.

17. See citations in note 15.

18. Aptheker, *Slave Revolts,* 224.

19. Ibid., 246.

20. Urich B. Phillips, *American Negro Slavery,* Paperback edition (Baton Rouge: Louisiana State University, 1966), 476.

21. Ibid.

22. Aptheker, *Slave Revolts,* 258.

23. The story of the pre-1822 struggles of the black Methodists of Charleston is developed most fully in Phillips, *American Negro Slavery,* 420–21.

24. Richard Wade, in his works cited in note 2 above, expresses strong doubts about the extent and significance of the insurrectionary plans.

25. Phillips, *loc. cit.*

26. Wade, "The Vesey Plot," 160.

27. See Aptheker, *Slave Revolts,* 268–76; Higginson, 215–75; John W. Lofton, Jr., "Denmark Vesey's Call to Arms," *Journal of Negro History,* xxxiii, 4 (October, 1948), 195–417; Sterling Stuckey, "Remembering Denmark Vesey," *Negro Digest,* xv, 4 (February, 1966), 28–41—a direct response to Wade's questions; Marion L. Starkey, *Striving to Make It My Home* (New York: W. W. Norton and Company, 1964), 192–210; Corporation of Charleston, *An Account of the Late Intended Insurrection,* Charleston: n.p. 1822).

28. Higginson, 228.

29. Corporation of Charleston, 34 [italics in original].

30. Higginson, 404.

31. On Gullah Jack see especially Starkey and Corporation of Charleston, as cited in note 27.

32. Corporation of Charleston, 39.

33. Wish, 410.

34. Phillips, 421.

35. Quoted in Perkins, "Religion for Slaves," 232.

36. Donald G. Mathews, *Slavery and Methodism* (Princeton: Princeton University Press, 1965), 41.

37. Ibid., 42.

38. Turner's *Confession, Trial and Execution* was originally published in 1881 by T. R. Gray in Petersburg, Virginia. However it is most accessible in Herbert Aptheker, *Nat Turner's Slave Rebellion* (New York: Humanities Press, 1966). I have used the same text as it appeared in "The Confession, Trial and Execution of Nat Turner." *Negro Digest*, xiv, 9 (July, 1965), 28–48. The source will not be cited again until it seems appropriate in the development of Turner's story.

39. For the story of the Münsterites see George H. Williams, *The Radical Reformation* (London: Weidenfeld and Nicolson, 1962), 362–86.

40. Aptheker, *Nat Turner's Slave Rebellion*, 38.

41. From the lives of Frederick Douglass and Harriet Tubman to "The Ballad of Nat Turner" in a recently published book of poems by Robert Hayden, *Selected Poems* (New York: October House, 1966), the tradition has been carefully and faithfully maintained.

42. Quoted in George Washington Williams, *History of the Negro Race in America*, 2 vols, (New York: G. P. Putnam's Sons, 1883), II, 90.

43. Du Bois (ed.), *The Negro Church*, 25.

44. Ibid.

45. *Narrative of the Tragical Scene . . . in Southampton County* (n.p., Werner and West, 1831), 23.

46. Ibid., 20.

47. Douglass, 111.

48. Quoted in Edwin A. Miles, "The Mississippi Slave Insurrection Scare of 1835," *Journal of Negro History*, xlii, 1 (January, 1957), 51.

49. Quoted in Wade, *Slavery in the Cities*, 83.

50. Ibid., 83–84.

51. A brief account of the *Amistad* story is most conveniently found in Louis Filler, *The Crusade Against Slavery 1830–1860* (New York: Harper and Row, 1963), 167–68.

52. Quoted in Williams, *History* II, 96.

53. See reference to the Bauers's work in note 1 above, especially pp. 415–18.

54. Ibid., 417.

55. Perkins, 236.

56. Henry Bibb, *Narrative of the Life and Adventures of Henry Bibb* (New York: the author, 1850), 24.

57. Ibid.

58. Quoted in Perkins, 237.

59. Douglass, 91.

60. Samuel Ringgold Ward, *Autobiography of a Fugitive Negro* (London: John Snow, 1855), 19. The family ran away in 1820.

61. Brown, *Narrative*, 79.

62. Three of Harriet Tubman's most widely read biographers tend to encourage the legendary aspects: Henrietta Buckmaster, *Let My People Go* (Boston, Beacon Press, 1959); Earl Conrad, *Harriet Tubman* (Washington, D.C.: Associated Publishers 1943); and Dorothy Sterling, *Freedom Train: The Story of Harriet Tubman* (New York: Doubleday and Company, 1954). In a recent study of the Underground Railroad Larry Gara attempts to suggest Harriet's real life size. See his *The Liberty Line* (Lexington, University of Kentucky Press, 1961).

63. Conrad, 35.

64. See Buckmaster for an account of Burns' situation, especially 230–36.

65. Herbert Aptheker (ed.), *A Documentary History of the Negro People in the United States*, 2 vols. (New York: Citadel Press, 1965), 1, 372.

66. Sterling, 81.

67. See references in note 62 above.

68. For an account of this fascinating story, see Aptheker, *Documentary History*, I, 378–80 and Moses Dickson, *Manual of the International Order of Twelve* (St. Louis: A. R. Fleming, 1891), 7–17.

69. Ibid., 15.

70. Ibid., 16.

71. Aptheker, *Documentary History*, I, 380.

72. Ibid.

73. Ibid., 441.

74. Ibid.

75. Sterling, 129–33.

76. Du Bois, *The Souls of Black Folk* (Greenwich, Conn.: Fawcett Publications, 1961), 183. Du Bois' justly famous work contains a number of important essays on black religion. See especially chapters X, XII, and XIV.

77. Frazier, 12.

78. Mays, 28–29.

79. Miles Mark Fisher, *Negro Slave Songs in the United States*, Paperback edition (New York: Citadel Press, 1963), 66–67, 181–185.

80. Ibid., 67.

81. Douglass, 159–60.

82. Introduction to Marx and Engels, *On Religion*, viii.
83. After I completed this paper my attention was called to a sociological study which will attempt to relate Negro religion to protest in the modern era: Gary T. Marx, *Protest and Prejudice* (New York: Harper and Row, forthcoming).

SELECTED BIBLIOGRAPHY FOR FURTHER READING

Aptheker, Herbert. *American Negro Slave Revolts*. New York: International Publishers, 1963.

Frey, Sylvia R. *Water From the Rock: Black Resistance in a Revolutionary Age*. Princeton: Princeton University Press, 1991.

Harding, Vincent. *There is a River: The Black Freedom Struggle in America*. New York: Vintage Books, 1983.

Wood, Peter H. *Black Majority: Negroes in Colonial South Carolina from 1670 through the Stono Rebellion*. New York: Alfred A. Knopf, 1974.

THE BLACK CHURCH
NORTH OF SLAVERY

III::

7 ::

Will B. Gravely

:: The most commonly attributed cause of the rise of independent black churches is discrimination in biracial churches symbolized by the famous incident in Philadelphia when Richard Allen and other black members were forcibly removed from the church while praying on their knees because they were seated in a section reserved for whites. While not discounting the importance of black reaction to white discrimination, Will Gravely argues that the rise of the African church movement was more complex and included the factors of black communities desiring their own institutions, the achievement of religious freedom, the rise of denominationalism, and the compromise over slavery within white denominations by 1820. ::

:: 7

THE RISE OF AFRICAN CHURCHES IN AMERICA (1786–1822)

Re-examining the Contexts

Will B. Gravely

:: At the end of his antislavery pamphlet published in 1810, Daniel Coker, a black Methodist preacher and schoolmaster in Baltimore, appended four significant lists. He named thirteen ordained black clergy (including himself), another eleven licensed local preachers, and eight writers and orators whose public works had proven "their talents." His compilation of fifteen "African churches," representing four denominational polities and ten cities, is an early primary source of what has been called "the independent church movement" in black American religion.[1] Despite the fact that he took pride in the enumeration of "African Methodists" at 31,884 in 1809, Coker downplayed denominational identifications.[2] At the time he wrote, all of the local black churches were still linked to biracial denominational jurisdictions; however, Coker was emphasizing an African church movement spanning the Atlantic seaboard from Charleston, South Carolina, to Boston, Massachusetts.

Black churches and their ministers, for Coker, were a biblical embodiment of the cultural and religious transformation of enslaved Africans into free Afro-Americans. He indicated as much by framing the entire appendix of lists with biblical images drawn from I Peter 2:9–10: "chosen generation," "royal priesthood," "holy nation," and "peculiar people." This passage gave Coker the symbolic references for "what God [was] doing for Ethiopia's sons in the United States of America." Indeed, another part of the biblical quotation—"which in time past were not a people, but are now the people of God"—testified to the emergence of an Afro-American community in the new United States. Hence, Coker gave Afro-American peoplehood biblical and theological sanction, calling attention to its institutional expression in the network of African churches and identifying the leaders of church and community.

The rise of the independent "African" churches has attracted the interest of several scholars with differing views. A classic debate concerning African survivals was first held by Melville Herskovits and E. Franklin Frazier. More recently their interpretive insights have been synthesized by Albert Raboteau.[3] But their concern is not the most fundamental historiographical issue in free black church history. The terms of the debate have shifted from the degree of syncretism in black Christianity to a consideration of *the causes* for racial separation in American religion, beginning in the late eighteenth century, continuing throughout the antebellum period (South as well as North), and culminating in the era of Reconstruction across the states of the old Confederacy.[4] It may well be, of course, that the assertion of black religious independence, as an identifiable movement for more than a century, merely recasts the debate between Herskovits and Frazier, suggesting that black religious sensibilities cannot be contained within biracial, Euro-American structures. This would keep alive the large question of how the peoples of European and African descent interacted in other ways besides their religious traditions. However, the linkage has not usually been made.

If the primary historiographical question regarding the rise of African churches is to search for *the causes* of racially based religious separatism, interpretive traditions have commonly emphasized one of two alternatives. The focus has either been on the story of white discrimination and the moral failure of American Christianity, or it has been a celebration of the origin of a black culture with separate churches—an important feature of its infrastructure. Even though these two contexts are not mutually exclusive interpretive options, they have tended to function that way.[5]

One factor which is perennially relevant to a consideration of the origins of black religious independence is white proscription, the conscious exclusion from positions of power of black members in biracial congregations and denominations. This historiographical emphasis is based on the famous incident, traditionally dated as November 1787, when trustees from St. George's Methodist Episcopal Church in Philadelphia pulled several black members and local preachers from their knees during prayer at a public service. Blamed for refusing to go to the seats set aside for their race in the gallery, they abruptly left the service. With Richard Allen and Absalom Jones as leaders, they embarked on a course that formed in 1794 the first two African congregations with their own buildings in the city.[6] Even though no contemporary account of the fracas at St. George's Church survives, it has been many times retold in black religious and social history, serving by the 1960s as the historical impetus for kneel-ins during the civil rights movement's challenge to white churches.[7]

Proscriptive practices by white Christians directed against black members and auditors in local churches were potentially the motivation behind the separatist movement. Events less overt, but symbolically as powerful as the confrontation at St. George's Church, often provoked a schism. Incidents of white pastors refusing to take black infants into their arms to christen them (Washington, DC), of blacks having to wait until all whites were served the Lord's Supper before being admitted to the table (Ohio), of conflicts over access to burial grounds (Charleston, South Carolina), and of constraints on freedom of expression in worship (Cincinnati, Ohio) served to set off black resistance.[8]

During the period from Richard Allen's first separate class meeting for blacks in Philadelphia (1786) to the formation of the third black Methodist denomination in 1822, examples abound which confirm a recalcitrant white opposition to equal privileges for blacks in every denominational movement having a noticeable black membership. Although Episcopalians were not far behind, Methodists were especially culpable. Their leading bishop, Francis Asbury, performed at least eight ordinations of black local preachers to the office of deacon, but the Methodist Episcopal general conferences never officially recognized the anomalous rank, never accepted the deacons into annual conferences of the Methodist preachers, and never advanced the black deacons (including Allen, who remained one for seventeen years) to eldership or full priesthood.[9] In 1822, the Mother Zion Congregation in New York eventually lost patience in its efforts to obtain full ordination for its pastors, who were local black deacons, as Allen had been in Philadelphia. It had endured refusals from three white Methodist Episcopal bishops, the Protestant Episcopal bishop of New York, and two white Methodist annual conferences.[10] The black Methodist movement for independence in Wilmington, Delaware, involved two secessions in eight years before denominational autonomy was secured by Peter Spencer and his followers. The issues involved arbitrary exercises of power against blacks by the white elders and conflicts over seating and use of buildings.[11] The Episcopalians, on the other hand, did give full priestly orders to Absalom Jones in 1804, but refused St.

Thomas African Congregation membership in its convention until 1862.[12] A similar exclusion (until 1853) hampered St. Philip's Church in New York, organized in 1809.[13]

Despite the contention of George Levesque that the origin of the first northern black Baptist church did not lie in discriminatory treatment by whites, a contemporary source strongly suggests otherwise. Elias Smith, a white pastor in Woburn, wrote in 1804, "When Thomas Paul [the first pastor of the African Baptist church in the city] came to Boston the Dr. [Samuel Stillman, a Baptist minister] told him it was Boston, and they did not mix colours." Another white Baptist in Boston, Thomas Baldwin, concurred by saying, "There are some of my congregation who would leave the meeting if Paul should preach here."[14] Although the details are less clear, tensions between white and black members of New York's Gold Street Church led to a black exodus in 1808 to form the Abyssinian Baptist congregation.[15]

At many points in the evolution of black religious independence, white control and black assertion clashed. The struggle was a competition for power and a test of the viability of biracial religious community. Especially among Episcopalians and Methodists, less so with Baptists and Presbyterians, whites were unwilling to share authority with and extend modes of participation to blacks. Many black churchfolk, on the other hand, insisted that their religious freedom could not be compromised. The sacred power that they felt, shared, and mediated could not be contained or isolated from more mundane forms of power. They wanted to elect and be elected to church office, to ordain and be ordained, to discipline as well as be disciplined, to preach, exhort, pray, and administer sacraments—in sum, to have their gifts and graces acknowledged by the whole community. Where that acknowledgement was withheld, blacks resisted and sought other alternatives. In their "Founders' Address" of 1820, three Zion Methodist preachers stated the dilemma. "So long as we remain in that situation [of being deprived of ordination]," they declared, "our Preachers would never be able to enjoy these privileges which the Discipline of the white Church holds out to all its Members that are called to preach, in consequence of the limited access our brethren had to those privileges, and particularly in consequence of the difference of color."[16]

A second historiographical tradition, less dramatic but no less significant, shifts the concern from black reaction to white discrimination. This second interpretive context is seen as a natural part of an expanding black community which had other racially separate institutions. Their origins must be explained in terms of the demography of black communities, the effects of migration and economic change on their composition, the presence of intra-religious competition and social dissent from within. Preeminently, this interpretation posits the prior existence of black communities within which separate churches were conceived and in which they would function.[17]

Black Philadelphia was also an example of this corollary interpretation of the emergence of the independent black churches. Before the walkout at St. George's, Allen and Jones, with others, had formed the Free African Society as a benevolent voluntary association.[18] It both assumed and fostered a community consciousness among black Philadelphians. Its religious dimension was so prominent that W. E. B. Du Bois would later interpret it as an example of continuity with African communal life. When, after six years, it disbanded, the members catalyzed communal energies into new institutional directions by founding the St. Thomas African Episcopal and Bethel African Methodist Episcopal congregations.[19]

Outside Philadelphia, before there were independent African congregations, voluntary associations met some black religious needs, besides those found in biracial churches. Early in 1776, Prince Hall, with fourteen other men, founded African Lodge No. 1 in Boston in connection with a British Army lodge. After the new organization got an official warrant in 1787, it regularly celebrated the Festival of St. John the Baptist on June 25, heard Hall and Chaplain John Marrant preach, and conducted masonic rites for public funerals of its members. In 1792, Hall's sermon recollected the time in Christian history when there was "an African church," referring to early church organizations in North Africa.[20] The hope of restoring an African Christian tradition permeated the petition signed by Hall and seventy-five other blacks from Boston in 1787, asking the General Court for permission to emigrate. Their plan specified the formation of "a religious society, or a Christian church" in Africa, with "one or more blacks [to be] ordained as their pastors or bishops."[21]

Similar features marked the history of Newport's African Union Society, which, by 1783, began to hold religious services in members' homes. Constituted in 1780, and embracing women in the membership, it had by the end of the decade sponsored a unified scheme of emigration with comparable organizations in Boston, Providence and Philadelphia. Appropriately, the Society invited a common religious effort, to seek God's guidance "by extraordinary fasting and prayer," naming on one occasion the first Tuesday in July 1789, for that purpose.[22]

The emigration schemes in Boston and Newport failed to develop beyond exploratory ventures, but the early benevolent societies had reached out to each other across several states, before the appearance of the first separate black congregation in the North in 1794, or of the first independent black denomination in 1813. By 1792, the black masonic movement had new lodges in Philadelphia, Providence, and New Haven.[23] The Newport African Unionists in June 1793 sent a contribution to the African church building project in Philadelphia, which later became St. Thomas church.[24] Locally, fraternal and benevolent associations had experimented with forms of religious life sponsored within their black communities which were not yet fraught with denominational competition and schism. The next logical step, to organize a community or union church, never took hold at the time when a significant option to denominationalism could have been shaped. Implicit in Boston, Newport, and Philadelphia, the concept did not catch on, though it was resurrected in attenuated form nearly a generation later in Providence between 1819 and 1821, and in Newport in 1824.[25]

The Union Church, as a racially separate institution, embodied the elusive dream of black communal unity. It expressed one form of religious freedom and demonstrated the persistent symbiosis between churches and other voluntary associations in black life. Left behind by black denominationalism, the local focus of the Union Church limited its contribution to the formation of independent churches, lacking what emerged in 1830 with the colored convention movement. The alternative, black churches both within biracial and separate denominational structures, was a concession to the organizational religious patterns of the larger society.

At the same time, the formation of separate black churches repeatedly made visible the black community's maturation. They became the institutional core of free black community life, serving as an educational venture, housing literary societies and libraries, and hosting schools and benevolent associations. Their buildings were the meeting-houses of the black freedom—and often of the white abolitionist—movement. Mirroring the communities they served, the churches enabled blacks to celebrate themselves as a collectivity, and they provided the protective space whereby each could contend with the other about common concerns. And always, the churches were houses of prayer, song, sermon, and sacrament in a distinctive Afro-American medium.

Despite the fact of white discrimination, and beyond the reality of an evolving free black culture, it is important also to remember that the founders of the African churches openly commended white sympathizers whose support they courted and received. Dr. Benjamin Rush drew up "sundry articles of faith and a plan of church government" in 1791 for a committee of "a dozen free Blacks" from the Free African Society. His Episcopal proposal was adopted three days later as another step toward the creation of St. Thomas church. Dr. Rush and other whites raised and contributed money from their community for the project, as blacks were also doing.[26] In 1799, Richard Allen thanked Rush particularly for his assistance in building three African churches in the city.[27] When no one else would come to their aid, the Zion Methodists got their black local deacons ordained by James Covel, Silvester Hutchinson, and William M. Stillwell, three supportive white elders, originally from the Methodist Episcopal organization but more recently founders of a new (Stillwellite) Methodist connection in New York.[28]

In the absence of black preachers in the early years after their organization, the African and Abyssinian Baptist congregations depended on the supply of white preachers from the Philadelphia and New York associations.[29] White Presbyterians in the Evangelical Society of Philadelphia were primary sponsors of the African Presbyterian Church in that city, first as a mission in 1807 and then as a building with its congregation beginning in 1811.[30] Even after the formation of separate churches, especially for Baptists and Presbyterians, the new congregations held membership in biracial associations, presbyteries, and synods.

If the relationship of whites to the African church movement is more complex than first appears, the presence of blacks in significant numbers in some aspects of biracial denominational structures before 1813 and after 1822 poses other interpretive problems. They may be seen within the contexts of three previous historiographical emphases during the period: the legal achievement and guarantee of religious freedom; the rise of denominationalism in the Second Great Awakening as part of an organizational revolution in American Protestantism; and the compromise within mainstream American religion before 1820 over slavery. A comprehension of how these factors interact with the rise of the African churches will help to explain how the patterns of racial organization set in the first generation still generally describe black-white interaction in American Christianity.

The major motif, as seen in the influential career of Sidney Mead, is the celebration of the revolutionary development of religious freedom in the late eighteenth century. Curiously, Mead never made any application of that achievement to the history of black religion in America. That omission may have been because the first black churches did not entirely correspond to his generalizations about religious freedom. "What individuals and groups do when given religious freedom depends upon what they are when such is offered," he wrote.[31] But for blacks, religious freedom was neither offered nor given, but seized and implemented in the independent church movement.

The chronological correspondence between the legal securing of religious

freedom and the idea, leading to the institutional embodiment of African churches was not coincidental. The early black churches met the legal requirements for
incorporation of religious bodies, most of which were directed to the ownership
and use of property. They passed articles of association, published their bylaws
and constitutions, and amended their incorporation to further protect their own
interests. They appealed, unsuccessfully and successfully, in court for their rights
to religious independence. The legal structures within which they worked were
newly enacted, so that they both tested and expanded the state's role in religious
litigation. As they were solidifying new institutional channels for themselves,
they were also contributing to a larger stream of religious freedom in the national polity.

Speaking before a jubilant audience in Baltimore on January 23, 1816,
Daniel Coker claimed that the recent Supreme Court decision in Pennsylvania
that freed Philadelphia's Bethel Church from Methodist Episcopal control vindi-
cated religious liberty, "Contrary to the predications of many," he declared, "we
have found to our great consolation, that the wholesome and friendly laws of our
happy country will give us protection in worshipping God according to the
dictates of our conscience."[32] The court decision gave African Methodists,
who later in the year would form the second black denomination, "the opportunity . . . of being free," and that meant to Coker being able "to sit down under our
own vine to worship and none shall make us afraid."[33]

If blacks were employing the necessary legal tactics to defend and extend
their own religious freedom, they were further involved in the organizational
revolution of denominationalism, "new measures" revivalism, and other modes
of church extension. In the post-Revolutionary generation, there was a fluidity in
the process of forming denominations because of the new context of religious
freedom. All of the denominational polities and structures within which African
churches were formed were being shaped, revised, challenged, defended, and
implemented. In the 1780s, Episcopalians and Methodists were moving from a
colonial to an American organization of church government. Presbyterians did
not hold their first general assembly until 1789. Baptists were only regionally organized until 1813, when they established the first national network for the purpose of missionary cooperation called the Triennial Convention.[34]

Denominational formation, therefore, was coterminous with the first generation of the independent church movement. It was a complex process, fraught
with conflict and debate. The Methodists, for example, endured between 1792
and 1822 three major secessions, *besides* the three African Methodist breaks, over
questions like the powers of the episcopacy, the legislative function of the gener-

al conference, and the role of the laity and the preachers.[35] Those conflicts were occurring at the same time that African Methodists in Philadelphia, New York, and Wilmington were organizing at the local level and confronting white authorities about innovative ways to involve the growing black constituency. Writing to inform the Philadelphia Conference of 1807 that they had legally adopted "The African Supplement" to their articles of association with the Methodist Episcopal Church, Richard Allen and the trustees of Bethel Church put the challenge bluntly. "Our only design," they claimed, "is to secure to ourselves our rights and privileges, to regulate our affairs, temporal and spiritual, the same as if we were white people."[36]

The rise of the African churches out of biracial connections cannot be isolated from such issues central to the internal life of Christian churches as access to ordination, representation in denominational governance, consultation about pastoral appointments and services, the ownership and use of property, and participation in congregational discipline. Those were the power factors being contended for generally in the shaping of the popular denominations, and black members and preachers were in the middle of the conflict.

Black denominationalism became a reality in three African Methodist organizations between 1813 and 1822. In partial forms, it expanded with the American Baptist Missionary Convention in 1840, the Congregational and Presbyterian evangelical associations and conventions of the 1840s and 1850s and in regional black Baptist associations and conventions in the midwest, like the Western Colored Baptist Convention (1853ff.) and the Northwestern and Southern Baptist Convention (1964).[37] These black church bodies usually maintained the government and doctrines of the denominations and local churches from which they separated. Because they had participated in the life of biracial congregations and denominations from the outset, black Protestants who removed themselves from white supervision and connections were merely continuing their own experience. That experience, was to affirm, audaciously to many whites, an elemental core within each denominational tradition, and behind that, within Christianity itself, which was not created or controlled by white Christians. That core was as accessible to blacks as to whites, and it was thereby appropriated. In the process, black Methodists, Baptists, Episcopalians, Presbyterians, and later Congregationalists, were redefining perhaps unwittingly the nature of the American denominational families. Their very presence, within biracial connections or separately alongside whites, transformed the landscape of Christianity in the United States.

As the founders of the African church movement perpetuated their own experience in the organizational revolution of the Second Great Awakening focused particularly on denominational formation, they also found themselves in competition with each other. Denominational differences in black communities were assured from the time some members of Philadelphia's Free African Society became Episcopalian under Absalom Jones, and others became African Methodists under Richard Allen.

Some of the religious options resulted from the refusal of some black Protestants to move into separate denominations. In 1796, a second black Methodist congregation, Zoar, was established in Philadelphia as a mission in the northern part of the city. The congregation never desired the independence toward which the Bethel society worked. Hence, in 1816, it remained loyal to the Methodist Episcopal Church and did not join Allen's new denomination. Similarly, in Baltimore, where Daniel Coker led the secession of 1815, the two largest congregations with their own buildings, Sharp Street Church and Asbury African Church, continued within the Methodist Episcopal denomination and insisted on calling themselves for another decade at least, "African Methodists." The separatists, who linked up with the Philadelphia independents, left behind all claims to church property.[38] In Wilmington, some blacks in Ezion Church kept unaltered their denominational connection after Peter Spencer led thirty-nine of his followers into a new organization in 1813.[39]

Denominational differences were further extended, when Spencer, after attending the organizing convention for the Allenite denomination in Philadelphia in 1816, refused to merge the African Union congregations into the new movement. Likewise, in New York, the Zion Methodists, following an exploratory interview with Bishop Allen in 1820, refused to bring their organization under his authority.[40]

African Methodists were not alone in their competitive denominational styles, for schism and division marked the early histories of the African Baptists and Presbyterians. In 1816, the Philadelphia Association debated for three days the competing claims of two groups, each representing itself as the authentic African Baptist party. Turning aside a protest from the white First Baptist Church, the Association sided with the claimants who owned the meetinghouse and other properties.[41] First in 1824, with the creation of a Second African Presbyterian Church with Jeremiah Gloucester as pastor, and then two decades later with the founding of Central Church with Stephen Gloucester as pastor, black Presbyterians in Philadelphia resolved problems in internal dissent by forming new congregations.[42]

There is a final context of white-black interaction which affected the African church movement. Between 1785 and 1818, three of the Protestant denominations within which African churches were established backed away from explicit opposition to slavery, both in the larger social and political order and in the disciplinary norms for membership and ordination.[43] Without providing the primary documentation, Woodson rooted the birth of the African Baptist Church of Philadelphia in 1809 in the waning "anti-slavery ardor" of the First Baptist Church during pastorates of southern-born whites.[44] That factor may have weighed in the decisions of other black secessionists during the period, though the evidence in the form of explicit justification is lacking. In other words, there is no document that defends black separatism on grounds that the denomination's antislavery standards had been compromised. At the same time, the African Methodist Episcopal denomination did reassert the original, forthright condemnations of slavery, which the Methodist Episcopal Church had abandoned.[45]

It is likewise noteworthy, in the case of the Methodists, that all three African separations occurred *after* the failure of the general conferences between 1800 and 1808 to remove slaveholders from membership and from clerical orders. Indeed, the conferences of 1804 and 1808 printed expurgated copies of the Church's Discipline for the southern states without the legislation on slavery. Even Asbury, who had despised slavery from the first, gave in to proslavery pressures, conceding in his journal that it was more important to save the African's soul than to free his body.[46]

Those events were taking place during the same period when Richard Allen, Daniel Coker, and William Miller (with other black Methodists in New York) were publicly condemning slavery. With Absalom Jones, Allen had published an appeal to slaveholders to set free their oppressed chattels in 1794. He echoed similar sentiments in an appendix to the Articles of Association of the Bethel Society in 1799.[47] In 1804 and 1805, he financed publication of two works by Thomas Branagan, a white antislavery author.[48] In 1810, Coker published in Baltimore his *Dialogue Between a Virginian and an African Minister*. On New Year's Day of that same year, one of the Zion Methodist ministers, Miller, was orator for black New Yorkers to commemorate the second anniversary of the end of the foreign slave trade.[49]

These antislavery activities reinforce a reminder. Blacks, unlike other Americans, had to consider the issue of personal freedom as the first freedom. It was only after emancipation in the northern states, between 1777 and 1818, that the attention of free blacks riveted on religious freedom, and their energies became directed to independent churches. Sometimes the separate churches became the routes to obtaining freedom for southern slave preachers. Henry Cunningham from Savannah, Georgia, served the African Baptist Church of Philadelphia from 1809 to 1811 in order to earn enough money to secure his freedom, to be ordained, and to return South. Josiah Bishop, an early pastor for the Abyssinian Church in New York, was formerly a slave in Virginia, who bought his own freedom and that of his family.[50] The first pastor of the African Presbyterian Congregation in Philadelphia, John Gloucester, traveled widely to raise funds to purchase the liberty of the rest of his family. Worn out at age forty-six, he died in 1822, but not before inducing his three sons—Stephen, James, and Jeremiah—to follow in his footsteps as black preachers.[51]

Always, the independent black churches stood as institutional symbols of human liberation. They did not often get the headlines which marked white abolitionist activity, but within their communities they carried on a continual struggle to defend, protect, extend, and expand black freedom.[52] Unlike white Christians of the period, black churchfolk did not have a choice as to whether they would work for black freedom, for their own liberty was inescapably bound up with the liberation of their people. That fact makes for a crucial, qualitative distinction between black and white Christian traditions in American history. Efforts to ignore it negate the ethical ground for the study of black and white interaction in American religion—a study which David Wills has appropriately requested.[53] Only when the fact is acknowledged can Sidney Ahlstrom's insight—that the black religious experience is the paradigm for the reinterpretation of American church history—be appreciated. Such an agenda is clearly more than the simple matter of addition or inclusion, for the black religious story has normative, fundamentally moral dimensions at its center.[54] To ignore it is to insure that we will never comprehend what Martin Delaney, the inveterate black nationalist, meant when he observed in 1849, "As among our people, generally, the Church is the Alpha and the Omega of all things."[55]

NOTES

1. Carter G. Woodson, *History of the Negro Church* (Washington: The Associated Publishers, 1921), Chap. 4; Daniel Coker *A Dialogue Between a Virginian and an African Minister* (Baltimore: Benjamin Edes for Joseph James, 1819; reprint, Dorothy Porter, ed., *Negro Protest Pamphlets*, New York: Arno Press, 1969).

2. Coker's figures correspond to the number of "colored" members in *Minutes of the Methodist Conferences, Annually Held in America: From 1773 to 1813, Inclusive* (New York: Daniel Hitt and Thomas Ware, 1813), 447–53 (for 1809).

3. Albert J. Raboteau, *Slave Religion: The "Invisible Institution" in the Antebellum South* (New York: Oxford University Press, 1978), 48–60, 86, 89.

4. See H. Shelton Smith, *In His Image, But . . . Racism in Southern Religion, 1780–1910* (Durham: Duke University Press, 1972), chap. 5; Will B. Gravely, "The Social Political and Religious Significance of the Formation of the Colored Methodist Episcopal Church (1870)," *Methodist History*, 18 (October, 1979):3–25.

5. George A. Levesque's suggestive essay, "Inherent Reformers—Inherited Orthodoxy: Black Baptists in Boston, 1800–1873)," *Journal of Negro History*, 60 (October, 1975): 491–99, wrestles with both motivating factors.

6. See *The Life Experience and Gospel Labors of the Rt. Rev. Richard Allen* (1833; reprint, New York: Abingdon Press, 1960); Sernett, *Black Religion and American Evangelism: White Protestants, Plantation Missions, and the Flowering of Negro Christianity, 1787–1865* (Metuchen: Scarecrow Press, 1975), 116ff, 218ff. Sernett revises the date for the confrontation to five or six years later.

7. *The Doctrines and Discipline of the African Methodist Episcopal Church* (Philadelphia: John H. Cunningham, 1817), 4. A dissident member, Jonathan Tudas, claimed that the event at St. George's never happened, forcing Allen to refute him in Trustees of Bethel and Wesley Churches, *The Sword of Truth* (Philadelphia: J.H. Cunningham, 1823), 13. On the popularization of the event, besides denominational histories and publications, see Lerone Bennett, Jr., "Pioneers in Protest: Richard Allen," *Ebony* 19 (May 1964): 142–52.

8. There were comparable conflicts over the segregate seating in Providence and Cleveland and of black pewholders being harassed in Bridgewater and Stoughton Corner, Massachusetts. John H. Cromwell, "The First Negro Churches in the District of Columbia," *Journal of Negro History* 7(1922): 65; B.W. Arnett, ed., *Proceedings of the Semi-Centenary Celebration of the African Methodist Church of Cincinnati, Held in Allen Temple, February 8–10, 1874* (Cincinnati: H. Watkin, 1874), 14, 16; Alan Peskin, ed., *North into Freedom: The Autobiography of John Malin, Freed Negro, 1795–1880* (Cleveland: Western Reserve University Press, 1966), 55–56; *Incidents in the Life of the Rev. J[eremiah] Asher* (London: Charles Gilpin, 1850), 44–48; William C. Nell, *The Colored Patriots of the American Revolution* (1855; reprint, New York: Arno Press, 1969), 33–34; *The "Negro Pew": Being an Inquiry Concerning the Propriety of Distinctions in the House of God, on Account of Color* (Boston: Isaac Knapp, 1837); Ulrich Bonnell Phillips, *American Negro Slavery* (1918; reprint, Baton Rouge: Louisiana State University Press, 1966), 420.

9. Reginald F. Hildebrand, "Methodist Episcopal Policy on the Ordination of Black Ministers, 1784–1864," *Methodist History* 20 (April 1982): 125–27.

10. Christopher Rush, *A Short Account of the Rise and Progress of the African M.E. [Zion] Church in America* (New York: Christopher Rush, et al., 1866), 38–40, 42, 46, 61–67, 75, 77.

11. Lewis J. Baldwin, "'Invisible' Strands of African Methodism," (Ph.D. diss., Northwestern University, 1980); John D.C. Hanna, ed., *The Centennial Services of the Asbury Methodist Episcopal Church, Wilmington, Delaware, October 13–20, 1889*

(Wilmington: Delaware Printing Co., 1889), 146; *The Discipline of the African Union Church of the United States of America and Elsewhere*, 3d ed. (Wilmington: Porter & Kukel, 1852), iii–v.

12. William Douglass, *Annals of the First African Episcopal Church, in the United States of America, Now Styled the African Episcopal Church of St. Thomas, Philadelphia* (Philadelphia: King & Baird, 1862), 85–106, 140–71.

13. Leon Litwack treated the action of the New York diocese as setting the policy of excluding black Episcopal congregations from convention membership; it had first been established in Pennsylvania. See Leon Litwack, *North of Slavery: The Negro in the Free States 1790–1860* (Chicago: Phoenix Books, 1961), 199–200; Rhoda Golden Freeman, "The Free Negro in New York City before the Civil War," (Ph.D. diss., Columbia University, 1966), 352–53, 356–60.

14. Levesque, "Inherent Reformers," 489–99; Elias Smith, *Five Letters* (Boston, 1804), 18, quoted in William G. McLoughlin, *New England Dissent 1630–1883: The Baptists and the Separation of Church and State* (Cambridge: Harvard University Press, 1971), 765.

15. Mechal Sobel, *Trabelin' On: The Slave Journey of an Afro-Baptist Faith* (Westport: Greenwood Press, 1979), 265–66; David Benedict, *General History of the Baptist Denomination in America, and Other Parts of the World* (Boston: Lincoln & Edwards, 1813), 542; *Minutes of the New York Baptist Association, Held in the City of New York, May 23 and 24* (1810), (n.p., n.d.), 4–5.

16. From the first A.M.E. Zion Discipline, quoted in William J. Walls, *The African Methodist Episcopal Zion Church: Reality of the Black Church* (Charlotte: A.M.E. Zion Publishing House, 1974), 49.

17. See Theodore Hershberg, "Free Blacks in Antebellum Philadelphia," *Journal of Social History* 5 (1971–72):183–209; Ira Berlin, "The Structure of the Free Negro Caste in the Antebellum United States," *Journal of Social History* 9(1975–76):297–318; and "Time Space, and the Evolution of Afro-American Society on British Mainland North America," *American Historical Review* 85 (February 1980):44–78; Emma Jones Lapsansky, "Since They Got Those Separate Churches: Afro-Americans and Racism in Jacksonian Philadelphia," *American Quarterly* 32 (Spring, 1980):54–78.

18. Gayraud S. Wilmore repeats, in his new edition of *Black Religion and Black Radicalism* (Maryknoll: Orbis Books, 1983), 81, the argument that Jones and Allen formed the Free African Society *after* the walkout at St. George's Church. David Wills has investigated the historiographical traditions about the incident, privately circulated as "A Note on the Origins of the A.M.E. Church," May 1980, Amherst College.

19. Douglass, *Annals*, 10–11, 15–17, 46; Du Bois, *The Philadelphia Negro: A Social History* (1889; reprint, New York: Schocken Books, 1967), 197.

20. For Hall's orations see Dorothy Porter, ed., *Early Negro Writing 1760–1837* (Boston: Beacon Press, 1971), 63–78, especially 68; see also John Marrant, *A Sermon Preached the 24th Day of June 1789. Being the Festival of St. John the Baptist* (Boston: The bible Heart, n.d.).

21. Massachusetts State Archives, House Files 2358, quoted in Floyd John Miller, *The Search for a Black Nationality: Black Colonization and Emigration 1787–1863* (Urbana: University of Illinois Press, 1975), 5.

22. Douglass, *Annals*, 25–29; Dorothy Sterling, ed., *Speak Out in Thunder Tones: Letters and Other Writings by Black Northerners, 1787–1865* (Garden City: Doubleday, n.d.), 3–12; Miller, *Search*, 6–15.

23. Lorenzo J. Greene, "Prince Hall: Massachusetts Leader in Crisis," *Freedomways I* (Fall, 1961), 249; George W. Crawford, *Prince Hall and His Followers: Being a Monograph on the Legitimacy of Negro Masonry* (New York: The Crisis, 1915), 49–50.

24. Manuscript records of the Free African Society of Newport, 20 June 1793, Newport Historical Society.

25. *Short History of the African Union Meeting and School-House, Erected in Providence (R.I.) in the Years of 1819, '20, '21: with Rules for Its Future Government* (Providence: Brown & Danforth, 1821); Robert Glenn Sherer, "Negro Churches in Rhode Island before 1860," *Rhode Island History* 25 (January 1966): 12–17.

26. David Freeman Hawke, *Benjamin Rush: Revolutionary Gadfly* (Indianapolis: Bobbs-Merrill Co., Inc., n.d.), 336; L. H. Butterfield, ed., *Letters of Benjamin Rush* (Princeton: Princeton University Press, 1951), Vol. 1, 602–03, 609–10, 716–17; vol. 2, 1071; George W. Corner, ed., *The Autobiography of Benjamin Rush* (Princeton: Princeton University Press, 1948), 202–03, 221; Douglass, *Annals*, 45–46.

27. *Articles of Association of the African Methodist Episcopal Church, of the City of Philadelphia, in the Commonwealth of Pennsylvania* (Philadelphia: John Ormrod, 1799; reprinted Philadelphia: Historic Publications, n.d.), 17–19.

28. Rush, *A Short Account*, 78.

29. *Minutes of the Philadelphia Baptist Association,* 1810, 5; 1811, 6; *Minutes of the New York Baptist Association,* 1810–1822, inclusive.

30. William T. Catto, *A Semi-Centenary Discourse, Delivered in the First African Presbyterian Church, Philadelphia on the Fought Sabbath of May, 1857: With a History of the Church from Its First Organization* (Philadelphia: Joseph M. Wilson, 1857), 19–27; Broadside, "To the Pious and Benevolent," Leon Gardiner Collection, and Minutes of the Evangelical Society, 1808–17, Pennsylvania Historical Society; Evangelical Society manuscripts, Presbyterian Historical Society.

31. Sidney E. Mead, *The Lively Experiment* (New York: Harper & Row, 1963), 108.

32. *The Act of Incorporation. Causes and Motives of the African Episcopal Church of Philadelphia* (n.c.: Whitehall, 1810): "The Articles of Association" of the African Union Church of Wilmington, 1813, Hall of Records, Dover, Delaware; *Articles of Association between the General Conference of the Methodist Episcopal Church, and the Trustees of the African Methodist Episcopal Church, in the City of New York* (Brooklyn: Thomas Kirk, 1801); *Articles of Association* (Philadelphia), cited in n.27.

33. Coker's sermon is apparently only available in an extract in Herbert Aptheker, ed., *A Documentary History of the Negro People of the United States* (1951; reprint, New

York: The Citadel Press, 1969), 67–69 and in summary form in Charles H. Wesley, *Richard Allen: Apostle of Freedom* (Washington: Associated Publishers, 1935), 141–42, 150.

34. Smith, *In His Image, But . . .*, 38, 58, 117.

35. The secessions were led by James O'Kelly, who founded the Christian Connection, William Hammet, who led a schism in Charleston, South Carolina, and William Stillwell of New York.

36. Elmer T. Clark et al., eds., *The Journal and Letters of Francis Asbury* (New York: Abingdon Press, 1958), vol. 3, 366–67.

37. *Minutes of the Organization of the Western Colored Baptist Convention. Held in the City of Alton, March 11, 12, and 13, 1853* (St. Louis: Charles & Hammond, 1853); *Minutes of the Northwestern and Southern Baptist Convention, Held in the Second Colored Baptist Church, St. Louis, Mo. June 16th, 17th, 18th, 20th, and 21st, 1865 [sic. 1864]* (Chicago: H. A. Newcombe & Co., 1864); *Reports of the American Baptist Missionary Convention, 1849, 1853–55, 1857–60*. Amos Gerry Beman Scrapbooks, Yale University, on Congregations and Presbyterian Conventions, 1844 (vol. 2, 57); 1859 (vol. 2, 133, 136, 141); 1860 (vol. 2, 103, 132); *Frederick Douglass' Paper* (Rochester), December 18, 1851.

38. James M. Wright, *The Free Negro in Maryland* (New York: Columbia University, 1921), 216; Baltimore City Station Class Records, Lovely Lane Museum, Baltimore; Glenn A. McAninch, "We'll Pray for You: Methodist Ethnocentrism in the Origins of the African Methodist Episcopal Church in Baltimore," (Master's thesis, University of North Carolina, Chapel Hill, 1973), 41, 50.

39. Hanna, ed., *The Centennial Services,* 160–61; "Articles of Association" of the African Union Church of Wilmington, 1813.

40. Daniel A. Payne, *History of the African Methodist Episcopal Church* (Nashville: Publishing House of the A.M.E. Sunday-School Union, 1891; New York: Arno Press, 1969), 13–14; Rush, *A Short Account,* 39–42, 57, 76.

41. *Minutes of the Philadelphia Baptist Association, 1816,* 4–6; William Keen, ed., *The Bi-Centennial Celebration of the Founding of the First Baptist Church of the City of Philadelphia 1898* (Philadelphia: American Baptist Publication Society, 1899), 86.

42. Catto, *A Semi-Centenary Discourse,* 78ff., 110.

43. Smith, *In His Image, But . . .*, chap. 1.

44. Woodson, *History of the Negro Church,* 74.

45. *The Doctrines and Discipline of the A.M.E. Church, 1817,* 190.

46. Will B. Gravely, "Early Methodism and Slavery: The Roots of a Tradition," *The Drew Gateway* 30 (Spring, 1964), 150–65; Smith, *In His Image, But . . .*, chap. 6. Copies of the expurgated edition of the Methodist Episcopal Disciplines are in the Rare Book Room of the Perkins Library, Duke University.

47. Jones and Allen, *A Narrative of the Proceedings of the Black People, During the Late Awful*

Calamity in Philadelphia in the Year 1793. 19–21, reprint, Porter, ed., *Negro Protest Pamphlets; Articles of Association* (Philadelphia), 17–19.

48. James D. Essig, *The Bonds of Wickedness: American Evangelicals Against Slavery* (Philadelphia: Temple University Press, 1982), 198–99.

49. Miller, *A Sermon on the Abolition of the Slave Trade, Delivered in the African Church, New York, on the First of January 1810* (New York: John C. Totten, 1810).

50. Sobel, *Trabelin' On*, 192, 324.

51. Catto, *A Semi-Centenary Discourse*, 35–41.

52. Carol V.R. George's study of black preachers in the abolitionist movement carries this issue in new directions. See "Widening the Circle: The Black Church and the Abolitionist Crusade, 1830–1860," in Lewis Perry and Michael Fellman, eds., *Antislavery Reconsidered: New Perspectives on the Abolitionists* (Baton Rouge: Louisiana State University Press, n.d.), 75–95.

53. For a recent essay which obscures this distinction *see* Winthrop Hudson, "The American Context as an Area for Research in Black Church Studies," *Church History* 52 (June, 1983), 157–71. Cf. David Wills' perceptive assessment of the historiographical importance of black religious history in its larger American context in his introduction to Wills and Richard Newman, eds., *Black Apostles at Home and Abroad: Afro-Christians and the Christian Mission from the Revolution to Reconstruction* (Boston: G.K. Hall, 1982), xi-xxxiii.

54. Sidney Ahlstrom, *A Religious History of the American People* (New Haven: Yale University Press, 1972), 12–13. The statement in his preface implies more than merely adding the black religious story to the larger picture; but it has rarely been realized in the scholarship thus far. See Will B. Gravely review in *Journal of Religious Thought* 33 (Spring-Summer, 1976), 106–08.

55. *The North Star* (Rochester), 16 February 1849.

SELECTED BIBLIOGRAPHY FOR FURTHER READING

George, Carol V.R. *Segregated Sabbaths: Richard Allen and the Rise of Independent Black Churches*. New York: Oxford University Press, 1973.

Levesque, George A. "Inherent Reformers—Inherited Orthodoxy: Black Baptists in Boston, 1800–1873." *Journal of Negro History* 60 (1975): 491–525.

Nash, Gary B. *Forging Freedom: The Formation of Philadelphia's Black Community, 1720–1840.* Cambridge, Mass: Harvard University Press, 1988.

Smith, Edward D. *Climbing Jacob's Latter: The Rise of Black Churches in Eastern Cities, 1740–1877.* Washington DC: Smithsonian Institution, 1988.

Woodson, Carter G. *The History of the Negro Church*. Washington DC: Associated Publishers, 1921.

8 ::

Carol V. R. George

::In his 1901 classic, *The Souls of Black Folk*, W. E. B.
Du Bois characterized the black preacher as "a leader,
a politician, an orator, a 'boss,' an intriguer, an idealist."
A similar statement could be made of black churches,
which have historically served many functions of community center, political forum, and employment agency.
Calling for a new appreciation of these multiple functions and a broader understanding of civil rights, Carol
George demonstrates that a history of the abolitionist
movement must include the often overlooked practical
abolitionism of black churches and ministers.::

:: 8

WIDENING THE CIRCLE

The Black Church and the Abolitionist Crusade, 1830–1860

Carol V. R. George

::A::ccording to a friend's report, the Reverend Noah C.W. Cannon, a black Methodist itinerant preacher and aspiring author, had just finished his service one Sunday evening in 1830 at a rural charge near Denton, Maryland, when he became involved in a potentially life-threatening situation. As the friend recalled, shortly after returning to his stopping place to spend the night, Cannon was confronted by a group of men who arrested him, alleging his resemblance to a man accused of murdering several women and children. The local magistrate subsequently released him, after acknowledging that Cannon's features in no way conformed to the description of the suspect, and the preacher left town the following morning. But it was not long before he realized that several men were still pursuing him; he rode his horse into a swamp and lay down along the side of the road until they passed. "He began to pray that the Lord would send rain to drive his pursuers in the house." The rain came, Cannon cautiously moved around the house to which his would-be captors had retired, and, successfully eluding the dogs sent out to track him, mounted his horse, and bolted across a stream to safety, the current carrying the dogs away. The minister rested that night at the home of friends in Georgetown, Delaware, before assuming his next preaching assignment in Washington. In the meantime, his pursuers had returned to Cannon's host in Maryland, where they broke into a trunk he had left behind, hoping its contents would "throw some light on the movements they supposed were going on among the colored people." They found only papers and Masonic books.

While Cannon went on to have a useful, and in some respects unique, career in the ministry of the African Methodist Episcopal church—writing books and traveling on various circuits that took him to virtually all the free states and into Canada—for the next three decades he and other A.M.E. itinerants steered cautiously around that rural Maryland district.[1]

Some twenty years later, in October, 1851, another black Methodist minister, Jarmain Wesley Loguen, was also threatened with arrest. Loguen, himself a self-proclaimed fugitive slave, purportedly participated in the "Jerry rescue" in Syracuse, New York, when another runaway, Jerry McHenry, was boldly seized by antislavery men from local arresting officers, in violation of the Fugitive Slave Law. Faced with the prospect of not only arrest but a return to slavery, Loguen nevertheless spoke to a crowd that collected at Syracuse City Hall. The clergyman had made no secret of his status as a fugitive, indeed, it had become part of his public image as antislavery lecturer and personal host to hundreds of runaways. Loguen told the Fugitive Slave Law, saying, "The time has come to change the tones of submission into tones of defiance—and to tell Mr. Fillmore and Mr. Webster, if they propose to execute this measure upon us, to send on their bloodhounds." Noting that friends had urged him either to purchase his own freedom or to allow them to do so, he rejected the principle behind their attractive and generous offer. "I owe my freedom to the God who made me," he said, "and who stirred me to claim it against all other beings in God's universe. I will not, nor will I consent, that anybody else shall countenance the claims of a vulgar despot to my soul and body." Denouncing the hated measure, Loguen concluded, "Whatever may be your decision, my ground is taken. . . . I don't respect this law—I don't fear it—I won't obey it! It outlaws me, and I outlaw it, and the men who attempt to enforce it on me."[2] Loguen did accept the judicious counsel of friends who advised him to seek a temporary haven in Canada until the passions aroused by the Jerry rescue cooled down. But he returned the following year and resumed his activities as a preacher, antislavery lecturer, land agent, and conductor on the underground railroad. In 1864 he was elected a bishop of the African Methodist Episcopal Zion church, a post he filled until his death in 1872.

Their dramas played out some twenty years apart in time, what do Cannon and Loguen have in common besides their experiences with oppression and their Methodist affiliation? Their personal dissimilarities are a matter of record: Cannon, erratic and eccentric, spent most of his career virtually unnoticed in the itinerant field, while Loguen, methodical and comparatively more settled, achieved national recognition as an antislavery activist. Yet they and other black ministers apparently shared certain assumptions about the role of the black church in the quasi-free society of the antebellum North.

The purpose of this essay is twofold: first, by drawing on the careers of some forty black clergymen in the period between 1830 and 1860,[3] to suggest the need for a new appreciation of the multidimensional quality of black clerical leadership, mindful that the parochial role of the clergy was as much a response to the interests of their constituent communities as their public, political, activities, and helped foster a kind of parochial abolitionism, and second, to consider the various ways the black church and its ministers contributed to the abolitionist and civil rights movement, and the heightening of black self-awareness. The two objectives are interrelated.

One must begin by shaping a broader, more inclusive working definition of leadership, stripped of the cultural accretions, elitist overtones, and white expectations that have long been associated with it. In a recent study of black abolitionism, Jane and William Pease have noted that a leadership gap separated those black spokesmen at the top of the movement from those they were supposed to serve, an observation echoing that of some contemporary critics of the black church in the nineteenth century.[4] While it may be true that a competency gap distanced the members of the clerical elite at the top of the social pyramid from the mass of common laborers and black servants below, the structure was composed of several levels of leadership. Leadership was more dispersed than a narrow definition of the term would allow. Not confined to a few notables selected and patronized by white [and other black] antislavery activists, it was as likely to be found among men in small parishes and on the itinerant circuit who, despite their less favorable circumstances, were able to stoke the fires of antislavery sentiment by suggesting new options to the black folks who heard them from day to day. The church was as close to a grass roots movement as the free black community could sustain at that stage in its development, and Cannon was one model of a grass roots leader. There were, in fact, a variety of clerical styles, three of which are outlined in the discussion that follows.

A redefinition of black clerical leadership requires a new perception of the efforts of those who advanced the objectives of the antislavery movement in significant but generally unheralded ways. Thus, a reassessment of what qualified as legitimate abolitionist activity also is clearly in order, with major revisionist effort only hinted at here. While members of the clerical elite traveled, wrote books, and addressed antislavery audiences, as noted in the press, their less distinguished brothers built Sunday schools, raised money, and joined or sponsored local groups responsive to community needs, all efforts which had the effect of heightening the racial consciousness and collective identity of black people. Measurable sociopolitical progress alone is an inadequate gauge for evaluating the effectiveness of the churchp; its enduring contributions lie primarily in other areas.

The particular mission of most black churchmen was to improve the quality of life for black people. While long-range goals were often blurred, many of these clergymen were engaged in the short-run with activities that would promote self-respect, self-worth, and control over one's life. Some did this by supporting moral improvement, others by focusing on local and denominational growth, and still others by promoting political involvement. They were aided in these endeavors by the fact that the church could draw from a well of shared history and common experiences to fill a collective need for liberation. Furthermore, if one agrees with James Cone's contention that the fundamental theme of black biblical exegesis has been liberation,[5] then one can speak as well of the development of a committed community of interest, albeit in an embryonic sense. The church gave black people a chance to exercise institutional control and an opportunity to gain self-respect. One result was that by 1860, although material circumstances for free blacks had deteriorated, church members were able to point to progress of a different kind: they witnessed a new sense of personal and racial pride, and a developing ability to exert autonomous control over an important area of their lives.

When organized immediatist abolitionism appeared on the public scene in 1830, the black church was simultaneously entering a new, more secure and outward-turning phase in its development, a congruence that increased the likelihood of interaction between the two efforts. Although the centrality of the church and the role of the clergyman in the black community had long been accepted, the corporate existence of the institution in America dated only from 1773, when the first formally organized black church appeared. In the years immediately following, churchmen were of necessity preoccupied with challenges to institutional legitimacy and autonomy; by 1830, however, having weathered the attacks of critics and demonstrated the viability of black religious separatism in the faraway states (though it was still suppressed in southern and border states), clergymen had acquired sufficient confidence and experience to move beyond concern with more survival to matters of program. That black clerical leaders and white abolitionists would borrow ideas and personnel from each other seemed inevitable, many of their goals appeared similar, and both groups were testing their approaches in a society unreceptive, when not openly hostile, to them.

Participation in antislavery activities was one of the factors that helped produce a black clerical elite. A much larger group of ministers served in middle-class
or historically notable black parishes, and a still greater number worked in small
congregations and on the itinerant circuit. But those relatively few men who were
prominent in abolitionist circles received maximum exposure and hence national and international stature. A selection process—response to indications of personal talent as well as external pressures—helped catapult these men into the
limelight, celebrating a nineteenth-century equivalent of what W. E. B. Du Bois
termed in the twentieth century a "talented tenth," that is, a small minority of gifted and educated people whose efforts would hopefully contribute to the elevation
of the race. Thanks to the efforts of recent historians and biographers, we are coming to know more about these prominent black abolitionists, and can trace their
tortuous paths through Garrisonianism and, for most, into the Liberty party. Yet
it is misleading to regard this elite as representative of black clerical abolition;
most black clergymen were engaged on more mundane levels, attracting minimal
attention outside their communities. As a consequence, we know little about the
ministries of these historically obscure figures, and even less about their role in
the intellectual filtering process by which ideas were transmitted from the top
down and received from the bottom up.

The black clergymen who publicly participated in the antislavery crusade
were privileged in ways not directly related to their involvement with the movement. Although many of them were former slaves or fugitives, they were gifted
with personal qualities that may have placed them further along on what William
and Jane Pease have described as the "continuum of freedom." According to the
Peases, "Where individuals found themselves on the continuum of freedom and
how they understood its meaning was, in short, the most important single fact
shaping the black crusade [for abolition and civil rights] in the antebellum
North."[6] Where a black clergyman found himself on the continuum of freedom
depended, of course, on a host of variables, some of which were beyond his control—talent, skill, education, luck, appearance, location. Higher social status
might be achieved, or it might be conferred.

If a competency gap separated members of this clerical talented tenth from
the mass of poor black workers, it generally did not correspond to their relationship with their immediate constituencies, where members, some of them advan-
taged themselves, supported the political activism of their ministers. In the
vanguard of antislavery activity, the ranks of this clerical elite included
Congregationalists Amos Beman, J.W.C. Pennington, Charles Ray, and Samuel
Ringgold Ward; Episcopalians Alexander Crummell, James T. Holly, and Peter

Williams; Presbyterians Samuel Cornish, Henry Highland Garnet, James Gloucester, and Theodore Wright; African Methodist Episcopal Zionists J.W. Loguen and Christopher Rush; and the African Methodist Daniel Payne. Out of this group of fourteen, only three belonged to independent black denominations, the majority served in traditionally white religious societies. They interacted regularly with white abolitionists, and while they respected the tolerance displayed by upper-middle-class whites, they were not misled by what passed for white altruism. Most would have agreed that white patronage had somehow facilitated selective black mobility, while simultaneously rejecting the notion that white standards were the only measure of black "leadership."

The prominence these men enjoyed set them apart from not only the disadvantaged laity but from their less renowned colleagues as well. There were, however, two harsh realities that served to remind all of them of their shared history and existential situation. One was the continuing pressure of discrimination, and the other was the lack of economic security.

While the passage of the Fugitive Slave Law posed a collective threat to the security of all free blacks, it was the daily acts of intolerance and discrimination that most deeply affected those victimized by them. Itinerant preachers and missionaries feared for their very lives; prominent ministers and settled pastors in socially prestigious cures suffered less dramatic but perhaps equally demoralizing forms of injustice. Peter Williams was forced by his bishop to resign from the board of the American Antislavery Society, and in 1834 his church was sacked by mobs; Alexander Crummell, Isaiah DeGrasse, J.W.C. Pennington, and Amos Beman were denied admission to educational institutions; Theodore Wright was harassed at Princeton Seminary by a group of rowdies; Henry Highland Garnet, Crummell, and Pennington were ejected from public conveyances; Samuel Cornish was refused tea at an inn.[7] William Douglass, rector of the prominent parish of St. Thomas Episcopal Church in Philadelphia, where the carpets were thick and the organ music first-rate, reportedly had "no more seat in the Episcopal Convention of that State than if he were a dog."[8] The list of abuses is long, and then incomplete. For while clergymen who were public figures could call attention to acts of injustice, local preachers like Noah Cannon had to fight their battles unaided and unnoticed.

Economic insecurity was as much a part of the fabric of life for black clergymen as was discrimination. It acted as a great leveler, reducing the possibilities for individual success, at least in an economic sense, to insignificance.

The inability of most clergymen to achieve economic security from their parish work alone did have the advantage, not always perceived by them as such, of keeping them close to the secular world where the members of their congregations earned their daily bread. The clerical talented tenth, whose visibility extended beyond the parish limits, were frequently able to supplement their earnings with vocationally related tasks, such as teaching, writing, and antislavery lecturing, but such income was unpredictable and debt was common.

It was an economic strain for black people to support a church and its program. The ubiquitous financial crunch was as much a part of black church life as family life. Church membership in the free black community was proportionately smaller than it was in the white, although the census of 1850 indicated that the ratio of clergy to laity was roughly comparable in both communities.[9] Nonmembers might develop informal associations with particular churches, and even contribute to their support, but generally the burden of devising ways to meet expenses fell to a faithful remnant. And their personal resources were meager. In New York City, for example, the largest class of free black workers in 1850 was made up of servants whose cash income was negligible.[10] For purposes of comparison, it is useful to note that white employees engaged in working with cotton goods in the state in that year earned a monthly income of $18.32, representing an annual income double that received by traveling A.M.E. preachers.[11] Allowing for a handful of notable exceptions, black churches were financially poorer than white churches of comparable size, because their members earned less and endowments were nonexistent. Few congregations could maintain the salary of a clergyman of the stature of Henry Highland Garnet, who in 1857 earned $500, including $200 from the American Missionary Association for serving as a city missionary.[12] A comfortable church like St. Philip's Episcopal in New York City, which even in the nineteenth century had an endowment growing out of property grants from the wealthy, white Trinity parish, was unique; in most black churches the budget was too tight to be stretched to make ends meet. The result was that black ministers had to devise ingenious ways to cover their expenses, including resorting to white patronage.

The financial strain was even greater for those clergymen who did not share the prominence of the talented tenth. If the members of the talented tenth formed a clerical elite, visible, active on the antislavery circuit, comparatively more privileged than their colleagues, another and larger category of ministers was made up of those who served in what might be termed middle-class (or historically notable) parishes. As concerned about abolitionism and civil rights as their more distinguished brothers, they tended to be not as well educated nor as well positioned socially as the others, and consequently had fewer resources to draw upon. Their tenuous financial circumstances forced them to look for additional income in farming, teaching, shopkeeping, barbering, smithing, or any number of other skilled tasks. Economic considerations also had the effect of limiting the amount of time they could give to the abolitionist campaign. Samuel Ringgold Ward, himself prominent in antislavery circles, noted, "The anti-slavery cause does not, cannot, find bread and education for one's children."[13] Not that ministers in this second group did not assume leadership positions, but rather the nature of their circumstances was such that they were limited to participation in local, regional, and denominational activities. The Reverend Lewis Woodson, for example, recently referred to as the "father of black nationalism," was an A.M.E. minister in Pittsburgh and a prominent figure at the 1841 meeting of the Pennsylvania State Convention of Colored Freemen, who supplemented his income by working as a barber.[14]

But the vast majority of antebellum black ministers belonged neither to the talented tenth nor to what might be conveniently termed the clerical middle class. The members of this third and largest group passed their careers in ministries to the local community or in traveling circuit. Primarily preachers, in their own eyes and those of others, they were compelled to seek secular employment to meet personal and family economic burdens. Unsophisticated by the standards of antislavery audiences, and isolated from that reformist milieu, they worked at tasks similar to those of their parishioners. A random sample of preachers who fit into this category indicate that most were African Methodists, either A.M.E. or A.M.E.Z.; in the period before the Civil War the total number of black men ordained to the Episcopal priesthood, for example, amounted to only seventeen, while in 1856 there were that number of A.M.E. preachers on the New York circuit alone.[15] Typically, ministers in this category received the "call" to preach in late adolescence or early adulthood, moved about regularly after ordination, and were minimally literate in the conventional sense. They left few records or printed sermons, and emerge from history only in the minutes of denominational conventions, where their presence and parochial activities are noted along with their rare statements to the delegates. There was no leadership gap in the field; a favorite expression among African Methodists was "like priests, like people."[16] In fact, where a leadership gap did exist, it tended to operate in a negative way, with members of the congregation readily filling any power vacuum they perceived. The paradoxical result was that the African Methodists' inability to implement clerical authority in the field encouraged the growth of lay leadership, with members vying for control of budgetary matters, ministerial selection, and program direction. But even a professionally ineffective local preacher provided both a role model and a symbolic center for the congregation.

While most northern church-going blacks in the period before the Civil War were Methodists by persuasion or adoption, a glance at the religious affiliation of members of the clerical elite reveals that Methodists were underrepresented in the circle of antislavery activists. The denomination did not contribute leadership to the formal organizations of the abolitionist movement in proportion to its members. There were, of course, notable exceptions, such as Christopher Rush, Richard Allen, J. W. Loguen, and Daniel A. Payne. But one generally looks in vain to find the names of black Methodists among those who traveled the established antislavery route, or who held high office in abolitionist organizations. This limited involvement may be related to the original decision Methodist clergymen made to join with a racially separated religious body, as well as to their generally straitened circumstances. It is also true that parochial concerns began to demand more attention from ministers and bishops than had been the case when the groups were small and members were few. But perhaps when evaluating black Methodist involvement, or lack thereof, we need to refocus our frame of reference. Instead of asking why so few black Methodist clergymen held prominent positions in abolitionist organizations, one might well ask what defined a particular activity as authentically abolitionist or pro-civil rights. Or one may ask, why white antislavery activists failed to join with local black clergymen to advance the civil rights of a particular congregation, as in Noah Cannon's situation. If Abolitionist activity were redefined along these lines, black Methodists and others would occupy more conspicuous places in accounts of the reform crusade. Furthermore, such a redefinition would encourage a new appreciation for the effectiveness of the church as a grass roots movement, along with a willingness to acknowledge the efforts of less distinguished members of the clergy whose form of parochial abolitionism appeared as important to the members of their congregations as the political activism of their more prominent colleagues.

If a new, more inclusive understanding of civil rights activity incorporated the following efforts—strengthening a black witness in American life, promoting black institutional growth in churches and schools, and counseling racial cooperation, and aid to fugitives—then the work of black bishops William Paul Quinn and Daniel A. Payne, for example, would qualify. Payne, the better known of the two primarily because of his writings as a church historian, was vitally interested in educational development, while Quinn, elected an A.M.E. bishop in 1844, was more concerned with expansion and membership growth. Quinn successfully extended A.M.E. influence into Ohio and the western territories; Payne, with somewhat less immediate success, waged what was at times an unpopular, single-handed campaign for A.M.E. educational development for clergy—as in his founding of Wilberforce University—and for young children and adults as well. Although denominational needs took precedence, neither man neglected the larger issues confronting free blacks. In his episcopal address to the A.M.E. conference in 1851, Bishop Quinn charged his listeners to honor their commitment to preach despite the difficulties created by "prejudice and persecution." Advising cooperation, he said, "We should work together. Nine times out of ten when we look into the face of a white man we see our enemy. A great many like to see us in the kitchen, but few in the parlor. Our hope is in God's blessing on our own wise, strong, and well-directed efforts."[17] Similarly, Bishop Payne urged the judicious exercise of power in church governmental affairs by noting, "[T]he American republic oppresses and enslaves every man who has a drop of African blood in his veins, and hunts the panting fugitive like a wild beast. . . . It is a fact as disgraceful as it is painful that no despot in Asia, Europe, or Africa is as cruel and relentless in the persecution of its victims as the American republic."[18] In consequence of that fact, Payne urged denominational reconciliation and understanding. Both men, like many of the clergy in the field, offered informed leadership to the members in their care, whose needs were allegedly at the heart of reform efforts to improve civil rights. It may also appear that by describing their episcopacies in this way, Payne and Quinn agreed with the board members of the New York Committee of Vigilance who expressed a preference for "practical abolitionists."[19] But their printed sermons suggest that their practical programs emerged out of theological-philosophical presuppositions.

Their theology, like that of most of their colleagues, was nineteenth-century evangelical Protestantism, heavily weighted in the direction of a humanized, liberating Christology. But they took special pains to balance the claims of the sacred and the secular, a reflection, in part, of the duality of Protestantism itself. More than that, it was the result of seeing God acting in history on behalf of oppressed peoples. Bishop Benjamin Arnett was presumably describing the collective mind of the A.M.E. church when he said, "Our organization, like others, had its general and special purposes. The general purpose was to assist in bringing the world to the foot of the cross of Christ, and the special was to assist in relieving the African race from physical, mental, and moral bondage."[20] Christ presumably brought relief, release, and liberation, but there was plenty of room for human agency, and that was the special purpose of the A.M.E. church. Theoretically, this high mission not only made every church a unit in a relatively broadly based civil rights organization, but also harmonized with an important aspect of the abolitionist crusade insofar as reformers were concerned about the physical, mental, and moral bondage of blacks. In practice, however, the church often fell short of its special mission.

It is not being unduly defensive of the A.M.E. church to observe that institutional change develops at a snail's pace, the result of the cautious, protective inclinations of those in decision-making positions. In the antebellum period, black Methodism was a neophyte organization, its members, according to Bishop Payne, largely untutored, underemployed, and regularly subjected to intimidation.[21] While Presbyterians and Congregationalists could flex their spiritual muscles on the slavery muscles on the slavery issue, guardedly confident that state legislatures would not close their doors, African Methodists enjoyed no such assurance. When a majority report on slavery, denying membership to those who held slaves, was presented to the 1856 A.M.E. general convention, it was labeled radical and hotly debated. Not that A.M.E. delegates seriously believed that there were many, if any slaveholders in their midst, but rather that the statement would be regarded as a symbol of the church's political stance. A milder, compromise report was finally passed, essentially because participants were persuaded that adoption of the stronger statement would result in the closing of struggling southern black churches and encourage the arrest or intimidation of itinerants in border states. To pass the more radical report simply as a witness was useless, said one delegate, because "Every colored man is an abolitionist, and slaveholders know it."[22]

Black churches witnessed to their antislavery sympathies in other, less overtly political ways. Settled pastors promoted Sunday schools and tried in addition to maintain day and evening schools. Most congregationalists had women's auxiliaries; in the A.M.E. church they were known as Dorcas societies and reportedly served as "an auxiliary of the Vigilance Committee, and as such gathered the necessary clothing and food for the passing runaway." Harboring fugitives qualified anyone willing to take the risk as a practical abolitionist, and the degree to which one publicized such activity enhanced its value as a political act. J.W. Loguen's reception of runaways was as generally known as his stance against the Fugitive Slave Law; he claimed that 1,500 fugitives had passed through his door at 293 East Genesee Street in Syracuse.[23]

Some individual A.M.E. churches had a better opportunity than others to implement their mission to relieve the physical and spiritual bondage of Africans. Perhaps a brief sketch of the development of one A.M.E. parish can serve to illustrate some of the general problems that pastors and parishioners confronted as they tried to shape a viable black institution. Allen Temple, Cincinnati, is admittedly not typical of A.M.E. congregational development. Founded in 1823, it had a tradition which contributed to its enduring prestige and size. Its early history was also determined in part by its geographical location at the very edge of free soil. But its local problems did reflect some common struggles.

The A.M.E. church first planted its branch of Zion in Ohio in 1823, and the circuit was served by a series of itinerant preachers. Before that time, black Methodists had to worship in white congregations, and according to A.M.E. Bishop Arnett, were denied the freedom of emotional expression granted to whites. On a particular Sunday in Cincinnati, says Arnett, a black man, overcome by the evangelical fervor of the white preacher and straining against the urge to leap or shout—practices specifically denied blacks—stuffed a handkerchief in his mouth. He burst a blood vessel and had to be carried out.[24] That event catalyzed black support for a separate church, and after some jockeying with white authorities, the black Methodists were given permission to meet separately. Still officially associated with the white denomination, the black congregation objected to being supplied by a white preacher, and asked to have a man of their own choosing, James King, a slave in Lexington, Kentucky, who was allowed to hire his time, and was permitted to fill their pulpit for several years, traveling regularly between Ohio and Kentucky, until an antislavery jude forged freedom papers for him. Settled in Ohio, King was responsible for leading the exodus of black Methodists out of the white denomination and into the African Methodist Episcopal church. Further discriminatory behavior by whites precipitated the second move. Father King, as he came to be known, was insulted when, in the company of another local black preacher, Philip Brodie, he attended a Methodist camp meeting and was told to wait to take communion until all the whites had been served. The two men reportedly said that they did not believe in two saviors, one for whites and one for blacks. When news reached them in 1823 of the success of the A.M.E. church in Baltimore, they determined to change their allegiance to African Methodism.

According to the church's chronicler, Bishop Arnett, the society soon acquired a number of labels; it was known variously as the "antislavery church," the "black abolitionists," and "King's niggers." The church aided fugitives, became a station on the underground railroad, and in the mid-1830s invited Lane Seminary students to come and teach in their Sunday and day schools. Arnett contended that there were many "appeals to Jehovah to come in his own way and deliver his people from worse than Egyptian bondage. Thus the fire of liberty continued to burn and the ministers fanned the coals and raised the fire to flames."[25]

Arnett's flowery prose aside, his basic outline can be taken seriously as it fits a pattern common to other black churches. Refusal to accept white discrimination, coupled with a desire for free religious expression and an avowedly antislavery stance describe a significant part of the story of autonomous black religious institutional development.

There is also a demonstration of growth and maturation in Arnett's account. Once the initial fight over separate identity was resolved, the campaign moved to higher ground. Seemingly parochial concerns, over the budget and the Sunday school, had wider ramifications for the cause of antislavery and civil rights. Struggles between clergy and laity over matters of priority and finances, Arnett believed, taught black people "knowledge of business and power of control over men." In the South, it "stimulated the hope of the people," by giving them glimpses of freedom and black mobility.[26]

By the 1850s, a separatist undertone pervaded the message of most black churches, which is not surprising given the increasingly oppressive racial climate of opinion. Separation corresponded to renewed interest in emigration, which was then being argued by some supporters as a way of acknowledging race pride and collective identity. Notable clerics like Henry Highland Garnet and Daniel Payne became converts to emigration, and both men became officers in the African Civilization Society, an organization intended for the "civilization and Christianization of Africa," which quickly became embroiled in the politics of the antislavery movement since it was perceived as an offshoot of the American Colonization Society.[27] Both the new appeal for emigration, based on racial integrity, and the churchmen's continued insistence on the need for self-respect, sprang from a common source.

Despite the pervasiveness of discrimination, the church, according to its supporters, did achieve some success in developing in its members a renewed sense of dignity, hope, and self-worth. Arnett addressed the issue when he said, "Here, then, is a key to explain the success of this [A.M.E.] church: Self-Respect. Its founders respected themselves, and they demanded respect from others. If the whites would not respect them, they could at least respect themselves." In 1859, J.W.C. Pennington found cause for optimism: "The race has been preserved mainly by the desperate hope for a better time coming. Their night has been long and their darkness dense. But their day has been slowly dawning, till, even now, while we speak, the sunbeams appear." Less poetically, M.H. Freeman noted that the essential goals for free blacks were "self-appreciation" and a "higher manhood." These spokesmen were addressing a widely held racist perception of blacks, which the Reverend Hosea Easton identified as the assumption that the slave was a mindless amoral "machine," and the freeman was something less than human. William Douglass commented that the slave system "blots out the moral image traced by God and says 'it is a thing.'"[28] For free blacks, self-respect and civil rights were two sides of the same coin, payment against the debt of "thing-ness."

Black churches not only preached self-respect, they gave people practical experience in acquiring it by opening up opportunities to exercise authority and gain new skills. An elderly parishioner of Arnett's in Cincinnati recalled in 1874 that "the great question proposed for solution fifty years ago was, can colored men conduct successfully a religious organization?" Citing the half-century of growth and achievement of the A.M.E. church, he concluded, "If these are not a full and complete refutation of the position assumed by our opposers, and a clear vindication of the correctness of our views, nothing can be." But the Episcopal minister James T. Holly demurred from such a view, suggesting instead that only by emigrating to Haiti could blacks hope "to inflame the latent members of self-respect." The young African Methodist clergyman Henry McNeal Turner saw things differently. Attempting to convince a southern black youth to join the A.M.E. church in the 1850s, Turner said, "We have our own bishops, and we, as a race, have a chance to be somebody, and if we are ever going to be a people, now is the time." This sense of growing self-confidence is also evident in Howard Bell's assessment of emigrationist sentiment, and can apply to the church. In Bell's opinion, "Had conservative leaders of Negro thought been further removed from their own problems, they might have been able to see more clearly the growing faith of the colored man in himself which was, to some extent at least, responsible for the demand for emigration and Negro nationalism. Perhaps this new faith which [Martin] Delany and [J.M.] Whitfield were preaching, was understood better outside of abolitionist circles, than within."[29]

The question of whether all, some, or only a few black churches were outposts of the abolitionist and reform crusade cannot be answered without reevaluating what should be considered valid, useful contributions to the movement. Certainly our vision needs to extend beyond the efforts of the clerical talented tenth. Black churches varied in the extent to which they provided moral, physical, and intellectual training grounds for their members. Some, like Allen Temple, were busy stations on the underground railroad; others, like the congregations of Lewis Woodson and Henry Highland Garnet, supported the political activism of their ministers. Most offered regular and heavy doses of moral reform. All black churches provided ideological supports not found in the dominant white society. Whether that made all of them agents of the abolitionist and civil rights campaign depends on how widely we draw the circle describing such activity. The church, like abolitionism, helped foster the development of self-respect and black consciousness.

NOTES

1. Alexander W. Wayman, *My Recollections of African Methodist Episcopal Ministers, or Forty Years' Experience in the African Methodist Episcopal Church* (Philadelphia: A.M.E. Book Rooms, 1881), 7–11; Daniel A. Payne, *History of the African Methodist Episcopal Church* (Nashville: A.M.E. Sunday School Union, 1891), 253–55. Like all memoirs, Wayman's account needs to be read critically. Both Wayman and Payne were nineteenth-century A.M.E. bishops, the latter serving also as a very conscientious church historian.

2. Jarmain Wesley Loguen, *The Reverend J. W. Loguen, as a Slave and as a Freeman* (reprint, New York: Negro Universities Press, 1968), 391–93. More biography than autobiography, Loguen's life story nevertheless conforms to what is known about his stand and his activities.

3. Information on the forty clergymen whose careers are relevant to this study is uneven in quantity—generous for those whom I have referred to as a clerical "talented tenth," limited for those who served in a small parishes or the itinerary. It is also important to remember that during the thirty-year period being examined, 1830–1860, men frequently changed jobs and roles, resulting in some cases in a change of status. Henry McNeal Turner, for example, who was a young clergyman in 1860, was elected an A.M.E. bishop in 1880.

    The categories which follow are drawn impressionistically, and are intended for reference. Theodore Hershberg's quantified study of faraway blacks in Philadelphia is useful, and might well be adapted for other cities.

    BLACK CLERICAL ROLES, 1830–1860

    Group I—The "Talented Tenth"

    Amos Beman (Cong., Conn.), Samuel Cornish (Pres., N.Y., N.J.), Henry Highland Garnet (Pres., N.Y.), James Gloucester (Pres., N.Y.), James T. Holly (Epis., Conn.), Jarmain Wesley Loguen (A.M.E.Z., N.Y.), Daniel A. Payne (A.M.E., Md., Pa.), J. W. C. Pennington (Cong., N.Y.), Charles Ray (Cong., N.Y.), Christopher Rush (A.M.E.Z., N.Y.), Samuel Ringgold Ward (Cong., N.Y.), Peter Williams (Epis., N.Y.), Theodore Wright (Pres., N.Y.)

    Group II—Denominational or Regional Ministries

    Morris Brown (A.M.E., Pa.), Daniel Coker (A.M.E., Md.-West Africa), William Douglass (Epis., Pa.), Hosea Easton (Cong., Mass.), George Hogarth (A.M.E., N.Y.), J. Sella Martin (Bapt., Mass.), Nathaniel Paul (Bapt., N.Y.), Thomas Paul (Bapt., Mass., N.Y.), John Peterson (Epis., N.Y.), William Paul Quinn (A.M.E.,

Pa.), Henry McNeal Turner (A.M.E., Ga.), Alexander Wayman (A.M.E., Ohio), Lewis Woodson (A.M.E., Pa.)

Group III — Essentially Local Ministries

Philip Brodie (A.M.E., Ohio), Noah Cannon (A.M.E., Pa., Itineracy), John Cornish (A.M.E., Pa.), Isaiah DeGrasse (Epis., N.Y.), Clayton Durham (A.M.E., Pa.), Moses Freeman (A.M.E., Ohio), James King (A.M.E., Ohio), J.W. Lewis (Bapt,. R.I.), William Levington (Epis., Md.), Daniel Peterson (A.M.E., N.Y., Liberia), Elymas Rogers Pres., N.J.), Samuel Snowden (Mass.) Edward Waters (A.M.E., Md., Pa.)

NOTE: Denominational abbreviations: Congregationalist (Cong.), Presbyterian, (Pres.), Episcopalian (Epis.), African Methodist Episcopal Zion (A.M.E.Z.), African Methodist Episcopal (A.M.E.), and Baptist (Bapt.).

4. Jane H. Pease and William H. Pease, *They Who Would Be Free* (New York: Atheneum, 1974), 186–93. The Peases conclude, "Whether assessed by its goals or its organizational efficiency, black abolitionism was a failure," (page 297). The existence of a leadership gap, they suggest, was one of the reasons for the failure, too many black leaders were guilty of "numberoneishness." Their study surveys the full spectrum of black abolitionism, although clergymen figure largely in it, as they did in the movement itself. Their work supplements Benjamin Quarles's fine study, *Black Abolitionists* (New York: Oxford University Press, 1969), and the numerous autobiographical and/or biographical accounts of members of the clerical "talented tenth." A helpful new contribution is Joel Schor, *Henry Highland Garnet: A Voice of Black Radicalism in the Nineteenth Century* (Westport, Conn.: Greenwood Press, 1977).

5. James Cone, *Liberation: A Black Theology of Liberation* (New York: J.B. Lippincott, 1970), 23ff.

6. Pease and Pease, *They Who Would Be Free*, 286.

7. Cornish described the incident in *The Emancipator*, August 17, 1837; it is quoted in Roi Ottley and William J. Weatherby, *The Negro in New York: An Informal Social History* (New York: Oceana Press, 1967), 42. Ottley and Weatherby contend that there was a group of white toughs in New York City, called the Blackbirders, who made it a practice of harassing free blacks for the purpose of capturing them as fugitives and selling them as slaves to traders.

8. Samuel Ringgold Ward, *Autobiography of a Fugitive Negro* (reprint, New York: Arno Press, 1968), 283. Ward also cites the indignities suffered by other free black men of stature. The circumstances that led to the founding of St. Thomas Church are discussed in Carol V. R. George, *Segregated Sabbaths* (New York: Oxford University Press, 1973), 63.

9. Report of the Superintendent of the Census, *The Seventh Census* (Washington: Armstrong, 1853), 29, 30.

10. J. D. B. DeBow (comp.), *Statistical View of the United States, Compendium of the 7th*

Census (Washington: Nicholson, 1854), 80, 81. DeBow's figures for those jobs in New York City requiring education that were filled by blacks is as follows: clerks, 7; doctors, 9; druggists, 3; lawyers, 4; merchants, 3; printers, 4; student, 1; teachers, 8; ministers, 21.

11. *The Seventh Census, 1850*. The figures for those working in "Cotton Goods" in the state were: $18.32, males; $9.68, females. The New York African Society for Mutual Relief, a black benevolent organization founded in 1810, would have confirmed the existence of a much larger group of black professionals and businessmen in New York City. See John J. Zuille (comp.), *Historical Sketch of the New York African Society for Mutual Relief* (New York: n.p., 1897), available on microfilm. See also Edgar J. McManus, *Black Bondage in the North* (Syracuse: Syracuse University Press, 1973).

12. Quarles, *Black Abolitionists, 80;* Schor, *Henry Highland Garnet*, 29, 144, 210. Clerical compensation is difficult to calculate, in part because supplementary income is rarely recorded. J.T. Holly, the rector of St. Luke's Episcopal Church, New Haven, was supposed to receive $150 per year, but in three years' time (between 1857 and 1860), the salary fell in arrears by $139.24. In 1839, Amos Beman, a Congregationalist minister, was scheduled to receive the handsome salary of $400; he managed to raise most of it among his members, but finally had to call on white aid. See Robert Austin Warner, *New Haven Negroes* (New Haven: Yale University Press, 1940), 78–94. The large and prestigious A.M.E. church in Cincinnati in 1858 listed an annual stipend for its minister of $437, although the budget for the entire denomination in 1846, with 69 ministers, was only $7,231.03. See Benjamin W. Arnett (ed.), *Proceedings of the Semi-Centenary Celebration of the African Methodist Episcopal Church of Cincinnati* (Cincinnati: Watkin, 1874), 25, and Henry McNeal Turner, *The Genius and Theory of Methodist Polity, or The Machinery of Methodism* (Philadelphia: A.M.E. Church Publication Department, 1885), 241.

13. Ward, *Autobiography of a Fugitive Negro*, 117.

14. Schor, in *Henry Highland Garnet*, 154, refers to Floyd J. Miller's study, "The Father of Black Nationalism," *Civil War History*, XVII (December, 1971), 310–19. See also *Proceedings of the State Convention of the Colored Freeman of Pennsylvania* (Pittsburgh: Matthew Grant, 1841), 16. There were seven Methodist clergymen along with Woodson (who served as secretary) who answered the roll at the convention.

15. George P. Bragg, *History of the Afro-American Group of the Episcopal Church* (Baltimore: Church Advocate Press, 1922), 15; Payne, *History of the A.M.E. Church*, 416.

16. Payne, *History of the A.M.E. Church*, 179.

17. Ibid., 256–57.

18. *Bishop Payne's First Annual Address to the Philadelphia Conference of the A.M.E. Church* (Philadelphia: Sherman, 1853), 17. This address is also found in Charles Killian (ed.), *Bishop Payne's Sermons and Addresses, 1853–1891* (reprint, New York: Arno Press, 1972).

19. New York Committee of Vigilance, *First Annual Report, 1837*. Theodore Wright and Samuel Cornish were among those who signed the report.

20. Arnett, *Proceedings of the Semi-Centenary Celebration*, 12.

21. *Bishop Payne's First Annual Address*, 11, 12. The same year that Payne gave his address (1853), the Pennsylvania Society for Promoting the Abolition of Slavery reported that Bethel Church had the largest black Sunday school, with 524 students, followed by St. Thomas with 183. See Benjamin C. Bacon (comp), *Statistics of the Colored People of Philadelphia* (Philadelphia: T. Ellwood Chapman, 1856), 10, 11.

22. Payne, *History of the A.M.E. Church*, 337–45. Quarles, *Black Abolitionists*, 56, quotes a black editor in 1849: "The mind does not take its complexion from the skin. To be a colored man is not necessarily to be an abolitionist."

23. Ottley and Weatherby, *The Negro in New York*, 85; Loguen, *The Reverend J.W. Loguen*, 444, J.W. Loguen to Gerrit Smith, July 14, 1855, Ms., Syracuse University Library.

24. Arnett, *Proceedings of the Semi-Centenary Celebration*, 14.

25. Ibid., 19–20.

26. Ibid., 100–101. Arnett's experience, as pastor of what became known as Allen A.M.E. Temple in Cincinnati, a large and important parish, may have influenced his perspective somewhat. In 1861, Alexander Crummell had the impression that Cincinnati had more wealthy blacks than any other city in the country. Crummell, *Charitable Institutions in Colored Churches* (Washington, n.p., 1892).

27. Payne, *History of the A.M.E. Church*, 170, 171. Useful information on the African Civilization Society is available in Schor, *Henry Highland Garnet*. The society, formed in 1858, and dominated by Garnet and also Martin Delany, grew out of the heat of emigrationist ferment in the fifties. See *Constitution of the African Civilization Society*, and *Board of Directors*, on microfilm, Schomberg Collection, New York Public Library.

28. Arnett, *Proceedings of the Semi-Centenary Celebration*, 99; J. W. C. Pennington, "The Self-Redeeming Power of the Colored Races of the World," *Anglo-African Magazine* 1 (October, 1859), 314; M.H. Freeman, "The educational Wants of the Free Colored People," *Anglo-African Magazine* 1 (April, 1859), 119; Hosea Easton, *A Treatise on the Intellectual Character and Civil and Political Condition of the Colored People of the United States* (Boston: Isaac Knapp, 1837), 51; William Douglass, "The Forbearance and Retributive Justice of God," *Sermons* (reprint, Freeport, N.Y.: Books for Libraries Press, 1971).

29. Arnett, *Proceedings of the Semi-Centenary Celebration*, 31; James T. Holly, "A Vindication of the Capacity of the Negro Race for Self-Government and Civilized Progress," in Howard Brotz (ed.), *Negro Social and Political Thought, 1850–1920* (New York: Basic Books, 1966), 142 (Holly's "Vindication" appeared in 1857); Robert Anderson, *The Life of the Reverend Robert Anderson* (Atlanta: Foote and Davies, 1900), 46; Howard H. Bell, *The Negro Convention Movement, 1830–1861* (reprint; New York: Arno Press, 1969).

SELECTED BIBLIOGRAPHY FOR FURTHER READING

Essig, James D. *The Bonds of Wickedness: American Evangelicals Against Slavery, 1770–1808.* Philadelphia: Temple University Press, 1982.

Ofari, Earl. *"Let Your Motto Be Resistance": The Life and Thought of Henry Highland Garnet.* Boston: Beacon, 1972.

Quarles, Benjamin. *Black Abolitionists.* New York: Oxford University Press, 1975.

Swift, David E. *Black Prophets of Justice: Activist Clergy Before the Civil War.* Baton Rouge: Louisiana State University Press, 1989.

David W. Wills and Richard Newman, ed. *Black Apostles at Home and Abroad: Afro-Americans and the Christian Mission from the Revolution to Reconstruction.* Boston: G.K. Hall, 1982.

EMANCIPATION, MISSION, AND BLACK DESTINY

IV::

9 ::

William H. Becker

::African Americans have had to assert continuously their humanity in light of a society that sought to dehumanize them. Written in 1972, this essay by William Becker examines the slave preacher and the independent black church as important "models of manhood," and argues that missions to Africa after the Civil War provided African Americans a unique opportunity and a dramatic symbol of self-assertion, independence, black identity, and vocation.::

:: 9 THE BLACK CHURCH

Manhood and Mission

William H. Becker

:: Students of the black Christian church today tend to emphasize its long and honorable association with the cause of black liberation, its tradition of protest, whether overt or covert, against white racism. "The Black Revolution was born in the 'invisible' Black Church of the slave era." "The independent Black Church emerged as a protest—a protest against the racist theology and the racist ecclesiology of the church in America."[1]

This emphasis, as Vincent Harding has pointed out, serves as a necessary counterbalance to "classic" interpretations of the black church, by such scholars as Benjamin Mays and E. Franklin Frazier, as passive, other-worldly, not inclined to struggle for racial justice. Any definite judgment on the black church will undoubtedly have to give some weight to both these interpretations, thereby recognizing what Harding terms "the ambiguity, the doubleness, of black religious experience, indeed of all religious experience."[2]

Yet even recognition of this "doubleness"—this polarity between religion as an opiate and religion as a stimulus to protest—does not constitute a full appreciation of the contribution the black church has made to the earthly liberation of its people. That contribution goes beyond the simple either/or of passive submission and active resistance to encompass the realm of communal nurture in which a people develops and symbolizes its answer(s) to the question, What does it mean to be a man? Every human community defines and authenticates those models of manhood that serve to guide its members in their growth toward mature humanity, and within the black community the church has played a key role in this process.

Manhood is an important term in the tradition of the independent black church (Bishop B. W. Arnett described the organizing conference of the African Methodist Episcopal Church in 1816 as "the Convention of the friends of Manhood Christianity"),[3] and there can be no doubt that the models of black manhood provided by the black church constituted one of its most important contributions, over the years, to the cause of black liberation. These models are delineated in the biographies, sermons, histories, and conference minutes of the black churches, and are manifested in the lives and work of significant black churchmen such as Daniel A. Payne and Henry M. Turner.

It is proper to speak here of models and not a single model. The changing situation of the black church in different periods of its history, the varying temperaments of its leaders, the ebb and flow of white racism—these and other factors have led to the development in the church of different styles of black manhood. While we cannot, therefore, speak of some single model of manhood, we can begin to identify various aspects of manhood which have been (and are) emphasized by the black church, and embodied in its heroic figures. This essay represents a preliminary effort in that direction.

There are four distinguishable but interrelated aspects of manhood, as manifested in the black church tradition, to be discussed here: (1) leadership, self-assertion, (2) independence, (3) black identity, and (4) vocation. With the reminder that these are understood as interdependent and not as mutually exclusive, it may be suggested that the first aspect is especially prominent in the slave preacher, the first three are prominent in the founders of the black church, and all four are evident in the developed black church, especially as it defines its role as a missionary church following Emancipation.

The two interrelated theses of this essay are that (1) the definition and assertion of black manhood has been a conscious motive and dominant theme throughout the history of the black church, and that (2) the assertion of black manhood was in turn a conscious motive and dominant theme in the black appropriation of the common nineteenth-century dogma that it was the black American's special providential calling to win his African brother to Christianity. Black manhood and black mission in Africa came to be tied together in the black Christian mind, and they remain tied together (though with some different emphases) to this day.

THE SLAVE PREACHER

The policy of white slaveholders concerning the religious instruction of their slaves varied greatly, not only from region to region, but even from one plantation to the next. Some forbade any religious instruction or practice; some required attendance at prayer services and Sunday worship.

It was not long after slaves began to appropriate the Christian faith as their own that there stepped forth from among them effective, although often illiterate, preachers of the gospel. We do not know very much about these "prophets" and "judges" of the black church, but we know enough to realize that they were among the first slaves who had opportunity to assert themselves in a public, dramatic role of leadership. Where slaves' meetings were prohibited and, therefore, held secretly in the woods or slave quarters, the charisma of the slave preacher was known only to those whom he led. Where slave worship was permitted, an able preacher might become widely known among both blacks and whites. Several known preachers attracted considerable white audiences, and sometimes, as in the case of George Lisle, Andrew Bryan, Josiah Bishop, and "Uncle Jack," white persons either manumitted slave preachers of recognized ability or raised money to purchase their freedom.[4]

Leadership by charismatic preachers is, according to W. E. B. Du Bois, one of the three dominant characteristics of slave religion (the other two being music and "frenzy" or shouting).

> The Preacher is the most unique personality developed by the Negro on
> American soil. A leader, a politician, an orator, a "boss," an intriguer, an ideal-
> ist—all this he is, and ever, too, the center of a group of men, now twenty,
> now a thousand in number.[5]

It is the preacher's place at "the center of a group of men" that especially concerns us here. As one who knew something of the Bible's sacred mysteries, who had the power to transform biblical imagery into the affections of the heart, who had the confidence to stand before others with shouting voice and pounding fist, the preacher was manifestly a man and a leader of men. In addition to whatever other symbolic functions he had, he symbolized self-assertive masculinity and integrity for the slaves who watched and heard him.

Unconsciously at least, he may also have symbolized the slave's previous independence in Africa, in that he was an Afro-American reincarnation, Du Bois suggests, of the "Priest or Medicine-Man" who played such a central role in African social organization.

THE INDEPENDENT BLACK CHURCH

Separate black congregations led by black preachers were formed in the eighteenth century, the first one between 1773–75 by Baptists in Silver Bluff, South Carolina. But it was not until the formation of the African Methodist Episcopal Church in 1816 that any black church achieved complete independence—i.e., control of its own property and freedom from the jurisdiction of white denominational officials. Because it was the first fully independent black denomination, and also because there is more published historical material available on it than on any other black denomination, the A.M.E. Church will be the focus of study in this essay.[6]

What we know of the causes and motives which led to the founding of the A.M.E. Church suggests that two interrelated factors, one negative and one positive, were primarily responsible. Undoubtedly these two factors, accompanied sometimes by others, were present in the formation of virtually all separate black churches. The negative factor is of course discrimination by whites against black fellow-worshippers. The positive factor is the assertion by black men of their essential dignity as men, as children of God, as citizens of the nation.

Richard Allen reports that soon after he arrived in Philadelphia in February, 1786, he saw the necessity of establishing a separate meeting house for "our colored brethren [who] were destitute of a place of worship [and] were considered as a nuisance" in the St. George's Methodist Church where some did worship. White discrimination and black pride collided in that dramatic incident in 1787, in which the trustees of St. George's sought physically to remove Absolom Jones, Richard Allen, and other blacks from a "white" section of the gallery in which they were on their knees at prayer. What someone has called the first "freedom march" occurred when the "prayer was over, and we all went out of the church in a body, and they were no more plagued with us in the church."[7]

Daniel Coker, with Richard Allen a founder of the A.M.E. denomination, in 1816 compared the newly independent churchmen with "the Jews in Babylon [who] were held against their will" but then gained their freedom. Like many A.M.E. spokesmen who were to come after him, he hoped and assumed that the A.M.E. Church would serve to build the unity, and therefore enhance the security, of the black people. "May the time speedily come, when we shall see our brethren come flocking to us like doves to their windows. And we as a band of brethren, shall sit down under our own vine to worship, and none to make us afraid."[8]

Given these dramatic beginnings, it is not surprising that the A.M.E. Church has viewed itself, its very existence as an independent, black-controlled de-nomination, as a manifestation of black self-assertion. Bishop Daniel A. Payne (1811–1893), the first official historian of the A.M.E. Church, says that the sep-aration of that black denomination from the predominantly white Methodist Episcopal Church was "beneficial to the man of color" in two ways. "First: it has thrown us upon our own resources and made us tax our own mental powers both for government and support." So long as he was simply a small minority within the M.E. Church, Payne argues, the colored man "always was, still is, and ever must be a mere cipher." His dependent status tended to "confirm the oft-repeated assertions of his enemies, that he really is incapable of self-government and self-support." In Payne's view, "the existence of the African Methodist Episcopal Church" constitutes a "flat contradiction of this slander."

The second benefit of separation is closely related to the first: It gave the black man "an independence of character which he could neither hope for nor at-tain unto, if he had remained as the ecclesiastical vassal of his white brethren." It has produced "independent thought," "independent action," and an "independent hierarchy," and the latter "has made us feel and recognize our individuality and our heaven-created manhood."[9]

Bishop Payne did more than simply write about the "heaven-created man-hood" nurtured within the A.M.E. Church. Like the black preacher of slavery times, he *embodied* that manhood—in a career as a teacher, pastor, and A.M.E. Bishop. He had numerous occasions during that career to display his personal courage and commitment. As an educator he overcame his own bitter discour-agement at the enforced closing of his flourishing school in Charleston, South Carolina, a closing forced upon him in 1835 by the "white backlash" which fol-lowed Nat Turner's uprising (1831). As pastor and bishop, he fought—against determined opposition within his own church—on behalf of some important causes: an educated ministry, racial inclusiveness in the church, sound planning in foreign missions.[10] When he was in his seventies he once chose to get off a train and walk, carrying his luggage, rather than be seated in Jim Crow condi-tions. "Before I'll dishonor my manhood by going into that car, stop your train and put me off," he said.[11]

Charles Spencer Smith (1852–1922), who like Payne was both a bishop and the official historian of the A.M.E. Church, produced Volume Two of the *History of the A.M.E. Church* in 1922. It covers the period from the end of Payne's history (1856) through World War I. A dominant theme of Smith's history is precisely the one we are discussing: the self-assertive manhood manifest in the leaders and spirit of the A.M.E. Church. The book begins with this dedication, "To the

Trailblazers, whose self-sacrificing and heroic labors made possible the expansion and development of the African Methodist Church in the West and South." It ends with a chapter entitled "After-war Problems" which quotes the well-known, militant poem of Claude McKay:

> If we must die, let it not be like hogs
> Hunted and penned in an inglorious spot,
>
> Like men we'll face the murderous, cowardly pack
> Pressed to the wall, dying—but fighting back![12]

In at least three different ways Smith associates black manliness and integrity with the A.M.E. Church. First, in the words he characteristically uses to describe the leaders (pastors, missionaries, and bishops) of the Church during the period treated. Elder William P. Quinn, missionary to states west of Ohio (1840), "had the faith and daring of Paul, the intrepidity of Francis Asbury, and the blood and iron of Bismarck. He was matchless in heroism, superb in courage, and relentless in his attacks on the foes of his people. He was a militant soldier of the Cross. He was a giant in his day." James Lynch and J. O. S. Hall, the first A.M.E. missionaries to South Carolina (1863), are characterized as men of "courage, daring, and self-sacrificing spirit." The Rev. A. W. Wayman, preaching in Norfolk, is "another Daniel [who by going South did] dare to enter the lion's den of American slavery." Wayman, J. M. Brown, and D. A. Payne are a "trio of red-blooded pioneers."[13]

> May 15, 1865, when Bishop Daniel Alexander Payne proceeded to organize the South Carolina Annual Conference, a new Chapter was opened in the history of the African Methodist Church, . . . one filled with deeds of heroism, daring, self-sacrifice, and indomitable will, which matches the story of the Crusaders.[14]

In highlighting the Church's continuing protest against slavery and (after Emancipation) against white racism and lynching, Smith finds a second way to associate the A.M.E. Church with what is now termed black liberation. Bishop William P. Quinn (1851): "Nine times out of ten when we look into the face of a white man, we see our enemy. . . . Our hope is in God's blessing on our own wise, strong, and well-directed efforts."[15] Resolutions on Civil Rights adopted unanimously by the General Conference of 1872:

> Resolved, that we, the representatives of the largest body of Christians of the African race in this country, hereby enter our solemn protest against this relic of barbarism and American slavery [i.e., Southern Jim Crow railroad laws]. . . .

> Resolved, that we hereby pray the Congress of the United States, now in session, to pass the "Civil Rights Bill," now pending, . . . to the end that equal rights may be awarded to every American citizen traveling on the highways of the nation.[16]

A memorial to the Congress of the United States from the "Commission on After-War problems of the African Methodist Episcopal Church" (1919): Many black American citizens have "sworn by the blood of their kinsmen who fell on the battlefields of France . . . to help make the world safe for democracy, that they will no longer tamely submit to a denial of the rights guaranteed them by the National Constitution."[17]

MANHOOD AND MISSION IN AFRICA

There is yet a third way in which C. S. Smith suggests an association of A.M.E. Church with black manhood—an association more subtle than the two already discussed, but nevertheless highly significant. This association has to do with those closely related aspects of manhood we have called identity and vocation. As the nineteenth century unfolded, the identity of the A.M.E. Church came to be more closely associated in the minds of its leaders with the idea of a special vocation to evangelize Africa.

The General Conference of 1872, for example, adopted the following statements in a report on Church Union:

> We are now more than ever convinced that the African Methodist Episcopal Church has yet a mission to perform, not only in the elevation and religious training of our long-neglected people in the United States, but in the perfect evangelization of African and the islands of the seas. . . .

> When prejudice on account of color shall be swept from the Church and shall disappear . . . then, and not until then, will the grand mission of the African Methodist Episcopal Church, as a separate organization, be at [an] end.[18]

Affirmation of blackness over and against white prejudice necessitates the existence and constitutes the identity of the A.M.E. Church; the mission of the Church, correlative with this identity, is to evangelize the black man, including those in Africa.

There is no surprise, of course, in the fact that the A.M.E. Church was concerned with missionary work. Such work was seen as the responsibility of all

Christians, deriving from Christ's Commandment in Matt 28:19–20. The Methodist Episcopal Church, parent body of the A.M.E., had a strong missionary tradition, and Richard Allen was himself a M.E. home missionary preacher during the 1790s, before he organized his own church. Moreover, the nineteenth century was the "great century" for Christian missionary expansion, and the black church, in its missionary fervor, reflected the fervor of the white Christian bodies surrounding it. Nor is it surprising that the black church should focus its missionary efforts on black men. There the need was greatest, the opportunities most obvious—especially after Emancipation in 1863—and the prospects of success highest.

What is surprising, at least at first blush, is the emphasis on *African mission*. Why should the independent black church—dependent upon a constituency of the poorest classes for its support, faced with great financial difficulties and a shortage of educated leaders, confronted in 1863 with the task of serving literally millions of newly freed slaves—undertake foreign missions across the seas in Africa? Why look so far, when the need is so great at one's back door—indeed, in one's own house?[19]

There were those within the A.M.E. Church who raised these very questions, as is illustrated by these words from the Episcopal Address to the General Conference of 1856:

> The cause of missions demands our serious and careful consideration. But whether we are able to cultivate the foreign as well as the home field is a grave and important question. Some think we ought to cultivate both. One thing however is certain, for it is a fact of history that we have made two attempts to occupy foreign fields [i.e., "in Africa and Haiti"] but have never maintained ourselves in them.[20]

Bishop Daniel Payne argued in 1884 that, rather than attempt to re-establish its foreign ministry efforts in Africa, the A.M.E. Church should concentrate its efforts on its already existing mission in Haiti. "The A.M.E. Church is too poor to attempt to establish more than one challenge at a time," Payne insisted, and the same principle must be applied to foreign missions. "The A.M.E. Church ought not to establish a mission in Africa until she has made her mission in the island of Haiti a grand success." Moreover, Payne warned against what he saw as a tendency toward "Ecclesiastical Imperialism" in missions at a time when "thousands of our own churches are suffering for lack of moneys to support them. All of our schools are suffering for lack of endowment."[21]

But Payne's words of caution were not heard in the black church during the

1880s and 90s, at least not on the subject of missions in Africa. During 1891, Bishop Henry M. Turner (1834–1915) traveled to West Africa, organizing the Sierra Leone Annual Conference of the A.M.E. Church on November 10 and the Liberian Annual Conference on November 23. In the eleventh of his series of fourteen "African Letter" (dated December 4) Turner said of Africa, "There is no reason under heaven why this continent should not or cannot be brought to God in twenty-five years—say thirty at most."[22]

In part, of course, Turner's enthusiasm for African mission simply echoed that of white churchmen. Whites were already missionizing blacks in Africa—why should the black church exclude itself from this task? As Bishop Nazrey said in 1856: "We have as much right to look after perishing Africa and the West India Islands as any other Christian Church upon the face of the earth."[23] The Episcopal Address to the General Conference of 1896 puts it more strongly: "Our church is better adapted to the redemption of Africa than any other organization."[24]

Moreover, black churchmen were being told over and over again during the 1880s and 90s, by both blacks and whites, that they were "better adapted" and in fact divinely commissioned to play the key role in missionizing Africa. As part of the "African fever" which gripped Europe and the U.S. during the period 1880–1900, it was widely assumed by statesmen, educators, journalists—as well as churchmen—that Africa would be Christianized "in this generation," and that the Afro-American would bear a major responsibility in this task.

This latter idea was not new; it had been broached before by the New England divine Samuel Hopkins, and by the American Colonization Society, organized in 1817. But following emancipation the idea was put forward with new force, and by a great variety of spokesmen. These appeals for black mission in Africa, as Josephus Coan has pointed out, generally emphasized one or more of the following points: (a) the American black man has been prepared for mission work by divine providence, through Christianization and education in the U.S.; (b) being thus blessed by God, Afro-Americans are obligated to bring these blessings to their African brothers; (c) Afro-Americans possess a "superior fitness" for African mission because of their racial kinship with Africans and because they can adapt to the African climate more successfully than white missionaries.[25]

But, acknowledging the pervasiveness and appeal of these arguments, why should the black church have accepted them—given its pressing tasks at home? Why didn't the A.M.E. Church respond to them with a resounding "No," as it had to earlier arguments, put forward by the American Colonization Society, that the proper destination of the American black man was Africa?[26]

The basic answer, I think, has to do with the issue of black manhood: African mission provided a dramatic symbol of the Afro-American as man, as leader, as authoritative carrier of God's word to those racial brothers who do not possess it. The power of this symbol can be see in an engraving used as the frontispiece in the Arnett book, which shows a group of dark-skinned peoples—Orientals, Africans, American Indians—approaching a preacher with the question, "Which way to God?" The preacher holds in his right hand an open Bible, and with his extended left arm points to a cross on a distant mountain peak, a cross from which radiate the word, "Lo I am the Way." The preacher is a young, vigorous, American black man. He is tall and well built; he stands a full head taller than any of the other figures. He is manifestly a man, and he is showing the way to the other men. The caption reads: "The Special Mission of the A.M.E. Church to the Darker Races is to 'Teach the Mind to Think, the Heart to Love, the Hand to Work.'"

This symbol of the black man as missionary to other men of color had appeal for both black and white Americans. It was a symbol which portrayed the Afro-American as exercising leadership and independence, as having a definite identity (educated, Christian, chosen of God) and a definite vocation (to evangelize the "darker races," especially in Africa). It was a symbol which sought to make some sense of the suffering of a slave past (that past was a preparation for this vocation), and which held out high hopes for the future (God will reward his faithful missionaries, and no man will be able to doubt their courage or effectiveness). Moreover, and this is a vital point, here is a symbol which, by dramatizing the manhood of the Afro-American *in another land*, made it clear, at one and the same time, that he was a man, but that he had to leave America to be recognized as a man.

All these aspects of the symbol, which are implicit in the engraving, became fully explicit in numerous statements by A.M.E. churchmen during this period. The Reverend S. F. Flegler, who as pastor led a group of thirty A.M.E. settlers to Liberia in 1878, addressed the South Carolina Conference of the Church in 1890 as follows:

Africa is the home of the Negro, the land where he is free, and where he has the best opportunity for the best development. It is much in need of the Gospel. What the Church expends in the interests of missionary operations in Liberia will return to you in glory and grandeur. The work is before us, and we will do it if we are possessed of race pride. I would not be here today, if I could have induced my family to have joined me when I was in Africa. I have too much soul in me to be satisfied with the condition that presents itself here. I

recognize no man to be my superior, nor any race to be naturally in advance of
ours . . . God Almighty never made a soul with more elements of manhood
than mine; and I thank God there is sufficient African blood in me to thrill me
with aspirations of manhood.[27]

In addition to the motifs already mentioned, one detects in this quotation a
certain ambivalence concerning Africa, a double-mindedness which follows
from what Du Bois called the "twoness" of the American Negro. On the one
hand, Africa is viewed positively: it is "home," the place of freedom and "opportunity," the source of "manhood." In these respects, the American black can identify with and affirm Africa. On the other hand, Africa is not source and giver, but
in need of what the Afro-American has to give. It is "Much in need of the
Gospel. . . . The work is before us, and we will do it, if we are possessed of race
pride." If this "race pride" includes the effort to Christianize Africa, as well as a
proper affirmation of what Africa is, it is clearly a complex concept, involving
ambivalence.

To recognize this complexity and ambivalence is to understand the basis for
significant differences which emerged between blacks of this period as to exactly
what constitutes the mission (and consequently, the manhood) of the black missionary to Africa. Most A.M.E. leaders reflected the dominant biases of western
culture, assuming that the role of the missionary was to replace African darkness
with Western Christian light. "Pursuing our onward march for the Dark Continent," says the Episcopal Address at the A.M.E. General Conference of 1896,

> we will speak to more than two hundred million of men and women, bone of
> our bone, and flesh of our flesh, and say to them, "Arise, and shine, for the
> light of civilization is waiting for thee."[28]

L. J. Coppin, A.M.E. Bishop of South Africa, writing on the topic "The Negro's
Part in the Redemption of Africa," said in 1902 that "In their isolated condition,
the people [of Africa] have for long centuries become the victims of customs
and habits not in keeping with the better life which is the result only of Christian
civilization."[29]

But there were a few A.M.E. leaders, the most noteworthy being Bishop
Henry M. Turner, who were convinced that Africa had as much to give the
American black as he had to give Africa—perhaps more. As a bishop, Turner was
concerned with Christianizing Africa, and he devoted great effort to raising
funds for African mission work, especially through publications such as the *Voice
of Missions*, which he founded in 1893 and edited until 1900. But he went beyond

missions, seeing emigration to Africa as the only satisfactory solution to the race problem in America, and he promoted and even sponsored various African colonization programs.

Turner saw the American black, surrounded as he was by a racist white majority, as schooled in contempt for himself, and as inevitably passing on this feeling of inferiority to his own children.

> Any people oppressed, proscribed, belied, slandered, burned, flayed and lynched will not only become cowardly and servile, but will transmit that same servility to their posterity, and continue to do so *ad infinitum*, and as such will never make a bold and courageous people. [30]

Therefore Turner concluded (in italics), "*There is no manhood future in the United States for the Negro*. He may eke out an existence for generations to come, but he can never be a *man*—full, symmetrical and undwarfed."[31] In contrast, the African black impressed Turner as embodying manliness in his very posture. "One thing the black man has here," he wrote from Africa, "and that is manhood, freedom and the fullest liberty. He feels like a lord and walks the same way."[32]

In Turner's view, Afro-American manhood could not be fulfilled simply by mission *to* Africa; it required mission *in* Africa, i.e., a large scale back-to-Africa movement by American blacks. "I believe that two or three millions of us should return to the land of our ancestors, and establish our own nation, civilization, laws, customs . . . and cease to be grumblers [in] the white man's country, or the country he claims and is bound to dominate."[33]

Like Turner, Professor Edward W. Blyden, who was among other things a clergyman, scholar, and Liberian government official, put forward in its most uncompromising form the argument that the manhood and mission of the black man was not here but in Africa. In his view, God had allowed African slaves to be brought to America so that they could be educated in Christianity, and then return home to Christianize Africa. In this way, Africans would receive Christianity through the tutelage of other Africans, instead of via the white man. "God sent us here to be trained that we might return to the land of our fathers and take charge of it, develop it and defined it."[34]

As these words suggest, Blyden went further in his analysis of divine providence than most black churchmen of the time: American blacks will not only teach Africa, they will emigrate to Africa and govern that land.

> You see then the field that lies before you. You see the reason that God is giving

you this schooling. It is to train you for the important duties, not here, but where there is a welcome field for your talent.[35]

Since the American black has this divine commission, he violates God's will when he seeks to deny his blackness.

> I have taken so much care, says the Lord, to preserve these black skins, and they are trying to extinguish themselves. You ought to see the importance of trying to preserve your race as purely as you can.[36]

African mission requires a pure black race, and black manhood will be fulfilled when it carries out its providential African mission.

MANHOOD AND MISSION TODAY

In the past the black church has, as we have seen, defined and embodied models of black manhood, and has associated that manhood with mission to Africa. This past tradition, so obviously relevant to many concerns of the contemporary black community, poses many questions for today's black church. Four such questions will be stated in this concluding section; the first two pertain to models of manhood, the second two have to do with the concept of mission to Africa.

1. Does the black church possess within itself, potentially if not actually, models of manhood adequate for the present, or must it look outside itself—to other black movements or ideologies—for models fully adequate for today?

This may seem at first like a strange question, one which must obviously be answered in the affirmative. But the answer is not so obvious. Criticism of the black church by black militants has forced some churchmen to be very sensitive, even defensive, about the church's "establishment" character. "To some Black people, especially many of the young Blacks, the very life, thought and style of the Black Church is seen as a gigantic sell-out of Black people."[37] Some black pastors have felt a pressure to identify with programs initiated by militants outside the church, or to turn over church facilities for use in these programs, without much time to ask whether the church has (or should have) its own program, and whether the church's program, if articulated, would harmonize with the militant one.

Some contemporary black theologians, while stressing the church's past contributions to the realization of black manhood, seem ready now to argue that, in the future, the church's contributions must be judged according to criteria from outside the church per se.

> It is this common experience among black people in America that Black
> Theology elevates as the supreme test of truth. To put it simply, Black
> Theology knows no authority more binding than the experience of oppression
> itself. . . . Concretely, this means that Black Theology is not prepared to accept
> any doctrine of God, man, Christ, or Scripture which contradicts the black
> demand for freedom now.[38]

Other black theologians show more awareness of the genuine tension that will
and must continue to exist between the church, which has traditional manhood
models of its own, and non-church black groups with which the church must
now work.

> Coalition formation is not always easy or smooth. It involves give and take . . .
> The Black Church will be pushed perhaps more than it will pull. . . . As coali-
> tions are formed, Black churchmen will need to clarify the distinct contribu-
> tion they have to offer out of their religious or theological perspective. . . .
> How does the Black Church distinguish itself from other organizations, even
> in coalitions, so that it can be itself and make its unique contributions?[39]

It seems clear that deciding between these two perspectives, or working out
some viable compromise between them, constitutes a major task for the black
church in the immediate future.

2. To what extent, and in what ways, can/does Jesus the Christ function in
the black church as a model of manhood adequate for the present, and what interpretive terms and symbols are required for a contemporary black christology?

Again, a strange-sounding question. If Jesus the Christ is not an adequate
model of manhood for the black church, who would be? In earlier decades, such
an answer—which dismisses the question—would have been quite appropriate.
Daniel Payne, for example, was quite clear that "The glorious manhood of Jesus
Christ is the only true type of real manhood. . . . Study him, study him as your
model; study the perfect model of manhood until he shall be conformed in
you."[40]

Today Payne's words are not sufficient because they take no account of what
Vincent Harding has called "the deep ambivalence of American Negroes to the
Christ we have encountered here."[41] This ambivalence has been there from the
beginning (see David Walker's *Appeal* of 1829), but only now is it fully and freely
articulated by blacks, many of whom are influenced by Malcolm X's forceful attacks on Christianity in his *Autobiography*. Addison Gayle, for example, addresses
this charge to the Christ: "You are the greatest slave master of them all. You

taught us to be good to our enemies, to love them, to forgive them. Holding out promises of heaven, you tied our hands and made us weak."[42]

Now that blacks, including black theological students, are speaking out against a Christ who has been co-opted as divine guardian of a white racist society (who has himself been "painted white and pink, blond and blue-eyed—and not only in white churches but in black churches as well"), the question is, Can Jesus the Christ function in the black church as a model of manhood adequate for the present, and if so, what interpretative terms and symbols will be most helpful in disclosing the "Black Messiah"?[43]

3. How should the black Christian church in America today understand its relation with black Africa: is the church the giver, or is it the recipient of Africa's gift?

I pose the question in this either/or form advisedly. Of course the black church may be *both* giver and receiver, just as it was in time past when, as we noted above, it recognized Africa as both the source of the black American's manhood and as in need of what the black American church had to give. But I am not sure the black church has ever, either in the past or the present, clearly recognized and analyzed its complex and perhaps ambivalent relation to Africa.

Most often the church of the past has spoken confidently of itself as the giver, as in the Episcopal Address of 1896 quoted above which invited Africa to "Arise, and shine, for the light of civilization is waiting for thee." Today black theologians reject such language as unconsciously reflecting the white-supremacist, Western-supremacist ideology so pervasive in white American Christianity. My question seeks to get at the issue: after this language is rejected, what language *should* be used? If Africa does not receive her light from the (Western) church, does she receive anything? If so, what? Does the black church in America receive from Africa? If so, from Christian Africa, or "traditional" Africa? And what does she receive?

These are anything but merely abstract questions. When John S. Mbiti, an African Christian theologian from Uganda, addressed black students at the Interdenominational Theological Center (October, 1970) on the topic "African Traditional Religions," the first question asked—and one that recurred again and again in a series of discussion sessions with Mbiti—was, Did Christian missionary work in Africa serve only to destroy African traditional religion and values, or did it also have some positive effects? Were this question posed by a black who has rejected the church, e.g., a Muslim, it would not be an expression of ambivalence. But when it is asked by a young black man preparing to enter the ministry of the Christian church, it is an expression of profound ambivalence toward the church and its mission. It suggests the need for some radical reflection on the relation between the black church and black Africa.

4. Does the black church (and more broadly, the black community) in America today possess a special mission beyond America, and if so is that mission best understood as having primarily a literal or a rhetorical-symbolic character?

This is a complex question, and one which receives quite divergent answers from different voices within the black community today. Some of these voices insist that the American black should abandon all thought of any mission to others, and concentrate his efforts on healing himself.

> We still have too much missionary zeal. We want to *light the lamp* for other
> nonwhites and whites as well. . . . It may be viewed as a come-down, as a withdrawal to halt our rhetoric (we still use it!) about showing the way for the balance of humanity but until we fully realize our responsibility to self, we'll be
> the laughing stock of the oppressed portion of the world.[44]

More common is the view that the American black should see his struggle as part of and essentially identical with the struggle of "oppressed," "colonized," "non-white," or "Third Word" peoples the world over. "We black Americans are . . . part of that fellowship of the disinherited which will surely inherit the earth in this century."[45]

It is easy to move from thinking of oneself as part of the oppressed to thinking of oneself as that vanguard which leads the oppressed (and perhaps the oppressor also) to freedom. "We are the ones who will save the world and bring a new day, a brilliantly alive society that swings and sings and rings out the world over for decency and honesty and sincerity and understanding and beauty and love. . . ."[46]

This view has had great impact on the thought of black churchmen and theologians. It led Martin Luther King, Jr., for example, to associate the black freedom movement with the worldwide struggle of the oppressed, and to suggest the possibility that the American black might constitute, through his nonviolent protest, the "new spiritual dynamic" required to save the world from self-destruction.

It makes a considerable difference, though, whether the black American's unity with the Third World and his special mission in that world is understood as having primarily a literal or a rhetorical-symbolic character.[47] If the unity/ mission concept is understood literally, we would not expect to find *fundamental* dissimilarities in the experiences, motives, concerns, and ideologies of black Americans and other nonwhites. If on the other hand the concept is rhetorical and symbolic, it may have great ideological value and significance, while still allowing for many and real differences to exist between the peoples involved.

To give a specific example, "Black Theology" is often discussed as if it were literally universal, a theology applicable to oppressed and/or nonwhite peoples the world over. Yet as David G. Gelzer has pointed out, "black theology and African theology are by no means the same." African theology was not born of slavery, does not aim at liberation from white racism, is "not a theology of blackness as forged by blacks for blacks," and does not in general pursue its task in a "hostile society."[48]

The concept of the unity of the darker races and of a special black mission in Africa has in the past had a tremendous rhetorical and symbolic significance within the black church and community. The power of the concept Black Mission in Africa during the period 1890–1900 went, as we have seen, far beyond the black church's actual, very limited commitment of funds and personnel to foreign mission work. It may be that this concept will continue to be of significance in the black church primarily for its symbolic rather than its literal truth, primarily for its expressive rather than its descriptive value.

NOTES

1. *Christianity and Crisis*, 30/18 (Nov. 2 and 16, 1970), 225, 229.

2. Vincent Harding, "Religion and Resistance Among Antebellum Negroes, 1800–1860," in August Meier and Elliott Rudwich (eds.), *The Making of Black America*, 1 (New York: Atheneum, 1969), p. 181.

3. B. W. Arnett (ed.), *Proceedings of the Quarto-Centennial Conference of the A.M.E. Church of South Carolina, May 15–17, 1889* (Charleston, S.C., 1890), p. 384.

4. Cf. Chapter 3, "Pioneer Negro Preachers," in Carter G. Woodson, *The History of the Negro Church* (Washington, D.C.: Associated Publishers, 1921).

5. W. E. B. Du Bois, *The Souls of Black Folk* (New York: Fawcett Publications, 1961), p. 141.

6. While it is true that the concept of black manhood and the explicit association between that manhood and mission to Africa are more pervasive and emphatic in the A.M.E. tradition than in that of other black churches, this is a difference of degree and not of kind. Study of historical works on other black denominations, both Baptist and Methodist, indicates that the generalizations which follow apply, in greater or lesser degree, to these as well as to the A.M.E. Church. This view will be documented in appropriate places by footnotes which refer to the National Baptist Convention, U.S.A., Inc., which is the largest of the black Baptist Churches—even as the A.M.E. Church is the largest black Methodist today.

7. Richard Allen, *The Life Experience and Gospel Labors of the Rt. Rev. Richard Allen*, n.d. (reprinted New York and Nashville: Abingdon Press, 1960), p. 25.

8. David Coker, "Sermon Delivered . . . January 1816 . . .," in Herbert Aptheker (ed.), *A Documentary History of the Negro People in the United States*, 1 (New York: Citadel Press, 1951), p. 68.

9. Daniel A. Payne, *A History of the A.M.E. Church, I, 1816–1856* (Nashville: A.M.E. Sunday School Union, 1891; reprinted New York: Arno Press, 1968), pp. 9–10, 12.

10. Cf. Josephus R. Coan, *Daniel Alexander Payne: Christian Educator* (Philadelphia: A.M.E. Book Concern, 1935).

11. Daniel A. Payne, *Recollections of Seventy Years* (Nashville: A.M.E. Sunday School Union, 1888; reprinted New York: Arno Press, 1968), p. 287.

12. Charles S. Smith, *A History of the A.M.E. Church, II, 1856–1922* (Philadelphia: A.M.E. Book Concern, 1922; reprinted New York: Johnson Reprint Corp., 1968), p. 395.

13. Ibid., pp. 17, 52, 54.

14. Ibid., p. 67. Similar language is found in the histories of the National Baptist Convention, U.S.A., Inc. Edward A. Freeman, in his *The Epoch of Negro Baptists and the Foreign Mission Board* (Kansas City, KA: The Central Seminary Press, 1953), describes John Jasper, one of the pioneer Baptist preachers, as a "personality who towers like a mighty oak above the horizon of the past and his contemporaries." He was "full of dangerous energies, almost gigantic in his muscles, . . . with a self-assertion that made him a leader within the circles of his freedom. . . . He was too decided, too aggressive . . . to be popular" (pp. 39–40). Freeman quotes a contemporary of the Baptist preacher Walter H. Brooks, who wrote: "Dr. Brooks . . . believed in Negro manhood; he opposed anything or anybody who antagonizes the manly development of the Negro" (p. 54). *The Story of the National Baptists,* by Owen D. Pelt and Ralph L. Smith (New York: Vantage Press, 1960), treats the early black Baptist preachers in a chapter entitled "The Heroic Age," arguing that, given the conditions under which they had to work, "the early pioneers of the Negro Baptist Church can certainly be called heroes—heroes both in mind and of spirit" (p. 34).

15. Smith, *History of the A.M.E. Church*, p. 22.

16. Ibid., pp. 101–02.

17. Ibid., p. 395.

18. Ibid., pp. 102–03.

19. It must be stressed that the question being posed here has to do, not with the *quantity* of effort and treasure expended by the black church in Africa (which was relatively small), but rather with the issue, why did the church attempt *any* effort in Africa, and why did the church make that effort so central in its missionary rhetoric, given its shortage of money and trained leaders, and the tremendous mission task it faced at home. The black church was terribly poor, and in spite of eloquent pleas and programs, never mustered either a large number of missionaries, nor sufficient funds to support them. The *Voice of Missions* published many poignant

letters sent home by A.M.E. missionaries in Liberia and Sierra Leone during the 1890s, letters which plead for financial support from the church, and which sometimes betray the disappointment of troops who feel abandoned in the field.

The average annual receipts of the Department of Missions *(both* home and foreign) of the A.M.E. Church during the period 1881–84 were $8,702.95, less than 3% of the $381,878 appropriated for missions by the Methodist Episcopal Church in 1884. (Cf. Coan, *Expansion of Missions*, p. 39).

The Foreign Missionary Board of the National Baptist Convention, Inc., raised a little more than four thousand dollars in 1897, about eighty-five hundred dollars in 1901. (Cf. Freeman, pp. 118, 122).

20. Smith, *History of the A.M.E. Church*, p. 332.

21. Daniel A. Payne, "The Past, Present and Future of the A.M.E. Church," *A.M.E. Church Review*, 1/4 (April, 1885), 314–15, 318–19.

22. Smith, *History of the A.M.E. Church*, p. 178.

23. Ibid., p. 26.

24. Josephus Coan, *The Expansion of Missions of the African Methodist Episcopal Church in South Africa, 1896–1908*. Unpublished doctoral dissertation (Hartford Seminary Foundation, 1961), p. 50.

25. Cf. Ibid., p. 61.

26. Cf. Smith, *History of the A.M.E. Church*, p. 21. Black Baptists were speaking and hearing similar calls to African mission during this same period. W. W. Colley, who had served as an African Missionary (commissioned by the Southern Baptists) from 1875–79, returned to the South in 1879 to organize the Foreign Mission Convention of black Baptists. "He urged upon his brethren the moral responsibility that, since God had blessed them with the light of his Word, it was their sacred responsibility to send it to their brethren in that benighted land." (Freeman, *Epoch of Negro Baptists*, p. 70). The Preamble of the Convention's Constitution, adopted in 1880, contains the statement that "African Missions claim our most profound attention, and [we feel] that we are most sacredly called to do work in this field and elsewhere abroad" (p. 73). Since the organization of this missionary Convention preceded, and to some extent precipitated, the organization of the National Baptist Convention, Inc., in 1895, Pelt and Smith conclude that "it is hardly an exaggeration to say that the wish to do missionary work in Africa created the National Baptist Convention" (*Story of National Baptists*, p. 149). This wish sometimes led Baptists, as it did the A.M.E., to put aside home mission tasks for the sake of African mission. "In view of the low state of our funds, and the importance of the prosecution of the african Missions, therefore we recommend that our strength and means be mostly directed to that field until the mission there is established." (C.C. Adams and Marshall A. Talley, *Negro Baptists and Foreign Missions* (Philadelphia: National Baptist Convention, U.S.A., 1944), p. 31).

27. Arnett, *Proceedings*, p. 139.

28. Coan, *Expansion of Missions*, p. 51.

29. L. J. Coppin, "The Negro's Part in the Redemption of Africa," *A.M.E. Church Review*, 19/2 (Oct., 1902), p. 507.

30. Henry M. Turner, "The American Negro and the Fatherland," in J. W. E. Bowen (ed.), *Africa and the American Negro: Addresses and Proceedings of the Congress on Africa, December 13–15, 1895* (Atlanta: Franklin Press, 1896), p. 197.

31. *Ibid.*, p. 195.

32. Turner as quoted in Edwin S. Redkey, *Black Exodus: Black Nationalist and Back-to-Africa Movements, 1890–1910* (New Haven: Yale Univ. Press, 1969), p. 44.

33. Turner, *American Negro and Fatherland*, p. 196.

34. Arnett, *Proceedings*, p. 133.

35. Ibid., p. 136.

36. Ibid., pp. 135–36.

37. *Christianity and Crisis*, 30/18, p. 232.

38. James H. Cone, *Black Theology and Black Power* (New York: Seabury Press, 1969), p. 120.

39. *Christianity and Crisis*, 30/18, p. 234.

40. Charles S. Smith (ed.), *Sermons Delivered by Bishop Daniel A. Payne Before the General Conference of the A.M.E. Church* (Nashville, 1888), pp. 58, 64.

41. Vincent Harding, "Black Power and the American Christ," *Risk*, 4/1, (1968), p. 26.

42. Addison Gayle, *The Black Situation* (New York: Horizon Press, 1970), p. 132.

43. For some preliminary efforts to deal with this question see Albert B. Cleage, Jr., *The Black Messiah* (New York: Sheed and Ward, 1968); James H. Cone, *A Black Theology of Liberation* (New York: J.B. Lippincott Co., 1970), especially chap. 6; and W.H. Becker, "Black Power in Christological Perspective," *Religion in Life* 38/3 (Autumn, 1969).

44. Robert Bowen in a letter published in *The Black Scholar*, 2/4 (December, 1970), p. 55.

45. John Oliver Killens, as quoted in Vincent Harding, "The Religion of Black Power," *The Religious Situation: 1968*, ed. by Donald Cutler (Boston: Beacon Press, 1968), p. 14.

46. Ronald Fair, as quoted in Vincent Harding, "The Religion of Black Power," *The Religious Situation: 1968*, ed. by Donald Cutler (Boston: Beacon Press, 1968), p. 14.

47. In our literalistic (yet somehow fantastic) age, I should stress that I use the terms rhetorical and symbolic as terms of high value, and in no sense as pejorative. Rhetoric, according to Webster, is "the art of expressive speech or of discourse, originally of oratory"; the symbol, according to Tillich, points beyond itself to some other reality, "participates in that to which it points," and thereby "opens up levels of reality which otherwise are closed for us."

48. David G. Gelzer, "Random Notes on Black Theology and African Theology," *The Christian Century*, 87/37 (September 16, 1970), 1091–92.

SELECTED BIBLIOGRAPHY FOR FURTHER READING

Angell, Stephen Ward. *Bishop Henry McNeal Turner and African-American Religion in the South*. Knoxville: University of Tennessee Press, 1992.

Jacobs, Sylvia M., ed. *Black Americans and the Missionary Movement in Africa*. Westport, CT: Greenwood, 1982.

Litwack, Leon. *Been in the Storm So Long: The Aftermath of Slavery*. New York: Random House, 1979.

Walker, Clarence E. *A Rock in a Weary Land: The African Methodist Episcopal Church During the Civil War and Reconstruction*. Baton Rouge: Louisiana State University Press, 1982.

Williams, Walter L. *Black Americans and the Evangelization of Africa, 1877–1900*. Madison: University of Wisconsin Press, 1982.

Evelyn Brooks Higginbotham

:: As the reader might rightly note, it is impossible today to pose important questions about the models of "black manhood" without any question of gender. In the following essay, Evelyn Brooks Higginbotham demonstrates that a fuller understanding of the African-American church must address gender as well as race and class, and argues that a more complete examination of women in black churches must also look beyond female preachers. ::

THE BLACK CHURCH

A Gender Perspective

Evelyn Brooks Higginbotham

*As I look about me today in this veiled world of mine, despite
the noisier and more spectacular advance of my brothers,
I instinctively feel and know that it is the five million women
of my race who really count. Black women (and women whose
grandmothers were black) are . . . the main pillars of those
social settlements which we call churches; and they have with
small doubt raised three-fourths of our church property.*

——W. E. B. DU BOIS, *Darkwater* (1918)

:: **M**uch has been written about the importance of the black church in the social and political life of black people. Much less has been written about black women's importance in the life of the church. This book is a study of women in the black church between 1880 and 1920—a period that has come to be known simultaneously as the "woman's era" and the "nadir" in America race relations. I argue that women were crucial to broadening the public arm of the church and making it the most powerful institution of racial self-help in the African-American community. During these years, the church served as the most effective vehicle by which men and women alike, pushed down by racism and poverty, regrouped and rallied against emotional and physical defeat.

In some instances, church women contested racist ideology and institutions through demands for anti-lynching legislation and an end to segregation laws. They expressed their discontent with both racial and gender discrimination and demanded equal rights for blacks and women—advocating voting rights or equal employment and educational opportunities. Black women even drew upon the Bible, the most respected source within their community, to fight for women's rights in the church and society at large. During the late nineteenth century they developed a distinct discourse of resistance, a feminist theology. More often, however, their efforts represented not dramatic protest but everyday forms of resistance to oppression and demoralization. Largely through the fund-raising efforts of women, the black church built schools, provided clothes and food to poor people, established old folks' homes and orphanages, and made available a host of needed social welfare services.

This study attempts to rescue women from invisibility as historical actors in the drama of black empowerment. Since women have traditionally constituted the majority of every black denomination, I present the black church not as the exclusive product of a male ministry but as the product and process of male and female interaction. In offering a corrective to the near exclusion of women in most studies of the black church, my book departs from the more recent and positive discussion of exceptional women, the early women preachers.[1] Research on women preachers, while of great value, does not capture the more representative role of the majority of women church members. If taken alone, such discussion continues to render women's role as marginal. Left obscured is the interrelation between the rising black churches in the late nineteenth and early twentieth centuries and the indefatigable efforts of black women's organizations. Left unheard are women's voices within the public discourse of racial and gender self-determination. In short, the focus on the ministry fails to capture adequately the gender dimension of the church's racial mission. Ultimately, my study provides a vantage point for viewing the interplay of race, gender, and class consciousness, for it presents the church, like the black community it mirrors, as social space of unifying and conflicting discourses.

I have focused my attention on the movement that brought into existence the National Baptist Convention, U.S.A., Inc. This movement represented and continues to represent the largest group—religious or secular—of black Americans. To persons not versed in church history, the term "convention" might bring to mind an annual meeting or tangential association. In the history of black Baptists, however, "convention" has almost the same meaning as "denomination." The black Baptist convention is distinct from that of white Baptists and emerged only because otherwise autonomous black Baptist churches voluntarily and freely come together.[2] Their collective association, beginning first at the state level and eventually embracing a national constituency, effected an unprecedented arena for public discussion and mobilization of resources on the part of African Americans.

Although conventions did not originate with late nineteenth-century black Baptists, their profound importance rests in their deployment as vehicles of black identity and empowerment. Ironically, it was the issue of slavery in 1844 that divided white Baptists into northern and southern conventions.[3] The close of the

Civil War did not heal the rift among white Baptists, but it did give black Baptists the opportunity to forge a national unity and identity of their own. The decision to form a black national convention was motivated by discriminatory policies on the part of white Baptists, as well as by the growing support among African Americans in general for racial self-determination.[4]

James Melvin Washington's *Frustrated Fellowship: The Black Baptist Quest for Social Power* (1985) remains the most comprehensive discussion of the racial tensions that spurred the evolution of the black Baptist movement. Washington and others have described its separatist, indeed nationalist character as informed by philosophies of racial self-help and racial self-determination. But in chronicling the events that led to the development of the black Baptist church as a potent national force, they have focused overwhelmingly on the contributions of outstanding ministers within male-dominated state and national conventions.[5]

Black Baptist churchmen certainly recognized the importance of women's active support for the denomination's efforts toward racial self-help and self-reliance. Yet male-biased traditions and rules of decorum sought to mute women's voices and accentuate their subordinate status vis-à-vis men. Thus tainted by the values of the larger American society, the black church sought to provide men with full manhood rights, while offering women a separate and unequal status. As we will see in the chapters that follow, however complex the black Baptist women's own ideas were concerning separate roles for men and women—or the approximate sexual division of labor—they would not lightly accept their own subordination in the struggle of their people.

THE BLACK CHURCH DURING THE NADIR

The nationalist consciousness of the black Baptist church came of age during the years of heightened racism that followed Reconstruction. In 1880, when black Baptists took the first step toward creating a permanent national structure, the halcyon days of voting and political ferment among southern blacks had given way to growing disillusionment.[6] By 1890, it had become preeminently clear that the black community would have to devise its own strategies of social and political advancement. In that year Mississippi adopted a disfranchisement plan that served as a model to the rest of the South. Disfranchisement formed part of the larger process of "depoliticalization": literacy tests, poll taxes, and other state election laws, along with social and psychological sanctions such as economic reprisal, violence, and threats of violence, effected the mass removal of blacks from the nation's political life. Political institutions and representative government became simply inaccessible and unaccountable to American citizens who happened to be black.[7]

Black men lost more than the ballot on election day. They lost many other rights, which theoretically the constitution and federal civil rights laws protected: the right to hold public office, sit on juries, allocate tax dollars for schools and other social services, protect their women and themselves from insult and victimization, and share in other basic human and citizenship rights. Black women, like all American women, had never shared political equality with their men. Once black men were denied the suffrage, however, black women became ever more powerless and vulnerable to southern racial hostility.[8]

As southern state after state during the 1880s and 1890s set in motion a barrage of discriminatory laws that routinized the separate and inferior status of blacks, violence and intimidation solidified the "Negro's place" in the New South. Between 1884 and 1900 more than 2,500 lynchings of blacks were recorded. American race relations reached an all-time low—the "nadir," as Rayford Logan termed the disquieting times.[9] "Jim Crow," as segregation was called, quickly pervaded every part of life and made itself felt even in death. In employment, housing, places of amusement, public transportation, schools, hospitals, and cemeteries, segregation daily produced and reproduced racial identities, power, and disempowerment. During the nadir, black communities turned increasingly inward. They struggled without the aid or protection of the federal government; worse yet, they suffered its policies of betrayal. In 1883 the Supreme Court had declared unconstitutional the federal Civil Rights Act of 1875, a law prohibiting racial discrimination in places of public accommodation. In 1896 the Court announced its sanction of the "separate but equal" doctrine.[10]

Powerless to avert the mounting tide of racist public opinion, black people struggled to maintain family and community cohesiveness in an environment that sought to tear them asunder. African Americans, looking now to themselves to educate the masses of their people, care for the needy, facilitate economic development, and address political concerns, tapped their greatest strength from the tradition of their churches.[11] From the early days of slavery, the black church had constituted the backbone of the black community. Truly African American in its origins, it provided a spiritual cohesiveness that permitted its people to absorb, interpret, and practice the Christian faith—to make it their own. As the "invisible institution" of the slaves, the church had long promoted a sense of individual and collective worth and perpetuated a belief in human dignity that countered the racist preachings of the master class.[12] In the decades following

Reconstruction, the church's autonomy and financial strength made it the most logical institution for the pursuit of racial self-help. It functioned not only as the house of worship, but also as an agency of social control, forum of discussion and debate, promoter of education and economic cooperation, and arena for the development and assertion of leadership.

Recognizing its diverse roles, E. Franklin Frazier termed the black church a veritable "nation within a nation."[13] At the individual level, but especially when collectively joined in association, black churches represented not an escapist and otherworldly orientation but the only viable bastion of a community under assault. If for many of its members the black church remained a focus for the perpetuation of community identity, for many of its leaders it became the vehicle for consolidating every existing strength into a concerted campaign for racial self-reliance. Those who sought to make the church the flagship of black dignity espoused strong race-conscious views concerning the preservation of the black community, and, just as important, they sought to shape the community so that preservation could become progress.

Race consciousness reached its apogee with the creation of the National Baptist Convention, U.S.A. in 1895. Determined to create a forum through which black people could voice their spiritual, economic, political, and social concerns, the convention's leaders equated racial self-determination with black denominational hegemony. These ideas were not unique to the black Baptist church. The African Methodist Episcopal Church had emerged as a separate denomination during the dawning years of the nineteenth century.[14] By the late nineteenth and early twentieth centuries all the black denominations had established community institutions and advanced the philosophy of racial self-help. But it was in the black Baptist church where this philosophy found its largest following.

Black Baptists constituted the most numerically significant attempt to counter the debilitating intent and effects of American racial exclusivism, and thus their story broadly characterizes the black church and black community. The National Baptist Convention, which existed apart from the powerful white Northern Baptist Convention and Southern Baptist Convention, constituted the largest and most representative sample of the black churchgoing population. In 1906 it had 2,261,607 members, while the second largest denominational membership, African Methodist Episcopal, had only 494,777. The National Baptist Convention included 61.4 percent of all black church members in the United States.[15] By 1916 National Baptists numbered 2,938,579. The convention was larger than any other black religious group and larger than either of the two major white Baptist groups, namely, the Northern Baptist Convention with 1,232,135 or the Southern Baptist Convention with 2,708,870.[16] The numerical power of the black Baptist convention appears even more dramatic when compared against the other white denominations. In 1916 it ranked as the third largest religious body in the United States—trailing only the Roman Catholic and Methodist Episcopal churches.

The great majority of the convention's members, like the great majority of blacks themselves, lived in the South and in areas with populations under 25,000. But its leaders hailed from towns and cities, and thus the bulk of its programs were there. The convention's urban presence steadily increased as blacks began to migrate in larger and larger numbers to southern and northern cities. In 1906 the National Baptist Convention constituted the largest denomination, black or white, in Atlanta, Memphis, and Richmond. By 1916 it took the lead in Birmingham and Nashville, while continuing to dominate in Memphis and Richmond. In Louisville, Washington, DC, and New Orleans, it was second only to the Catholic church, while its numbers grew exponentially in Philadelphia, Pittsburgh, and Chicago.[17] By sheer size alone, the black Baptist church formed a microcosm of the black population in America and included men and women from all social classes and geographic regions.

THE BLACK CHURCH AS PUBLIC SPHERE

By law, blacks were denied access to public space, such as parks, libraries, restaurants, meeting halls, and other public accommodations. In time the black church —open to both secular and religious groups in the community—came to signify public space. It housed a diversity of programs including schools, circulating libraries, concerts, restaurants, insurance companies, vocational training, athletic clubs—all catering to a population much broader than the membership of individual churches. The church served as meeting hall for virtually every large gathering. It held political rallies, clubwomen's conferences, and school graduations. It was the one space truly accessible to the black community, and it was this characteristic that led W.E.B. Du Bois, long before E. Franklin Frazier, to identify the black church as a multiple site—at once being a place of worship, theater, publishing house, school, and lodge.[18]

The church also functioned as a discursive, critical arena—a public sphere in which values and issues were aired, debated, and disseminated throughout the larger black community. The black Baptist convention movement facilitated the sharing and distribution of information through periodic statewide and national meetings, where thousands gathered and discussed issues of civic concern. Since black women constituted two-thirds of this movement, they had a crucial role in the formation of public sentiment and in the expression of a black collective will. Particularly through women's efforts, black communities with very limited income raised funds sufficient to build and sustain churches, schools, and social welfare services. At times in concert and at times in conflict with their men, black women initiated race-conscious programs of self-help.

The very nationalist discourse that unified black men and women betrayed inherent gender conflict. As a deliberative arena, the National Baptist Convention sought to speak for both men and women, but it did not encourage expression from men and women as equals. The convention's masculine bias was evident in its institutional structures and discourses. Positions of authority and power were monopolized by men. Thus women sought to develop their own voice and pursue their own interests, which at times overlapped and at other times contested the men's. Rising gender consciousness was part of a complex of ideas that informed black Baptist denominational work as a whole.

In 1900 women succeeded in forming an alternate sphere of deliberation within the larger denominational context of the National Baptist Convention. The Woman's Convention, defined as an auxiliary to the NBC, summoned a sisterhood more than one million strong and culminated nearly three decades of work by women's organizations at the local and state levels. Through their convention, black women shared knowledge of their state and local activities. They governed their own members, initiated their own agenda, elected their own leaders, and developed criteria that won respect and emulation from other women. In 1909 the convention boasted of having established the first school for black women that black women themselves owned. Through their school and their national convention, black Baptist women challenged many of the real and symbolic barriers that others—white Americans in general and even black men—sought to impose upon them in the church and larger society.[19] Rather than diminishing racial solidarity, rising gender consciousness made possible the effective drive toward a national black Baptist identity.

Through a racial and gender-based movement, black women confronted and influenced their social and political milieu, and they did so through the mediating influence of the church. According to Peter Berger and Richard Neuhaus, "mediating structures" constitute part of the public realm. They stand between private citizens and the large, impersonal institutions of public life, such as the government, and produce meaningful value systems as well as concrete mechanisms for ordering people's lives and addressing needs.[20] More effectively than any other institution, the church stood between individual blacks, on the one hand, and the state with its racially alienating institutions, on the other. The church's ability to sustain numerous newspapers, schools, social welfare services, jobs, and recreational facilities mitigated the dominant society's denial of these resources to black communities. And it was primarily the fund-raising activity of black women that undergirded the church's mediating function.

In characterizing the black church as a public sphere, my analysis moves in a different direction from such conceptual models as "civil religion" or "public religion." The concept of civil religion, made popular and controversial by Robert N. Bellah, calls attention to the character and role of religious symbolism in American political life. It locates religious symbols outside the confines of the church and asserts their life and meaning in expressions of patriotism, the general understanding and articulation of American national identity, and in public rituals and ceremonies such as holidays and presidential inaugurations.[21] Instead, my book stresses the public character and role of the black church. This is no small difference. The religious symbolism of the nation's public life—its collective thanksgivings and civic piety—held problematic and contradictory meanings for African Americans.[22] Frederick Douglass conveyed this point eloquently before a crowd of white Americans on the Fourth of July in 1852. Contrasting their celebration of liberty with the enslavement of his own people, Douglass called the Independence Day festivities "sacrilegious" and proceeded with this jeremiad: "Your prayers and hymns, your sermons and thanksgivings, with all your religious parade and solemnity, are to Him [God], mere bombast, fraud, deception, impiety, and hypocrisy."[23]

For African Americans, long excluded from political institutions and denied presence, even relevance, in the dominant society's myths about its heritage and national community, the church itself became the domain for the expression, celebration, and pursuit of a black collective will and identity. At issue here is the public dimension of the black church, not the religious dimension of the public realm. The question is not how religious symbols and values were promoted in American politics, but how public space, both physical and discursive, was interpolated within black religious institutions. Indeed, scholars of African-American religion do not tend to utilize the concept of civil religion. For example, James Melvin Washington inverts Sidney Mead's usage of Chesterton's phrase—the "nation with the soul of a church"—by describing black Baptists as having a "church with the soul of a nation."[24]

In the closed society of Jim Crow, the church afforded African Americans an interstitial space in which to critique and contrast white America's racial domination. In addition, the church offered black women a forum through which to articulate a public discourse critical of women's subordination. A gender perspective on the black church facilitates understanding the church's public dimension, since, in emphasizing discursive interaction between men and women, such a perspective more accurately portrays the church's extensive activities and influence at the grass roots level. I describe the black church not as the embodiment of ministerial authority or of any individual's private interests and pronouncements, but as a social space for discussion of public concerns. During the late nineteenth and early twentieth centuries, the church came to represent a deliberative arena, whose character derived from the collective nature of the church itself, namely, as a body of many diverse members, and from race-conscious feelings of nationalism.[25]

My analysis of the black church finds conceptual utility in the scholarly literature that has been inspired by Jürgen Habermas's formulation of the "public sphere." Habermas identified the public sphere as a historically situated and institutionalized discursive realm. It mediated between private citizens (civil society) and the state and afforded an arena for the rational formation and functioning of information, in other words, public opinion. In the collective effort to arrive at a "common good," public opinion emerged, Habermas posited, as "the tasks of criticism and control which a public body of citizens informally—and, in periodic elections, formally as well—practices vis-à-vis the ruling structure organized in the form of a state."[26] Thus separate and independent of the state and also the market economy, the public sphere operated as a realm where all citizens interacted in reasoned discourse, even in criticism of governmental authority.

Critics of Habermas question his idealization of the liberal or bourgeois public sphere, and they especially criticize his failure to explore more fully competing, non-bourgeois publics.[27] They pluralize the "public sphere" concept in order to represent, at specific historical moments, a number of groups and interests that stand in oppositional relationship within societies stratified along racial, class, and gender lines. These numerous "publics" may overlap, but more often conflict—becoming oppositional or "counter-publics."[28] While these scholars focus upon neither the black church, nor black women, their critiques of Habermas are especially illuminating for asserting a variety of public arenas in which people participate.

When E. Franklin Frazier termed the black church a "nation within a nation," he conveyed the meaning of a "counter-public sphere." Frazier's metaphor of the black church as nation suggests a public distinct from and in conflict with the dominant white society and its racist institutional structures. The church-spon-

sored press played an instrumental role in the dissemination of a black oppositional discourse and in the creation of a black collective will. As black literacy
rose from a mere 5 percent in 1860 to 70 percent in 1910, the church served as a
major site of print production in black communities. Penelope Bullock's study of
the black periodical press notes that churches, particularly the Baptist, A.M.E.,
and A.M.E. Zion churches, took the lead in the publication of general magazines
in the post-Reconstruction era. For example, the anti-lynching newspaper *The
Free Speech and Headlight* of Memphis, which was made famous by Ida B. Wells,
was a black Baptist-owned newspaper.[29] Black Baptist state conventions, men's
and women's, figured prominently in newspaper publication during the late
nineteenth century. In 1900 black Baptists at the local and state levels published
forty-three newspapers, the great majority of which were located in the South.[30]
This role of the church cannot be overstated, since there were no black newspapers with massive national distribution; nor were the ideas and activities of
blacks considered newsworthy to the white press except in the most derogatory
and repressive way.

The role of publishing was vital to the creation of a black civic vision. The
National Baptist Magazine, publication of the National Baptist Convention, defined its scope as "devoted to the interests of the Negro Race in general."[31] The
magazine featured articles and editorials on a variety of subjects, including black
history, lynching, presidential elections, industrial education, and segregation on
railroads. The publishing board of the National Baptist Convention reported a
circulation of more than 13 million issues of various tracts and booklets between
1900 and 1903. The press published religious materials, but it also conceived of
its mission as "moulding the doctrines and opinions and shaping the destiny of the
future church and race." The National Baptist Convention unquestioningly
viewed itself as a public in opposition to white America, and it referred to the
importance of its press in this context: "The Negro Baptists of this country . . .
must discuss, produce or provide literature capable of keeping the identity and
increasing race pride of the rising generation or they must be entirely overshadowed by the dominant race of this country."[32]

The formation of the National Baptist convention, U.S.A. and its auxiliary
women's convention afforded black men and women social space in which to
critique openly the United States government, its laws, and its institutions. In
fact, the level of public discussion caused one of the leaders of the Woman's
Convention to come under government surveillance.[33] There were also subtle,
perhaps more far-reaching political implications. The Baptist convention offered
black men and women a structure for electing representatives, debating issues,

and exercising many rights that white society denied them. Benjamin Mays and Joseph Nicholson, pointing to this surrogate political role, state that the "local churches, associations, conventions, and conferences become the Negro's Democratic and Republican Conventions, his Legislature and his Senate and House of Representatives."[34] Through their conventions, African Americans refuted notions of their inability or unreadiness for equal political participation. Among women, this understanding heightened support of women's suffrage. The political rhetoric espoused at black women's annual meetings included the demand not only for voting rights, but for full inclusion in American public life.

The black church constituted a public that stood in opposition to the dominant white public, and yet as the case of women illustrates, it did not form a monolith. Nor did it reveal values completely independent of white America. A gender perspective on the church lends clarity to this matter, since it locates different sites in which black women both embraced and contested the dominant values and norms of northern white Baptists, white women, and even black men. For example, during the 1880s and 1890s, southern black and northern white Baptist women worked in a cooperative fashion rare for the times.[35] Their cooperation was not based upon identical motives and interests, but it indicated that divergent motives did not preclude mutual goals. Together, black and white women spread the Gospel, supported one another's organizations, financed black education, and alleviated the plight of the poor. The women's movement in the black Baptist church imagined itself both as part of the black community and as part of an evangelical sisterhood that cut across racial lines.[36] That black women voiced the race-conscious interests and agenda of the male-dominated movement precluded neither interracial cooperation with white women nor conflict with black men.

CHURCH WOMEN'S MULTIPLE CONSCIOUSNESS

During the late nineteenth and early twentieth centuries, laws and changing social attitudes were chipping away at barriers to women's right to property, to education, to the professions, and even to suffrage in the western states of Wyoming in 1890 and in 1896 in Utah, Colorado, and Idaho.[37] During the latter decades of the nineteenth century white and black women joined in religious associations and secular clubs to bring about social reform. They fought for temperance, educational opportunity, suffrage, and a variety of gender-related issues. "To be alive at such an epoch is a privilege, to be a woman then is sublime," proclaimed the black educator and feminist Anna J. Cooper during the heady times of the "woman's era."[38] Cooper's exhilaration expressed nothing less than the black Baptist women's rising expectations.

The years between 1890 and 1920 witnessed significant strides for women. The number of all women with professional degrees rose by 226 percent.[39] Hazel Carby notes the increase of black women writers during the decade of the nineties. Anna J. Cooper published her feminist critique *A Voice from the South* (1892); other publications included Ida B. Wells, *On Lynchings* (1892) and Gertrude Mossell, *The Work of the Afro-American Woman* (1894). Black women established their literary presence in novels: Amelia E. Johnson's *Clarence and Corinne* (1890) and *The Hazely Family* (1894); Emma Dunham Kelley's *Megda* (1891); Frances Ellen Watkins Harper's *Iola Leroy* (1892); and Victoria Earle's *Aunt Lindy* (1893). Moreover, black women's writings drew attention and praise in the burgeoning field of journalism, as was reflected by the chapter devoted to them in I. Garland Penn's *The Afro-American Press and Its Editors* (1890).[40]

The cynical era of Jim Crow and the optimistic woman's era stood entangled one with the other—their imbrication giving shape to the black Baptist women's nationalist, yet feminist appeal. The complexity of the racial and gender meanings of the age suggests both the multiple consciousness and multiple positioning of black women, and also the complexity of the black church itself—an institution overwhelmingly female in membership. The church, like the black community, cannot be viewed solely through the lens of race. A gender perspective on the black church reminds us that the history of African Americans cannot be excluded from the important effort to identify and study social relations between men and women.

The history of black Baptist women discloses not only the gender dimension of the church's racial mission, but its class dimension as well.[41] The leadership of the women's convention movement formed part of an emergent class of school administrators, journalists, businesswomen, and reformers who served an all-black community. This educated female elite, frequently consisting of teachers or wives of ministers associated with educational institutions, promoted middle-class ideals among the masses of blacks in the belief that such ideals ensured the dual goals of racial self-help and respect from white America. Especially in the roles of missionary and teacher, black church women were conveyers of culture and vital contributors to the fostering of middle-class ideals and aspirations in the black community. Duty-bound to teach the value of religion, education, and hard work, the women of the black Baptist church adhered to a politics of respectability that equated public behavior with individual self-respect and with the advancement of African Americans as a group. They felt certain that "respectable" behavior in public would earn their people a measure of esteem from white America, and hence they strove to win the black lower class's psychological allegiance to temperance, industriousness, thrift, refined manners, and Victorian sexual morals.

On the one hand the politics of respectability rallied poor working-class blacks to the cause of racial self-help, by inspiring them to save, sacrifice, and pool their scant resources for the support of black-owned institutions. Whether through white-imposed segregation or black-preferred separatism, the black community's support of its middle class surely accounted for the development and growth of black-owned institutions, including those of the Baptist Church. On the other hand, the effort to forge a community that would command whites' respect revealed class tensions among blacks themselves. The zealous efforts of black women's religious organizations to transform certain behavioral patterns of their people disavowed and opposed the culture of the "folk"—the expressive culture of many poor, uneducated, and "unassimilated" black men and women dispersed through the rural South or newly huddled in urban centers.[42]

The Baptist women's preoccupation with respectability reflected a bourgeois vision that vacillated between an attack on the failure of America to live up to its liberal ideals of equality and justice and an attack on the values and lifestyle of those blacks who transgressed white middle-class propriety. Thus the women's pronouncements appeared to swing from radical to conservative. They revealed their conservatism when they attributed institutional racism to the "negative" public behavior of their people—as if rejection of "gaudy" colors in dress, snuff dipping, baseball games on Sunday, and other forms of "improper" decorum could eradicate the pervasive racial barriers that surrounded black Americans. The Baptist women never conceded that rejection of white middle-class values by poor blacks afforded survival strategies, in fact spaces of resistance, albeit different from their own. Equally important, while the female leaders of the black Baptist church sought to broaden women's job opportunities and religious responsibilities, they revealed their conservatism in their unquestioning acceptance of man's sole right to the clergy.

LEGACY OF RESISTANCE

Despite the limits of their movement, black Baptist women left an impressive record of protest against the racist and sexist proscriptions of their day. Eugene Genovese has written that "the living history of the church has been primarily a history of submission to class stratification and the powers that be, but there has remained, despite all attempts at extirpation, a legacy of resistance that could appeal to certain parts of the New Testament and especially to the prophetic parts of the Old."[43] Exposing the black church's public dimension does not invalidate the centrality of its spiritual dimension in the private lives of black people or in the life of the black community. However, my interpretation of the church and black church women stresses the imbrication of the social and the spiritual within a context akin, but not identical, to what C. Eric Lincoln and Lawrence Mamiya call the "dialectical model of the black church." For Lincoln and Mamiya, this model postulates the black church to be in "dynamic tension" within a series of dialectical polarities: priestly versus prophetic functions; other-worldly versus this-worldly; particularism versus universalism; privatistic versus communal; charismatic versus bureaucratic; and accommodation versus resistance.[44]

I characterize the church as a dialogic model rather than dialectical, recognizing "dynamic tension" in a multiplicity of protean and concurrent meanings and intentions more so than in a series of discrete polarities. Multiple discourses—sometimes conflicting, sometimes unifying—are articulated between men and women, and within each of these two groups as well. The black church constitutes a complex body of shifting cultural, ideological and political significations. It represents a "heteroglot" conception in the Bakhtinian sense of a multiplicity of meanings and intentions that interact and condition each other.[45] Such multiplicity transcends polarity—thus tending to blur the spiritual and secular, the eschatological and political, and the private and public. The black church represented the realm where individual souls communed intimately with God and where African Americans as a people freely discussed, debated, and devised an agenda for their common good. At the same time that church values and symbols ordered the epistemological and ontological understandings of each individual and gave meaning to the private sphere of family—both as conjugal household and as "household of faith"—church values and symbols helped to spawn the largest number of voluntary associations in the black community. It follows logically, then, that the church would introduce black women to public life. The church connected black women's spirituality integrally with social activism.

Although women's historians tend to focus overwhelmingly on the secular club movement, especially the National Association of Colored Women, as exemplary of black women's activism, clubwomen themselves readily admitted to the precedent of church work in fostering both "woman's consciousness" and a racial understanding of the "common good." Fannie Barrier Williams, a founding member and leader of the National Association of Colored Women, acknowledged in 1900: "The training which first enabled colored women to organize and successfully carry on club work was originally obtained in church work. These churches have been and still are the great preparatory schools in which the primary lessons of social order, mutual trustfulness and united effort have been taught. . . . The meaning of unity of effort for the common good, the development of social sympathies grew into woman's consciousness through the privileges of church work."[46]

The club movement among black women owed its very existence to the groundwork of organizational skill and leadership training gained through women's church societies. Missionary societies had early on brought together women with little knowledge of each other and created bonds of sisterly cooperation at the city and state levels. Not only Baptists, but also black Methodists, Presbyterians, and women in other denominations came together in associations that transformed unknown and unconfident women into leaders and agents of social service and racial self-help in their communities. For black Baptist women during the 1880s, the formation of state societies nurtured skills of networking and fund-raising. For more than a decade before the founding of the National Association of Colored Women, church-related societies had introduced mothers' training schools and social service programs, many of which were later adopted into the programs of the secular women's clubs.

More than mere precursors to secular reform and women's rights activism,[47] black women's religious organizations undergirded and formed an identifiable part of what is erroneously assumed to be "secular." The black Baptist women's convention thrust itself into the mainstream of Progressive reform, and conversely such clubs as those constituting the secular-oriented National Association of Colored Women included church work as integral and salient to their purpose. This complexity precludes attempts to bifurcate black women's activities neatly into dichotomous categories such as religious versus secular, private versus public, or accommodation versus resistance.

Even such quotidian activities as women's fund raising, teaching in Sabbath schools, ministering to the sick, or conducting mothers' training schools embarked a politically subversive character within southern society. In many respects, the most profound challenge to Jim Crow laws, crop liens, disfranchisement, the dearth of black public schools, and the heinous brutality of lynching rested in the silent, everyday struggle of black people to build stable families, get an education, worship together in their churches, and "work the system," as Eric Hobsbawm terms it, "to their minimum disadvantage."[48] Arguments over the accommodationist versus liberating thrust of the black church miss the range as well as the fluid interaction of political and ideological meanings represented within the church's domain. Equally important, the artificiality of such a dichotomy precludes appreciation of the church's role in the "prosaic and constant struggle" of black people for survival and empowerment.[49] Edward Wheeler persuasively argues for the paradoxical implications of social uplift and accommodation: "Accommodation, which of course had a submissive tone, also had a subversive quality. On the one hand, uplift meant accommodation and surrender to the concepts, principles, and ideals of the dominant society. On the other, uplift was a denial of what white society meant by accommodation, for it spoke of a possibility to move beyond the limits prescribed by the dominant society."[50]

In the 1909 Atlanta University study of social betterment activities among African Americans, Du Bois attributed the greater part of such activities to the black church and specifically to church women.[51] In the final analysis the women's movement in the black Baptist church may be likened more to Harriet Tubman's repeated, surreptitious efforts to lead slaves step by step away from bondage than to Nat Turner's apocalyptic, revolutionary surge. Women's efforts were valiant attempts to navigate their people through the stifling and dangerous obstacle course of American racism. Committed to the causes of racial self-help and advancement, the convention movement among black Baptist women contributed greatly to the church's tremendous influence in both the spiritual and secular life of black communities. But the women's movement did something more. It gave to black women an individual and group pride that resisted ideologies and institutions upholding gender subordination. The movement gave them the collective strength and determination to continue their struggle for the rights of blacks and the rights of women.

NOTES

1. See Jualynne Dodson, "Nineteenth-Century A.M.E. Preaching Women: Cutting Edge of Women's Inclusion in Church Polity," in Hilah F. Thomas and Rosemary Skinner Keller, eds., *Women in New Worlds: Historical Perspectives on the Wesleyan Tradition,* vol. 1 (Nashville: Abingdon Press, 1981), 276–292; Jean McMahon Humez, ed., *Gifts of Power: The Writings of Rebecca Jackson, Black Visionary and Shaker Eldress* (Amherst: University of Massachusetts Press, 1981), 1–50; William L. Andrews, ed., *Sisters of the Spirit: Three Black Women's Autobiographies of the Nineteenth Century* (Bloomington: Indiana University Press, 1986), 25–234.
2. C. Eric Lincoln and Lawrence H. Mamiya, *The Black Church in the African American Experience* (Durham, N.C.: Duke University Press, 1990), 25–26; Leroy Fitts, *A History of Black Baptists* (Nashville: Broadman Press, 1985), 64–79; Joseph H. Jackson, *A Story of Christian Activism: The History of the National Baptist Convention, U.S.A., Inc.* (Nashville: Townsend Press, 1980), 23–27.

3. Winthrop Hudson, *Religion in America: An Historical Account of the Development of American Religious Life,* 2nd ed. (New York: Charles Scribner's Sons, 1973), 202–203; Sydney E. Ahlstrom, *A Religious History of the American People* (New Haven: Yale University Press, 1972), 719–725.

4. See James Melvin Washington, *Frustrated Fellowship: The Black Baptist Quest for Social Power* (Macon, Ga.: Mercer University Press, 1985), 22–45.

5. Sandy D. Martin draws some attention to women's organized involvement in foreign mission support during the formative years of the National Baptist Foreign Mission Convention, but his discussion is brief. Most scholarly works on the black Baptist church identify a few individual women by name, but they fail to discuss women as a group and as significant contributors to the church's historic role. See Sandy D. Martin, *Black Baptists and African Missions: The Origins of a Movement, 1880–1915* (Macon, Ga.: Mercer University Press, 1989), 129–134; Washington, *Frustrated Fellowship,* 139; Jackson, *Story of Christian Activism,* 87–90, 135–145; Fitts, *History of Black Baptists,* 121–134; Lewis G. Jordan, *Negro Baptist History* (Nashville: Sunday School Publishing Board, National Baptist Convention, 1930); Owen D. Pelt and Ralph Lee Smith, *The Story of the National Baptists* (New York: Vantage Press, 1960).

6. The Baptist Foreign Mission Convention was founded in 1880. It was one of three organizations to merge in the formation of the National Baptist Convention, U.S.A. in 1895. Because of this, the NBC uses the 1880 date as its founding date. For a history of this convention, see Martin, *Black Baptists and African Missions,* 56–106.

7. Joel Williamson, *A Rage for Order: Black/White Relations in the American South since Emancipation* (New York: Oxford University Press, 1986), 171.

8. For a discussion of women during the Reconstruction and post-Reconstruction period, see Jacqueline Jones, *Labor of Love, Labor of Sorrow: Black Women, Work, and the Family from Slavery to the Present* (New York: Random House, 1985), chap. 2.

9. Rayford W. Logan, *The Negro in American Life and Thought: The Nadir, 1877–1901* (New York: Dial Press, 1954); Logan, *The Betrayal of the Negro: From Rutherford B. Hayes to Woodrow Wilson* (New York: Collier Books, 1965), 292–302; Neil R. McMillen, *Dark Journey: Black Mississippians in the Age of Jim Crow* (Urbana: University of Illinois Press, 1989), 197–253; Williamson, *Rage for Order,* 117–151.

10. In a series of cases between 1876 and 1896, the Supreme Court moved in a conservative direction, which culminated with the Plessy case and the euphemistic doctrine of "separate but equal." *United States v. Cruikshank,* 92 U.S. 542(1876); *Civil Rights Cases,* 109 U.S. 3 (1883); *Plessy v. Ferguson,* 163 U.S. 537(1896). See Derrick A. Bell, Jr., *Race, Racism, and American Law,* 2nd. ed. (Boston: Little, Brown, 1980), 34–38, 83–91.

11. Early scholars of black history called attention to the importance of the home mission and educational work of the black church during the decades that followed the demise of Reconstruction. They especially emphasized the church's racial self-help

efforts in response to diminishing civil and political rights. See William Edward Burghardt Du Bois, ed., *The Negro Church* (Atlanta: Atlanta University Press, 1903), 111–152; Carter G. Woodson, *History of the Negro Church* (Washington, D.C.: Associated Publishers, 1921), chaps. 4, 5.

12. The most comprehensive studies of slave religion are Albert J. Raboteau, *Slave Religion: The "Invisible Institution" in the Antebellum South* (New York: Oxford University Press, 1978), and Mechal Sobel, *Trabelin' On: The Slave Journey to an Afro-Baptist Faith* (Westport, Conn.: Greenwood Press, 1979). See also Eugene D. Genovese, *Roll Jordan Roll: The World the Slaveholders Made* (New York: Random House, Pantheon Books, 1974), 232–284.

13. E. Franklin Frazier, *The Negro Church* (New York: Schocken Books, 1964), chap. 3.

14. Gary Nash, *Forging Freedom: The Formation of Philadelphia's Black Community, 1720–1840* (Cambridge, Mass.: Harvard University Press, 1989), 227–233, 259–267; Gayraud Wilmore, *Black Religion and Black Radicalism: An Interpretation of the Religious History of Afro-American People,* 2nd ed. (Maryknoll, N.Y.: Orbis Books, 1989), 78–89; Lincoln and Mamiya, *Black Church in the African American Experience,* 47–75.

15. The figure for black Baptists in 1906 represents the number of Baptists under the National Baptist Convention and does not reflect those black Baptists who are listed under the Northern Baptist Convention, or those found among the Primitive Baptists, Two Seed Baptists, and Freewill Baptists. When all these groups are considered, black Baptists numbered 2,354,789 in 1906. I have also distinguished the A.M.E. church from such black Methodist groups as the A.M.E. Zion and the Colored Methodist Episcopal. The entire black Methodist population in 1906 was 1,182,131. See U.S. Department of Commerce and Labor, Bureau of the Census, *Special Reports: Religious Bodies, 1906*, vol. 1, (Washington, D.C.: Government Printing Office, 1910), 137–139; Sobel, *Trabelin' On*, 182.

16. For statistics of religious denominations, see Bureau of the Census, *Religious Bodies, 1906*, vol. 1, 137–139; Bureau of the Census, *Religious Bodies,* 1916, Part I (Washington, D.C.: Government Printing Office, 1919), 40.

17. For statistics on black Baptists, see Bureau of the Census, *Religious Bodies, 1916*, vol. 1, 121, 123–128. For a survey of the black population's predominantly rural and southern character during this period, see U.S. Department of Commerce, Bureau of the Census, *Negro Population, 1791–1915* (Washington, D.C.: Government Printing Office, 1918), 88–94.

18. Philip S. Foner, ed., *W. E. B. Du Bois Speaks, 1890–1919* (New York: Pathfinder Press, 1970), 97.

19. A wealth of materials related to the Woman's Convention, Auxiliary to the National Baptist Convention is found in the papers of Nannie Helen Burroughs, former corresponding secretary and president of the organization and also founder and president of the National Training School for Women and Girls. See Nannie Helen Burroughs Papers, Library of Congress.

20. Berger and Neuhaus are not concerned with historical perspective, nor do they see the church as the only such structure. Their concern is with mediating structures in the contemporary welfare state. They observe: "Not only are religious institutions significant 'players' in the public realm, but they are singularly important to the way people order their lives and values at the most local and concrete levels of their existence." They go on to note that the black community cannot be understood from a historical perspective without looking at the role of the black church. Peter L. Berger and Richard John Neuhaus, *To Empower People: The Role of Mediating Structures in Public Policy* (Washington, D.C.: American Enterprise Institute for Public Policy Research, 1977), 26–28.

21. For differing interpretations of "civil religion," see essays in Donald G. Jones and Russell E. Richey, eds., *American Civil Religion* (San Francisco: Harper and Row, 1974), especially chaps. 1, 2, 6, 7, 10; Robert N. Bellah and Phillip E. Hammond, *Varieties of Civil Religion* (San Francisco: Harper and Row, 1980), 3–23.

22. See the discussion of "mythic patterns of national mission" and the idea of national community in the form of covenant in John F. Wilson, *Public Religion in American Culture* (Philadelphia: Temple University Press, 1979), 34–39.

23. Frederick Douglass, "The Meaning of the Fourth of July to the Negro, 1852," in Philip E. Foner, ed., *The Life and Writings of Frederick Douglass,* vol. 2 (New York: International Publishers, 1950), 192; also see an analysis of Frederick Douglass's millennialist vision in David W. Blight, *Frederick Douglass' Civil War: Keeping Faith in Jubilee* (Baton Rouge: Louisiana State University Press, 1989), 101–121.

24. See Sidney E. Mead's usage of Gilbert Chesterton's phrase in his discussion of civil religion. Sidney E. Mead, "The 'Nation with the Soul of a Church,'" in Jones and Richey, eds., *American Civil Religion,* 45. However, the black scholar Charles Long writes from the point of view of African Americans: "The distinction between civil religion and church religion is not one that would loom very large for us." See Charles H. Long, "Civil Rights—Civil Religion: Visible People and Invisible Religion," in ibid., 211–221, especially 216; and Washington, *Frustrated Fellowship,* 135–157.

25. Benedict Anderson defines nation as "an imagined political community—and imagined as both inherently limited and sovereign." For black Baptists, the "imagined community" was racially bounded and its sovereignty was perceived as free of white control—hence black denominational hegemony. See Benedict Anderson, *Imagined Communities: Reflections on the Origin and Spread of Nationalism* (London: Verso, 1983), 14–16.

26. Jürgen Habermas, "The Public Sphere: An Encyclopedia Article (1964)," *New German Critique,* 1 (Fall 1974): 49–55; Habermas, *The Structural Transformation of the Public Sphere: An Inquiry into a Category of Bourgeois Society,* trans. by Thomas Burger with the assistance of Frederick Lawrence (Cambridge, Mass.: MIT Press, 1989), especially chap. 2. For differing interpretations that draw upon Habermas in discussing the role of religion in the public sphere, see Robert Wuthnow, *The*

Restructuring of American Religion (Princeton, N.J.: Princeton University Press, 1988), chap. 4; Wuthnow, *The Struggle for America's Soul: Evangelicals, Liberals, and Secularism* (Grand Rapids, Mich.: William B. Eerdmans, 1989), 11–15; and José Casanova, "Private and Public Religions," *Social Research*, 59 (Spring 1992): 17–57.

27. Critics of Habermas do not share his assessment of the breakdown and decline of the public sphere itself, nor do they agree with him when he attributes decline to the historical emergence of competing interest groups (the non-bourgeois strata) and the resultant diminution of the state's accountability to its citizenry. In contradistinction to Habermas, Nancy Fraser submits that "in stratified societies, arrangements that accommodate contestation among a plurality of competing publics better promote the ideal of participatory parity than does a single, comprehensive, overarching public." Nancy Fraser, "Rethinking the Public Sphere: A Contribution to the Critique of Actually Existing Democracy," *Social Text*, 25/26 (1990): 56–80.

28. They are responding to Habermas's discussion of the emergence of the public sphere as a distinct phase of bourgeois social formation in late seventeenth- and eighteenth-century Europe. His critics note instead a multiplicity of competing publics, which existed then and continue to exist now based on racial, ethnic, class, and gender interests. For treatment of various types of counter-publics, see ibid., 61–68; John Keane, *Public Life and Late Capitalism: Toward a Socialist Theory of Democracy* (New York: Cambridge University Press, 1984), 92–94; Rita Felski, *Beyond Feminist Aesthetics: Feminist Literature and Social Change* (Cambridge, Mass.: Harvard University Press, 1989), 154–182.

29. *The Free Speech and Headlight* was published by the Reverend Taylor Nightingale, pastor of the Beale Street Baptist Church, although Ida Wells was its editor and chiefly responsible for voicing its social message. Wells does not figure as a participant of the women's movement of the black Baptist church, since she was a member of the A.M.E. Church and was active with the organized women's movement of that denomination. See Samuel Shannon, "Tennessee," in Henry Lewis Suggs, ed., *The Black Press in the South, 1865–1979* (Westport, Conn.: Greenwood Press, 1983), 325.

30. For example, black Baptist newspapers are discussed for the states of Alabama, Arkansas, Florida, and Missouri in Suggs, ed., *The Black Press in the South*, 30, 34, 38, 70–71, 103, 105, 212–214; also see National Baptist Convention, *Journal of the Twentieth Annual Session of the National Baptist Convention, Held in Richmond, Virginia, September 12–17, 1900* (Nashville: National Baptist Publishing Board, 1900), 191; Du Bois, ed., *Negro Church*, 121.

31. For discussion of the *National Baptist Magazine*, see Penelope L. Bullock, *The Afro-American Periodical Press, 1838–1909* (Baton Rouge: Louisiana State University Press, 1981), 73–76.

32. This statement can be found in the combined report for 1901 and 1902 of the National Baptist Convention, U.S.A., which is printed in Du Bois, ed., *Negro Church*, 115.

33. In 1917 the Department of War monitored the activities and mail of Nannie Helen Burroughs, corresponding secretary of the Woman's Convention, for remarks in condemnation of Woodrow Wilson. Records of the War Department, General and Special Staffs, Military Intelligence Division, "Black Radicals (Church of God)," from Record Group 165, National Archives.

34. Benjamin E. Mays and Joseph W. Nicholson, *The Negro's Church* (New York, 1933; rpt. New York: Arno Press and the *New York Times,* 1969), 9.

35. The most extensive holdings of northern white Baptist women are the records of the Woman's American Baptist Home Mission Society and the Women's Baptist Home Mission Society, which are located in the American Baptist Archives Center in Valley Forge, Pennsylvania, and the American Baptist—Samuel Colgate Historical Library, Rochester, New York. Materials are also housed at the Franklin Trask Library in Andover-Newton Theological Seminary in Massachusetts.

36. The women's movement in the black Baptist church reflected a trend found in all the denominations in the late nineteenth century. Studies of white women's societies include Lois A. Boyd and R. Douglas Brackenridge, *Presbyterian Women in America: Two Centuries of a Quest for Status* (Westport, Conn.: Greenwood Press, 1983); Virginia Lieson Brereton and Christa Ressmeyer Klein, "American Women in Ministry: A History of Protestant Beginning Points," in Rosemary Ruether and Eleanor McLaughlin, eds., *Women of Spirit: Female Leadership in the Jewish and Christian Traditions* (New York: Simon and Schuster, 1979), chap. 11; Ruether and Rosemary Skinner Keller, *Women and Religion in America: The Nineteenth Century* (San Francisco: Harper and Row, 1981), 243–293.

37. Suzanne Lebsock, "Women and American Politics, 1880–1920," in Louise A. Tilly and Patricia Gurin, eds., *Women, Politics, and Change* (New York: Russell Sage Foundation, 1990), 35–59.

38. Anna J. Cooper, *A Voice from the South* (Xenia, Ohio, 1892; rpt. New York: Negro Universities Press, 1969), 143.

39. For black women's educational and social reform activities, see Dorothy Salem, *To Better Her World: Black Women in Organized Reform, 1890–1920,* 7–103, vol. 14 in Darlene Clark Hine, ed., *Black Women in United States History: From Colonial Times to the Present* (Brooklyn: Carlson Press, 1990); Bettina Aptheker, "Black Women's Quest in the Professions," in Aptheker, *Woman's Legacy: Essays on Race, Sex, and Class in American History* (Amherst: University of Massachusetts Press, 1982), 89–110; Cynthia Neverdon-Morton, *Afro-American Women of the South and the Advancement of the Race, 1895–1925* (Knoxville: University of Tennessee Press, 1989), 78–103; Jacqueline Rouse, *Lugenia Burns Hope: Black Southern Reformer* (Athens: University of Georgia Press), 41–85. Also see for white women, Lynn D. Gordon, *Gender and Higher Education in the Progressive Era* (New Haven: Yale University Press, 1990); Rosalind Rosenberg, *Beyond Separate Spheres: Intellectual Roots of Modern Feminism* (New Haven: Yale University Press, 1982); Robyn Muncy, *Creating a Female Dominion in American Reform, 1890–1935* (New York: Oxford University Press, 1991).

40. Hazel V. Carby, *Reconstructing Womanhood: The Emergence of the Afro-American Woman Novelist* (New York: Oxford University Press, 1987), 96–115; I. Garland Penn, *The Afro-American Press and Its Editors* (Springfield, Mass.: Willey, 1891), 366–427.

41. See E. Franklin Frazier's recognition of the middle-class orientation of the National Baptist Convention in Frazier, *Black Bourgeoisie* (New York: Macmillan, 1957), 89.

42. Houston Baker, in his discussion of the black vernacular, characterizes the "quotidi-an sounds of black every day life" as both a defiant and entrancing voice. Similarly, John Langston Gwaltney calls the "folk" culture of today's cities "core black cul-ture," which is "more than ad hoc synchronic adaptive survival." Gwaltney links its values and epistemology to a long peasant tradition. See John Langston Gwaltney, *Drylongso: A Self-Portrait of Black America* (New York: Random House, 1980), xxv–xxvii; also Houston Baker, Jr., *Afro-American Poetics: Revisions of Harlem and the Black Aesthetic* (Madison: University of Wisconsin Press, 1988), 95–107; Baker, *Blues, Ideology, and Afro-American Literature: A Vernacular Theory* (Chicago: University of Chicago Press, 1984), 11–13.

43. Genovese, *Roll Jordan Roll,* 163.

44. Lincoln and Mamiya, *Black Church in the African American Experience,* 10–16.

45. The Russian linguist and critic Mikhail Bakhtin discusses "dialogism" and "het-eroglossia" in specific regard to his theory of language: "Everything means, is under-stood, as part of a greater whole-there is a constant interaction between meanings, all of which have the potential of conditioning others." See M. M. Bakhtin, *The Dialogic Imagination: Four Essays,* ed. Michael Holquist and trans. Caryl Emerson and Michael Holquist (Austin: University of Texas Press, 1981), 293, 352, 426.

46. See Fannie Barrier Williams, "The Club Movement among Colored Women of America," in Booker T. Washington, N. B. Wood, and Fannie Barrier Williams, *A New Negro for a New Century* (Chicago: American Publishing House, 1900), 383.

47. For discussion of black and white women's church work as a forerunner to secular reform, see Ann Firor Scott, *The Southern Lady: From Pedestal to Politics, 1830–1930* (Chicago: University of Chicago Press, 1970), 141; Jean Friedman, *The Enclosed Garden: Women and Community in the Evangelical South, 1830–1900* (Chapel Hill: University of North Carolina Press, 1985), 111, 113, 115–126; Jacquelyn Dowd Hall, *Revolt against Chivalry: Jessie Daniel Ames and the Women's Campaign against Lynching* (New York: Columbia University Press, 1979), 70–77; Kathleen C. Berkeley, "'Colored Ladies also Contributed': Black Women's Activities from Benevolence to Social Welfare, 1866–1896," in Walter J. Fraser, Jr., R. Frank Saunders, Jr., and John L. Wakelyn, eds., *The Web of Southern Social Relations: Women, Family, and Education* (Athens: University of Georgia Press, 1985), 181–185.

48. Eric Hobsbawm, "Peasants and Politics," *Journal of Peasant Studies,* 1 (1973): 12, 16.

49. James Scott uses the phrase "prosaic and constant struggle" in his study of everyday forms of resistance in a Malaysian community. See James Scott, *Weapons of the Weak: Everyday Forms of Peasant Resistance* (New Haven: Yale University Press, 1985), 301.

50. Edward L. Wheeler, *Uplifting the Race: The Black Minister in the New South, 1865–1902* (Lanham, Md.: University Press of America, 1986), xvii.
51. W. E. Burghardt Du Bois, ed., *Efforts for Social Betterment among Negro Americans* (Atlanta: Atlanta University Press, 1909), 16, 22.

SELECTED BIBLIOGRAPHY FOR FURTHER READING

Andrews, William L., ed. *Sisters of the Spirit: Three Black Women's Autobiographies of the Nineteenth Century*. Bloomington: Indiana University Press, 1986.

Dodson, Jualynne E. "Nineteenth-Century AME Preaching Women" in *Women in New Worlds: Historical Perspectives on the Wesleyan Tradition*. edited by Hilah Thomas & Rosemary Keller. Nashville: Abingdon, 1981.

Humez, Jean M. "'My Spirit Eye': Some Functions of Spiritual and Visionary Experience in the Lives of Five Black Women Preachers, 1810–1880" in *Women and the Structure of Society: Selected Research from the Fifth Berkshire Conference on the History of Women*. edited by Barbara J. Harris and JoAnn K. McNamara. Durham, NC: Duke University Press, 1984.

Sterling, Dorthy. *We Are Your Sisters: Black Women in the Nineteenth Century*. New York: W. W. Norton, 1984.

Wills, David W. "Womanhood and Domesticity in the AME Tradition: The Influence of Daniel Alexander Payne" in *Black Apostles at Home and Abroad: Afro-Americans and the Christian Mission from the Revolution to Reconstruction*. edited by David W. Wills and Richard Newman. Boston: G.K. Hall, 1982.

"THE FUTURE GOLDEN DAY OF THE RACE"

Timothy E. Fulop

::In his *The Negro in American Life and Thought: The Nadir, 1877–1901* (1974), Rayford W. Logan named the quarter century after Reconstruction the "nadir" for African Americans because of the period's increasing brutality and decreasing prospects for racial harmony and justice. Though many African Americans remained hopeful for change in the United States, this period saw increasing attention given to hopes for racial justice outside of white society and the United States. Timothy E. Fulop examines the intersection of historical realities, politics, and religious symbols as African Americans addressed their hopes and envisioned the future.::

:: I I "THE FUTURE GOLDEN
DAY OF THE RACE"

Millennialism and Black Americans
in the Nadir, 1877–1901

Timothy E. Fulop

:: At the turn of the century, Edward W. Blyden, resident of Liberia and former Presbyterian missionary from America, read to some African natives the following description from the New York *Independent* of the burning of a black man in Georgia:

> Sam Hose was burned on Sunday afternoon in the presence of thousands of people. Before the fire had been kindled the mob amused themselves by cutting off the ears, fingers, toes, etc. to carry away as mementos. After the burning and before the body was cool, it was cut to pieces, the heart and liver being especially cut up and sold. Small pieces of bone brought 25 cents, and "a bit of liver, crisply cooked, sold for 10 cents." So eager were the crowd to obtain souvenirs that a rush for the stake was made, and those near the body were forced against and had to fight for their escape.[1]

The story was so shocking, Blyden recounted, that the African audience did not know whether to respond with indignation or incredulity:

> Their imagination had never pictured any tragedy so frightful or revolting. Nothing in their experience or their traditions could afford any parallel to such hideous barbarities practiced as they were by people supposed to be Christian and highly civilized.[2]

The last twenty-five years of the nineteenth century have appropriately gone down in African-American history as "the Nadir." Disenfranchisement and Jim Crow laws clouded out any rays of hope that Reconstruction had bestowed in the American South. Darwinism and phrenology passed on new "scientific" theories of black inferiority, and the old racial stereotypes of blacks as beasts abounded in American society. The civil, political, and educational rights of black Americans were greatly curtailed, and lynching reached all-time highs in the 1890s.[3] Conditions were not much better in Africa as European nations carved the continent into colonies and spread Western civilization, according to one critic, in "the proportion of hundreds of gallons of gin to a Bible or missionary."[4] The Nadir was accompanied by a cacophony of black voices seeking to make sense of the history and destiny of African Americans.[5] One strand of these voices proclaimed in song, sermon, and theological treatise that the millennial reign of God was coming to earth.

The study of millennialism in American religion has been a rich and popular field of study, yet as Leonard Sweet stated in a historiographical survey of American millennialism, "the manner in which millennial ideology fired faith and forged it to works in the black experience, and not just among insurrectionists like Nat Turner, has not been explored."[6] From the images of a future Canaan held by slaves to the dream of the Promised Land in the sermons of Martin Luther King, Jr., millennialism in African-American religion remains largely unexamined. This article sheds further light on how African Americans in the Nadir period understood their destiny by exploring the neglected subject of black millennialism.

Millennialism is the belief rooted in Christian tradition and thought that history will be fulfilled in a golden age. The term itself comes from Rev 20:1–7, which predicts a thousand-year reign of Christ with the resurrected martyrs while Satan is bound and confined to the abyss. Though the millennium is explicitly mentioned only in this New Testament passage, older Hebrew Bible images and metaphors of a time of felicity on earth have played an important role in millennial movements.[7]

Of particular importance in African-American thought is the biblical story of the Exodus and the image of Canaan. Thomas Wentworth Higginson in an 1867 article on Negro spirituals claimed that the books of Moses and the Revelation of St. John composed the Bible of American blacks, and "all that lay between, even the narrations of the life of Jesus, they hardly cared to read or to hear."[8] It will become evident that the identification with ancient Israel and the hope for entering the Promised Land played an important role in black millennialism.

TOWARD A TYPOLOGY OF BLACK MILLENNIAL THOUGHT

Several scholars claim that American slaves were primarily millennialists of the quietest sort who waited for Christ to intervene in history, release them from slavery, and usher them into Canaan as God had done for the ancient Israelites in delivering them from bondage in Egypt, though there were those, like Nat Turner, who were of a revolutionist sort and claimed a role for themselves in the apocalyptical drama.[9] In contrast, black millennialism in the Nadir period exhibits great variety. Before proceeding, however, to an examination of the varieties of black millennial thought, it is useful to categorize black millennial thought in the Nadir period according to three types: cultural millennialism, millennial Ethiopianism, and progressive millennialism.

Cultural millennialism denotes the type of black millennial thinking most closely akin to the ideology of the United States as the redeemer nation of the world. The emphasis is on the working out of the millennium through the forces of Western civilization, education, Anglo-Saxon culture, American democracy, and republicanism.

Millennial Ethiopianism, as will become apparent in this article, is the most distinctively African-American millennial tradition, though there are elements unique to the black experience in each of these millennial types. In contrast to white millennial theories that emphasize America, Anglo-Saxon culture, and the radical break with the Old World, millennial Ethiopianism posits a pan-African millennium, a future golden age continuous with a glorious African past accompanied by God's judgment of white society and Western civilization.

Progressive millennialism is a more traditional type of millennial thought that emphasizes the role of the church, evangelism, missions, and reform in giving birth to the millennium on earth. This type is not without notes of pan-Africanism and strong social criticism concerning race relations, but, unlike millennial Ethiopianism, it reveals an optimism that the millennium will be marked by racial equality and harmony. Progressive millennialism is optimistic about the power of Christianity to transform and perfect American society, but it is not naive and takes a more religiously prophetic stance toward the United States than does cultural millennialism.

DESCRIPTIONS OF THE MILLENNIUM

Different varieties of black millennial thought can be delineated by addressing questions of what the millennium will look like, where its location will be, how it will come about, and when it will occur. Attention to these issues makes it possible to distinguish between cultural millennialism, millennial Ethiopianism, and progressive millennialism.

Since the millennium is only mentioned formally in one opaque passage of scripture open to many different interpretations, a description of the millennium reveals much about the particular group that espouses this vision. The millennium proclaimed by African Americans during the Nadir period shared many of the spiritual priorities of white nineteenth-century American millennialism. J. W. E. Bowen, president of Gammon Theological Seminary, preached an enthusiastic sermon titled "What Shall the Harvest Be?"

> A belief in the future golden day of the race when men shall see, not through a glass darkly, but face to face, gives buoyancy and courage to the efforts of Christians in bringing all men to the knowledge of the truth as it is in Christ. The golden age is not in the past as the heathens ignorantly taught, but it is before us somewhere in the dim tracery of the future, and possibly we have come to the edge of this new heaven. I do not believe that that age will find its characteristics so much in the material acquisitions as in the spiritual triumphs of the soul and in a proper knowledge of our relation to God.[10]

George W. Clinton, African Methodist Episcopal Zion Church bishop and editor of the *Star of Zion*, claimed that the tense of one well-known hymn "Jesus *shall* reign," would need to be changed to "Jesus *doth* reign where'er the sun. . . ."[11] The unification of all Christians was anticipated by the African Methodist Episcopal (A.M.E.) Church bishop Daniel Alexander Payne:

> The name Christian—that and that alone—will be able to stand before enlightened, progressive humanity, the glory of the millennium and the consuming fires of the judgment-day, to which we all are hastening, and for which we all ought to live.[12]

Black millennial visions also included social and political concerns common to reform-minded nineteenth-century evangelicals. Lucius H. Holsey, self-taught bishop of the Colored Methodist Episcopal Church, proclaimed a millennium without wars, "corrupting institutions," "massive conclaves of sin and infidelity," saloons, drunkenness, the opium traffic, "slavery in every form," "heathen priests and their superstitious systems," kingdoms and empires, and "every opposing foe and antagonizing power."[13] Concerns of contemporary populists and progressives are detected in an *A.M.E. Church Review* article by a layman, R. Henri Herbert of Trenton:

The Government of the Future! A government whose primary object will be to make two blades of grass grow where but one did before; a government in which Taxation shall go hand in hand with Representation; a government in which every man shall be protected in the full enjoyment of his equal legal, political and religious liberty; a government in which education shall be as universal as the star-decked canopy of Heaven; a government in which there shall be no Pagan, no Mahomedan, no Catholic, no Protestant, no Negro, no Caucasian, no distinction of race or creed, but which will ever remember that "of one blood were created all the nations of the Earth;" a government in which there shall be neither wars nor rumors of wars but over which shall everlastingly rest the sweet benison of Peace; a government so vast in its territory, so wonderful in its wealth, so stupendous in its resources, so God-like in its beneficence that the human mind can but poorly compass its grandeur—A GOVERNMENT THAT SHALL EMBRACE THE WHOLE EARTH, *THE RE-PUBLIC OF THE WORLD!* . . . Then shall have come the time of which sages have written and poets sung and which the great Jehovah Himself hath prophesied. Then upon earth shall be—THE MILLENNIUM![14]

Contemporary descriptions of the millennium by white Americans like Samuel Harris's *The Kingdom of Christ on Earth* lack a racial component, but in black depictions of the millennium, resolution of the "race problem" is primary. The millennium, according to James T. Holly, would "dissipate the darkness that has so long brooded over the sons of Ham."[15] Holsey looked for an era of racial reconciliation inspired by "the fatherhood of God and the brotherhood of men."[16] The fullest vision of racial harmony and equality is offered by the South Carolina politician and A.M.E. bishop R. H. Cain:

Happy for the great country, happy for the negro and the nation when the great principles upon which our government is founded, when the genius of liberty as understood by the fathers, shall permeate this whole land, mold the opinions of statesmen, fix the decrees of judges, settle the decisions of Supreme Courts and executed by every law officer of this broad land; then there will need be no more discussion as to what of the negro problem. . . . There will be one homogeneous nation governed by intellectual, moral worth and controlled by Christian influences. Then there will be no East, no West, no North, no South, no Black, no White, no Saxon, no Negro, but a great, happy and peaceful nation.[17]

Unlike white millennial thought, which was nearly unanimous about the focus of the millennium being on the United States,[18] black millennial thought proposed a variety of locations for the millennium. A large segment of black millennial thought did locate the millennium in America, which was congruent with the dominant ideology of America as a redeemer nation and a "city upon a hill."[19] Herbert is in this tradition for he reminds his readers that the Old World with its aristocracy, militarism, and despotism is in decay and that the future republic of the world has its foundation in the American republic.[20] Many black Americans looked for the millennium to be located in America because they believed that America would also be as exceptional in race relations as it was thought to be in its republicanism, availability of "virgin land," growth of missions, expansion of evangelical religion, and technological accomplishments.

The myth that the world's peoples were divided according to the three sons of Noah provided an important foundation for thinking about black destiny, race relations, and millennialism. Accordingly, the educator J. Augustus Cole argued for the unique status of America:

> The American Negro has a share in the New World. He need not rush out of
> the land which he bought with two hundred and fifty years of servitude to find
> his destiny in Africa . . . in the case of the Negro he is entitled to America as he
> is to Africa. In the plan of Providence America seems to be reserved as the fu-
> ture home of the surplus of all the races: Asia was allotted to Shem, Europe to
> Japtheth and Africa to Ham. But America was given to no race.[21]

Likewise, the influential Baptist minister and editor Rufus Perry stated that "God has beneficently reserved Africa for *Africans*—the sons of Ham,—just as Asia is reserved for the sons of Shem, Europe for the sons of Japheth, and America as a common continent for the reunion of all the sons of Adam in the bond of common brotherhood."[22]

In his Atlanta Exposition address of 1895, Booker T. Washington proposed that racial brotherhood and black advancement would be accomplished in the South by his accommodationist program stressing material development rather than social and political equality—a program that he claimed, in a flourish of millennial rhetoric, would "bring into our beloved South a new heaven and new earth."[23] Others went beyond this rhetoric to speak of a providential "new race" in America. George L. Ruffin, Baptist layman and judge in Massachusetts, argued for racial amalgamation:

> The New World comes to the front to take up civilization where the Old
> World has left it; to bear it onward and upward the New World must have new
> institutions and a new race; the aggregated experience and wisdom of the Old

World nations is here, and for a purpose; the aggregated races of the Old
World are here; the Saxon, the Celt, the Latin and the African are here, not to
rebuild their several nations and races, but to build one nation and one race—
the American—superior to all others, a new race, fit in intellect, heart and
power to occupy and sway the destiny of the imperial New World.[24]

Another proponent of amalgamation argued that the Negro must merge with
Anglo-Saxon civilization, and recommended Ruth's word to Naomi (Ruth 1:16):
"Entreat me not to leave thee, . . . thy people shall be my people, and thy God
my God. . . ."[25] This may appear to be a complete capitulation to the redeemer
nation ideology of Anglo-Saxon America as exemplified in Josiah Strong's *Our
Country* (1886), but these writers also included strong notes of social criticism
against a society in which racial strife is so great that they believe only amalgamation can solve the race problem. Amalgamation is not merely a bleaching process
of blacks, for, as Ruffin stated, "the white must also go and lose his identity."[26]
Though there was disagreement concerning racial segregation, full social and
political equality, and racial amalgamation, many African-Americans sought their
destiny in the United States.

Not all African-Americans, however were so confident about their future in
the South or the United States in general. Evidence of the former is the declaration by a forerunner organization of the National Baptist Convention that the
South was dangerous and hostile territory for blacks, and that young black men
should take their families to the West and start a new life. Biblical imagery was
employed in this prophetic advice: "The exodus of the Israelites from Egypt will
be a small sized excursion compared to the move there will be [from] the
South."[27]

One such movement with millennial overtones, as Nell Painter has argued,
was the exodus of blacks to Kansas in 1879. Though the movement was not
monolithic in leadership or religious meaning, the biblical exodus imagery
loomed large and one leader, Benjamin "Pap" Singleton, called himself the
"Moses of the Colored Exodus." An old "Exoduster" in St. Louis enlarged on this
biblical imagery:

> Moses . . . took 'em out o' bondage, and wen dey was all a-waverin' an'
> mighty feared he took 'em 'cross de Red Sea an' den dey was safe . . . Dis is
> our Red Sea, right hyah in St. Louis, atween home an' Kansas, an' if we sticks
> togeder an' keeps up our faith we'll get to Kansas and be out o' bondage for
> shuah . . . Dem as is a-waverin' an' is a'feared is goin' to sink in dis hyah Red
> Sea.[28]

Popular exodus songs included lines such as, "We are on our rapid march to Kansas, the land that gives birth to freedom," "In the midst of earth's dominion, Christ has promised us a kingdom," and "It seems to me that the year of jubilee has come; surely this is the time that is spoken of in history."[29] Whether the rush to the Union lines during the Civil War, Kansas in the 1870s and 1880s, or Northern cities in the next century, many black Americans looked for Canaan, with varying degrees of millennial fervor and rhetoric, in Northern and Western areas of the United States.

Some of the Africans who heard the story of Sam Hose asked, "Why don't those Africans return to the land of their fathers and escape from the hands of them that hate them?"[30] Some African-Americans also wondered the same thing, for they could not envision any future for themselves, let alone the millennium, in the United States. A.M.E. bishop Henry M. Turner, the foremost advocate of black emigration to Africa during this time, argued: "Every man that has the sense of an animal must see there is no future in this country for the Negro . . . we are taken out and burned, shot, hanged, unjointed and murdered in every way."[31] The famed journalist John Edward Bruce denounced America and white Christianity for making caste prejudice the chief god of the country and predicted apocalyptic doom in an 1891 article:

> The nation is standing upon a volcano. It is a living, breathing lie, and the judgment of almighty God, will overtake it as surely as night follows day . . .
> Judgement is coming! The noisome pestilence, the destruction that wasteth at noonday, the arrow that flieth by day, the Pestilence that walketh in darkness will have no terrors for the Godly, but they will as surely overtake the great majority of the Negro-hating white Christians as that God is just.[32]

For these black nationalists and critics of American society, Africa replaced America as the focus of their hopes and dreams, and some of this focus was accompanied and undergirded by millennial belief and rhetoric.

Thomas Wentworth Higginson made a glaring omission in his characterization of what scripture served as loci for interpreting black experience when he left out Ps 68:31: "Princes shall come out of Egypt and Ethiopia shall stretch out her hands unto God." Albert Raboteau claims that this verse was "without doubt the most quoted verse in black religious history" and notes that the very obscurity of the verse extended its explanatory range though the various interpretations "clustered around three major themes: the African Race, the Redemption of Africa, and the Mission of the Darker Races."[33]

The golden age of the mythic past and the belief in a future golden age often collapse together in millennial thought.[34] Nineteenth-century black Americans believed that Egypt and Ethiopia in Ps 68:31 referred to the African race and looked to these ancient civilizations as proof of a glorious Africa past that rivaled European civilization and discredited any pseudo-scientific theories of black inferiority. This glorious past, in turn, inspired belief and confidence in a millennial future. In *The Cushite, or the Descendants of Ham*, Rufus Perry complained that the black mummy had been "transformed by the art of Pythagorean metempsychosis into a white mummy with a look of disdain upon its former self." Perry's aim was to prove that the ancient Ethiopians and Egyptians were black descendants of Ham:

> Then the Negro of the nineteenth century may point to them with pride; and, with all who would find in him a man and brother, cherish the hope of a return to racial celebrity, when in the light of a Christian civilization, Ethiopia shall stretch out her hands unto God.[35]

In addition to the ancient civilizations attributed to Ham's sons—Mizraim (Egypt), Cush (Ethiopia), and Canaan—George W. Brent argued that the important role of Africa in biblical history confirmed "Africa's Future glory" according to Ps 68:31.[36]

Black Americans in the late nineteenth century believed that the "redemption of Africa" was at hand, which meant, in varying degrees, Western civilization and Christianization. One conservative Southern lawyer argued that Anglo-Saxons had "wantonly overlooked" the prophecy of Ps 68:31 and greatly underestimated African ability "until our Heavenly Father, in His own time, caused to arise a Livingstone and a Stanley, who, in the belief that God did not make the great continent of Africa without a purpose nor the people without capacity for development, entered the heart of Africa and explored its resources."[37] Many black Americans, however, were critical of how Western civilization was being introduced into Africa. George B. Peabody argued that the redemption of Africa be sought primarily in the spread of the Christian gospel:

> But civilization does not save men; for civilization itself is self-destructive! That which is tamed by her is a *foe* to her, even as a tamed lion devours his master. Christianity *alone* can make the lion and lamb lie down together, and be led by a little child. The day is dawning. Hark! I hear a better song—the song of the saints, who are nearing with their banner to transplant the saving

> power which alone preserves the world from hopeless corruption. . . . This is
> the hope of Africa: First to be purged by the Redeemer's blood. Then may she
> welcome civilization and all its attendants with her door.[38]

As with nineteenth-century missions in general, the press for missions to Africa
was accompanied by millennial expectations.[39]

In his article "The Negro at Home and Abroad: Their Origin, Progress and
Destiny," J. Augustus Cole synthesized many themes of Ps 68:31. He began with
an examination of Hamitic origin and argued, in opposition to those who "attribute [Negro] origin to the ouran-outang, date his existence from a pre-
Adamic age, or teach him that he is a developed chimpanzee," that the builders of
the pyramids were black. Stressing that the name Ham means black or burnt, he
castigated those "jet black and professedly educated men in America" who advocated the name American or Afro-American in place of African or Negro. Though
Cole believed that blacks have an equal right to America as other races and did
not recommend emigration to Africa, he exhibited a pan-Africanism and concern for the destiny of Africa and the African race:

> There is no reason why the distribution of the Negro in America and West
> Indian Islands should impede the progress of African advancement, if all could
> labor for one end and keep the integrity of the race. . . . It is in the Christianity
> of the Negro that his destiny will be realized."[40]

Christianity, however, must not be the white man's variety:

> But in embracing Christianity the Negro has made a very sad mistake, which
> will always hinder his progress. When we accept Christianity from the white
> man, we do not regard it so much as the religion of Christ, as the "white man's
> religion." Consequently we have imitated the white man instead of imitating
> Christ, and we have retained both the white man's vices as well as his
> virtues.[41]

In order to progress toward Canaan instead of regressing to Egypt, the black
church must "make it her duty to instruct the race as to the right principles of religion by expunging from African Christianity all idolatrous imitations, which we
have acquired from the white man."[42] If the black church succeeds:

> Then God will be honored, the Church will be powerful, and we will no more
> "do evil that good may come." Then the millennium of the Negro will be near,
> when the sheep of other folds in Africa shall be united with those in America

and the West Indies by the cord of Christianity, and then there shall be one flock under one Shepherd, Jesus Christ.[43]

The third theme of Ps 68:31, according to Raboteau, is the mission of the darker races. Cole hinted of this in his emphasis on the black church working toward a pure Christianity, but this theme is found best in the writings of W.E.B. Du Bois. In the pamphlet *The Conservation of Races* he wrote:

We are Negroes, members of a vast historic race that from the very dawn of creation has slept, but half awakening in the dark forests of its African fatherland. We are the first fruits of this new nation, the harbinger of that black tomorrow which is yet destined to soften the whiteness of the Teutonic today.[44]

Du Bois followed by proposing a creed for the American Negro that extols the unique mission of blacks in the attainment of "human brotherhood."[45] A.M.E. bishop W. J. Gaines, who was born a slave, related this exceptional role to slavery:

History presents no sublimer spectacle than the patience and non-resistance of this race who, though smarting under the wrongs of more than two hundred years, refused to take revenge into their own hands and rebel with violence and bloodshed against their oppressors. No race ever acted more like Jesus Christ, whose life was one long patient non-resistance to wrong.[46]

In a tentative argument for racial amalgamation, George T. Downing stated that it was the destiny of America that the three divisions of Shem, Ham, and Japheth "meet as brother and form one people that will excel" for all three make an indispensable contribution, "none of which is more essential than the one the African branch specially contributes—that is the heart element—the element which Christ ingrafted into the religion of His day, an element which all Christendom now joins in extolling above all others."[47] Raboteau traces this concept of the mission of the darker races to the tradition of criticism against American Christianity by black Americans as exhibited by David Walker's *Appeal to the Coloured Citizens* and Frederick Douglass's *Narrative*: "In effect the jeremiad did more than enable blacks to vent their righteous indignation: it placed black Christians in a stance of judgment over white Christians; it consolidated a position of moral superiority for the descendants of the African Race."[48]

The ideas of the mission of the black race and moral exceptionalism of black Christians as they relate to millennialism are most fully elaborated in the writings of James Theodore Holly and Theophilus Gould Steward. In "The Divine Plan of Human Redemption in its Ethnological Development," Holly argued that this divine plan unfolds in three historical dispensations related to the three sons of Noah:

> The Semitic race had the formulating, the committing to writing and primal guardianship of the Holy Scriptures during the Hebrew dispensation. The Japhetic race has had the task committed to them of translating, publishing and promulgating broadcast the same Holy Scriptures, as completed by the Canon of the New Testament, during the apostolic phase of the Christian dispensation. But neither the one nor the other of those two races have entered into or carried out the spirit of those Scriptures. This crowning work of the will of God is reserved for the millennial phase of Christianity, when Ethiopia shall stretch out her hands directly unto God. Hence it may appear that the Semitic race has given us the written *thought* of God's Divine Plan; the Japhetic race has openly proclaimed this thought in the printed and preached WORD; but both alike await the forthcoming ministry of the Hamitic race to reduce to practical ACTION that spoken word, that written thought.[49]

Though the white nations have spread the gospel, they have lacked the peace that exemplifies the millennium:

> The most warlike and predatory nations of this nineteenth century of the grace of Jesus Christ are precisely the most enlightened Christian nations, which we must confess are at the same time very busily engaged in publishing and circulating the Bible in all languages and in sending Gospel missionaries among all peoples, even unto the very ends of the earth . . . the apostolic phase of the Christian dispensation is to terminate in a deluge of blood, shed by those warlike nations in fratricidal combat, at Armageddon in the great battle of God Almighty, when He shall declare war and assemble the bloodthirsty nations for slaughter . . . then the millennial phase of the Christian Dispensation will begin. The reign of peace and justice will be established on this earth for a thousand years, under the Lord Jesus.[50]

The African race, argued Holly, will experience a reversal from curse to blessing, from being the servants to having "the post of honor under the heavenly government of God."[51]

Steward, an A.M.E. minister and educator, wrote *The End of the World Country*, and argued that the millennium will be a special time for the darker races. Identifying the present age as the fourth, or Roman, age depicted in Daniel 7,

Steward argued that this age would soon end in judgment. Judgment is coming because of Anglo-Saxon pride, militarism, and betrayal of Christianity into a clan religion. Contrary to conceited beliefs about the success of foreign missions, Steward argued that the Indian, Asian, and African races have been excluded from Christianity "not because of the character of Christianity, all honor to its holy teachings! but because of the character of the representatives of the so-called Christian nations who come among them."[52] Fratricidal warfare between the "Christian nations" will end the age, but the darker races will escape the judgment and will convert to a pure gospel purged of Anglo-Saxon prejudice in the dawning millennium. Steward suggested that God has maintained the "Church of Abyssinia" in order that it may be a leader in the millennium:

> Who knows but this is the church that God is nourishing in the wilderness during the age that Jerusalem shall be trodden under foot, that is, until that time when the fullness of the Gentiles, the more than one billion who are still beyond the pale of Christianity, shall be brought in? . . . then the really righteous, unobscured by the perverse civilization—a civilization which is called Christian, but which is essentially Saxon, shall shine forth as the sun, and this hidden church of the wilderness shall come forth to lead Africa's millions, as part of that fullness of the Gentiles which is to come to welcome the universal Christ.[53]

Though Steward did see the end of the world and the ensuing millennium as having its focus in America, this is a result not of the triumphs but of the apostasy and failure of Anglo-Saxon civilization and missions.

In a discussion of how African American envisioned the millennium would come and when, it is helpful to be aware of the distinction between premillennialism and postmillennialism.[54] Premillennialism locates the second coming of Christ before the millennium and is usually associated with apocalyptic tones of judgment and divine intervention. Postmillennialism argues that Christ will return after the millennium and is usually associated with a more evolutionary and optimistic view of the establishment of the kingdom of God in the world through spiritual and material triumphs.

James Holly's millennialism provides an example of premillennialism. He stated that "Christ shall come with His saints and give to our weary and sin cursed earth its long-lasted Sabbath by inaugurating a reign of a thousand years."[55] There is a radical disjunction between the present and the millennium, as Holly believed that the "Christian" nations embody the spirit of the Antichrist and would aid the coming of the millennium only by destroying themselves at

Armageddon.[56] Steward is also a premillennialist in terms of judgment and a radical disjunction between the present and the future, though he is unsure whether Jesus will personally inaugurate the millennium: "The culminating stages of the Redeemer's glory will be marked by the coming of Jesus as King on earth, whether in a visible, personal form, or in effectual power only, it is not to our purpose to inquire."[57]

The traditional, but tenuous, correlation between premillennialism and inaction or quietism is not found in the millennialism of Holly or Steward. Though Christ will inaugurate the millennium, Holly and Steward criticized the present social and racial situation through their theories and reserved an active role for blacks in spreading the millennium.

The driving force behind the coming of the millennium for postmillennialists is also God, though not in such a manner that the present and future is marked by a radical disjunction. Some postmillennialists, those I identify as cultural millennialists, found the millennium arising out of the forces of Western civilizations. Gaines, for example, saw God working through Anglo-Saxon civilization:

> Providence, in wisdom, has decreed that the lot of the negro should be cast with the white people of America. Condemn as we may the means through which we were brought here, recount as we may the suffering through which, as a race, we passed in the years of slavery, yet the fact remains that today our condition is far in advance of that of the negroes who have never left their native Africa. We are planted in the midst of the highest civilization mankind has ever known, and are rapidly advancing in knowledge, property and moral enlightenment. We might, with all reason, thank God even for slavery, if this were the only means through which we could arrive at our present progress and development.[58]

Herbert claimed that the millennium was arising from the spread of republicanism, justice, education, and civilization.[59]

Most black millennialists who may be described as postmillennialists were not so naive and optimistic as to identify the kingdom of God with Western civilization. Their optimism lay, rather, in their belief that Christianity could be a leaven in history, transforming and redeeming it until the millennium emerged. I refer to this kind of millennialism as progressive. Bishop Clinton spoke for churchmen in emphasizing the role of the church as a leaven "for purifying, preserving and seasoning the world till 'Righteousness abound, As the great deep profound, And fill the earth with purity.'"[60]

In addition to his statement that the millennium inspires Christians to evan-gelize, J. W. E. Bowen called black Americans to take the future into their own hands and acquire "Christian character"; actions that he optimistically believed would "assert and prophesy the incoming of the gray dawn of the millennium which shall ultimately usher in the blazing midday."[61] The millennium, argued Holsey, will come about by the "hybridization" of Jesus' love, presence, and power in the world:

> Shiloh's empire still abides, and its magnetic embodiment in the person of the living Christ, marches on in stately tread, transversing the breadth of cen-turies, measuring the decades, and wrapping the string of days and the fibre of hours around his hand, and buckling the aged cycles and the countless trend of years to his belt. . . . But the Kingdom of Shiloh is progressive. It is educative and consequently slow in its progress. It is slow to the ideas and conceptions of men, but not slow to God. . . . The perfection of character is the ultimate end for which time is given, and the process and progress toward perfection can-not cease until the effort is coronated with the brightest gems of nature. The Kingdom of Shiloh cannot stand still, because its very life is in its thrift and activity.[62]

Many black ministers in the "New South" were optimistic about the transforming powers of Christianity on race relations, according to Edward L. Wheeler, be-cause of their belief in the "fatherhood of God and the brotherhood of man."[63] This optimism is visible in the belief that the kingdom of God would triumph in the world.

The premillennial, or more appropriately millennial Ethiopian, beliefs of both Holly and Steward are accompanied by an apocalyptic urgency that sees the millennium as very near at hand. Holly argued for an imminent millennium both from the appearance of the spirit of the Antichrist in the "Christian nations" and the manipulation of "sacred chronology." He suggested that the "millennial Sabbath" would begin six thousand years after creation, which he claims was in 4124 BC and, thus, puts the end at 1876. Interestingly, Holly then added forty years of tribulation, a biblical number of "Trial and humiliation" (roughly the years of the Nadir period under study!), which points to 1916, though the mil-lennium might come sooner because God "has promised to cut short those evil days for the sake of the elect."[64] Steward was more tentative than Holly about calculating the end times by biblical prophecy and suggested several different tabulations. In addition, Steward argued for an imminent millennium based on the signs of the times (social and political unrest, increase in knowledge and travel, apostasy, and the emergence of the Antichrist).[65]

James H. Moorhead has argued that postmillennialism, by placing the second coming after the achievements of evangelical Christianity in the world, "represented a compromise between an apocalyptic and an evolutionary view of time, between a history characterized by dramatic upheavals and supernatural events and one governed by natural laws of organic development.[66] Apocalyptic elements can also be detected in the coming of the millennium in many of the millennial schemes under study that may loosely come under the rubric of postmillennialism. Though Holsey emphasized that the coming of the millennium is slow, it is also throbbing with an apocalyptic nearness:

> Everywhere Shiloh's empire touches the deep chores of human nature and human hearts, stirring, revolutionizing and unifying its forces and agencies, exhibiting those far-reaching plenitudes of power and throbbing energies and plenipotent activities that make up its irresistible character. Everyday the empire of Shiloh is making its onslaughts and encroachments upon the ramparts of sin and hell.[67]

Likewise, Bowen preached that "the times are ominous; ominous I believe not for evil, but for good,"[68] and argued that the millennium would arise in the new century:

> I repeat, my hope is fixed, and standing upon the top of this present Mt. Nebo, and letting my eyes sweep through the dark past up along the shores of the river we have crossed, and now into the wilderness with our churches, school houses, trade schools, and various christian and civilizing agencies, with faith in God, I am certain that I see, though the thick darkness that envelopes us, the gray rays of a new morn, and I hear the tramp of a new civilization and the music of its avant courier joyfully shouting: "There's a good time coming boys, a good time coming."[69]

Though there may be some overlap between cultural millennialism, millennial Ethiopianism, and progressive millennialism due to the elusive and elastic nature of millennial symbols as well as shared concerns and traditions, I contend that these three types portray distinct major themes. Likewise, I believe that the different types can be assigned to the great variety of millennial thought presented, while recognizing a degree of overlap between the types.

Cultural millennialism, with its strong identification with Western culture and American society, and its optimism that the forces of western civilization were working out into a millennial golden age is exemplified by the articles of Cain, Herbert, and Gaines. In a way, the racial amalgamation of Ruffin, Minton, and Downing represents an extreme form of cultural millennialism, yet falls short of complete identification with Anglo-Saxon culture because of notes of social criticism and black exceptionalism. Capitalism and economic growth are another such force of progress, according to Booker T. Washington and William Matthews. The latter, a wealthy lawyer and businessman in Washington, D.C., wrote an article in the *A.M.E. Church Review* titled "Money as a Factor in Human Progress" in which he argued that money is an indispensable "soldier" in the spread of Christian civilization:

> Those most deeply interested in the redemption of Africa frankly admit that their great hope is in the spirit of commercial enterprise; not in it alone to be sure, but that commerce will be the John the Baptist opening up a way and that the Christian missionary with an open Bible following in the furrows made by the invincible and remorseless plough of commerce, will drop his seed of truth, which will spring up into a magnificent harvest.[70]

The religious nature of cultural millennialism is similar to what Robert Bellah has called civil religion.[71] Though God is given recognition as working through the forces of culture, the prominent place of the deity in traditional Christian theology is either replaced or shared by a profound trust in American cultural principles and institutions. It may be more appropriate to consider this a rhetorical millennialism than a developed theological and biblical millennialism, though it is difficult to make a clear distinction. There is a certain elastic vagueness to millennial symbols that extends their powerful influence in culture, resulting in a millennial theory that may be diffuse, diluted, and secular.

The emphasis on pan-Africanism, the criticism or rejection of white society and culture, and the elevation of the African past characteristic of millennial Ethiopianism are found in the millennial language and thought of Perry, Brent, Cole, Bruce, Holly, and Steward. An extreme form is the millennialism of the latter three who espouse the total rejection of white society in terms of apocalyptic judgment. In general, millennial Ethiopianism stresses the supernatural intervention of God, a broader understanding of history in which Western civilization is seen as a stage and not the fulfillment of history, the importance of biblical prophecy centering on Ps 68:31, the moral leadership and prophetic insight of black peoples, and the judgment of American cultural forces.

Progressive millennialism is a more traditionally theological millennialism most akin to the prevailing white postmillennialism of the middle of the nineteenth century. Unlike millennial Ethiopianism, progressive millennialism as seen in the thought of Bowen, Clinton, Payne, and Holsey stresses the power of Christianity through the church's involvement in evangelism, missions, and reform in transforming American society and bringing about the millennium on earth. This type, however, does not share the more secular and uncritical optimism of cultural millennialism.

A discussion of millennial types is not complete without looking at a-millennialism among African-Americans. This theory interprets Revelation 20 symbolically as either the age of the church or the realm beyond this world. In the only biblical commentary on Revelation written by an African-American during this period, A.M.E. Zion bishop J. W. Hood argued that if there is to be a millennium and partial resurrection of the saints, it will occur in heaven. There will be no establishment of the millennium on earth, for the second coming of Christ will be at the end of time, and the "new heaven and new earth" will be beyond time. The only establishment of the kingdom of God, according to Hood, is within the heart, when Christ rather than Satan dwells in the hearts of men and women.[72] In a collection of black Baptist sermons published to assure white missionaries that their work in the South had not been in vain, S. W. Anderson addressed the subject of eschatology in a-millennial fashion and argued that the only golden "world to come" would be in heaven.[73] The Presbyterian minister Francis J. Grimke castigated this-worldly and otherworldy millennial talk of "golden streets, and pearly gates, and white robes, and a land flowing with milk and honey" because he believed that it distracted black Americans from the more pressing need for "character" and "Christian manhood and womanhood."[74]

An a-millennial position tends to look toward the world with neither extreme optimism nor extreme pessimism. In an *A.M.E. Church Review* article from 1900, Du Bois looked to the dawning century with caution and modesty:

> The progress of the nation toward a settlement of the Negro is patent—the
> movement with all its retrogression is a spiral not a circle, and as long as there
> is motion there is hope. At the same time we must indulge in no fantastic
> dreams, simply because in the past this nation has turned back from its errors
> against the Negro and tardily sought the higher way is no earnest for the fu-
> ture. Error that ends in progress is none the less error.[75]

Progress is neither inevitable nor impossible, but dependent on the hard work of Christian men and women rather than a millennial vision.

CONCLUSION

It is generally accepted by scholars today that millennialism should be described, as Hillel Schwartz states, "less often as the products of disease, more often as an arsenal of world-sustaining forces."[76] Timothy L. Smith argues that black Americans in the nineteenth century grasped the radical and liberating nature of Christianity:

> Africans were pressed up against the wall by American slavery's vast assault upon their humanity. This tragic circumstance compelled them to discover in the religion of their white oppressors a faith whose depths few of the latter ever suspected, enabling the Black Christians to reconcile suffering and hope, guilt and forgiveness, tyranny and spiritual freedom, self-hate and divine acceptance. In that faith some of them found the strength to throw off their bonds, and many others the dignity, when once emancipated, to stand up free.[77]

In like manner, many black Christians found great strength in the Christian millennial tradition because of its divinely inspired criticism and rebellion against the present social order. Regardless of form or type, millennialism sets a future perfect state over against the present and sows the seeds of social and religious criticism. Inherent in black millennialism is criticism against the unjust and unequal treatment of African Americans as well as criticism against white Christianity, which did little if anything to solve the "race problem."

Black millennialism of the Nadir period reveals several important things about the experience of African Americans. Blacks of this period were deeply religious and influenced by biblical symbols and passages. Jean Quandt has argued that postmillennialism during this period became secularized into a theory of human and natural progress.[78] Although this can be see in cultural millennialism, the greater part of black millennialism retained a strong emphasis on divine and spiritual activity, perhaps related to the fact that black Americans did not have many secular powers and institutions at their disposal. This religious emphasis, however, did not translate into a quietism or withdrawal from social criticism. Some of the strongest criticism of white Christianity and American society can be found in black millennialism.

It becomes clear in a study of black millennialism that a very important ingredient of the African-American Christian faith was the belief that history is divinely ordained, controlled by God, and moving toward its fulfillment. The belief in the millennium and the special destiny of the black race was part of a theodicy African Americans sought in order to make sense of their past in slavery, reaffirm meaning in their lives, and strengthen their trust in God.[79] In the midst of the deteriorating conditions of the Nadir, black Americans may have differed in how they understood their destiny in different types of millennialism, but they were united in the strong belief that God was in control of history and their future.

NOTES

A version of this paper was presented at the Mid-Atlantic Regional Meeting of the American Academy of Religion, 20–21 March 1991, Barnard College, New York City. The author would like to thank James H. Moorhead, Albert J. Raboteau, and John F. Wilson for their careful reading of this essay and their helpful comments.

1. Edward W. Blyden, "The Negro in the United States," *A.M.E. Church Review* 16 (January 1900) 309.

2. Ibid.

3. See Rayford W. Logan, *The Negro in American Life and Thought: The Nadir, 1877–1901* (New York: Dial, 1954).

4. George B. Peabody, "The Hope of Africa," *A.M.E. Church Review* 7 (July 1890) 59.

5. For background on this era, see Wilson Jeremiah Moses, *The Golden Age of Black Nationalism, 1850–1925* (Camden, CT: Archon, 1970); George M. Fredrickson, *The Black Image in the White Mind: The Debate on Afro-American Character and Destiny, 1817–1914* (New York: Harper & Row, 1971); Ronald C. White, *Liberty and Justice for All: Racial Reform and the Social Gospel, 1877–1925* (San Francisco: Harper & Row, 1990); and August Meier, *Negro Thought in America, 1880–1925: Racial Ideologies in the Age of Booker T. Washington* (Ann Arbor: University of Michigan Press, 1963).

6. Leonard Sweet, "Millennialism in America: Recent Studies," *Theological Studies* 40 (1979) 530. Other important bibliographic surveys of millennialism include David E. Smith, "Millenarian Scholarship in America," *American Quarterly* 17 (1965) 535–49; and Hillel Schwartz, "The End of the Beginning: Millenarian Studies, 1969–1975," *Religious Studies Review* 2 (1976) 1–14.

7. Sweet, "Millennialism in America," 523–24; one must keep in mind Sweet's warning of the "infestatious definitional imprecision" endemic in studies of millennialism, though I would add that one must also recognize a certain elasticity in millennial language.

8. Thomas Wentworth Higginson, "The Negro Spirituals," *Atlantic Monthly* 19 (1867) 687–88. See also Lawrence W. Levine, *Black Culture and Black Consciousness: Afro-American Folk Thought from Slavery to Freedom* (New York: Oxford, 1977), 33–55.

9. See Donald G. Mathews, *Religion in the Old South* (Chicago: University of Chicago Press, 1977) 223–25; James H. Moorhead, "Millennialism," in Samuel S. Hill, ed.,

Encyclopedia of Religion in the South (Macon, GA: Mercer University Press, 1984) 477–79; and Albert J. Raboteau, *Slave Religion: The "Invisible Institution" in the Antebellum South* (New York: Oxford University Press, 1978) 311–13.

10. J. W. E. Bowen, "What Shall the Harvest Be?" in Idem, ed., *What Shall the Harvest Be? A National Sermon; or, a Series of Plain Talks to the Colored People of America, on their Problems* (Washington, DC: Howard University Print, 1892) 2. Background information for most of the African-Americans under study in this essay can be found in William J. Simmons, *Men of Mark* (Cleveland: George Rewell, 1887); Rayford W. Logan and Michael R. Winston, eds., *Dictionary of American Negro Biography* (New York: W. W. Norton, 1982); and the appendix in Edward L. Wheeler, *Uplifting the Race: The Black Minster in the New South, 1865–1902* (Lanham, MD: University Press of America, 1986).

11. George W. Clinton, "Christianity Under the Searchlight," in idem, ed., *Christianity Under the Searchlight* (Nashville: National Baptist Publishing Board, 1909), 36.

12. Daniel Alexander Payne, *Recollections of Seventy Years* (Nashville: Publishing House of the A.M.E. Sunday School Union, 1888) 303.

13. Lucius H. Holsey, "From Repentance to Final Restitution," in idem, ed., *Autobiography, Sermons, Addresses and Essays* (Atlanta: Franklin Painting & Publishing Co., 1898) 122–23.

14. R. Henri Herbert, "The Government of the Future," *A.M.E. Church Review* 1 (October 1884) 148–49.

15. Samuel Harris, *The Kingdom of Christ on Earth* (Andover, MA: W. F. Draper, 1874); James Theodore Holly, "Sacred Chronology and the Inspired Arithmetic of Divine Revelation," *A.M.E. Church Review* 2 (July 1885) 13.

16. Holsey, "The Trend of Civilization," in *Autobiography*, 274.

17. R. H. Cain, "The Negro Problem of the South." *A.M.E. Church Review* 2 (January 1886) 145. The numbering of the *Review* is problematic in this issue, and the dating may not be exact.

18. The major exception being premillennial dispensationalism, cf. Timothy P. Weber, *Living in the Shadow of the Second Coming: American Premillennialism, 1875–1982*, (rev. ed.; Chicago: University of Chicago Press, 1987).

19. See Ernest Lee Tuveson, *Redeemer Nation: The Idea of America's Millennial Role* (Chicago: University of Chicago Press, 1968).

20. Herbert, "Government of the Future," 144–48.

21. J. Augustus Cole, "The Negro at Home and Abroad: Their Origin, Progress and Destiny," *A.M.E. Church Review* 4 (April 1888) 401.

22. From the symposium "What Should Be the Policy of the Colored American Toward Africa?" *A.M.E. Church Review* 2 (July 1885) 69.

23. Louis R. Harlan, ed., *The Booker T. Washington Papers, vol. 3: 1889–1895* (Urbana: University of Illinois Press, 1974) 586–87.

24. George L. Ruffin, "A Look Forward," *A.M.E. Church Review* 2 (January 1885) 33.

25. Theophilus J. Minton, "Is Intermarriage Between the Races to be Encouraged?" *A.M.E. Church Review* 2 (January 1887) 286.

26. Ruffin, "A Look Forward," 29. Though Strong (*Our Country* [Cambridge, MA: Belknap Press, 1963] 202, 209–11) defined Anglo-Saxon "somewhat broadly to include all English-speaking peoples," it is doubtful that he included black Americans in his definition. For an argument that black Americans be designated "Negrosaxons," see William H. Ferris, *The African Abroad, or His Evolution in Western Civilization* (2 vols.; New Haven, CT: Tuttle, Morehouse & Taylor, 1913) 1. 296–311.

27. *Washington Bee* (District of Columbia, 9 November 1889) quoted in James M. Washington, *Frustrated Fellowship: The Black Baptist Quest for Social Power* (Macon, GA: Mercer University Press, 1986) 155.

28. *Globe-Democrat* (St. Louis, 19 March 1879) quoted in Nell Irvin Painter, "Millenarian Aspects of the Exodus to Kansas of 1879," *Journal of Social History* 9 (1976) 333. Painter argues that there was also a non-millenarian movement to Kansas that was more deliberate about the move in contrast to the millenarian exodus that she characterizes as imminent, collective, and total. The former group, however, also made use of the biblical exodus imagery, which demonstrates the elasticity of religious symbols and millennial rhetoric. See also Nell Irvin Painter, *Exodusters: Black Migration to Kansas after Reconstruction* (New York: Alfred A. Knopf, 1977) and Robert G. Athearn, *In Search of Canaan: Black Migration to Kansas, 1879–80* (Lawrence, KS: Regents Press of Kansas, 1978).

29. See Walter G. Fleming, "'Pap' Singleton, The Moses of the Colored Exodus," *American Journal of Sociology* 15 (1909), 67–68.

30. Blyden, "The Negro in the United States," 309–10.

31. "The Negro Has Not Sense Enough," *Voice of Missions* (Atlanta, 1 July 1900); reprinted in John H. Bracey, et al., *Black Nationalism in America* (Indianapolis: Bobbs-Merrill, 1970) 173. The standard history of black emigration to Africa is Edwin S. Redkey, *Black Exodus: Black Nationalist and Back-to-Africa Movements, 1890–1910* (New Haven: Yale University Press, 1969), but Redkey does not discuss millennialism.

32. Peter Gilbert, ed., *The Selected Writings of John Edward Bruce: Militant Black Journalist* (New York: Arno, 1971) 47–49. In a 1900 article, Bruce (*Selected Writings*, 65) counseled parents to teach children that "in God's own time Ethiopia will suddenly stretch her hands unto him who shapes the destinies of nations and individuals." He later became an official in the Universal Negro Improvement Association and identified Marcus Garvey as the Jesus of the black race; cf. Randall K. Burkett, *Black Redemption: Churchmen Speak for the Garvey Movement* (Philadelphia: Temple University Press, 1978) 149–56.

33. Albert J. Raboteau, "'Ethiopia Shall Soon Stretch Forth Her Hands': Black Destiny

in Nineteenth-Century America," University Lecture in Religion, Arizona State University, 27 January 1983, 5. See also Moses, *Golden Age of Black Nationalism*, 156–69.

34. Tuveson (*Redeemer Nation*, 78) argues "more than anything else, the end of history is not the establishment of things new, but the restoration of the very oldest—the primeval heritage of mankind, of which man has been defrauded by a super-human Enemy."

35. Rufus Perry, *The Cushite, or the Descendants of Ham* (Springfield, MA: Willey, 1893) ix, x.

36. George W. Brent, "The Ancient Glory of the Hamitic Race," *A.M.E. Church Review* 12 (October 1895) 272–75.

37. D. Augustus Straker, "The Congo Valley: Its Redemption," *A.M.E. Church Review* 2 (January 1896) 146–57.

38. Peabody, "The Hope of Africa," 56–61.

39. Studies of black missions to Africa are found in Walter L. Williams, *Black Americans and the Evangelization of Africa* (Madison, WI: University of Wisconsin Press, 1982) and Sylvia M. Jacobs, ed., *Black Americans and the Missionary Movement in Africa* (Westport, CT: Greenwood, 1982). For a study of the theological background of the foreign mission movement, see William R. Hutchison, *Errand to the World: American Protestant Thought and Foreign Missions* (Chicago: University of Chicago Press, 1987).

40. Cole, "The Negro at Home and Abroad," 401.

41. Ibid.

42. Ibid, 402.

43. Ibid., 394–402. See also the poem based on Ps 68:31 by L. J. Coppin in "The Negro's Part in the Redemption of Africa," *A.M.E. Church Review* 19 (October 1902) 511–12.

44. W. E. Burghardt Du Bois, *The Conservation of Races* (Washington, DC: American Negro Academy Occasional Papers, No. 2, 1897) 12.

45. Ibid., 15. William H. Becker ("The Black Church: Manhood and Mission," *JAAR* 40 [1972] 316–33) argues that the nineteenth-century dogma that it was the black American's divine calling to evangelize Africa was related to the need to demonstrate black leadership, independence, identity, and vocation.

46. W. J. Gaines, *The Negro and the White Man* (Philadelphia: A.M.E. Publishing House, 1897) 65.

47. George T. Downing, "The Afro-American Force in America," *A.M.E. Church Review* 1 (October 1884) 159. See also Alex Crummell's 1877 sermon, "The Destined Superiority of the Negro," in idem, *The Greatness of Christ and Other Sermons* (New York: Thomas Whitaker, 1882) 332–52; and Wilson Jeremiah Moses, *Alexander Crummell: A Study of Civilization and Discontent* (New York: Oxford University Press,

1989). For an identification of blacks with the suffering servant of Isaiah, see Kelly Miller, *Race Adjustments: Essays on the Negro in America* (New York: Neale Publishing Company, 1908) 150–51.

48. Raboteau, "Ethiopia Shall Soon Stretch Forth Her Hands," 11. The selections from Walker and Douglass are reprinted in Milton C. Sernett, ed., *Afro-American Religious History: A Documentary Witness* (Durham, NC: Duke University Press, 1985) 100–108, 188–95. Perry (*The Cushite*, 146–47) traces this belief of the moral superiority of blacks to the ancient Cushites. Wilson Jeremiah Moses (*Black Messiahs and Uncle Toms: Social and Literary Manipulations of a Religious Myth* [University Park, PA: Pennsylvania State University Press, 1982]) examines what he calls the "Afro-American messianic myth."

49. James T. Holly, "The Divine Plan of Human Redemption in its Ethnological Development," *A.M.E. Church Review* 1 (October 1884) 79–85.

50. Ibid., 81.

51. Ibid., 84.

52. T. G. Steward, *The End of the World; or, Clearing the Way for the Fullness of the Gentiles* (Philadelphia: A.M.E. Church Book Rooms, 1888) 4–7, 18–20, 67–75, 79–99, 112–27.

53. Ibid., 125–26.

54. I contend for my threefold typology in contrast to the more common categories of premillennialism and postmillennialism, which do not adequately describe black millennialism. The later are retained, however, as helpful secondary heuristic devices that also orient the discussion to other works on nineteenth-century millennialism.

55. Holly, "The Divine Plan of Human Redemption," 81.

56. Holly, "Sacred Chronology," 9–13.

57. Steward, *The End of the World*, 20.

58. Gaines, *The Negro and the White Man*, 213.

59. Herbert, "Government of the Future," 148–49.

60. Clinton, "Christianity under the Searchlight," 80. See also A. H. Newton, *Out of the Briars* (Philadelphia: A.M.E. Book Concern, 1910) 177–85, 245, 248.

61. Bowen, "What Shall the Harvest Be?" 7, 8.

62. Holsey, "Christianity Shiloh's Empire," in idem, *Autobiography*, 71–74. In this sermon, Holsey identifies "Shiloh" in Gen 49:10 with Christ but expands this identification to the millennial reign of Christ.

63. Wheeler, *Uplifting the Race*, 37–59.

64. Holly, "Sacred Chronology," 12, 13. In addition, Holly argued that the secret number of the elect, known only by God, must be accompanied by the "faithful preaching of the Gospel of the coming Kingdom." In conversation with the author, James Moorhead has noted the similarities between Holly's dates and those of Charles Taze Russell of the Millennial Dawn (Jehovah's Witnesses) movement. I am un-

aware of any direct connection, but this interesting similarity may warrant further research.

65. Steward, *The End of theWorld*, 79, 110.

66. James H. Moorhead, "The Erosion of Postmillennialism in American Religious Thought, 1865–1925," *Church History* 53 (1984) 61–62.

67. Holsey, "Christianity Shiloh's Empire," 77. In another sermon, Holsey ("From Repentance to Final Restitution," in idem, *Autobiography*, 111–23) demonstrated that the postmillennial and premillennial typology is not always clearly marked and cannot be forced, for he speaks of a conflation of the millennium with the apocalyptic second coming.

68. Bowen, "What Shall the Harvest Be?" 1.

69. Bowen, "The Disciplinary Character of Affliction," 18.

70. William Matthews, "Money As a Factor in Human Progress," *A.M.E. Church Review* 1 (April 1885) 327, 238.

71. See Robert N. Bellah, "Civil Religion in America," *Daedalus* 96 (1967) 1–21.

72. J. W. Hood, *The Plan of the Apocalypse* (York, PA: Anstadt, 1900) 164–77. See also idem, *The Negro in the Christian Pulpit* (Raleigh, NC: Edward, Broughton, 1884) 148–64, 178–89. The formal exposition of theology by B. T. Tanner contains no discussion of the millennium, cf. *Theological Lectures* (Nashville: A.M.E. Church Sunday School Union, 1894).

73. S. W. Anderson, "The World to Come," in E. M. Brawley, ed., *The Negro Baptist Pulpit: A Collection of Sermons and Papers on Baptist Doctrine and Missionary and Educational Work* (Philadelphia: American Baptist Publication Society, 1890) 175–87. Another essay in the volume, however, exudes with millennial confidence that all of America will soon be converted to Christianity; cf. M. Vann, "Baptists and Home Missions," 251.

74. See Grimke's 1892 sermon to the Washington, D.C. Ministers Council, "The Afro-American Pulpit in Relation to Race Elevation," in Carter G. Woodson, ed., *The Works of Francis J. Grimke*, vol. 1: *Addresses Mainly Personal an Racial* (Washington, DC: Associated Publishers, 1942) 223–34.

75. W. E. B. Du Bois, "The Present Outlook for the Dark Races of Mankind," *A.M.E. Church Review* 17 (October 1900) 100.

76. Schwartz, "The End of the beginning," 1.

77. Timothy L. Smith, "Slavery and Theology: The Emergence of Black Christian Consciousness in Nineteenth-Century America," *Church History* 41 (1972) 512.

78. See Jean Be Quandt, "Religion and Social Thought: The Secularization of Postmillennialism," *American Quarterly* 25 (1973) 390–409.

79. See Raboteau, "Ethiopia Shall Soon Stretch Forth Her hands," 4–7.

SELECTED BIBLIOGRAPHY FOR FURTHER READING

Drake, St. Clair. *The Redemption of Africa and Black Religion.* Chicago: Third World Press, 1970.

Moses, Wilson Jeremiah. *Alexander Crummell: A Study of Civilization and Discontent.* New York: Oxford University Press, 1989.

Moses, Wilson Jeremiah. *The Golden Age of Black Nationalism, 1850–1925.* New York: Oxford University Press, 1978.

Redkey, Edwin. *Black Nationalist and Back-to-Africa Movements, 1890–1910.* New Haven: Yale University Press, 1969.

Stuckey, Sterling. *The Ideological Origins of Black Nationalism.* Boston: Beacon Press, 1972.

URBANIZATION, NEW RELIGIOUS MOVEMENTS, AND SOCIAL ACTIVISM

V ::

Hans A. Baer and *Merrill Singer*

::The first half of the twentieth century saw the development of great religious diversity as large numbers of African Americans migrated to Northern cities attracted by jobs in industry, and propelled by the codification of Jim Crow laws and the decline of farming opportunities in the South. Interpretations of this religious diversity have focused on the influences from different African and white ethnic cultures, and the multiple religious options available in the Northern cities compared to the relatively homogenous evangelical South. Hans A. Baer and Merrill Singer stress social factors and different experiences of racism within American culture as central factors in explaining the resulting religious diversity among African Americans. ::

:: 12 TOWARD A TYPOLOGY OF
BLACK SECTARIANISM AS
A RESPONSE TO RACIAL
STRATIFICATION

Hans A. Baer and *Merrill Singer*

:: Several years ago, a Black anthropologist lamented the tendency, particularly in recent decades, to overlook the diversity among persons of African descent within the United States (Green 1970). Although Green cited examples of diversification along class, cultural, historical, and regional lines along Afro-Americans, her argument would also apply to Black religion. Despite the fact that there now exists a voluminous literature on the plethora of religious movements and organizations existing in our society, the vast majority of these studies focus on groups with predominantly White memberships. As Szwed (1971:v) notes, " . . . it is a sad fact that we have better descriptions—incomplete as they are—of religious beliefs and practices in West Africa, Brazil, and the Caribbean than we have of Black people in the United States."

The few studies which do consider Black religion tend to focus on various aspects of the more conventional religious groups in the Black community (Du Bois 1903; Mays and Nicholson 1933; Powdermaker 1939; Lewis 1955; Frazier 1974). But as Wilmore (1972:210) indicates, " . . . The period between 1890 and the Second World War was one of luxuriant growth and development for many forms of Black religion in the United States and Africa that challenged the bourgeois character of the main-line Black denominations and the racist posture of the White churches." Only a few scholars have given any attention to the great variety of unconventional religions that are found among Black Americans (Jones

1939; Fauset 1971; Washington 1973; Simpson 1978). Even fewer have provided us with detailed accounts of some of these groups (Lincoln 1962; Essien-Udom 1962; Brotz 1970; Williams 1974; Burnham 1979). As a result of our own research with certain relatively unknown religious movements in the Black community, we have come to believe that there is a need for a typology which systematically recognizes the diversity of Black religious groups and simultaneously places them into a context that they all share.[1] Such a typology will not only order the extensive pluralism of the Black religious experience, but will also serve as an analytical guide for future research in this area.

In this paper, we shall first discuss the need for a new typology of Black sectarianism. Second we present our own typology through an analysis of established sects, messianic-nationalists sects, conversionist sects, and thaumaturgical-manipulationist sects. Finally, we deal with the Father Divine movement as a special example of a mixed type.

PAST TYPOLOGIES OF BLACK RELIGIOUS GROUPS
AND THE NEED FOR A NEW TYPOLOGY

Much ink has been spilled in the social scientific literature on typologies and even more has been spilled in recent years questioning their utility. It is not our desire to elaborate upon, revise, or even modify the traditional church-sect typology. In fact, it is not clear to us whether or not our scheme is absolutely dependent upon this venerable nemesis of the sociology of religion, although some of our terminology and thinking will be borrowed from some of its principal proponents.

Our typology is by no means the first one applied to religious groups in the Black American community. Based upon his study of thirteen religious groups in New York and Washington, D.C., Jones (1939) proposed the presence of the following types of "evangelistic churches and cults" in his sample: (1) those with strong charismatic leaders, (2) "spirit possession" cults, and (3) "utopian, communal, or fraternal" cults. While Jones made no pretense that this scheme encompasses the diversity of religious groups among Blacks, in the appendix he presents a more complete "classified table of religious cults" among Black Americans. This consists of the following types: (1) faith-healing cults, (2) Holiness cults, (3) Islamic cults, (4) Pentecostal cults, (5) Spiritualist cults, (6) cult personalities, and (7) others. A major problem with both of Jones' typologies is that they fail to differentiate between "cults" and other religious organizations in the Black community. It appears that the term "cult" is applied to any group that is not either Baptist, Methodist, or one of the religious bodies which is considered to be "mainstream" in the Black community or in the larger society. The second typology is also confusing in that it fails to differentiate faith-healing groups from the Holiness, Spiritualist, or other groups which often also include healing dimensions.

On the basis of his research with forty Black churches, Daniel (1942) proposed a somewhat more inclusive typology. He classified forty churches in "that part of Chicago which has the densest Negro population" on the basis of their ritual, ceremonial, and emotional content. It was his contention that ritual performs different functions for different classes among urban Blacks while at the same time enhancing the morale of a subordinate racial group. On the basis of these criteria, Daniel proposes a scheme which include the following "ritual types": (1) "ecstatic sects or cults," (2) "semidemonstrative groups," (3) "deliberative," and (4) "liturgical denominations." This typology has the added advantage of placing Black religious within the context of the social structure of the larger society as well as that of the Black community. Its major drawbacks are that it is confined to a restricted sample of congregations in an urban area and fails to discuss strategies that religious Blacks have devised for coping with racial stratification.

Some social scientists, such as Simpson and Yinger (1972) and Yinger (1970) make note of various sectarian movements among Blacks and cite them as examples of the types in their own classifications. Despite this, since the earlier work of Jones and Daniel, there have been no concerted attempts to provide a systematic typology for the diversity of religious movements and organizations in the Black community.

Perhaps the principal difficulty of classification and typologies is that of using them in some sort of meaningful context. With this in mind, it may be argued that the content, structure, and diversity of Black religion derives primarily from three sources: (1) influences from African cultures; (2) influences from religious patterns in Euro-American culture; and (3) religious responses on the part of Blacks to cope with their minority status in a stratified and racist society. In the delineation of our typology, we will focus upon the third source, largely because it appears to be the overriding factor which is shared by all Black religious groups in American society. As Essien-Udom (1962:30) notes, diverse religious groups in the Black community are ad hoc responses to "the unresolved problem of the Negro's status as a second-class citizen in the United States."

The typology delineated in this paper will concern itself only with religious movements and organizations that are composed primarily of Black members. This is in keeping with our view that Black religion is in large part a response to the stratification and racism which are inherent in American society. Our typology will not include white-controlled religious organizations that contain either predominantly Black congregations or have Black members scattered about among various predominantly White congregations. Exclusion of these groups from our typology does not imply that they are insignificant topics of research. Rather, we focus on Black-controlled groups in an effort to understand collective religious response to the exclusion Black Americans have experienced from mainstream roles and opportunities.

THE CONSTRUCTION OF A TYPOLOGY OF BLACK SECTARIANISM

Since relatively little research has been done on religious groups among Black Americans, we feel that a simple but inclusive typology is called for at this time. The response of one group to another group or to the larger society in which it is embedded includes both a behavioral dimension and an ideational dimension. In the construction of a typology of Black sectarianism, we will use these two dimensions as our axes. One axis considers the "strategies of social action" that Black religious groups adopt in addressing their structural position in American society. In this regard, the response of a particular group may be *instrumental*; that is it may focus upon the attainment of concrete goals that are expected to improve the objective status of its adherents, or it may be *expressive* in that it provides for the release of the emotional tensions accumulated through the experiences of its members in an oppressive situation. The second axis considers the general "attitudinal orientation" of the members of various religious groups to the cultural patterns of the larger society, or more specifically to those of the dominant or majority group in that society. A particular religious body may incorporate a positive orientation; that is, it tends to be attracted to or accept the values, norms, and beliefs of the dominant group, or it may develop a negative orientation; that is, it rejects or is repulsed by them, at least conditionally.

Figure 1 below illustrates the typology in the form of a four cell matrix.[2] Each cell represents a different type of religious sect. Much of the literature on religious organizations is devoted to making a distinction between the "sect" and the "cult." While such a distinction may be useful in many cases, we will dispense with it for the purposes of our paper. Instead, we will emphasize the sectarian nature of Black religious groups in that they all exist in a state of tension with the larger society. This is in keeping with the observation of many social scientists that sectarian groups are in essence protest movements that not only challenge the ability of established churches or religions to meet the needs of all people but that they also challenge certain aspects of the larger society (Troeltsch 1931; Pope 1942; Wilson 1969; Yinger 1970; Stark and Bainbridge 1979). In the case of Black religious groups, the racial status of their adherents adds an additional element to the nature of their conflict within the context of American society.

FIGURE I

RELIGIOUS RESPONSE TO THE LARGER SOCIETY AMONG BLACK AMERICANS

Strategies of Social Action

	Expressive	*Instrumental*
Positive	*thaumuturgical / manipulationist sects*	*mainstream or established sects*
Negative	*conversionist sects*	*messianic-nationalistic sects*

Attitudinal Orientation

It is important to stress that in reality there are no "pure" types. For example, no religious group is exclusively instrumental or expressive in the strategies of social action that it chooses to adopt. All that can be said is that there is a greater emphasis on one orientation than the other. In cases where it is not clear which classifactory category is the most appropriate one for a particular group, it is common to note the existence of "mixed" types. In addition, an inherent weakness of all typologies is their implication that social reality is static. In other words, they fail to recognize that specific religious groups may evolve from one type into another type. We will note the presence of such evolutionary shifts in our discussion of various religious movements and organizations. The remainder of this section will examine the four types of Black sectarian responses to the larger society that emerge out of our typology.

1. Established sects.

The established sects in the Black community are committed, at least in theory, to a reformist strategy of social activism which will enable Blacks to become better integrated into the political, economic, and social institutions of the larger society. Although many of the congregations of this type continue to exhibit a strong expressive side in worship activities, they are particularly strongly committed to various instrumental activities, such as lending support to various protest activities, raising funds to fight discrimination, and sponsoring college scholarships. Members of the established sects tend to accept the cultural patterns of the larger society and want to share in the benefits of the "American Dream." Congregations in this type are found in associations such as the National Baptist Convention, U.S.A., the National Baptist Convention of America, the African Methodist Episcopal Church, and the African Methodist Episcopal Zion Church. Although many of the congregations in these organizations include working-class and lower-class members, their leadership and orientation tends to be middle-class. Although within the context of the larger society, these groups still maintain a sectarian tension with the larger society, they constitute the "mainstream denominations" and the bastions of respectability within the Black community. The established sects have produced many of the renowned political leaders of the civil rights movement.

The established sects are drawn primarily from two religious protest movements: the first, included groups of free Blacks who separated from predominantly White congregations prior to the Civil War and the second, consisted of former slaves after the Civil War who separated from the White Baptists. The Methodists and Baptists won free Blacks as well as slaves over in great numbers during the Second Great Awakening (Washington 1973; 42). Although initially free Blacks enjoyed a relatively intimate fellowship with White people for a short period after the Revolutionary War, eventually they were assigned segregated sections on the main floors and balconies of churches. As a protest against such discriminatory practices, free Blacks began to establish their own congregations and later associations. In recent years, the status of the established sects has been somewhat undermined by the gradual but steady exodus of many middle-class Blacks into the White-controlled Episcopal, Presbyterian, Congregational, and Catholic churches (Simpson 1978:238).

2. Messianic-nationalist sects.

As the term implies, messianic-nationalism combines religious belief with the ideal of achieving cultural independence and political or even territorial self-determination. Central to the ideology of this sectarian movement is the repudiation of "Negro" identity as an oppressive creation by the White man and the substitution of a new ethnicity predicated on a belief in the unique spiritual importance of Black people. Rhetorically, at least, messianic-nationalist sects reject both mainstream goals and values. Additional characteristics that stand out as the core features of messianic-nationalism include: (1) acceptance of a belief in a glorious Black history and subsequent "fall" from grace; (2) adoption of various rituals and symbols from established millenarian religious traditions; (3) messianic anticipation of divine retribution against the White oppressor; (4) assertion of Black sovereignty through the development of various nationalist symbols and interest in territorial separation or emigration; and (5) rejection of certain social patterns in the Black community, including family instability, female-headed households, and male marginality. In its own way, each messianic-nationalist sect echoes the pivotal themes listed above. In one group emigration may be stressed, while in another it may play but a minor role in group ideology, likewise, some groups turn to Islam for their nationalist symbols and religious rituals, whereas rival assemblages look to Judaism or even Christianity. Because of its importance in structuring group ceremony and ideology, this latter feature will be used in the following discussion of the various sub-traditions within the messianic-nationalist movement. It must be stressed, however, that whatever their outward differences, the majority of messianic-nationalists are strikingly similar.

The messianic-nationalist groups best known within and outside the Black community are those that adopt an Islamic orientation. The initial move toward Islamization of Black religion occurred in Nobel Drew Ali's Moorish Science Temple founded in Newark in 1913. Drew, a self-proclaimed prophet of Allah, maintained that Black Americans are the descendants of a proud Moorish nation in Africa and, following the destruction of White people, will inherit a regal future (Essien-Udom 1962, Bontempts and Conroy 1966). Although no longer as prominent as in the past, storefront Moorish temples and record shops can still be found in several Northern cities. Contributing to the reduced importance of the Moors was the emergence in the early 1930s of the Nation of Islam, originally under W.D. Fard and later under Elijah Muhammad. The Black Muslims, as Lincoln (1962) labeled them, developed an elaborate mythology based on the deification of Fard and a view of White people as devils. Through the extensive proselytizing efforts of this group, and what has been described as their combination of "Dale Carnegie self-improvement techniques and a savvy sense of small business enterprise" (Albern *et al.*, 1977:21), Islamic ideology spread to thousands of individuals in the Black community. Because of fissioning, this ultimately led to the appearance of numerous (and often feuding) Black Muslim sects.[3]

Another, and probably even older shift toward messianic-nationalism in the Black community is characterized by its adoption of an Israelite identity (Brotz 1970). No doubt rooted in the early and long enduring identification of Black

Americans with the biblical accounts of the Children of Israel, this movement first gained outside attention at the turn of the century (Shapiro 1970). One of the first Black Jewish sects was called the Church of the Living God, the Pillar Ground of Truth for All Nations, organized by a Black seaman and railroad worker named F. S. Cherry. William S. Crowdy, also a railroad worker, was the founder of another early Black Jewish group called the Church of God and Saints of Christ.

In both these groups, now respectively centered in Philadelphia and Belleville, Virginia, there can be found various Jewish (as well as Christian) ritual symbols and practices and the teaching that Black people are the true descendants of the biblical Israelites. Currently, in Chicago alone, there are nearly twenty Black groups with titles such as "Israelites, . . . Jews, Hebrews, Cannanites, Essenes, Judaites, Rechabites, Falashas, and Abyssinians (now generally defunct and replaced by the term Ethiopian)" (Landing 1974:51). The most outstanding of these groups, because of its literal acceptance of the emigration theme in messianic-nationalism, is the Original Hebrew Israelite Nation founded in Chicago in the early sixties. In 1967 and 1968, several hundred members of this sect migrated to Liberia in hope of establishing an agricultural utopia. After a series of setbacks, group members followed their leader to Israel, where they were joined by a new wave of migrants from the United States. Today, approximately 900 members of this group live in three development towns in Israel (Singer 1979).

The last major wing of the messianic-nationalist movement[4] remained within the Christian fold, but modified certain Christian beliefs in its efforts to create a more satisfying Black identity. The most noteworthy of these groups is the African Orthodox Church, which grew out of Marcus Garvey's massive Universal Negro Improvement Association. This assemblage urged Blacks to forget the image of a White god and instead worship a Black Madonna and a Black Christ. A similar orientation developed in Albert B. Cleage's Shrine of the Black Madonna, headquartered in Detroit (Harding 1968).

In spite of their often revolutionary stance, messianic-nationalist groups not uncommonly move toward a position of accommodation vis-à-vis the dominant society. As early as 1964, Parneti noted that the Nation of Islam was "manifesting a growing inclination toward a *modus vivendi* with the larger community . . ." (Parenti 1964: 182–183). This shift accelerated rapidly following the death of Elijah Muhammad in 1975. Under the guidance of Wallace E. Muhammad (a.k.a. Imam Warith Deen Muhammad), the group, now known as the American Muslim Mission (A.M.M.), dropped its anti-White ideology and moved toward a more orthodox practice of Islam. In the last few years, the A.M.M. has begun to exhibit a noticeable introversionist tendency (e.g. see Khalifah 1980:5). This change is the result of a growing middle-class orientation of the A.M.M. and its members. As this example reveals, worldly success—a goal implied in the messianic-nationalist desire for politico-economic independence—can result in a muting of the more rebellious inclinations that exemplify this type of Black sect.

3. Conversionist sects.

Conversionist sects characteristically adopt an expressive strategy of social action, emphasizing the importance of various behavioral patterns, such as shouting, ecstatic dancing, and glossolalia (speaking in tongues), as outward manifestations of "holiness" or "sanctification." Wilson (1969:364) notes the following about the conversionist sect:

> . . . Its reaction towards the outside world is to suggest the latter is corrupted because man is corrupted. This type of sect takes no interest in programmes of social reform or in the political solution of social problems and may even be actively hostile towards them.

Conversionist sects tend to be "other-worldly" and apolitical in their orientation, and rely upon the willingness of the individual to undergo a process of conversion as the meaningful way to affect social transformation. It is this emphasis on personal change, rather than the promotion of religious conversion per se, that is the hallmark of these groups. As defined by conversionist sects, living a life of holiness requires adherence to a puritanical morality and an avoidance of carnal activities, such as drinking, smoking, dancing, and gambling. Next to the established sects, the conversionist sects, which consist primarily of a great multitude of small Baptist, Holiness, and Pentecostal congregations and organizations, appear to be the largest religious type in the Black community. A few of the many Black Holiness and Pentecostal organizations include associations such as the Church of God in Christ, Church of Christ (Holiness) U.S.A., and the Pentecostal Assemblies of the World (Simpson 1978:259). On the other hand, despite the close alliance between some of its adherents and the Ku Klux Klan, the Holiness movement did occasionally bring poor Whites and Blacks together in interracial revivals. Some Blacks also established Holiness sects. One of these, the Church of God in Christ, later became a Pentecostal group after its founder was influenced by the Azusa Street Revival and is presently the largest of the Holiness / Pentecostal groups in the Black community (Simpson 1978: 259–60). In contrast to the Holiness movement, the Pentecostal movement per se emphasized one form of ecstatic behavior over all others as a mark of sanctification, namely glossolalia. Although there were earlier scattered instances of individuals and small groups who had experienced glossolalia, the Pentecostal movement first took root at the Azusa street revival which occurred at a Black Holiness congregation in Los Angeles in 1906 (Bloch-Hell 1964:31). Despite some cooperative efforts between Black and White Pentecostalists, the majority of Pentecostal as well as holiness groups are divided along racial lines. It appears that the Holiness and Pentecostal Blacks split off from their White counterparts for many of the same reasons as did the independent Black Baptists and Methodists earlier.

Wilson (1969:372) notes that conversionist sects, if they manage to survive and grow, are particularly prone to a process of "denominalization." Thus, some Black Holiness and Pentecostal groups have become increasingly bureaucratic and are at times involved in social reform (e.g., Simpson 1978: 262). On the basis of such trends, it appears that some of the larger conversionist groups are being transformed into established sects with a more temporal view of the world and the possibilities for social change. On the whole, however, the great majority of conversionist groups in the Black community continue to provide their adherents with an escapist response to the problems of racism and social inequality.

4. Thaumaturgical / manipulationist sects.

Although Wilson (1969) makes a subtle distinction between thaumaturgical and manipulationist sects, he admits that there is little difference between the two, except that the response of the first is less universalist and more personal than the latter. Since in the Black community one finds certain religious groups which tend to combine these two orientations, we deem it convenient to combine the two terms in labeling them. Thaumaturgical/manipulationist sects maintain that the most direct way to achieve socially desired ends, such as financial prosperity, prestige, love, and health, is by engaging in various magico-religious rituals or by acquiring esoteric knowledge which both provide an individual with spiritual power over himself and others. These sects tend to promote individual responsibility for psychological well-being, and stress the need to overcome negative attitudes and develop a positive frame of mind. Thaumaturgical/manipulationist groups generally accept the cultural patterns, values, and beliefs of the larger society, but attempt to change the means for obtaining the "good life." Because of their individualistic orientation, such groups view themselves as open-minded and are very amenable to religious syncretism.

Of the four types in our scheme, the thaumaturgical/manipulationist sect has been the most neglected by scholars, despite its prevalence in the Black community. Most commonly representative of this type are those groups which refer to themselves as "Spiritual" churches. Various scholars refer to them as "Spiritualist" churches (Drake and Cayton 1945; Jones 1939; Hurston 1931; Mays and Nicholson 1933; Frazier 1974; Washington 1973). Research by one of us with these groups in several Northern and Southern cities indicates that the term "Spiritualist" was contracted to "Spiritual" at some point in the development of most contemporary Black Spiritual churches (Baer, n.d.). The Spiritual movement in the Black community essentially combines elements from Black Protestantism, Roman Catholicism, Spiritualism, Voodooism (or at least its diluted version generally known as "hoodoo" in the United States), and various other religious traditions.

The historical development of the Spiritual movement remains obscure, but it seems to have emerged in various large cities, particularly New Orleans, Chicago, and Detroit during the period after World War I. As was also true of many of the conversionist and messianic-nationalist sects, the growth of the Spiritual churches was a result of the migration of Blacks from the rural South to the urban centers of both the South and the North. Although most Spiritual churches are quite small and attract primarily lower-class individuals, some are quite large and cross-cut socioeconomic lines. Most Spiritual churches maintain at least a loose affiliation with a larger association.

The largest of these associations, the Metropolitan Spiritual Churches of Christ Association, has over one hundred congregations, many of which are located in Illinois and Michigan but also in many other areas of the U.S.A., as well as some in West Africa. One of the most unique Spiritual groups is the Universal Hagar Spiritual Churches which was established in 1923 in Detroit by Father George W. Hurley.[5] Unlike most Spiritual groups who direct their devotion towards the spirits and Jesus Christ, members of this organization view their founder as God Incarnate—the Christ and Savior of the Aquarian Age. Father Hurley, who is thought by his followers to have passed into the spirit world in 1943, taught that Christianity has been used as a means of oppressing Blacks by providing them with a "pie-in-the-sky" philosophy.[6]

Despite certain similarities between the Spiritual movement and Black Protestant groups, it is the emphasis on the manipulation of one's present condition through the use of various magico-religious rituals and the acquisition of esoteric knowledge, often referred to as "secrets" or "mysteries," that tends to distinguish the former from some of the more conventional religions among

Black Americans. For the most part, members of Spiritual churches do not adhere to the puritanical morality and the "other-worldly" perspective of many conversionist sects. The acquisition of the "good life" along with its worldly pleasures are central concerns. It is believed that these goals may be achieved by acquiring spiritual power or receiving a blessing. Specific techniques for achieving such objectives include the burning of votive candles, praying before the image of a saint, the use of various occult items, and receiving a "message" or "reading" from a prophet or spiritual advisor, either in a public religious service or during a private consultation. Many individuals who are not regular members of Spiritual groups attend services in these churches or visit privately Spiritual prophets and advisors. The Spiritual religion concerns itself with the concrete problems of its adherents and clients by attempting to provide them with the spiritual means to acquire needed finances, success in locating employment, love, or the improvement of a strained personal relationship. In fact, many Spiritual people note that heaven and hell are states of mind—the former being a result of a positive attitude and the latter of negative thinking.

A newer example of the thaumaturgical/manipulationist sect in the Black community is the United Church and Science of Living Institute founded in 1966 by the Rev. Frederick Eikerenkoetter II (better known as "Rev. Ike"). Rev. Ike teaches that the *lack* of money is the root of all evil and urges his followers to rid themselves of attitudes of deferred rewards in the afterlife and to start believing in their own abilities of acquiring a slice of the "American Dream" (Snook 1973 84–89).

It is somewhat difficult at this point to generalize about the evolutionary trend of thaumaturgical/manipulationist sects in the Black community. In the case of the Spiritual movement, there is a tendency on the part of some of the larger congregations to emulate the established sects. This may involve an attempt to disassociate themselves from the smaller Spiritual congregations, which often have the stereotype in the Black community of being involved in "witchcraft" and other illicit activities. On the other hand, some of the smaller Spiritual congregations which are also seeking a more respectable image tend to emulate the conversionist sects.

5. The Father Divine movement as an example of a "mixed" type.

As Wilson (1969: 362) notes, " . . . Sects are not easily marshalled into a few dichotomies." Consequently, one may encounter a "mixed type" which escapes easy classification because it prominently exhibits characteristics or orientations of two or even more categories. Of the multiplicity of religious groups in the Black community, one of the most elusive for purposes of classification is the Father Divine Peace Mission movement. This sect is one that to a greater or lesser extent, at least during its zenith in the 1930s and 1940s, incorporated aspects of all of the four categories in our typology. Therefore, we will discuss it here as an excellent example of the "mixed" type.

Although, apparently, Father Divine had been an itinerant preacher before settling down in Sayville, Long Island, in 1919, his movement emerged largely as a response to the hardships that not only Blacks, but also many Whites, experienced during the Great Depression. Unlike most other predominantly Black religious groups, the Father Divine movement attracted many White people despite an ideology which pictured Father Divine as an incarnation of God. Prior to Father Divine's death in 1965, the movement addressed itself primarily to the oppressive situation of Blacks in American society.

Like the established sects in the Black community, Father Divine was committed to a variety of programs of social reform. He represented his movement as a practical program which would provide his followers with health, food, clothing, shelter, and jobs. In addition to establishing schools for both children and adults, Father Divine urged his followers to register and vote in political elections. Despite Father Divine's sponsorship of cooperative ventures and a brief flirtation with the Communists (Harris 1971: 202), he was by no means a revolutionary but rather a reformer committed to working within the framework of the capitalist system. He was a staunch advocate of the Protestant ethic of work, self-support, savings and investments, and the sanctity of private property (Burnham 1979:51).

Although the Father Divine movement was similar to the established sects in the Black community in its emphasis on social reform efforts, it also took on some of the dimensions, at least in subtle manner, of the messianic-nationalist sects. According to Essien-Udom (1962:32), Father Divine's ". . . teachings, like those of black nationalists, display the mood of alienation from the existing society." Despite the fact that Father Divine taught that color is of no consequence, he also was a living testimony of the notion that "black is beautiful." After all, had not God decided to take on the body of not only a short, squat, bald man but also one who was Black?

In addition, like the conversionist sects, the Father Divine movement stressed salvation through profound change in oneself. Although ecstatic behavior *per se* was not a central focus as it is in many Black Holiness and Pentecostal groups, the elaborate banquets that Father Divine held were often characterized by dancing, shouting, clapping, testifying, and joyous singing on the part of his followers (Harris 1971: xxi–xxii). Members of the movement were also expected to abide by a strict code of ethics which prohibited the use of intoxicants, smoking, social dancing, gambling, theater-going, and all forms of sex.

Finally, the Father Divine movement exhibited and continues perhaps even today to exhibit many aspects of the thaumaturgical/manipulationist sects. Much like the latter, Father Divine advocated a temporal rather than an "other-worldly" orientation to solving the problems of his followers. He taught that the established churches had used religion to keep the masses of Blacks in their downtrodden and miserable condition. According to Harris (1971:128), "visualization of the positive is the philosophical basis" of this group.

Since the death of Father Divine in 1965, the group has been under the guidance of Mother Divine, a White woman. Although the sect still conducts communion banquets, services, and anniversary celebrations, and operates some of its former establishments, it appears that it has adopted a more introversionist posture than in its heyday (Burnham 1979).

SUMMARY AND CONCLUSIONS

It is often asserted that 11:00 AM on Sunday morning is the most segregated time in American society. Bearing in mind this thought as well as the historical background of Blacks in the United States, it may be argued that much of what one finds in Black religion is a response to the racism and stratification inherent in our sociocultural system. Powerless groups have often utilized religion as a way of coping with social reality, and, in this regard, Black Americans are no exception. Consequently, in attempting to develop a typology of Black sectarianism, we have focused on this dimension. Our effort has been prompted by a recognition of the need to order systematically the diversity of religious strategies that Blacks have created in attempting to cope with oppression. This approach is not intended to imply that Black religion is merely a coping mechanism, nor that its sources lie only in the nature of Black/White economic and social relations. Rather, we emphasize this dimension because it is around the issue of alternative strategies that much of the diversity of Black religion developed.

The established sects or the "mainstream denominations" within the context of the Black community, particularly those with large, middle-class Baptist and Methodist congregations, have adopted a reformist strategy which attempts to create improvements for Blacks by working within the system; they essentially accept the "American Dream." Perhaps because of their great sense of powerlessness, lower-class Blacks have been particularly creative in developing strategies which ultimately attempt to instill dignity and meaning in their often seemingly hopeless lives. The messianic-nationalist sects, such as the Black Muslim, Black Jewish and Black Hebrew groups, have tended to construct counter-cultures, which tend to reject many of the values and goals of larger society while at the same time developing utopian communities. Perhaps the majority of lower-class Blacks with a religions orientation have turned to various conversionist sects, such as the multitude of small Baptist, Holiness, and Pentecostal groups, which often tend to seek their salvation in some ill-defined afterlife. Finally, one finds the more temporal strategy of the thaumaturgical/manipulationist sects, particularly those which stress the acquisition of the "good life" as it is defined in the larger society by carrying out certain magico-religious acts and by subscribing to a philosophy of positive thinking.

The danger of any typology is that it may oversimplify the complexities of social reality, and we, of course, recognize the potential of this law in our typology of Black sectarianism. The mere fact that sects evolve over time due to both external and internal factors indicates the presence of mixed or transitional forms. A case in point, as mentioned earlier, is the conversionist sect which is being transformed into an established sect. Apparently, many of the larger Baptist and Methodist groups underwent such a change in the past and it now appears that various congregations in the Church of God in Christ (Pentecostal) are experiencing a similar development. Furthermore, it is particularly important to note that there is a tremendous amount of interweaving of religious patterns among the various sects in the Black community. This is perhaps most pronounced in the Spiritual movement in which groups blend aspects of a wide diversity of religious traditions. The Universal Hagar Spiritual Association and the Father Divine movement are specific examples of this syncretic tendency that one finds in Black religion. Similarly, among the messianic-nationalists, there has been a high degree of ideological diffusion among the various groups, despite the differences in orientation. Needless to say, no typology, regardless of how elaborate it may be, can do justice to such a phenomenon.

NOTES

1. Merrill Singer (1979) recently spent nearly a year doing fieldwork among members of the Original Hebrew Israelite Nation, a Black American sect now centered in

Israel. Between October 1977 and June 1979, Hans Baer (n.d.) worked with the eleven Black Spiritual congregations in Nashville, Tennessee. He also has visited Spiritual churches in seven other cities.

2. Using somewhat different variables (instrumental vs. expressive orientation and traditional vs. acculturated symbols), Fernandez (1964) devised a structurally similar typology of religious movements in Africa.

3. One of these, the Ansaru Allah community, underscores the similarity of messianic-nationalist groups, in that it combines Islamic and Judaic symbols in its ritual. There is even some indication that the Ansars previously were a Black Jewish group that has been Islamized in recent years.

4. At least one messianic-nationalist group, King Efuntola's Sacred Yoruba Village of Oyo Tunji, has rejected all of the major messianic relations and is attempting to re-adopt African beliefs and rituals. This group has established an agricultural colony near Beaufort, South Carolina.

5. The only reference that we have been able to find in the literature referring to this group is a brief comment by Parker (1937: 105) which claims that Father Hurley was vehemently opposed to the establishment of a Father Divine mission in Detroit.

6. Although Father Hurley spoke and wrote to his followers about the oppression of "his people" and emphasized their "Ethiopian" roots, the messianic-nationalism of the Universal Hagar Spiritual association has been rather muted compared to that of other sects, such as the various Black Muslim and Black Jewish/Hebrew groups.

REFERENCES CITED

Alpern, David, Stephen Lesher, and Sylvester Munroe. 1977. I fear only Allah. *Newsweek*, March 21.

Baer, Hans A. n.d. Black spiritual churches: A neglected socio-religious category. Phylon: *Atlanta University Journal of Race and Culture* (in press).

Bloch-Hoell, Nils. 1964. *The Pentecostal Movement*. London: Allen & Unwin.

Bontempts, Arna and Jack Conroy. 1966. *Any Place But Here*. New York: Hill & Wang.

Brotz, Howard M. 1970. *The Black Jews of Harlem*. New York: Schocken.

Burnham, Kenneth E. 1979. *God comes to America: Father Divine and the Peace Mission Movement*. Boston: Lambeth.

Daniel, Vattel Elbert. 1942. Ritual and stratification in Chicago Negro churches. *American Sociological Review* 7:352–61.

Drake, St. Clair and Horace R. Cayton. 1945. *Black Metropolis*. New York: Harper and Row.

Du Bois, W. E. B. 1903. *The Souls of Black Folk*. Chicago: A.C. McClurg.

Essien-Udom, E. U. 1962. *Black Nationalism: A Search for an Identity in America*. Chicago: University of Chicago Press.

Fauset, Arthur H. 1971. *Black Gods of the Metropolis*. Philadelphia: University of Pennsylvania.

Fernandez, James W. 1964. African Religious Movements—Types and Dynamics. *The Journal of Modern African Studies* 2:531–49.

Frazier, E. Franklin. 1974. *The Negro Church in America*. New York: Schocken.

Green, Vera. 1970. The Confrontation of Diversity within the Black Community. *Human Organization* 29:267–72.

Harding, Vincent. 1968. The Religion of Black Power. In *The Religious Situation*. Donald R. Cutler, ed. Boston: Beacon Press.

Harris, Sara. 1971. *Father Divine*. New York: Collier.

Hurston, Zora Neale. 1931. *Mules and Men*. New York: Perennial Library.

Jones, Raymond. 1939. A Comparative Study of Religious Cult Behavior among Negroes with Special Reference to Emotional Conditioning Factors. *Howard University Studies in the Social Sciences* 2(2).

Khalifah, Santi Aman. 1980. Iman Muhammed Issues Challenge. *Bilalian News*, July 19, p. 5.

Landing, James. 1974. The Spatial Expression of Cultural Revitalization of Chicago. *Proceedings of the Association of American Geographers* 6: 50–53.

Lewis, Hylan. 1955. *Pathways of Kent*. Chapel Hill: University of North Carolina Press.

Lincoln, C. Eric. 1962. *The Black Muslim in America*. Boston: Beacon Press.

Mays, Benjamin E. and Joseph R. Nicholson. 1933. *The Negro Church*. New York: Institute of Social and Religious Research.

Parenti, Michael. 1964. *The Black Muslims from Revolution to Institution*. Social Research 31:175–94.

Parker, Robert A. 1937. *The Incredible Messiah*. Boston: Little, Brown & Company.

Pope, Liston. 1942. *Millhands and Preachers*. New Haven, Conn.: Yale University Press.

Powdermaker, Hortense. 1939. *After Freedom*. New York: Viking.

Shapiro, Deanne Ruth. 1970. Double Damnation, Double Salvation: The Source and Varieties of Black Judaism in the United States. Unpublished M.A. thesis, Columbia University.

Simpson, George Eaton. 1978. *Black Religions of the New World*. New York: Columbia University Press.

_____ and J. Milton Yinger. 1972. *Racial and Cultural Minorities: An Analysis of Prejudice and Discrimination*. New York: Harper and Row.

Singer, Merrill. 1979. Saints of the Kingdom: Group Emergence, Individual Affiliation and Social Change among the Black Hebrews of Israel. Unpublished Ph.D. dissertation, University of Utah.

Snook, John. 1973. *Going Further: Life-and-Death Religion in America*. Englewood Cliffs: N.J.: Prentice-Hall.

Stark, Rodney and William Bainbridge. 1979. Of Churches, Sects and Cults:

Preliminary Concepts for a Theory of Religious Movements. *Journal for the Scientific Study of Religion* 18: 117–33.

Szwed, John F. 1971. Preface. In *Black Gods of the Metropolis*. Arthur H. Fauset. Philadelphia: University Press.

Troeltsch, Ernst. 1931. *The Social Teaching of the Christian Churches*. Translated by O. Wyon. New York: Macmillan.

Washington, Jr., Joseph. 1973. *Black Sects and Cults*. Garden City, N.Y.: Anchor/Doubleday.

Williams, Melvin D. 1974. *Community in a Black Pentecostal Church*. Pittsburgh: University of Pittsburgh Press.

Wilmore, Gayraud S. 1972. *Black Religion and Black Radicalism*. Garden City, N.Y.: Anchor/Doubleday.

Wilson, Bryan. 1969. A Typology of Sects. In *Sociology of Religion*. Roland Robertson ed. Baltimore: Penguin.

Yinger, J. Milton. 1970. *The Scientific Study of Religion*. New York: Macmillan.

SELECTED BIBLIOGRAPHY FOR FURTHER READING

Baer, Hans A. and Merrill Singer. *African-American Religion in the Twentieth Century: Varieties of Protest and Accommodation*. Nashville: University of Tennessee Press, 1992.

Brotz, Howard M. *The Black Jews of Harlem*. New York: Schocken, 1970.

Burkett, Randall K. *Garveyism as a Religious Movement: The Institutionalization of a Black Civil Religion*. Metuchen, NJ: Scarecrow Press, 1978.

Fauset, Arthur H. *Black Gods of the Metropolis: Negro Religious Cults of the Urban North*. Philadelphia: University of Pennsylvania Press, 1944.

Watts, Jill. *God, Harlem, USA: The Father Divine Story*. Berkeley: University of California Press, 1992.

13 ::

C. Eric Lincoln

:: One of the most prominent new religious movements found among African Americans in urban America was the Nation of Islam which taught that African Americans must find their identity in a radically different and separate culture and religion in order to achieve liberation. This new message resonated particularly among the most disaffected urban African Americans. C. Eric Lincoln was the first to bring this movement to the attention of a broader audience with the publication of his *Black Muslims in America* in 1961. In the following essay from 1983, Lincoln addresses the changing nature of Islam among African Americans. ::

:: 13 THE MUSLIM MISSION
IN THE CONTEXT OF
AMERICAN SOCIAL
HISTORY

C. Eric Lincoln

:: T he United States of America began as a Protestant Christian establishment, and after two hundred years was still close enough to her religious origins
for a prominent theologian to aver with confidence that "to be a Protestant, a
Catholic or a Jew are today the alternative ways of being an American."[1] Among
the vast array of challenging implications to be drawn from Professor Will
Herberg's famous aphorism are the following: religion in the United States is so
closely identified with cultural or civil values as to take on the character of nationalism; and being "American" presupposes the Judeo-Christian heritage or experience. There is an inescapable irony in both propositions. In the first place, to
the uncritical observer the most prominent feature of contemporary American
life is its secularism, not its piety. In the second place, the founding fathers went
to extraordinary lengths to insure the religious neutrality of the emergent nation
by constitutional fiat. There could be no religious establishment, and there could
be no religious test or requirement for equality of participation in the full range
of common values incident to American citizenship. Nor may the national legislature make any laws to the contrary.[2] Nevertheless, a close examination of
American secularism will reveal features that are startling in their religious
tenor. The principal elements of this "new" religion are derived principally from
the Judeo-Christian tradition, and from the idealistic sentiments of what is commonly called "the American Dream." This is the religion I call "Americanity,"[3]

and for all the prideful references to the separation of Church and State in the U.S., Americanity is the "established" faith, a fact of critical importance in understanding the implications of the Islamic presence in America.

However, despite a demonstrated sophistication in socio-political foresight, there is nothing to suggest that the founders of the United States of America had even a premonition of the eventual arrival of Islam upon these shores. While the first European settlers were themselves in search of religious freedom, their initial "errand into the wilderness" was to establish a Christian community—one which would become a beacon of perfection—a kind of religious demonstration project for all the world to see and emulate. But the "world" to which the notion of a "righteous empire"[4] was addressed was the turbulent, schismatic world of European Christianity. Islam, a "pagan" religion, was beyond consciousness and beyond contemplation. In the unfolding scenario of Western manifest destiny, the religions of the East, like the peoples of the East, belonged to an exotic history whose wheel had turned; in the peculiar balances of the historical order, the rise of the West meant the descent of the East. Eight hundred eighty-eight years separate the Battle of Tours from the landing of the Mayflower at Plymouth Rock, and in that interim of nearly a full millennium Islam had long been displaced in the critical concerns of those who found, in the New World beyond the Atlantic Ocean, a world from which to mold a more perfect image of the Old World. Although Islam had lingered on in the Spanish Peninsula, and was spread among the Indians by Blacks serving in the Spanish expeditions in the Americas in the sixteenth century,[5] it had never been an aspect of the English experience, and the American commonwealth was from the beginning a transplant of the Anglo-Saxon culture and expectations. That primary cultural impress has of course been modified by subsequent immigration, and by the development of an indigenous experience. But it has not been supplanted. Anglo-conformism remains the norm—indeed the *sine qua non* of American self-perception.

It is clear then that the religion of Islam is not in any substantial way a part of the critically valued American experience. It has no purchase in the antecedent European-American traditions, and it played no part in the critical development of the indigenous American culture. Exclusionist immigration policies were aimed at reserving the country for Caucasian people in general and people of Western European descent in particular. In consequence, the development of the "Western Empire" proceeded in what must now be perceived as a deliberately created cultural vacuum, denying itself the wisdom and the culture of the East in the vain, short-sighted pursuit of a chauvinistic racial chimera.

While American immigration policies excluded both Asians and Africans, its commercial interests did not. Among the millions of Blacks who were made *involuntary* immigrants under the aegis of slavery, there were inevitably numbers of Muslims from the Islamic kingdoms of the West Coast of Africa. How many thousands (or perhaps tens of thousands) we shall never know, for the slavemasters had no interest in recording the cultural and spiritual achievements of their chattels. What is more, the slave trade required and maintained a determined myopia regarding the religious interests of its hapless human commodities: first to avoid the embarrassment of possibly selling an occasional Black Christian, but more often in support of the fiction that the very religious depravity of the Africans made them legitimate targets for spiritual rehabilitation through the dubious ministrations of chattel slavery. Under that convenient sanction, even recognizably Muslim Africans would fare no better than the rest, for Islam was considered the supreme cabal of infidels, when it was considered at all. In spite of all this, the evidence of a substantial Muslim presence among the American slave population is compelling, while in South America and the Caribbean that presence was common enough to be taken for granted and the cultural impress of Islam remains in high relief in those areas to this day.[6]

In sharp contrast to the prevailing practices in Roman Catholic Latin America, the Anglo-Saxon Protestant hegemony that defined the cultural and religious parameters of the slaveholding South (in what was to become the United States) considered it expedient to suppress *all* African religions of whatever kind. The fear of insurrection or revolt under cover of religion was deep and unremitting, and the common precaution was to disperse as widely as possible all those slaves known to have common tribal or language affiliations. This practice effectively precluded the cultic apparatus by means of which religions survive and propagate themselves. In spite of such discouragements, accounts persist of Muslim slaves who committed the entire *Qur'an* to memory in an effort to keep the faith alive and to pass it on to others.[7] Inevitably, of course, such heroic efforts were unavailing, for the intransigence of the slave system, buttressed as it was by a formidable reticulation of customs and convention, could not and did not accommodate itself to the heroics of its victims. What the system did provide (after a hundred years of dereliction) was an alternative faith. As the generations succeeded each other, scarcely marked except by the momentary discontinuities of birth and death, into the vacuum left by the proscribed "native" religions of whatever sort of origin, Christianity, that is to say Protestant Christianity, eventually made its way. It took the better part of a century—from 1619 to sometime after the Society for the Propagation of the Gospel received permission to proselytize the slaves in 1701.[8]

It was not a permission easily obtained. At stake in sharing a religion with the Blacks was the spectre of sharing a community with them. The implications for economic prerogative, social status, political power, and even the transcendent bliss of the heavenly rest were unknown and troublesome in their anticipation. But the benefits, it was argued, would be many—not the least of which would be more tractable, more reliable, more loving, and more dedicated servants.[9] Was it worth the risk? Opinion was divided, and the compromise was a severely edited version of the faith dominated by careful selections of Pauline doctrine offered as Divine approval of the lowly condition of the slave. From the beginning of the Black experience in American Christianity, Black Christians were separated by race and by destiny. The churches were segregated and remain so to this day and sharing the faith has yet to accomplish the elementary principle of sharing the community. White churches and Black churches go their separate spiritual ways, while in the arena of social and political intercourse the mandates of the faith are still suspended in the interest of less respectable values.

Such is the backdrop against which Black Islam attempts resurgence. Why "Black" Islam? First, because it was the Black Muslims, that is, the "Moors" among the Spanish *conquistadores*, who first introduced Islam to the New World.[10] Second, because in the English colonies the only Muslim presence was among the slaves imported from Black Africa. Third, while there had been small enclaves of orthodox Muslims in America for many decades, their presence had been characterized by clannishness and quietism, not by proselytism or public identity and involvement.

The orthodox Muslims were more a spasm than an outpost of Islam, inundated by the floodtide of militant Christianity, the spirit and the symbol of Western ascendancy. In consequence, these "white Muslims" maintained a low profile. Perhaps subconsciously they considered themselves the logical targets for a Christian jihad, unaware, or more likely unconvinced, of the projections afforded all religions by the Constitution of the United States. In any case, they seemed content, or at least constrained, to keep Islam within the parameters of their ethnic associations. Certainly, the white Muslims provided no more opportunity and even less incentive for Black participation in the religion of Islam than the counterpart white church provided for a meaningful Black involvement in Christianity. And while their respective statuses within the American social structure were hardly analogous, their responses to the Black presence were not at all dissimilar.

Fortunately the African has a genius for religion that cannot be expunged. Blacks seldom wait to be won over by a religion. They take the initiative and whenever they adopt a faith they make it peculiarly their own. They had known Islam and Christianity in their homelands, a fact overlooked by their new masters. But in their new situation both were given new life and style; both became visible signs of a distinctive community.

The memory of Islam, however tenuous, was never completely lost to the slave experience. The major Black Christian denominations were formed long before the Civil War, and though routinely denigrated by the white church, were a recognized part of the Christian community. If they were considered exotic, it was because they were Black—not because they were alien—a problem Islam could not and did not escape.

There was no room and no occasion for a "new" religion in the post-Civil War United States. The Black church, split between Methodist and Baptist denominations, offered the newly emancipated Blacks the chance for self-respect in the form of religious self-determination, that is, the opportunity to *belong*—to be a part of an independent *Black* organization. Drawn by so heady and so novel an opportunity, and pushed by the white churches in which they had previously held a debased and segregated membership, the new Black Americans surged out of the white church and became proud members of "their own" Black churches— the African Methodist Episcopal Church, the Colored Methodist Episcopal Church, the National Baptist Conventions, Inc., and so on. Through all this, there was a memory of Islam, but its time was not yet. It was to be another half-century before that memory would find vocal and physical expression among the hapless Blacks struggling for a negotiable identity and searching for their cultural roots.

In 1913, a Black "prophet" from North Carolina established a "Moorish Science Temple" in Newark, New Jersey.[11] Timothy Drew was not an educated man, but he had somehow learned enough about Islam to consider it the key to what would fifty years later be called "Black liberation." Islam was the religion of the Moors, the Black conquerors from Africa who once ruled much of Europe. How could anyone with such a heritage suffer the debasement which was the common lot of Blacks in America? Drew had no training in the social sciences, but he did have the perception to realize that there is a very definite relationship between what you are called and how you are perceived, and between how you are perceived and how you are treated. "It is in the name," he concluded; the Black man's problems began with accepting a pejorative nomenclature. Drew, who was born in 1866 and given the Christian name of Timothy, now proceeded to give himself a name indicative of his "Moorish" heritage—Noble Drew Ali. His followers were no longer to be known as "Negroes" or "Africans" but as

"Moorish-Americans," thus preserving their newly won American citizenship, but making explicit their Islamic heritage. Each "Moor" was issued an appropriate name and an identity card making clear his religious and political status in a society where "Negroes," however pronounced their Christian pretensions, were not generally held in high esteem.

Drew's movement spread to Pittsburgh, Detroit, Chicago, and a number of cities in the South. Although it made use of what was known of the more romantic paraphernalia of Islam, including the Holy *Qur'an*, the wearing of *fezzes*, Muslim names, and the repudiation of certain fundamental Christian beliefs, Noble Drew Ali's movement was essentially a mélange of Black nationalism and Christian revivalism with an awkward, confused admixture of the teachings of the Prophet Muhammad. It was not Islam, but it was a significant recovery of the awareness of Islam.

After a violent eruption within the administration of his Moorish-Science Movement, Ali died of mysterious causes in 1929. Thereafter the movement languished, splintered, and was succeeded by a more vigorous, imaginative, and demanding version of Islam led by Elijah Muhammad.

Elijah Muhammad was born Elijah Poole in Sandersville, Georgia, on 7 October 1897.[12] One of 13 children born to an itinerant Baptist preacher, Poole was destined to become one of the most controversial leaders of his time. But controversy aside, in terms of the impress he made on the world he must be reckoned one of the most remarkable men of the twentieth century. Among his more commonly recognized achievements were his enormous contributions to the dignity and self-esteem of the Black undercaste in America. Beyond that, and with perhaps infinitely more far-reaching implications, Elijah Muhammad must be credited with the serious re-introduction of Islam to the United States in modern times, giving it the peculiar mystique, the appeal, and the respect without which it could not have penetrated the American bastion of Judeo-Christian democracy. If now, as it appears, the religion of Islam has a solid foothold and an indeterminate future in North America, it is Elijah Muhammad and Elijah Muhammad alone to whom initial credit must be given. After more than a hundred years, "orthodox" Islam in America had not titillated the imagination of the masses, White or Black, and was scarcely known to exist before the "Black Muslims"—Elijah's Nation of Islam—proclaimed Elijah's "Message to the Black Man" in the name of Allah.

Elijah learned what he knew of Islam from a shadowy, mysterious evangelist who went by a variety of aliases, but who was most popularly known as Wali Farrad, or Wallace Fard. Fard claimed to have come from the Holy City of Mecca on a mission of redemption and restoration of the Black undercaste. He taught that the Black African Diaspora were all of Muslim heritage, "lost-found members of the tribe of Shabazz." The essence of his message was that Black debasement had occurred over the centuries because Blacks were separated from the knowledge of Allah and the knowledge of self. They were estranged from the one true God to whom they owed allegiance, and ignorant of their own history and their previous high status in the hierarchy of human valuation. The problem was to restore to the Lost-found Nation the truth, the only truth that could make them free. This was the formidable task bequeathed to Elijah Muhammad, when after three years of instruction, Fard ostensibly returned to Mecca after designating Elijah, "Messenger of Allah."

In his own words, Elijah set out to "cut the cloak to fit the cloth." The complexity of his task was beyond imagination, for as Messenger of Allah he had committed himself to nothing less than the restoration of the most despised and brutalized segment of American Christianity to a level of dignity and self-appreciation from which informed choices about religion could be made. His methods were sometimes ad hoc, and usually controversial, but they were always addressed to the realities of the situation rather than to an abstract theory whose relevance to his peculiar task had nowhere been demonstrated. Against him was a formidable array of forces, not the least of which were three hundred fifty years of solid Christian tradition in an avowedly, consciously, Christian society. His initial "parish" was the slums and the Black ghettos of the industrial cities, and his potential converts were the slum-created outcasts of a developing technocratic society. His "people" were those who were most battered by racism and stifled by convention, and whose experience of the white man's "invincibility" made the acceptance of Black inferiority seem as reasonable as it was pervasive. The Black intellectuals would scorn him, and white-appointed Black leaders would denounce him; the Christian Church would oppose him, and the local enclaves of orthodox Islam would repudiate him. But Elijah Muhammad was a man for the times. He was as dedicated as he was fearless; he was as imaginative as he was charismatic. He persisted in challenging the formidable phalanx of forces confronting him, and ultimately he prevailed. In the midst of his harassment by federal agents, local police, and others determined to silence him, he declared with characteristic boldness:[13]

> I am not trembling. I am the man. I am the Messenger . . . I am guided by God.
> I am in communication with God . . . If God is not with me . . . protecting me,
> how can I come and say things no other man has said?

Muhammad drew freely upon the Bible, upon religious and secular mythology, and upon his own unique pedagogical constructs fashioned from experience. He met his converts where they were, ministering as far as he could to a spectrum of needs which transcended the spiritual to find their cruelest expression in more immediate exigencies, which were psychological, economic, social, and political. His "book" was the *Qur'an* but that was not the only book he found useful. His "law" was the law of Islam, but he created his own supplement to fit the limited understanding of his followers. His "God" was Allah, but how does one portray the reality of Allah to a people whose total experience is washed in the pus of racial oppression? He cut his cloak from the cloth available. Elijah Muhammad did not achieve orthodoxy for the Nation of Islam, but orthodoxy was not his goal. What he did achieve was a pronounced American awareness of Islam, its power and its potential. Because of him, there was a temple or mosque in a hundred cities where no mosques had existed before. There was a visible religious presence in the form of a hundred thousand Black Muslims—conspicuous in their frequent rallies and turnouts, and in their little groceries and restaurants and bakeries and other small businesses. The clean-shaven young Muslims hawking their newspapers on the streets, celebrating their rituals in the prisons, debating their beliefs in the media gave to the religion of Islam a projection and a prominence undreamed of in North America. Suddenly, the prison warden, and the social workers, and the people who depended on Black labor were saying that the Nation of Islam had done a better job of rehabilitating the Black *déclassé* than all of the official agencies addressed to that task. And there was a general, if grudging, awareness in the Black community that the Black Muslims had done more to exemplify Black pride and Black dignity, and to foster group unity among the Black masses than any of the more reputable, integrational-oriented civil rights organizations.

By the close of Elijah's *seigniory*, the Nation of Islam was no longer exclusively a community of the poor, the fallen and the *déclassé*. With Malcolm X as its chief public representative, the Nation of Islam had attracted a good number of college students and a showcase element of intellectuals and professionals, including doctors, college professors, and former Christian ministers. An increasing number of celebrities in the world of sports and entertainment, clearly influenced by the Nation, became Muslims. However, most of them joined more "orthodox" branches of Islam to avoid the stigma of belonging to an exclusively Black communion. A notable exception was Cassius Clay, who, after becoming the World Champion of heavyweight boxing, adopted the Islamic name Muhammad Ali.

Under Elijah Muhammad, the Nation of Islam became the prevailing Islamic presence in America. It was not *orthodox Islam*, but it was by all reasonable judgments, *proto-Islam*; and therein lies a religious significance that may well change the course of history in the West.

After shaping and guiding the Nation of Islam for more than 40 years, the Honorable Elijah Muhammad died on 25 February 1975. Shortly thereafter, the mantle of leadership devolved on Wallace Deen Muhammad, Elijah's fifth son. It was a progression rather than a succession of leadership, for Wallace Muhammad was destined to walk in his own way rather than in the tracks of his father. While he himself had no illusion and no anxieties about orthodoxy, Elijah Muhammad had promised his people that the day would come when they would fully understand their religion and its book, the Holy *Qur'an*, and when they would be universally recognized as full members of the worldwide Muslim community. The choice of Wallace Deen (later to be known as Warith Deen Muhammad), to head the Nation after Elijah's death seems intended to implement that promise.

Immediately following his election as Chief Minister of the Nation of Islam, Wallace began the decultification of the following he had inherited from Elijah. His procedures were bold and forthright, but they were fraught with dangers of many kinds. A distinctive feature of the cult phenomenon is that the allegiance of the followers is in large part a response to the personal charisma of the leader, and the charisma does not lend itself to transfer or succession. This does not mean that a new leader may not have charisma of his own, but it does mean that Wallace did not necessarily inherit his father's ability to obtain obedience and respect. That is why the characteristic cult seldom survives the death of its founder. In the cult phenomenon, few "successors" are able to hold intact the disparate forces controlled by a charismatic founder. Wallace was no exception. The transfer of power was neither complete nor intact, and while the widely predicted catastrophic implosion did not occur, there was dissatisfaction, disillusionment, and an inevitable erosion of membership. An undetermined segment of the Nation either drifted from involvement, or elected to follow the independent movement of Minister Louis Farrakhan, who remains the most prominent exponent of the original teachings of Elijah Muhammad. For the millions of Blacks whose lot has not been measurably improved by almost three decades of America's "new" racial policies, the romance of Elijah Muhammad's Nation of Islam still represents challenge and identity; and, above all, it is a visible expression of the rage and hostility that still pervades the Black undercaste. To them, it is quite clear that the denied and the disinherited are still Black; the *deniers* and the disinheritors are still white; and Armageddon[14] remains inevitable. They see no compelling reason now to doubt Elijah, or to re-interpret his teachings.

Wallace's task as chief *imam* is ultimately ordered by the magnitude of his own ambitions. Now that he is confirmed in his leadership role, it is conceivable that he could, if he chose, fashion for himself a comfortable spiritual suzerainty that would demand little more of him than the normative political housekeeping needed to keep him in power. The models for such are many and familiar, and whatever its directions, the Nation of Islam *was* a going institution when Wallace Muhammad took it over. However, Wallace has made it clear that his first priority of office is to eradicate completely the Black nationalist image of the erstwhile Nation by a dramatic reconstruction of its social and political understanding. The sweeping changes implied in this effort alone are enough to give pause to someone less determined, but for Wallace, social reconstruction is only an obvious and necessary prelude to a much larger and even more formidable task. His ultimate goal is, of course, complete orthodoxy for the cult Elijah fathered and made internationally famous as the Nation of Islam.

Wallace Deen Muhammad is a dreamer, but he is a dreamer-cum-realist, and gentle, sensitive, and self-effacing. History may yet prove him to be one of the most astute religious leaders of this age, regardless of communion. A lifelong student of Islam, fluent in Arabic, and well conversant with the nuances of Qur'anic ideology and its institutionalized projections, Wallace is no less a keen and perceptive observer of the American scene. Therein lies his potential for achievement and service to Islam. If he can bring the erstwhile Nation of Islam into fully recognized communion with orthodox Islam, he will have accomplished more for the propagation of that faith than any *Mujaddid* in modern times. The implications of such a feat are enormous, for they transcend at the outset the mere matter of a ready-made corps of new adherents, although a hundred thousand or so new additions to any religion is in itself a signal achievement. But beyond mere statistics, the presence of a prominently visible, orthodox Muslim community in the United States would have political, social, and economic implications, which might, in time, reverberate far beyond the realm of the spirit.

Ironically, perhaps the most imponderable obstacle between orthodoxy and the Nation of Islam is not the opposition of the purist keepers-of-the-gate inside Islam, but the far more elusive and impalpable body of tradition that defines Black religion in general. Black religion derives, in the first instance, from that aspect of the Black experience that made it difficult to resolve the apparent incongruities between Christianity and Black slavery. It was not only a repudiation of the concept that slavery was acceptable to God, but has always been a critical medium through which the Black community has institutionalized its efforts to effect Black liberation. Inevitably, this has meant a certain estrangement of the Black church from Christian "orthodoxy" as understood and practiced by the white church. Hence, the salient tradition of Black religion has always been the sufficiency of its own insight.

Since practically all members of the Nation of Islam trace their religious origins to the Black Christian Church, there is little reason to believe that the notion of "orthodoxy" holds for them any values of overwhelming significance. Further, since Islam is no stranger to the enslavement of Blacks, even in contemporary times, many of those who came to the faith via the Nation of Islam, may well view Islamic orthodoxy as the Islamic counterpart of white Christianity—a possibility probably not overlooked in the careful strategies of Elijah Muhammad. Since Blacks have had more than sufficient reason to question "orthodox" interpretations of any faith in the long travail that is the Black experience, they have learned to rely on feeling—the *direct* experience of the Divine—rather than on the official formulas and prescriptions of the experts. Indeed, the traditional Black answer to questions of orthodoxy has always been:

> If we ain't got it right
> Ain't it a mighty wonder
> De Spirit's over here
> Instead of over yonder?
> If this ain't true religion
> How come I got the feelin'
> My soul done caught on fire
> And left this world a'reelin'?

Certainly there is impressive evidence that Wallace Deen Muhammad has given such problems the most painstaking scrutiny before determining his own strategy for making Islam, in a relatively short period of time, the major religion in America after Christianity.[15] The catalogue of changes Wallace has accomplished in only five years of leadership tenure is already long and detailed. There have been changes of doctrine, changes of structure and administration, changes of name, style, role, and office. There were changes of official attitude about race, political involvement, and military service. High-ranking members of the ruling hierarchy were demoted or reassigned; financing of the movement's super-structure was redesigned and a strict accounting system introduced. The Fruit of Islam was disbanded. Key elements underpinning Elijah Muhammad's mythological doctrines were either allegorized, re-interpreted, or quietly abandoned altogether, and the "blue-eyed arch-enemy," that is, the "white devils," were rehabilitated and welcomed into the movement as brothers. The American flag is now displayed in every Muslim school, and the Pledge of Allegiance is made before morning prayers are offered. Still, the chief imam confesses with the candor of new revelation:[16]

> The former leader, the Honorable Elijah Muhammad, taught something that was un-American and un-Islamic. Now that I am leading the Community, following the Sunni (the way) of Prophet Muhammad, I find it now more difficult because it seems that many Americans liked it better when we were isolated—separated from the American people. Many that I thought would congratulate me, have not.

In opting for corporate legitimacy for his Nation rather than for the personal emoluments traditionally available to such offices as his, Wallace was never far from the risk of losing everything. That risk was defused to some degree by the nature of his investiture. Although his name was presented for consideration by the surviving members of Elijah Muhammad's family, his appointment to office as Chief Minister of the Nation of Islam was given unanimous ratification by 20,000 members of the Muslim Nation (assembled in Chicago) on 26 February 1975. Once he assumed office, the chief *imam* immediately moved to dissociate himself and his office from the commercial interests so long a feature of the Nation of Islam. This strategy not only removed his office from the possibility of a conflict of interest, but it freed the new leader for the implementation of the grand vision that he had held since the days he headed the temple in Philadelphia in the late 1950s.

The "Islamization" of the Nation of Islam reached deeper and deeper. Ministers of Islam became "*imams*"; temples of Islam became "mosques," and later, "*masjids*." Black people, believers and non-believers alike, were redesignated "Bilalians" in remembrance of Bilal Ibn Rabah, friend and confidant of the Prophet Muhammad. The fast of Ramadan, traditionally celebrated in December under Elijah Muhammad, was rescheduled to coincide with the lunar calendar used by other Muslims throughout the world; and the Nation's official newspaper, *Muhammad Speaks*, was renamed *The Bilalian News*. The roles of women were upgraded, military service was no longer forbidden, and believers were urged to take an active part in the civil process. Malcolm X was rehabilitated and the Harlem mosque was renamed in his honor. In October 1976, the Nation itself changed names, becoming thereafter "The World Community of Al-Islam in the West" (WCI). Four years later the name would change again to The American

Muslim Mission, "which," the imam explained, "speaks more to our aspirations and thrust."[17] During the same period the imam changed his own name from Wallace to "Warith" Deen Muhammad. He explained that this change was necessary because the man for whom he was named, Wallace Fard, had invested the name Wallace "with symbolism and mysticism," and that it had "an un-Islamic meaning."[18]

Finally, Imam Warith Deen Muhammad[19] made it clear that while most of the Mission's commercial holdings had been sold or placed in the hands of individual businessmen, the interest in the provision of economic opportunities for all who needed them was undiminished. This interest was made tangible in a dramatic development, which also exemplified the movement's new understanding of its civil responsibilities and opportunities. In February of 1979 the World Community of Islam signed a $22 million contract with the U.S. Department of Defense. The Muslims are teamed with Allen A. Cheng and Associates, a Chinese-American entrepreneur, and doing business as the American Pouch Food Company. They will manufacture an updated version of the C-rations previously used by the military. The marketing potential of the new industry is estimated at more than $60 million annually.[20]

Although the leadership of Warith Deen Muhammad has been aggressive and far-reaching, it has also been low-key. The Muslims are no longer "news" in the sense they were when Elijah Muhammad and Malcolm X were the regular sources of newspaper headlines or television commentaries. This may well be a blessing in disguise. The energy crisis and America's chief political crises are all centered in areas of the world where Islam holds sway, and a more pronounced visibility of the growing Muslim presence in America might well drench the efforts of Warith Muhammad in a backwash of anti-Islamic sentiment. No one is more aware of this possibility than is the imam himself, and while he has not retreated from the principles of his faith, he has been diligent in showing himself and his movement to consist of reliable and responsible Americans, open and receptive to dialogue and cooperation with all who are receptive to them. In a book called *As the Light Shineth From the East*[21] the imam attempts to spell out his position on the more controversial issues that nag at his leadership philosophy, or which otherwise threaten the rapprochement he wants between the American Muslim Mission and the diverse publics it wants to impress. Where Elijah advocated a separate Black nation, for example, Imam Warith declares: "I am a patriot of . . . the true blood of the Constituted of the United States";[22] "Now we are balancing [Elijah Muhammad's teachings] so we can develop an awareness in the children [of Islam] that they are not only members of a race but they are citizens—members of a nation—we want to grow in the full dimension of our country";[23] "My greatest desire for our community AMM is to . . . one day hear that a Muslim, a real Muslim, a genuine Muslim from our Community has become a governor, or senator, or head of some big American corporation."[24] The imam is a vocal supporter of the Equal Rights Amendment, and his work with prisoners and ex-convicts earned him an invitation to address the American Congress of Corrections composed of prison administrators from all over the United States and Mexico.

Obviously, the old Nation of Islam has come a long way under Warith D. Muhammad, but exactly how far is a very critical question yet to be determined. It is probable that those reforms designed to bring the movement into closer alignment with today's version of the American Dream will eventually be accorded the recognition and applause the imam has thus found elusive. (He has already been honored with the Walter Reuther Humanities Award, and he shares the Four Freedoms Award with such laureates as Eleanor Roosevelt and John F. Kennedy.) Nevertheless, considering the increasing polarities between East and West, there is no guarantee that the same reforms will not militate against the prize the imam wants most—unqualified recognition for the American Muslim Mission (AMM) as a legitimate segment of world Islam.

The signals from the East appear to be encouraging. Warith Muhammad enjoyed cordial relations with former Egyptian president Anwar Sadat (as did Elijah Muhammad with Sadat's predecessor, General Nasser). A more weighty significance however, may be suggested by the fact that Warith was the only American observer invited to the Tenth Annual Islamic Conference of Ministers of Foreign Affairs (which met in Fez, Morocco); or in Warith's new role as a conduit for Islam's varied missionary enterprises in America. In 1978, a number of the oil-rich Persian Gulf states, including Saudi Arabia, Abu Dhabi, and Qatar named the American imam "sole consultant and trustee" for the recommendation and distribution of funds to all Muslim organizations engaged in the propagation of the faith in the United States.[25] A mosque estimated at $14–16 million is on the drawing board for the south side of Chicago, to be financed by contributions from the international community of Islam. About two million dollars have already been donated by just two donors, with an additional quarter-million given to the imam by one of them to be used directly for his educational budget.[26] Such largess is not without its hazards. Some established Muslim groups in the United States are unhappy about the attention the American Muslim Mission has received since Warith Deen assumed leadership, and in their pique they are quick to dismiss him as a propagator of (Elijah Muhammad's) "lies," and "no Muslim."

Also, the risk that the American Muslim Mission will be seen to be manipulated by international politics is inescapable. Certainly, there is no lack of potential manipulators, as Imam Muhammad must readily admit; but the potential for manipulation is the critical test of both the man and the movement. If either should falter, Islam will be the loser in America, once again.

NOTES

1. See Will Herberg, *Protestant-Catholic-Jew* (New York: Doubleday, 1955), p. 274.
2. See *The Constitution of the United States of America*.
3. *Cf.* C. Eric Lincoln, "Americanity, the Third Force in American Pluralism," *Religious Education*, vol. 70, no. 5 (1975): 485.
4. *Cf.* Martin Marty, *Righteous Empire: The Protestant Experience in America* (New York: Dial Press, 1970).
5. For a discussion of Spanish (Roman Catholic) precautions against the threat of the spread of Islam among the American Indians through Black proselytization and intermarriage with Blacks, see Clyde-Ahmad Winters, "African American Muslims from Slavery to Freedom," *Islamic Studies* vol. 17, no. 4 (1978): 187–90.
6. Ibid., pp. 190–205.
7. Such a man was Ayuba Suleiman Abrahima Diallo of Annapolis, Maryland. Diallo, also known as Job ben Solomon, eventually gained his freedom after 1731 through British interests impressed by his knowledge and his strict observance of the Qur'an. Winters, "Afro-American Muslims," p. 191. *Cf.* Kunte Kinte, Muslim protagonist in Alex Haley's celebrated *Roots* (New York: Doubleday, 1978).
8. The Society for the Propagation of the Gospel in Foreign Parts was the missionary arm of the Church of England. Originally organized in the interest of converting the Indians, the society turned its attention to the Blacks after the Indians repeatedly rejected the "white man's religion."
9. *Cf.* Cotton Mather, *The Negro Christianized, An Essay to Excite and Assist the Good Work, The Institution of Negro Servants in Christianity* (Boston: B. Green, 1706). Mather catalogues a long list of benefits, including Divine approval, to be gained by bringing the Blacks to Christ, while refuting the popular arguments for excluding them from Christendom.
10. Betty Patchin Green, "The Alcades of California," *Aramco World Magazine* (November–December 1976): 26–29.
11. For an account of the Moorish-Science Movement, *see* the following: Arthur H. Fausett, *Black Gods of the Metropolis* (Philadelphia: University of Pennsylvania Press, 1944); Arna Bontemps and Jack Conroy, *They Seek a City* (Garden City, New York: Doubleday, Doran, 1945). See also C. Eric Lincoln, *The Black Muslims in America*, 1st ed. (Boston: Beacon Press, 1961), pp. 51–55.

12. *See* C. Eric Lincoln, *The Black Muslims in America*, 1973 rev. ed. (Boston: Beacon Press, 1973) for a definitive study of the development of the Nation of Islam under the leadership of Elijah Muhammad, and of the impact of the movement on American racial and religious practices.

13. *Mr. Muhammad Speaks*, May 1960.

14. Elijah Muhammad taught that "the Armageddon," a final clash between the forces of good (i.e. Blacks) and the forces of evil (i.e. Whites), must take place "in the wilderness of North America" before the Black Nation could be fully restored. *See* Lincoln, *Black Muslims in America*.

15. Such a projection assumes that since Judaism has only about six million adherents in the U.S., it could be numerically eclipsed by a crusading Islam in relatively short order.

16. From an interview with Dirk Sager, correspondent for Station ZDF, German television; "Communicating for Survival," World Community of Islam (WCI) news release, 27 December 1979.

17. WCI News Release, 30 April 1980.

18. WCI News Release, 2 April 1980.

19. His official title was changed later to Leader and President of the World Council of Islam in the West.

20. *The Bilalian News*, 16 February 1979.

21. Warith D. Muhammad, *As the Light Shineth From the East* (Chicago: WDM Publishing Co., 1980).

22. "Communicating for Survival," 27 December 1979.

23. Ibid., 28 September 1979.

24. From a personal interview with Warith Deen Muhammad, 9 April 1980.

25. "Communicating for Survival," "Imam Warith Deen Muhammad, a Biographical Sketch," n.d.

26. From a personal interview with Warith Deen Muhammad, 9 April 1980.

SELECTED BIBLIOGRAPHY FOR FURTHER READING

Austin, Allen D., ed. *African Muslims in Antebellum America: A Sourcebook*. New York: Garland, 1984.

Chevannes, Barry. *Rastafari: Roots and Ideology*. Syracuse: Syracuse University Press, 1994.

Lincoln, C. Eric. *The Black Muslims in America*. 3rd. ed. Grand Rapids, MI: Eerdmans, 1994.

McCloud, Aminah Beverly. *African American Islam*. New York: Routledge, 1995.

Mamiya, Lawrence H. and C. Eric Lincoln. "Black Militant and Separatist Movements." In *The Encyclopedia of the American Religious Experience*. Vol. 2, edited by Charles H. Lippy and Peter W. Williams. New York: Charles Scribner's Sons, 1988.

14 ::

Iain MacRobert

::On October 19, 1994, the white Pentecostal Fellowship of North America publicly repented of past racial
divisions and voted to disband in order to join with
African-American Pentecostals in forming a new multiracial umbrella organization of Pentecostal denominations known as the Pentecostal Churches of North
America. This was a significant development for although
the Pentecostal movement began at the 1906 Asuza
Street revival in Los Angeles as a multiracial movement
under black leadership, its subsequent development as
well as its historical and theological interpretation was
marred by racism and exclusion as examined by Iain
MacRobert in the following essay.::

:: 14 THE BLACK ROOTS OF PENTECOSTALISM

Iain MacRobert

∷ **I**n 1965, at a time when most white American Pentecostal authors had either written William Joseph Seymour and his black prayer group out of their movement's history or trivialized his central role, Walter Hollenweger recognized that:

> The Pentecostal experience of Los Angeles was neither the leading astray of
> the Church by demons . . . nor the eschatological pouring out of the Holy
> Spirit (as the Pentecostal movement itself claims) but an outburst of enthusiastic religion of a kind well-known and frequent in the history of Negro churches in America which derived its specifically Pentecostal features from Parham's
> theory that speaking with tongues is a necessary concomitant of the baptism of
> the Spirit.[1]

The historical origins of Pentecostalism in the United States lie primarily in the Wesleyan-Holiness, Keswick and Higher Life Movements, and in the black American church.[2] While the white influences on the early Pentecostal Movement have been recognized by Pentecostal historians, they have often disparaged and sometimes completely ignored the crucial influences of Afro-American Christianity. White pioneers and early leaders like Charles Fox Parham or Ambrose Jessup Tomlinson have been recognized—even eulogized—whereas Seymour, one of the most influential of the pioneers, has generally been marginalized and his important role even denied by the myth of no human leadership, and this in spite of the recognition accorded him by such diverse people as Frank Bartleman in the United States, Alexander A. Boddy in Britain, and G. R. Polman in the Netherlands.[3] Parham may have been accused of homosexuality and Tomlinson of financial mismanagement and megalomania, but Seymour was less acceptable to most North American Pentecostal historians than either of them. They were white, he was black.

A more scholarly and rigorous historian, James R. Goff, continues to maintain that "Parham, more than Seymour, must be regarded the founder of the Pentecostal movement," because "it was Parham who first formulated the theological definition of Pentecostalism by linking tongues with the Holy Spirit baptism."[4] For Goff, glossolalia as the initial evidence of Spirit baptism is "the *sine qua non* of the experience" and "the central theological corpus which has always defined the movement."[5] To characterize Pentecostalism in terms of the evidence doctrine is, however, to accept a narrow, inadequate, white, North American definition which is belied, not only by Pentecostals in the two-thirds world, but also by some white classical Pentecostals in Britain, and by many black-majority Pentecostal churches both in Britain and in the United States itself.[6]

Because Pentecostalism is primarily found not on a theological proposition, but on a shared perception of human encounter with the divine, it has roots in many Christian traditions and in a diversity of cultures; but it is first and foremost an experiential rather than a cognitive movement. Goff maintains that, "the primacy of theological formulation" labels Parham as chronologically the founder of Pentecostalism.[7] While doctrine was important to some early Pentecostals (though generally less so to black worshippers), all theological formulations were both secondary to their pneumatic experience and, to a greater or lesser extent, inadequate in their attempts to understand or explain the Pentecostal phenomena. The Pentecostal movement did not spread to fifty nations within two years of the Azusa Revival or grow to its current size of some 360 million adherents worldwide as a result of Pentecostal "theology" or Parham's evidence doctrine, although his understanding of tongues as *xenoglossa* did encourage early Pentecostal foreign missions.[8]

The particular attraction of Pentecostalism to people around the world and the ease with which it has been indigenized in non-Western societies lies in its black experiential roots which provide a substratum of enduring values and themes for the bulk of the Movement outside of white North America and Europe.

One historian who has taken Seymour's role seriously is the Methodist clergyman, Douglas J. Nelson. In 1981, Nelson completed his thesis—under Hollenweger's supervision—on "The Story of Bishop William J. Seymour and the Azusa Street Revival."[9] His historical and biographical research made Seymour's crucial role clear. Seymour, however, was not simply an American with a black skin. Nor was his socialization solely determined by his negative encounters with the aftermath of American slavery and enduring discrimination and racism. Seymour and the other black worshippers who brought to birth the Azusa Street revival and the world-wide Pentecostal Movement which flowed from it shared an understanding and practice of Christianity which had developed in the African diaspora out of a syncretism of West African primal religion and culture with Western Christianity in the crucible of New World slavery.

AFRICAN ROOTS AND THE BLACK LEITMOTIF

Africans, brought as slaves to the Americas, did not arrive *tabula rasa* nor did forced acculturation totally eradicate their primal religious beliefs. On the contrary, both in Africa and in the Americas these pre-literate beliefs were transmitted from generation to generation by oral tradition and symbolism. In narratives—myths, legends, and folk tales—songs, parables, and other aphorisms, ritual, drama, dance, and the rhythms and tones of "talking" drums, African religious ideas were preserved to be syncretized with the Christianity of white America and thus produce a distinctively black form of Christianity. Albert J. Raboteau has well summarized this process:

> Shaped and modified by a new environment, elements of African folklore, music, language, and religion were transplanted to the New World by the African diaspora. . . . One of the most durable and adaptable constituents of the slave's culture, linking African past with American present, was his religion. It is important to realise, however, that in the Americas the religions of Africa have not been merely preserved as static "Africanisms" or as archaic "retentions" . . . African styles of worship, forms of ritual, systems of belief, and fundamental perspectives have remained vital on this side of the Atlantic, not because they were preserved in a "pure" orthodoxy but because they were transformed. Adaptability, based upon respect for spiritual power wherever it originated, accounted for the openness of African religions to syncretism with other religious traditions and for the continuity of a distinctively African religious consciousness.[10]

The primal religious beliefs brought from Africa with the diaspora included a powerful sense of the importance of community in establishing and maintaining both the personhood of individuals and an experiential relationship with the spirit world of ancestors and divinities. They inhabited a world in which the sacred and profane were integrated and the ability to tap into the *force vitale* by means of divination and spirit possession was considered essential to the welfare of the community, the wholeness of the individual, and the success of any major undertaking in the material world.[11]

To attune themselves to the power of the spirits, both in Africa and in the New World, they used rhythm and music. Polyrhythmic drumming, singing, dancing, and other motor behavior opened up the devotee to spirit possession. In Africa, these were understood as the spirits of the ancestors and divinities. In the Americas new understandings grew out of the pragmatic syncretism of their primal religion with Western Christianity. The possessing spirits of Africa became identified with the apostles, prophets, saints, angels, and Holy Spirit of the white missionaries but phenomenologically there was considerable continuity.[12]

In spite of missionary attempts to demythologize the perceptions of slaves, literacy brought them into contact with the world of the Bible which, like their own, was concerned with the relationship between the spiritual and the natural. The biblical accounts of miracles, healings, exorcisms, spiritual power, and the presence of the Holy Spirit in peoples' lives did not seem so different from their own experiential ancestral religion. Furthermore, their identification with the story of Israel's bondage in Egypt and their subsequent Exodus to the promised land meant that freedom was understood as more than liberation from the power and consequences of personal sin. An African concept of sin as antisocial activities was reflected in an understanding of the work of the devil as predominantly in the concrete realities of enslavement. The Lord of Hosts who delivered his people from Pharoah's oppression was the God of liberation from political and social evil.[13]

The adventism of evangelical revivalism was also particularly attractive to black Christians for it proclaimed an apocalyptic revolution to be inaugurated by the Second Coming of Christ. The high, the mighty, and the oppressor were to be put down, while the humble, the powerless, and the oppressed—the Saints—were to be exalted. This eschatological status-reversal was believed to be immanent. Thus the black church in the Americas embraced an inaugurated eschatology which was congruent with an African sense of the future which is so close that it has almost arrived. And if at any moment they were to put on their golden slippers "to walk the golden streets" it was because—in spite of their bondage and sub-human status—they were the children of God now! Others were inspired by the scriptures and their Christian faith to plan insurrections during Sunday services and other ostensibly religious gatherings.[14]

The revivalism of the late eighteenth and early nineteenth centuries attracted black people because it stressed an experiential conversion of the heart rather than an intellectual or catechetical religion. "The powerful emotionalism, ecstatic behavior, and congregational responses of the revival," writes Raboteau, "were amendable to the African religious heritage of the slaves, and forms of African dance and song remained in the shout and the spirituals of Afro-American converts to evangelical Protestantism." "In addition," continues Robateau, "the slaves' rich heritage of folk belief and folk expression was not destroyed but was augmented by conversion."[15]

Thus much of the primal religion of West Africa was syncretized with Western Christianity and, in particular, with those themes which were of primary importance to the survival and ultimately the liberation of an oppressed people. Certain leitmotifs which echo both their African origins and their sojourn in the "Egypt" of chattel slavery surface again and again in the black church of the Americas. An integrated holistic world view, the immanence of the divine, belief in spirit possession, spirit healing and spirit power, the importance of dreams and trances, the extensive use of rhythm, certain types of motor behavior, antiphonal participation in worship, baptism (immersion) in water, and the centrality of community all had African antecedents and reemerged during the revivalist camp meetings of the eighteenth and nineteenth centuries where they also influenced whites.[16]

Other leitmotifs of white evangelical or biblical origin became particularly important in the black Christian community: the imminent Parousia, an inaugurated eschatology, and an "Exodus" theology which perceives freedom in sociopolitical as well as spiritual terms. These leitmotifs were expressed, not in systematic propositions but in the oral, narrative, sung, and danced liturgy and theology of the black Christian community.[17]

By the beginning of the twentieth century, many of the black churches in the United States—particularly in the North—had largely conformed to white, middle-class, conservative evangelicalism. Both the black and white Holiness people—who were mainly proletarian—were dissatisfied with the "deadness" and "worldliness" in many churches and looked for a world-wide revival as the harbinger of the imminent Second Advent of Christ. One such Holiness preacher was William J. Seymour.[18]

WILLIAM JOSEPH SEYMOUR AND THE AZUSA STREET REVIVAL

Born in the South in 1870, the son of emancipated slaves, Seymour grew up in the midst of violent racism. Nelson writes that during his first twenty-four years of life:

> Seymour receives little or no formal schooling but works hard, educates himself . . . drinks in the invisible institution of black folk Christianity, learns to love the great Negro spirituals, has visions of God, and becomes an earnest student of unfulfilled scriptural prophecy.[19]

That invisible institution of black folk Christianity with its black leitmotif formed the cultural and religious basis for Seymour's subsequent role as the leader of the Azusa Street Revival.

Seymour was "seeking for interracial reconciliation" but was aware that this could only be brought about with the aid of divine power.[20] Leaving the interracial Methodist Episcopal Church, he joined another less bourgeois interracial group, the Evening Light Saints, who taught—in addition to holiness, divine healing, racial equality, and a kind of ecumenism—that a final great outpouring of the Spirit was about to take place before the end of world history. Their holiness doctrine, like that of the rest of the Holiness Movement, was based on a simplistic understanding of Wesley's teaching and stressed that a second crisis experience of entire sanctification should follow conversion. Some, following the teaching of Charles G. Finney, also stressed the social aspects of Wesley's teaching and defined sanctification as a willingness to become involved in social action as an outworking of personal faith and consecration.

After recovering from smallpox, which left him blind in one eye, Seymour was ordained by the Evening Light Saints and, during the summer of 1905, was serving as the pastor of a black Holiness church in Jackson, Mississippi. In October he received reports that glossolalia as an evidence of the power of the Holy Spirit was being experienced at the Bible School of Charles F. Parham in Houston, Texas. While outbursts of glossolalia have recurred again and again throughout the history of the Church from the day of Pentecost to the present, in 1901 Parham was responsible for the teaching that it is both the initial evidence of Spirit baptism and the ability "to preach in any language of the world."[21] While the former tenet has become widely, but by no means universally, accepted by Pentecostals, the latter, like his Anglo-Saxon Israel, antimedicine, and conditional immortality teaching, has been largely rejected.[22]

Seymour enrolled at Parham's Bible School. At nine o'clock each morning, he attended classes "segregated outside the classroom beside the door carefully left ajar by Parham" who "practices strict segregation."[23] Leaving Houston, Seymour travelled to the cosmopolitan city of Los Angeles to become pastor of a small black (Church of the Nazarene) Holiness mission on Santa Fe Street. At nightly meetings he preached on conversion, sanctification, divine healing, and the imminent Second Advent; and on Sunday morning he spoke on glossolalia as a sign accompanying Spirit baptism, and this in spite of the fact he had not yet spoken in tongues himself. Returning to the mission for the evening service he found the doors locked against him. He lived and worshipped in the home of Edward S. Lee and his wife and later with Richard and Ruth Asbury. Both couples were black. On Friday the sixth of April, Seymour and a small group began a ten-day fast. Three days later Lee asked Seymour to pray for his recovery from illness. After anointing and prayer Lee felt better and requested that Seymour pray for him to receive the Holy Spirit with the evidence of tongues. He was not disappointed.[24]

Later that night in the Ashbury home, a group of black "sanctified wash women" were singing, praying, and testifying. As Seymour rose to preach on *Acts* 2:4, he recounted the events that had taken place earlier that evening but could preach no longer because as soon as he had completed his account of Lee's experience, Lee burst forth in tongues. Nelson describes what followed:

> The entire company was immediately swept to its knees as by some tremendous power. At least seven—and perhaps more—lifted their voices in an awesome harmony of strange new tongues. Jennie Evans Moore, falling to her knees from the piano seat, became the first woman thus to speak. Some rushed out to the front porch, yard, and street, shouting and speaking in tongues for all the neighborhood to hear. . . . Teenager Bud Traynor stood on the front porch prophesying and preaching. Jennie Evans Moore returned to the piano and began singing in her beautiful voice what was thought to be a series of six languages with interpretations.[25]

Within three days the original all-black group was receiving visits from whites as well as blacks to witness and experience glossolalia, trance, and healing. On the twelfth of April Seymour spoke in tongues himself.[26]

The revival rapidly outgrew the Asbury home and a rundown former African Methodist Episcopal chapel was leased at 312 Azusa Street. Cleared of construction materials which had been stored there, sawdust was spread on the dirt floor and pews fabricated from odd chairs, nail kegs, and boxes with planks laid across them. The three services which were conducted each day often overlapped.

Some meetings only attracted about a dozen people but within a month Sunday attendance had risen to 750 or 800 with a further four or five hundred, for whom there was no room, crowding outside.[27] Nelson declares that, "multitudes converged on Azusa including virtually every race, nationality, and social class on earth, for Los Angeles contained the world in miniature. . . . Never in history had any such group surged into the church of a black person."[28] Multiracial congregations were unusual. Black leadership of such congregations, while not unheard of, was extremely rare.

Spirit baptism was, for Seymour, more than a glossolalic episode. It was the power to draw all peoples into one Church without racial distinctions or barriers. Seymour's newspaper *The Apostolic Faith* of September 1906, declared that "multitudes have come. God makes no difference in nationality. Ethiopians, Chinese, Indians, Mexicans, and other nationalities worship together."[29] Black witnesses to those events recalled that, "everybody went to the altar together. White and colored, no discrimination seemed to be among them."[30] "Everybody was just the same, it did not matter if you were black, white, green, or grizzly. There was a wonderful spirit. Germans and Jews, black and whites, ate together in the little cottage at the rear. Nobody ever thought of color."[31] White witnesses echoed the same theme: "The color line was washed away in the blood."[32] Visiting from England, the Church of England clergyman, Alexander A. Boddy, recorded that

> It was something very extraordinary, that white pastors from the South were eagerly prepared to go to Los Angeles to the Negroes, to have fellowship with them and to receive through their prayers and intercessions the blessings of the Spirit. And it was still more wonderful that these white pastors went back to the South and reported to the members of their congregations that they had been together with Negroes, that they had prayed in one Spirit and received the same blessings as they.[33]

Within five months of the birth of this Movement, thirty-eight missionaries had gone out from Azusa. In only two years it had spread to over fifty nations worldwide, but the radical challenge to racism was by this time being subverted and rejected by some arrogant and pusillanimous whites. Parham, who propagated the Anglo-Saxon Israel teaching of white supremacy and wrote for the notoriously racist Ku Klux Klan, was horrified at the desegregation and the adoption of black liturgy by whites which had taken place and castigated Azusa for having "blacks and whites mingling" and "laying across one another like hogs."[34] In 1912 he wrote:

Men and women, whites and blacks, knelt together or fell across one another; frequently, a white woman, perhaps of wealth and culture, could be seen thrown back in the arms of a big "buck nigger," and held tightly thus as she shivered and shook in freak imitation of Pentecost. Horrible, awful shame![35]

DISSOCIATION AND REPLICATION

In 1914 the white-dominated Assemblies of God was formed, thus ending, in the world of Vinson Synan, "a notable experiment in interracial church development."[36] Two years later, the "new issue" controversy over the baptismal formula and the nature of the Godhead resulted in the withdrawal of the "Jesus Name" Oneness Pentecostals and the further purging of black people and elements of the black leitmotif from the Assemblies of God. Thus, writes Robert Mapes Anderson, "the Assemblies became an all but 'lily white' denomination . . . Since 1916, except for a few black faces here and there in urban congregations in the Northeast, the Assemblies has remained a white man's church."[37] The moralistic Oneness Pentecostals fared little better. The same desire for white "respectability," racial segregation, and the rejection of the black leitmotif tore them apart so that by 1924 there were separate white and black organizations. When the Pentecostal Fellowship of North America was set up in 1948 with the ostensible purpose of demonstrating to the world the fulfillment of Christ's prayer for Christian—in this case Pentecostal Christian—unity, only white organizations were invited to join. In 1965, having added a further nine organizations to the original eight, it was still exclusively white.[38]

What began in April 1906 as a black revival under Seymour's leadership incorporated the leitmotif of black Christianity in the Americas and Parham's distinctive doctrine of glossolalia as an evidence of Spirit baptism and the instrument of world evangelization. Almost immediately it became interracial and spread at a phenomenal rate, both in the United States and throughout the world. White Pentecostals in the United States, however, exploited doctrinal disagreements to dissociate themselves from their black brethren, to distance themselves from the black origins of the Movement, and to purge it of its more obviously black and radical elements which, however, re-emerge again and again wherever Pentecostals of the African diaspora meet for worship.

In Britain, for example, the black Pentecostal congregations which have been established by settlers from the Caribbean from the early 1950s, fall into three broad categories. Those which are part of the white-dominated, three-stage, Trinitarian organizations in the United States, like the Church of God (Cleveland) [known in Britain as the New Testament Church of God] and the Church of God of Prophecy, or the white-dominated, moralistic United Pentecostal Church, tend to be culturally ambivalent and there is often considerable tension between white-defined fundamentalist "orthodoxy" and "orthopraxis" and the black leitmotif which can never be totally stifled. Other three-stage, Trinitarian, "Church of God" type congregations have broken free from white headquarters in the United States and are significantly more "black" in their beliefs, liturgy, and practice. But the congregations which demonstrate the most overt commitment to the black leit-motif tend to be the Oneness groups with black headquarters in the United States or the Caribbean which pre-date the West Indian migrations of the late 1940s and early 50s.

These groups continue to pulsate most clearly with the liturgical characteristics of the Azusa Revival[39]: orality, narrativity, dance, and liturgical motor behavior with the extensive use of music and rhythm; an integrated and holistic world view incorporating Spirit possession[40] and trances; the importance of dreams, healing and the need for spiritual power to change the material (and social) world; the importance of community and human relationships—including the abolition of the color line—if life and religion are to be worthwhile; freedom as a sociopolitical as well as a spiritual issue; the imminence of a revolutionary world order inaugurated by the Second Advent of Christ, which is already to some extent present in an inaugurated eschatology. These themes were all in evidence at Azusa as they had been in the church of the African diaspora in the United States and they are replicated among black Pentecostals in Britain and in the two-thirds world where the overlay of white, North American "orthodoxy" is often quite superficial and in many situations—when the North Americans have gone home—totally absent. Parham's evidence doctrine, while of real importance to most white North American Pentecostals, some European Pentecostals, and a few mission churches, is largely irrelevant to most Pentecostals in the underdeveloped and developing nations and serves only as a redundant symbol of Pentecostal "orthodoxy" for most black Pentecostals in Britain.

DOES IT MATTER?

"Directly or indirectly," writes Synan, "practically all of the Pentecostal groups in existence can trace their lineage to the Azusa Mission."[41] If this is true, then Seymour rather than Parham or Tomlinson is the most significant historical figure in the early Pentecostal Movement. But does it actually matter who the person primarily responsible was: Parham, who taught that glossolalia is the evidence of

Spirit baptism and who advocated and practiced racial segregation; Tomlinson who forbade political involvement and led a racially divided church,[42] or Seymour who, as part of the African diaspora, believed in and lived out a Pentecostal experience with socially revolutionary implications? It matters to many black Pentecostals in the United States, Britain, and South Africa who have to confront the social, economic, and political sins of racism, discrimination, and apartheid.[43] It matters—though they may not realize it—for many white Pentecostals who in the denial of their Movement's roots perpetuate the racial arrogance and support for an oppressive socio-political and economic *status quo* which makes them the enemies of the Gospel to the poor. And it matters so that Pentecostalism does not become—or indeed remain—an individualistic ideology used by the powerful to control the powerless, or an alien ideology internalized by the powerless to control themselves, but returns to its original emphasis on God's pneumatic empowering of the powerless to be agents of transformation in both the Church and the wider society.

NOTES

1. Walter J. Hollenweger, *The Pentecostals* (London: SCM Press, 1972), 23–24; originally in his ten volume *Handbuch der Pfingstbewegung* (Geneva, 1965–67).
2. See Vinson Synan, *The Holiness-Pentecostal Movement in the United States* (Grand Rapids, Michigan: William B. Eerdmans, 1961), and Vinson Synan (Ed.), *Aspects of Pentecostal-Charismatic Origins* (Plainfield, NJ: Logos International, 1975).
3. Frank Bartleman, *Azusa Street* (Plainfield NJ: Logos International, 1980 [originally 1925]), especially 46; A.A. Boddy in *Confidence* (September, 1912); G.R. Polman, letter to G.A. Wumkes, 27th February 1915.
4. James R. Goff, *Fields White Unto Harvest: Charles F. Parham and The Missionary Origins of Pentecostalism* (Fayetteville: University of Arkansas Press, 1988), 11.
5. Ibid.
6. The Elim Pentecostal Church in Britain, following the teaching of George Jeffreys, maintains that any of the gifts of the Spirit are evidence of Spirit baptism. While most of the black Pentecostal organizations have articles of faith—largely inherited from their white co-religionists—which state their belief in glossolalia as the initial evidence—in practice it is largely ignored and displaced by an implicitly inclusive charismatology.
7. Goff, 15.
8. Barrett's estimate of 360 million Pentecostals may be a little to high for the narrower definitions of Pentecostalism because it includes traditions which pre-date both Parham (1901) and Seymour (1906). David B. Barrett, "The Twentieth Century

Pentecostal/Charismatic Renewal in the Holy Spirit, with its Goal of World Evangelization" in *International Bulletin of Missionary Research*, Vol. 12, No 3, (July 1988).

9. Douglas J. Nelson, "For Such Time As This: The Story of Bishop William J. Seymour and the Azusa Street Revival" (unpublished Ph.D. dissertation, University of Birmingham, 1981).

10. Albert J. Raboteau, *Slave Religion: the Invisible Institution in the Antebellum South* (Oxford: Oxford University Press, 1978), 4–5.

11. Iain MacRobert, *The Black Roots and White Racism of Early Pentecostalism in the USA* (Bassingstoke: Macmillan Press, 1988), 9–14.

12. Ibid., 14–15.

13. Ibid., 15–18.

14. Ibid., 20–23, 33–36.

15. Raboteau, 149.

16. Melville J. Herskovitz, *The Myth of the Negro Past* (Boston: Beacon Press, 1958), 227–31.

17. MacRobert, *Black Roots*, 31–34.

18. Ibid., 38–42.

19. Nelson, 31, 153–8.

20. Ibid., 161.

21. Sarah E. Parham (Comp.), *The Life of Charles F. Parham: Founder of the Apostolic Faith Movement* (Joplin, Missouri: Tri-State Printing Co, 1930), 51–52.

22. On Parham's theories of racial supremacy see: Charles Fox Parham, *A Voice Crying in the Wilderness* (Joplin, Missouri: Joplin Printing Co, 1944 [originally 1902]), 81–84, 92–100, 105–118; and Charles Fox Parham, *The Everlasting Gospel* (Baxter Springs, Kansas, 1942), 1–4.

23. Nelson, 35.

24. Ibid., 187–90; MacRobert, *Black Roots*, 51–52.

25. Nelson, 191.

26. Ibid., 191–92.

27. Ibid., 192–94, 196; *The Apostolic Faith* Vol. 1, No 1 (September 1906), 1, col. 1; Bartleman, 47–48.

28. Nelson, 196.

29. *The Apostolic Faith, op. cit.,* 3, col. 2.

30. Quoted in Synan, *Aspects*, 133.

31. Quoted in Nelson, 234, n. 91.

32. Barleman, p. 54.

33. *Confidence* (September 1912).

34. Parham, *Everlasting Gospel*, 1–3.

35. Charles Fox Parham, *Apostolic Faith*, Baster Springs, Kansas (December 1912).

36. Synan, *Holiness-Pentecostal*, 153.

37. Robert Mapes Anderson, "A Social History of the Early Twentieth Century Pentecostal Movement" (Ph.D. Thesis, Columbia University, 1969), 319–20; published in a revised form as *Vision of the Disinherited: The Making of American Pentecostalism* (New York: Oxford University Press, 1979).

38. Synan, *Holiness-Pentecostal*, 179–80.

39. Iain MacRobert, "Black Pentecostalism: Its Origins, Functions and Theology with special reference to a Midland Borough" (unpublished Ph.D. dissertation, University of Birmingham 1989), 39.

40. Even Bartleman, a white Pentecostal pioneer, constantly refers to the baptism with, in or of the Holy Spirit as "possession." Bartleman, 72 ff.; see also Seymour in *The Apostolic Faith* Vol. 1, No 4 (December 1906), 1, col. 4.

41. Synan, *Holiness-Pentecostal*, 114.

42. A. J. Tomlinson, *Answering the Call of God*, 9–10, quoted in Lillie Dugger, *A.J. Tomlinson* (Cleveland, Tennessee: White Wing Publishing House, 1964), 21; A. J. Tomlinson, quoted in C. T. Davidson, *Upon This Rock* (Cleveland, Tennessee: White Wing Publishing House and Press, 1973), 437–38, 448, 518, 552–53, 594; "Minutes of 45th Assembly (1950)", quoted in *Church of God of Prophecy Business Guide* (Cleveland, Tennessee: White Wing Publishing House and Press, 1987), 45.

43. See, for example, Nico Horn "The Experience of the Spirit in Apartheid South Africa" in *Azusa Theological Journal*, Vol. 1, no 1, Durban, South Africa: Relevant Pentecostal Witness Publications (March 1990), 19–42.

SELECTED BIBLIOGRAPHY FOR FURTHER READING

Cox, Harvey. *Fire From Heaven: The Rise of Pentecostal Spirituality and the Reshaping of Religion in the Twenty-first Century*. Reading, Mass.: Addison-Wesley, 1995.

Hurston, Zora Neale. *The Sanctified Church*. Berkeley: Turtle Island, 1981.

Nelson, Douglas J. "For Such a Time as This: The Story of Bishop W. J. Seymour and the Asuza Street Revival." Ph.D. dissertation, University of Birmingham, England, 1981.

Paris, Arthur. *Black Pentecostalism: A Southern Religion in an Urban World*. Amherst: University of Massachusetts Press, 1982.

Tinney, James S. "Exclusivist Tendencies in Pentecostal Self-Definition: A Critique from Black Theology." *The Journal of Religious Thought* 36 (1979): 32–49.

15 ::

:: A common explanation for why many African American migrants from the South sought refuge in new religious movements such as the Nation of Islam or Pentecostal storefront churches is that they found the established black Baptist and Methodist churches in northern cities to be too cold, large, formal, middle-class, and "deradicalized." For these reasons, many scholars of twentieth-century African-American religion have focused primarily on the innovative and new movements often referred to, problematically, as "cults and sects." Randall K. Burkett, however, argues that scholarly attention should be redirected to the mainline black churches, and their community involvement and social activism should not be underestimated. ::

:: 15 THE BAPTIST CHURCH IN
YEARS OF CRISIS

J. C. Austin and Pilgrim Baptist
Church, 1926–1950

Randall K. Burkett

::**A**fro-American religious life in the urban North, especially during the second quarter of the twentieth century, has often been described as the "era of sects and cults." It is generally argued that, in the face of a dramatic population increase resulting from an influx of southern migrants, coupled with economic dislocation and eventual massive unemployment that culminated in the Great Depression, the mainline Black denominations were unable to respond effectively to the spiritual and social needs of the Black community. Unable to cope with urbanization and its attendant secularization, the established churches are seen to have yielded center stage to myriad smaller religious institutions, which blended a sense of intimacy with an emphasis on religious ecstacy.[1]

Gayraud Wilmore, one of the most provocative and astute observers of Afro-American religious history, essentially takes this position in his book *Black Religion and Black Radicalism*.[2] The chapter that he devotes to this period is entitled "The Deradicalization of the Black Church," clearly reflecting his perspective. Wilmore posits, in effect, the "fall" of the Black church in the interwar years. He is especially harsh on the clergy, whom he characterizes as having adopted Booker T. Washington's gradualism and as having bought into a white Christian notion of a self-effacing white Christ. To the extent that the clergy became involved in civil rights organizations at all, Wilmore charges, they did so primarily as a way of entering the mainstream of American society, reflecting their growing identification with dominant white cultural norms. As a consequence, he concludes, the clergy served as a restraining influence on the potential militancy of certain Civil Rights organizations, keeping them on an accommodationist path. At the same time, the mainline churches themselves, in their search for respectability, "succumbed to the cajolery and bribery of the white power structure and became its foil."[3]

While the mainline denominations were moving toward the periphery of Black cultural life, through their own internal dynamics, according to Wilmore's analysis they were also being driven toward marginalization by external creative energies both from "below" and from "above." On the one hand, lower-class movements, typified by the storefront churches and the "sects and cults," were growing by leaps and bounds. Wilmore cites the traditional litany of these organizations—the Holiness and Pentecostal churches; the de-Christianized groups such as the Black Jews, the Moorish Science Temple, and the Nation of Islam; and the deific groups such as Daddy Grace's United House of Prayer for All People and Father Divine's Peace Mission Movement—as examples of the rich diversity of Black religious institutional life in this period.[4]

On the other hand, among the Black middle and upper classes, the mainline churches met with a growing indifference, if not outright hostility. Whether measured by the movement of upwardly mobile Blacks from Baptist and Methodist to Congregational, Presbyterian, and Episcopal denominations, or by the emergence of the predominately secular Harlem Renaissance, the traditionally Black denominations, according to conventional wisdom, were being abandoned as relics of a past age—that is, as institutions once useful but now essentially a drain and a restraining influence on future progress, especially as that progress was measured by full integration into the dominant white American society.[5]

It certainly is clear that Afro-American religious life was going through a period of extraordinary change in the interwar years. The religious vitality of the so-called sects and cults and of the storefront churches is a phenomenon well deserving of the attention it has received in the literature. Another important factor contributing to major change was the increasing differentiation of the Black community; specifically, a range of voluntary associations grew to prominence, removing from the mainline churches some of the responsibility they had borne in an earlier period as political, social, fraternal, and benevolent institutions, and antireligious and secular elements among a portion of the Black community. However, there was much more vitality in the mainline institutional churches during the post–World War I era—especially among the Baptists—than researchers have recognized. A comparison of the *Census of Religious Bodies* for the years 1926 and 1936, the last year such a census was conducted by the federal government, shows a nearly 9 percent increase in Black membership among all denominations, from 5.2 million to 5.7 million. Black Baptists alone, however, showed an even larger gain, from 3.2 million in 1926 to nearly 3.8 million a decade later. Literally all of this gain was registered among urban churches, whose rolls swelled from 1.2 million to 1.9 million in the period, and enabled the Baptists to claim fully two-thirds (67 percent) of all Black church members in 1936, up from 61.6 percent a decade earlier.[6]

While it is true that the Census Bureau undercounted smaller religious organizations and ignored others altogether (for example, Father Divine's Peace Mission Movement is not enumerated), this fact does not discount the striking increase in the number of Black Baptists. This increase is particularly noteworthy in light of the significant drop during the same period in the number of church members in other denominations (including not only the African Methodists but also smaller groups such as the Churches of Christ and the Churches of the Living God). In what follows, I redress the neglect of the historical Black denominations in general, and of Baptists in particular, in the interwar years by focusing on the life of one highly influential Baptist minister, Junius Ceasar Austin, whose ability, eloquence, and wide-ranging interests in preaching, politics, music, aviation, education, civil rights, and foreign missions placed him in the forefront of progressive clergy in urban America.

J. C. AUSTIN: EARLY YEARS

J. C. Austin (1887–1968) was born in the upper South, in New Canton, a rural village in Buckingham County, Virginia. He received the call to the ministry at the age of eleven and served in the Baptist pastorate for just a few months short of seventy years. His early theological and social outlook were shaped by his educational experience at the Virginia Seminary and College at Lynchburg, one of the oldest independent Black Baptist seminaries in the country.

Virginia Seminary was organized in 1887 by the Virginia Baptist State Convention.[7] From its earliest days, the school was staffed by a leadership that George Shepperson and Thomas Price describe as "highly independent in spirit, believing . . . that the Negro peoples were perfectly capable of carrying on with their work without the white man always at their elbows."[8] Its president, Gregory W. Hayes, was once chastised by white Baptists for his spirit of "foolish independence and self-assertion," which had turned Lynchburg into "a sort of hotbed of racism."[9] The school was one of a number of Black educational institutions formed in the late nineteenth century that "taught doctrines and inculcated attitudes which some call politely 'racial radicalism,' and others, more bluntly, 'sedition.'"[10]

J. C. Austin imbibed this aggressive and independent spirit as a student during the first decade of the twentieth century. Virginia Seminary awarded him a B.A. degree in 1905, a Bachelor of Divinity degree in 1908, and a Doctorate of Divinity in 1910. He later studied for several summers at Temple University.[11] In 1915, he was called to Ebenezer Baptist Church in Pittsburgh, where he served until 1926. His ministry in Pittsburgh was auspicious; before he had reached his fortieth birthday, Austin had already made his mark as one of the leading clergymen of the *National Baptist Convention of the U.S.A., Incorporated*.

By this time also, the fundamental themes and style of his ministry were set. First, his magnetic preaching style and creative organizational skills enabled him to build a congregation of more than five thousand members in Pittsburgh by 1926. Second, his strong denominational leadership was evidenced by his election in 1924 as president of the Pennsylvania State Baptist Convention and by his frequent speaking engagements at the most prestigious Black Baptist churches throughout the country. Third, he was actively involved in the political, economic, and social life of Pittsburgh, as demonstrated by his election as president of the Pittsburgh chapter of the NAACP, his encouragement of the exodus of the southern Blacks to the North, and his founding of such organizations as the Home Finder's league and the Steele City National Bank.[12] Fourth, he participated in the protest and Black nationalist organizations such as the International League of Darker Peoples, the National Race Congress, and the Universal Negro Improvement Association.[13] Fifth, he was firmly committed to the religious and political redemption of Africa, as both the American Negro's special destiny in the Divine Scheme and the sine qua non for Black America's own liberation from white oppression.[14] J. C. Austin would continue and expand his involvement in these five arenas during the period we turn to next: the first quarter century of his activities in Chicago, from 1926 to 1950.

PILGRIM BAPTIST CHURCH

The starting point for an appreciation of Austin's independence in all the arenas of his activity must be Pilgrim Baptist church in Chicago and the close-knit ties that bound Austin and his congregation together. Pilgrim Church was a classic "Black Diaspora" church,[15] organized during the period when European migration to the United States was being curtailed and when the massive internal migration of Afro-Americans from rural to urban and from southern to northern America was cresting. Pilgrim Baptist Church had begun as a prayer meeting of five individuals who first met in a private home on January 6, 1915. In 1919, the growing congregation called the Reverend Samuel E. J. Watson as its first pastor. Under Watson's leadership, church membership skyrocketed to several thousand. In 1921, the congregation moved to its present location at Thirty-third Street and Indiana Avenue, the former home of the synagogue built by the architects Dankmar Adler and Louis Sullivan. When Watson died unexpectedly in 1925, the congregation called as its pastor the Reverend Junius Ceasar Austin.[16]

Austin was first and foremost an extraordinary preacher. The testimony from friends and foes alike is unanimous: in his day, Austin was one of the three or four greatest preachers of the National Baptist Convention. Frequently people came two or three hours before the service in order to get a seat. The church, which held 2,500, was filled two and occasionally three times each Sunday. According to one source, Austin's sermon notes could not be left untended on the pulpit after the service, or some aspiring preacher was likely to pocket them.[17]

The sermons themselves were sometimes topical and direct, in the Black nationalist tradition by which Austin had been molded in the crucible of Lynchburg Seminary. Illustrative of his sermon topics is one that he preached in Pittsburgh shortly before he came to Chicago, based on the theme "Slavery! Slavery! Economic Slavery, Peonage, and race injustice . . . must go."[18] A published sermon from 1937, entitled "Advancing the Kingdom of God in Business," demonstrates that in Chicago Austin did not abandon his sharp critique of contemporary American society, and that his sermons were well-researched, thoughtful, and eloquent. In this sermon, Austin insists that "economics is inextricably interwoven with the issues of the good life which is the aim of the Kingdom of God." He characterizes the United States industrial system of laissez-faire capitalism as "a relic of 1776," and declares that the capitalist social order, which "clings to the moribund platitude that all men have equal opportunities to acquire and achieve," is predicated upon a "mistaken idea."[19]

Austin also preached powerful exegetical and devotional sermons. By 1930, Pilgrim was the third largest church in the National Baptist Convention, and one of the ten largest churches in the United States.[20] Austin's sermons were carried over radio both regionally and, on occasion, nationally, on programs such as "Wings over Jordan."

In addition to his potent oratorical skills, Austin had the organizational and financial acumen to take control of a very large church with an enormous debt—nearly $150,000. In the face of the ever-worsening Depression, he liquidated the debt within ten years and placed the church on a solid fiscal foundation that permitted a steady expansion of its programs. By 1950, more than $125,000 in building repairs and renovations had been completed, a parsonage had been acquired, $28,000 had been expended toward the development of a community center, and $17,000 had been raised toward construction of a gymnasium and housing project.

The church itself was organized into approximately one hundred auxiliary units, to assure that every member of the congregation had a "home" in Pilgrim's vast community. Austin was particularly effective in organizing groups of church women, who, among their other roles, functioned as social workers, "missionary women whose job it was to go out . . . into these tenements and hovels those folks were living in and teach them hygiene and how to care for their babies and make sure they had food."[21] With the aid of five assistant ministers and a deacon board of fifty-eight, Austin turned Pilgrim into a seven-day-a-week center for welfare, education, health care, job training and placement, youth activity, culture, and religion.[22]

The arena of musical programming provides an excellent window into Austin's aggressive and entrepreneurial style in bringing the best talent to Pilgrim. One of his first moves upon arriving in Chicago was to hire as musical director the renowned Edward H. Boatner, a prominent classically trained church musician. Boatner developed an array of musical programs that included a wide range of choral and instrumental presentations for Sunday mornings and other occasions throughout the year. In spite of the popularity of these programs, Austin was aware that classical religious music did not have the widespread appeal to attract newer migrants to the city. On the sixth anniversary of his pastorate at Pilgrim, he invited the Reverend J.H.L. Smith, from Ebenezer Baptist Church in Chicago, to bring his newly formed gospel chorus to perform under the direction of its founder, Thomas A. Dorsey. Austin immediately recognized the tremendous popular appeal of the jazz rhythm at the heart of gospel sound, and within one month (and over Boatner's objections) he had induced Dorsey to move to Pilgrim Church.

Dorsey remained at Pilgrim Church throughout his long career, and both he and Austin benefited immensely from their mutual association. As Michael W. Harris has concluded, Austin's embrace of this new musical form was pivotal to its acceptance in the church at large. "One can assume," Harris writes, "that had Austin not organized a chorus at Pilgrim, the advent of gospel blues in old-line churches would have stagnated in derision and for want of serious regard from the old-line establishment. . . . Only an old-line preacher and church of the

stature of Austin and Pilgrim could have imparted respect to gospel blues' notoriety. From this perspective, the February 1932 meeting between Dorsey and
Austin marked a turning point in the emergence of gospel blues. . . ."[23]

The point to underscore in reflecting on Austin's work at Pilgrim is one that
has been made succinctly by St. Clair Drake and Horace Clayton in summarizing
a discussion of the place of the churches in Black Chicago:

> Despite the dependence of Negro congregations upon the occasional friendly
> aid of white co-religionists, the Negro church is largely free of white control.
> Negro preachers have the greatest "freedom" of any Race Leaders. Politicians
> must fit themselves into machine politics. Most "civic" leaders are dependent
> upon white Philanthropy. Most of Bronzeville's preachers are answerable to no
> one except their congregations. They can say what they please about current
> affairs and race relations; there are no church superiors to discipline them and
> no white people to take economic reprisals. Because they are so largely free of
> the political and economic controls of the white community, Bronzeville ex-
> pects them to be *real* Race Men.[24]

If, in fact, J. C. Austin was able—in several areas of political, social, and denominational activity—to operate according to his own perception of the needs of his
church, race, and nation, he was permitted to do so because of the secular foundation he had built at Pilgrim Church. His eloquent preaching and his organizational and financial skills gave him a power base in the burgeoning Black populace
of Chicago that was substantially independent of the white community, and—
given Baptist polity—independent of denominational control as well. This left
him free to act essentially as he saw fit across a wide horizon of the political landscape before him.

THE NATIONAL BAPTIST CONVENTION

A second arena of Austin's activity was his denomination, the *National Baptist
Convention of the U.S.A., Incorporated (NBC)*. It is impossible to describe in any detail the Byzantine complexity of the politics that characterized the National
Baptist Convention during this period. What I would like to offer is a tentative
outline concerning the pattern of politics within the NBC, insofar as one can do
so, from the perspective of J. C. Austin, one of the pivotal figures in that denomination in the interwar years.

First, one must recognize that, excluding the Woman's Convention, the
National Baptist Convention for most of the twentieth century was dominated by

the powerful pastors of Pilgrim Church's cross-town rival, Olivet Baptist Church. The fact that for nearly fifty of the last seventy-five years the president of the Convention has also been pastor of Olivet is an indication of this control. Olivet is the oldest Baptist church in Chicago, founded in 1853. Like Pilgrim, it benefited enormously from the flood of Black migrants who poured out of the South after Reconstruction. Its ranks swelled from four thousand members in 1915 to more than twelve thousand in the 1930s, when it became the largest Protestant congregation in America.[25]

In 1915, Olivet Church called as its minister Lacey Kirk Williams, a Texan who had been educated at Arkansas Baptist College and Bishop College in Bishop, Texas. He ascended to the presidency of the National Baptist Convention in 1923 and held that post until his death in 1940.[26] In the early years of their association, Austin and Williams were apparently able to work together. In 1924, while still in Pittsburgh, Austin was elected to the influential position of chairman of the Foreign Mission Board, presumably with Williams's support or at least his acquiescence. However, Austin's first move upon reaching Chicago—hiring Edward Boatner as musical director—could only be interpreted as a direct challenge to Williams's leadership. Boatner had previously been employed at Olivet, and Williams had even installed him as musical director of the National Baptist Convention in order to keep him happily ensconced at Olivet. Austin's offer to double Boatner's salary in order to secure his services demonstrates not only Austin's confidence in being able to raise funds, but also his intention to compete head-on with the most powerful figure in the denomination. As Michael Harris points out, clergy in this period were fiercely competitive; this competition affected all aspects of their church programs and was by no means restricted to interdenominational rivalries.[27]

Austin's action undoubtedly infuriated Williams, who did not hesitate to respond. In 1929, at the annual meeting of the National Baptist Convention in Kansas City, Missouri, Williams publicly forced Austin out of the chairmanship of the Foreign Mission Board. Austin later described this action in a letter to his life-long friend and ally, Nannie H. Burroughs. Written in mid-September 1929, the letter began:

> Dear Sister Nannie,
>
> I have buckled on my war shoes, at least since war has been declared on me, and I am standing now right on the firing line facing the enemy with the sword of truth in hand determined to contend for every inch of the ground while counting upon the promises of God, and following no tricks, clicks, nor schemed but principles of righteousness.

Our man here [William] has pledged himself to the Devil to crush me for no other purpose than the fact that the National Baptist forces make a little too much noise over me, and I have been too successful at the head of the Foreign Mission Board. Whenever I appeared in Kansas, the demonstration was greater than when the President himself appeared, and my offerings surpassed any effort he put on. So determined was he to remove me from chairmanship, and realizing that he could not do it while I was on the ground, he waited until the messengers were gone and with only thirty-seven people in the hall late Monday afternoon, when I was near St. Louis. He with his tricksters ruled me out of office on the grounds that I didn't live in Philadelphia, and elected C. C. Scott.

I am receiving letters of protest every day from outstanding men also very firm invitations from the *other side of the* Baptist family.[28]

Nannie Burroughs's response to Austin was prompt, firm, and supportive:

I am absolutely disgusted with tricksters, hypocrites, and sycophants. You are altogether right to demand a public performance and square deal.

I heard of your matchless address and tremendous carrying power. Keep your head and keep your tongue. Someone asked a woman how to make a rabbit pie. She said "First catch you a rabbit." Don't start your war until you have your implements with which to fight, then go to it. I am with you world without end.[29]

The breach between the two men was widened a few months later, following the murder of the auditor of the National Baptist Convention, Edward D. Pierson. Pierson had apparently uncovered instances of fraud among some chief officers of the convention, and was en route from Nashville to Chicago in mid-April 1930 to present his charges when he was abducted, bound, and shot, and then tossed into a river in southern Indiana. His body was discovered the next day, and eventually several high officials of the NBC, including the secretary of the Sunday School Publishing Board, the Reverend A. M. Townsend, Sr., and his son were indicted for murder. Although no one was ever brought to trial, some Baptists insinuated that Williams himself was responsible for having Pierson eliminated.[30]

In a tumultuous convention in Chicago a few months after the murder, Williams was clearly on the defensive, and Austin sought to press his advantage by having his own name placed in nomination for the presidency. When his nomination was ruled ineligible, on the grounds (later proved to be false) that Austin had not registered his church or his delegates for the convention, pandemonium broke out, and Williams supporters quickly engineered his reelection by acclamation. At the end of the chaotic ten-day meeting, Austin publicly pledged his support to Williams, pointedly stating that he "was not contemplating a split from the convention."[31]

By the next year, however, newspaper reports described the creation of a "militant group led by the resourceful Dr. J. C. Austin of the Windy City"[32] which was opposing Williams and the NBC establishment. One of Austin's allies wrote in an open letter to him, printed in the *Pittsburgh Courier*: "Progressive Baptist leaders feel that the Baptist church, now claiming millions, must lose its hold on these people, unless it can offer an intelligent, educated and honest leadership. . . . They want to see the various Baptist boards relieved of absentee bossism and to have insinuations of dishonesty against leaders, such as [A. M.] Townsend, either proved or disproved."[33] This was probably the first reference in print to an identifiable group of "progressive" Baptists who had formed in opposition to convention leadership. These progressives included J. C. Jackson, president of the New England Baptist Missionary Society; Lewis G. Jordan of Philadelphia, former chairman of the Foreign Mission Board and historiographer of the convention; William H. Jernagin of Washington, D.C., president of the Baptist Sunday School Union and Baptist Teachers Union; Nannie H. Burroughs, founder of the National Training School for Women and Girls and one of the most powerful and dynamic women in the NBC; J. Raymond Henderson of the Second Baptist Church in Los Angeles; and William H. Moses of New York. The group also included younger men such as Adam Clayton Powell, Jr., Gardner C. Taylor, and many others.

Austin repeatedly sought the presidency of the convention during the next three decades. although he never succeeded in wresting control from the establishment. His best opportunity for victory probably came in 1941, when an open convention was held to elect a successor to L. K. Williams, who had died the previous year in a plane crash. When Austin lost that election to the "steamroller" tactics of the opposition,[34] there were widespread rumors of a denominational split, and the newspapers carried stories about the imminent creation of a "Progressive Baptist" convention. One article, appearing in September 1941, reported: "Dissatisfied with the outcome of the election, Dr. Austin called a meeting . . . Friday morning where more than 1,000 Baptist leaders became members of a newly formed organization to be known as the Progressive Baptists of the National Baptist Convention."[35] However, Austin and others apparently later decided that the eve of the entry of the United States into world war was not the time to divide their denomination, and the creation of the Progressive Baptist Convention did not come for another twenty years.

AUSTIN AND POLITICS

Austin's involvement in local Chicago as well as national politics merits an essay in itself, but two or three examples of his activities illustrate his vigorous participation. One of the first organizations that Austin created at Pilgrim Baptist Church was the Cooperative Business, Professional, and Labor League. As stated in a broadside describing its purposes, the league was predicated upon the belief "that there is a great community of interest existing among our business, professional, and laboring classes, which community of interest is so inseparable that none can make substantial progress without the support of the other. Our business people, our professional people, and our laboring people must go forward together or there will not be much going forward by any of us."[36]

The league's goal was to foster Black employment through the support of Black business. Austin was an advocate of the "Double-Duty dollar," and he clearly believed in "mixing" religion and business. He repeatedly admonished his parishioners, "Don't spend your money with a dealer who does not in turn provide some opportunity for us to live by labor." The league also sought to foster Black pride by teaching youth to be "proud of themselves and the accomplishments of Negro people." It sought, for example, to help secure education for talented young people; it supported the work of Carter G. Woodson and the Association for the Study of Negro Life and History; it recognized the accomplishments of Black leaders in all fields (such as commemorating the "pioneer aviatrix" Bessie Coleman); and it served as a forum for debate by inviting political figures to speak at Pilgrim Church.

To illustrate Austin's participation in local Chicago politics, one can cite the testimony of Harold Gosnell in his still-useful book *Negro Politicians: The Rise of Negro Politics in Chicago* (1935). Gosnell states that following the death of African Methodist Episcopal bishop Archibald J. Carey in 1931, Austin became a prominent clerical supporter of "Big Bill" Thompson, the old Republican political boss and Chicago mayor. Gosnell quotes an Austin campaign speech in which he declared:

> Let us follow the leadership of a man who knows nothing but forward and upward in the person of William Hale Thompson. . . . We saw Big Bill go down out of the confidence of the people, out of the love of the people. . . . He

struggled in the grave. . . . The *Tribune* wrote an obituary. I went back again and looked upon the grave. . . . But thank God, before the primary I heard the grave crack, the tombstone fall and saw William Hale Thompson rise (applause) and stand over his enemies and say "I am on the side of truth, of right, of justice." (Big applause.)[37]

Thompson was a Republican political boss of the old order who, as mayor, had weathered the crisis of the infamous Chicago race riot of 1919 and had still retained the overwhelming loyalty of the Black community. While a few clergy (including Lacey K. Williams) opposed Thompson for having "turned over the Negro communities of Chicago to the vice lords, policy kings, bootleggers and racketeers,"[38] Austin was more interested in the political gains to be made for the Black community by supporting the Thompson machine. As Alan Spear has pointed out, the Chicago Black political leadership was deeply suspicious of the reformist agenda of the "progressive" Republicans, who were led by Illinois governor Charles S. Deneen. These Black leaders saw political reform as the end of Black access to party bosses and patronage and the reinstitution of Blacks' subservience to a predominantly white electorate.[39]

We should not be surprised, then, that Thompson was praised by Austin in the most grandiloquent terms. Austin declared at one political rally: "God made just one William Hale Thompson and forgot the mold. Truth, courage, consecration, ideas of right, ideas of justice, let there be right, righteousness. Let it come to earth. Call it William Hale Thompson. . . . I would call him Napoleon, I would call him Abraham Lincoln. When history is written, they will write in the blue sky high above all of them the name of William Hale Thompson."[40] One suspects that although he may have accepted the analogy of Thompson to Napoleon, Gosnell personally must have had trouble with Austin's comparison of Thompson to Lincoln. Nevertheless, Gosnell concluded his chapter, entitled "The Second Lincoln," with the observation that "by furnishing Negroes with new jobs, by protecting them against mishandling by the police, by recognizing them as citizens, by fitting its appeals to the various groups found within the Negro community, the faction created a situation in which colored preachers could refer to Thompson as the 'Second Lincoln' and win applause."[41]

Austin was also active on the national political scene. Austin and his Cooperative Business, Professional, and Labor League hosted a debate on the fourth of July, 1931, between Benjamin J. Davis, a former Republican National Committeeman from Georgia, and Oscar DePriest, the Republican congressman from the South Side of Chicago who was the first Afro-American to be elected to the United States Congress in the twentieth century. The debate centered on Mr. DePriest's urging that Blacks in the South consider breaking their near-total allegiance to the Republican party, since the "lily white Republicans in the South . . . did not want to help [Negroes] and could not help them if they wanted to."[42]

In fact, six weeks prior to the debate, DePriest had called for creation of a "Non-Partisan Negro Conference," the goal of which would be "to determine the needs and grievances of colored citizens in American and formulate a plan for their amelioration."[43] The meeting was eventually held in Washington, D.C., on December 2–4, 1931. Some 179 delegates from twenty-five states plus the District of Columbia attended the meeting to debate such topics as disenfranchisement, lynching, civil service, economic opportunities, religion and politics, women in public life, and the distribution of federal educational funds. Austin, along with Kelly Miller, Judge W. C. Hueston, Bishop E. D. W. Jones, Nannie H. Burroughs, and publisher Robert L. Vann, were members of the Findings Committee. This committee concluded:

> We regard political parties as an instrument to be used and not as a fetish to be worshipped. Tools may wear out and grow blunt. They may be re-sharpened or cast aside for different or better ones. The ballot was given the Negro as a weapon of defense. The effectiveness of the ballot is appreciated and recognized mainly when the voter has the potentiality and evidences the disposition to change the result. . . . At this time of a wavering balance between the two parties, the Negro vote can easily be utilized for what it is most worth—political and civil equality and economic opportunity. One can always make a better bargain, when there are two bidders instead of one.[44]

One of the most fundamental and far-reaching political realignments in the first half of the twentieth century proved to be the shift of Black voters from the Republican to the Democratic party. Although there were isolated cases of Republican defections as early as the turn of the century, the move did not gather popular support until the Depression. The greatest shift to the Democrats was accomplished during the presidency of Franklin D. Roosevelt. While it is difficult to assess the effect of the Non-Partisan Negro Conference on this pivotal change in party affiliation, it is typical that Austin was centrally involved in the early debate.[45]

AUSTIN AND VOLUNTARY ASSOCIATIONS

J. C. Austin was involved with a wide range of voluntary associations organized for cultural, social, political, fraternal, and religious ends. He was a member of the Elks, the Masons, the Knights of Pythias, and the Independent Order of St. Luke. We have already noted that he was an avid supporter of the Association for the Study of Negro Life and History. His activities and interests were eclectic. He was early fascinated with air travel, and in May 1935 he founded one of the first organizations of Negro aviators in the United States, at Pilgrim Baptist Church. Many of its charter members were good friends and members of his congregation. He was founder and president of the Inter-Church Good Will Conference of Chicago, an interdenominational and interracial association of clergy. He was a key member (along with Chandler Owen, George Cleveland Hall, Irene McCoy Gaines, and others) of the Citizen's Committee organized in 1928 to support the Brotherhood of Sleeping Car Porters, and he took an active role on behalf of the Chicago Scottsboro Defense Committee in the mid-1930s. The list of organizations, associations, and committees to which he belonged is considerable.[46]

An episode in the mid-1930s involving Austin, the National Office of the NAACP, and the local Chicago Branch of the NAACP may serve to illustrate both the degree of Austin's activity and the complexity of his involvement (and that of other clergy) in voluntary associations. Austin had hosted a number of prominent national officers of the NAACP as speakers at Pilgrim Church in the early 1930s, including Daisy E. Lampkin, regional field secretary, and Robert W. Bagnall, director of branches. In late 1935, Austin agreed to devote an entire Sunday service to the NAACP, and the Chicago Branch president, A. C. MacNeal, wrote to many of Chicago's largest churches calling their attention to the "splendid type of cooperation on the part of Reverend Austin" and inviting them to follow Austin's example by setting aside a Sunday morning in their churches to speak about the work of the association.

Two years later, NAACP secretary Walter White wrote to MacNeal, informing him of an initiative that Austin had recently put forth. In a speech at a conference in Washington, D.C., Austin had urged that "instead of sitting down, passing resolution[s,] the conference should get behind the NAACP, which is the one organization which could make a fight for the association." At the close of the conference, Austin had offered a resolution to establish an NAACP lobby in Washington. Delighted with this show of support, White urged MacNeal to follow up on Austin's suggestions, and he himself agreed to Austin's invitation to speak at a "great anti-lynching meeting" at Pilgrim Church, where Austin foresaw "5,000 Negroes with buttons on and upturned faces and open hearts and receptive minds to receive your message." White and Austin had already agreed on a date for this meeting when the Chicago branch chief wired that the arrangements were acceptable only if the branch bore one-fourth of the traveling expenses and received three-fourths of the net proceeds. These terms were unacceptable to the national office, and the meeting had to be canceled.[47]

As this episode illustrates, the long history of hostility and jealousy between the NAACP national office and the Chicago branch often made cooperation between the two nearly impossible. In 1939, E. Frederick Morrow, coordinator of branches, wrote to national headquarters from Chicago that the situation was desperate:

> The branch too long has been dominated by a few individuals who run it as they see fit. There is little democracy. There is a distinct "class-caste" atmosphere. This militates against securing the membership of the man in the street. This has been told me so many times, it haunts me. There is a feeling that it is run by the lawyers, for the lawyers. No effort has been made to reach out and get new blood, or new contacts.
>
> You are already familiar with the rabid anti-national office attitude here. I do not know all the history of this, but it harms the program, for there cannot be harmony where distrust exists, and one has to explain every move and intention. Some have even warmly threaten[ed] rebellion against the N[ational] O[ffice], and running things to suit themselves.[48]

Austin was caught in this cross fire. With a small group of well-entrenched individuals controlling the local chapter, it was difficult for him or any other clergy to exert influence over local NAACP affairs in Chicago. They found it much easier to develop cordial relations with national officers; one can well imagine that this was a solution satisfactory to local officials as well, who did not want powerful clergy threatening their control of the branch.

AUSTIN AND AFRICA

J. C. Austin's commitment to Africa and to the redemption of Africa through the missionary efforts of Black Christians was at the core of his theology. From his college days at Lynchburg Seminary until his death more than a half-century later, African missions were a matter of central concern to him. It was this concern, more than any other single factor, that had attracted Austin to the Garvey movement, to which he spoke at the International Convention of Negro Peoples of the World in 1922, in a speech entitled "Representing the Negro Clergy." His first major denominational responsibility in the NBC was that of chairman of the Foreign Mission Board, a position to which he had been elected in 1924. Missions were a top priority at Pilgrim Baptist Church, and by the end of his first year as minister there, the church was already ranked as the denomination's third largest contributor to foreign missions, giving more than $1,200 to support their work. For years, Pilgrim Church paid the salary of Dr. Samuel W. Martin, a missionary in Issele-Uku, Nigeria.[49]

In February 1950, Austin was selected, along with nine of the National Baptist Convention's most prominent advocates of foreign missions, to review the denomination's work in Africa. This fact-finding and study commission, known among Baptists as the "Tall Pines," traveled throughout West Africa for more than a month. The group met with government officials as well as their own missionaries and congregations. The secretary of the Foreign Mission Board, C. C. Adams, described in his journal a visit to the Issele-Uku mission stations:

> Thursday, February 23, was a long-looked-for day at the Pilgrim Mission. The occasion: the formal dedication of the Teacher's Training College, known as the Austin Building, in honor of Dr. J. C. Austin of Chicago, Illinois. Brother [Samuel] Martin had prepared a wonderful program that called together people from far and wide—chiefs, civilian and educational authorities from the highest levels. Some of them were British of rare culture, all of whom were loud in praise of Brother Martin and his work and leadership. The impressive program of dedication was followed by colorful demonstrations of calisthenics by the student body on the campus. These were simply dazzling and beyond my power of description.[50]

Austin was also specially honored by ten African chiefs of the Benin region, who bestowed on him a royal chiefhood and a magnificent robe and cap. Typically, Austin sought to use this special status to advance a scheme that he hoped would benefit both Africans and Afro-Americans. On his return to the United States, he created an "African Exports and Imports N.B.C., U.S.A." and took the role of executive secretary in it. The goal of this organization was to provide a direct outlet in the United States for the cultural, artistic, and other products of West Africans, with the National Baptist Convention serving as intermediary in fostering trade between the two continents.

Austin's reports upon his return to the United States demonstrate that he was acutely sensitive to the powerful political forces that were taking shape in West Africa. "I found Lagos quite tense and ready to fight for freedom," he wrote to Claude Barnett of the Associated Negro Press. "The same spirit I found in the Gold Coast at Accra. I also met the governor who gave us a grand reception in the opening of his court. On the morning of our appearance, Gov. [Charles Noble Arden] Clarke of Nigeria delivered his address in favor of a new constitution which offers freedom and independence to the people of the Gold Coast." He saw in these political developments a potent message for Afro-Americans as well: "I saw and counselled with a black president and a black secretary of State. . . . I saw black clerks and managers working in stores and black officials high in government everywhere I went. I went to Africa only to be convinced that not only the hope of the black man, but the hope of peace and the hope of the world rests in Africa."[51]

J. C. Austin's perennial refrain that "the Negro in America will never be free until Africa gets her clothes on" reflected one of the most venerable traditions in Black religious nationalist thought. This was essentially the belief that the freedom of Africa and the freedom of Afro-America—indeed, of all Africa-in-Diaspora—were inextricably linked to one another and to an understanding of God's scrutable plan, epitomized in the biblical prophecy of Psalm 68:31: "Princes shall come out of Egypt, Ethiopia shall soon stretch forth her hands unto God."

CONCLUSION

In his provocative essay "Political Change in the Negro Ghetto, 1900–1940," the political scientist Martin Kilson describes several patterns of political adaptation that were available to Afro-Americans in the early twentieth century. He characterizes one of these patterns as "interest group articulation," in which cliques or interest groups seek to advance their own needs. Particularly intriguing among varieties of group formation, Kilson writes, "is the political movement based on the aggregation of voluntary associations." He explains:

> In this situation, a skillful and often charismatic leader first maximizes the
> politicization of his own voluntary association and then, having secured this
> initial base, branches out, penetrating first ideologically and then organization-
> ally other nonpoliticized voluntary associations. The penetration or aggrega-
> tion process was pursued by a highly politicized voluntary agency of the
> leader, and invariably ideology (usually racialist or black nationalist) proved
> the most important political resources.[52]

Kilson had in mind the political organization developed by Adam Clayton Powell, Jr., in the late 1930s, but he might have easily taken the work of J. C. Austin as his example. Coming to Chicago in the mid-1920s, well-grounded in the Black religious nationalism that he had learned at Lynchburg Seminary and refined during his association with the Garvey movement during his Pittsburgh years, Austin first set about to establish a firm base for activism at Pilgrim Baptist Church. He soon found himself increasingly at odds with the established leadership of his denomination and began a lifelong campaign to reform it along "progressive" lines.

At the same time, he immersed himself in local and national political activity. Through the formation of the Cooperative, Business, Professional, and Labor League, Austin sought to politicize and mobilize both the burgeoning Black middle class in Chicago (which, Kilson reminds us, was probably larger than the Black elite in any other city in the country, including New York City) as well as the lower-middle-class and poor laborers who constituted the majority of the Black population in Chicago. He became for a brief time a leading clerical supporter of William Hale Thompson, head of one of the few city political machines in America open to the idea of Black participation on terms of relative equality with other ethnic groups. Again, Kilson is instructive:

> Thompson's mode of organizing Negroes in Chicago in order to guarantee
> their support was even more important to the eventual inclusion of blacks in
> Chicago machine politics than the voting pattern. . . . Unlike those in any
> other major city in this period, the Republican leaders in Chicago cultivated
> the independent-minded Negro middle class leaders rather than those Negro
> political leaders inclined to neoclientage linkages with white power struc-
> tures. Equally important, the Negro leaders who organized Big Bill
> Thompson's Negro support insisted upon something other than neoclientage
> ties to the Chicago machine.[53]

Austin recognized and capitalized on the unique opportunity Thompson presented, and he utilized his connections to secure jobs, economic opportunity and political clout. Whether in helping to organize the Non-Partisan Negro Conference in 1931, in seeking to penetrate special interest groups like the Chicago NAACP, or in attempting to form an export/import association to benefit both Africans and Afro-Americans, Austin was a highly astute and effective preacher-politician. Although he chose not to seek elective political office himself, Austin understood the uses of political power, and he always believed that the church had a responsibility to address political, social, and economic issues as part of its mission.

In the *Intercollegian Wonder Book of the Negro in Chicago 1779–1927*, Pilgrim Baptist Church was described as "a great forum for race uplift and general interest. It is the business man's Clearing House, and a soul saving station for the sinful city. It is truly a church with a program, led on by a minister with a vision."[54] Whether or not it is appropriate to characterize Pilgrim Church and its pastor as among the "wonders" of the world of Black Chicago, Austin was certainly one of a number of clergy who responded creatively and effectively to the crisis of the interwar years. The independent, pan-Africanist, and Black religious nationalist spirit that Austin espoused epitomizes precisely the tradition in the historical Black denominations that Wilmore has identified as constituting the genius of the historical Black church. Its roots are deep in the nineteenth-century protest tradition of Richard Allen and Henry Turner, Nathaniel Paul and William Simmons, James Pennington and Henry Garnet, and Alexander Crummell and James Holly, about whom much is already known. The exemplars of this tradition in the twentieth century—not only both Powells and both Kings, but also Reverdy C. Ransom and R. R. Wright, Jr., Nannie Burroughs and Gardner C. Taylor, Mary McLeod Bethune and William Y. Bell, Anna Julia Cooper and George Freeman Bragg, Jr., and many others—deserve our attention. With careful study of their lives and work, we will have a much fairer view of the richness of Black religious life in the second quarter of the twentieth century. We may come to see that for a number of men and for a growing number of women, these critical years offered unparalleled opportunity for the creation of new institutional structures, both within the historic Black denominations and among newly formed groups known as "sects and cults," and that many of these individuals maintained a critical and even prophetic stance against the pervasive racism of the period.

NOTES

1. The classic articulation of the theme of the failure of the Black Church in the interwar years is found in E. Franklin Frazier, *The Negro Church in America* (New York: Shocken Books, 1963), particularly chapter 4, "Negro Religion in the City." See also Arthur H. Fauset, *Black Gods of the Metropolis* (Philadelphia: University of Pennsylvania Press, 1944); and Raymond J. Jones, *A Comparative Study of Religious Cult Behavior Among Negroes, with Special Reference to Emotional Group Conditioning Factors* (Washington, D.C.: Howard University Graduate School, 1939).

2. Gayraud S. Wilmore, *Black Religion and Black Radicalism: An Interpretation of the Religious History of Afro-American People*, 2d ed. (New York: Orbis Books, 1983), 144.

3. Wilmore, in *Black Religion and Black Radicalism*, 144, cites with approval a statement made by Joseph R. Washington in *Black Religion* (Boston: Beacon Press, 1964), 35.

4. Wilmore, *Black Religion and Black Radicalism*, 152–60. Robert Weisbrot, in his study *Father Divine and the Struggle for Radial Equality* (Urbana: University of Illinois Press, 1983), adopts the conventional view that black clergy in the 1920s and 1930s were preoccupied with an other-worldly spirituality and this-worldly concern for their own economic aggrandizement. His view of Father Divine as a socially conscious

reformer committed to racial equality, who was attempting to instill political awareness among his followers, is a valuable corrective to previous studies. He underestimates, however, the commitment of Black clergy to social Christianity throughout this period, and he ignores the central religious impulse that empowered the Peace Mission Movement. Father Divine's position as a fervent theocrat and self-declared messiah and his demand for absolute celibacy from his followers, for example, are surely more than unfortunate political liabilities in his reformist agenda. See especially Weisbrot, chapter 7, "The Politics of Racial Justice."

5. Wilmore, *Black Religion and Black Radicalism*, 160–66. The most forceful statement concerning the Black Church as a barrier to integration is found in Frazier's *Negro Church*, chap. 5 and conclusion.

6. U.S. Department of Commerce, Bureau of the Census *Census of Religious Bodies: 1936*, (Washington, D.C.: U.S. Government Printing Office, 1941), 1:900–3.

7. For a fascinating account of the origins of Virginia Seminary as a racially independent school, see Lester F. Russell, *Black Baptist Secondary Schools in Virginia, 1887–1957* (Metuchen, N.J.: Scarecrow Press, 1981), especially 49–57 and 140–48. The school was actually incorporated in the Commonwealth of Virginia on February 24, 1888.

8. George Shepperson and Thomas Price, *Independent African: John Chilembwe and the Origins, Setting, and Significance of the Nyasaland Native Rising of 1915* (Edinburgh: Edinburgh University Press, 1958), 114.

9. Gregory W. Hayes (1862–1907) became president of the Virginia Seminary in 1891 and was primarily responsible for charting the school's course of racial independence, which resulted in the splitting (in 1899) of the Virginia Black Baptists into two separate organizations, the Virginia Baptist State Convention and the Baptist General Association of Virginia (Colored). The former was composed of "racemen," who stood for racial independence in support of Hayes's philosophy, while the latter were "co-operationists," who were willing to share (or, some would insist, sacrifice) educational control with whites in exchange for financial support: see Russell, *Black Baptist Secondary Schools*, 52–56. Charges against Hayes by white Baptists are found in the text of a letter from Dr. M. MacVicar of the American Baptist Home Mission Society to the Reverend Z. D. Lewis, September 27, 1898, reprinted by Russell, ibid., 140–43.

10. Shepperson and Price, *Independent African*, 98. Among Lynchburg's most famous graduates was the African revolutionary leader John Chilembwe, who attended the school from 1898 to 1900. Chilembwe's education at Lynchburg had been financed by the Reverend Willis W. Brown, a close friend and mentor of Junius C. Austin, and the one who sold Marcus Garvey the building that became Garvey's headquarters, known as "Liberty Hall."

11. *Chicago Tribune*, October 19, 1957. *A Testimonial to the Reverend Junius Ceasar [sic] Austin: Pastor of Ebenezer Baptist Church of Pittsburgh, Pennsylvania 1915–1926* (n.p.,

n.d.) was a pamphlet published in commemoration of Austin's eleven years at Ebenezer Baptist Church. It states (though we have no independent documentation) that he did postgraduate work at Temple College in Philadelphia. The pamphlet also notes that Austin "did his apprentice work under Dr. W. E. Moore, then pastor of Zion Baptist Church, and later was ordained from this parish with the late Dr. Motts, former Dean of the Temple Theological department as his catechist" (6).

12. The Home Finder's League was organized by Austin to help Southern immigrants to Pittsburgh find housing. This effort was more successful than was the Steele City National Bank, which collapsed in January 1926, just as Austin left Pittsburgh for Chicago. Austin and other bank officers were blamed for the bank's failure and were accused of defrauding depositors of funds. Shareholders eventually recouped forty-two cents on each dollar invested, according to an article in the Chicago *Defender* (February 12, 1927), 1. See also Chicago *Defender* (April 2, 1927), 2.

13. The International League of Darker Peoples was organized in 1919 to ensure that Blacks would present a united front at the Paris Peace Conference. The National Race Congress had been founded in Washington, D.C., three years earlier to oppose lynching and mob violence, with Austin's friend and fellow Baptist clergyman William H. Jernagin as president. Austin's willingness to speak forthrightly on racial issues, in spite of the opposition of his more moderate and cautious colleagues, is evidenced by the sermon "Representing the Negro Ministry," which he gave as the keynote address of Marcus Garvey's Third International Convention of the Negro Peoples of the World on August 1, 1922. Austin was criticized, both by members of his own congregation and by some of his fellow clergy, for his support of the Universal Negro Improvement Association (UNIA). A Department of Justice undercover agent's report states, "I spoke to several of the leading preachers of Harlem during the day regarding the action of Rev. J. C. Austin in taking part in the program of the U.N.I.A. and they all were of the opinion that he should not have done so and was harming both himself and the Baptist cause by dealing with Marcus Garvey." For Austin's involvement in the UNIA, see the brief biographical essay of Austin in Randall K. Burkett, *Black Redemption: Clergymen Speak for the Garvey Movement* (Philadelphia: Temple University Press, 1978), and chapter 4 of Burkett's *Garveyism as a Religious Movement: The Institutionalization of a Black Civil Religion* (Metuchen, N.J.: Scarecrow Press, 1978), especially 114–16.

14. See Burkett, *Black Redemption*, 112–17. For general information about Black churches in Pittsburgh during this period, see Dennis Clark Dickerson's essay "Black Workers and Black Churches in Western Pennsylvania, 1915–1950," in *Blacks in Pennsylvania History: Research and Educational Perspectives*, ed. David McBride (Harrisburg: Pennsylvania Historical and Museum Commission, 1983), 51–62. Dickerson has made available to me a substantial amount of primary source material, oral interviews, and other information that he gathered on Austin during his own research. As St. Clair Drake has demonstrated, the image of the redemption of

Africa was "one important focus of meaningful activity among New World Negroes," and it served as "an energizing myth in both the New World and in Africa itself for those pre-political movements that arose while the powerless were gathering their strength for realistic and rewarding political activity." St. Clair Drake, *The Redemption of Africa and Black Religion* (Chicago: Third World Press, 1970), 11.

15. St. Clair Drake and Horace R. Cayton, *Black Metropolis: A Study of Negro Life in a Northern City* (New York: Harcourt, Brace and Company, 1945), 58ff.

16. A brief history of the origin of Pilgrim Baptist Church may be found in *Pilgrim Baptist Church Achievement Celebration, 1926–1939* (n.p., n.d., pamphlet), 6, 9. Rev. Samuel E. J. Watson died on June 16, 1925.

17. Interview with Austin's children, Dorothea Austin Brown and Junius C. Austin, Jr., Chicago, June 10 and 12, 1981. Harold Cooper, public relations officer for Lagos, Nigeria, may be taken as representative of the many visitors to Pilgrim Church who never forgot Austin's eloquence. Writing to Claude A. Barnett in 1953, several years after having heard Austin preach, Cooper wrote, "I should also be grateful if you could let me know the exact address of my old friend Dr. Austin, to whom I wish to write about a number of matters. I hope he is still in robust health and still packing the Pilgrim Baptist Church every Sunday morning. One of my most vivid memories is of that remarkable service which you and I attended. I have described it to many of my clerical acquaintances in the United Kingdom, who compared it glumly with their own weekly experience of preaching to almost empty churches." Harold Cooper to Claude A. Barnett, November 1, 1953, in Claude A. Barnett Papers, Chicago Historical Society, Chicago (henceforth cited as CHS). I am deeply grateful to Archie Motley and Linda Evans of the CHS staff, who have provided generous assistance in facilitating my research for this article.

18. *Pittsburgh Courier*, November 22, 1924, 5.

19. This sermon was published in the *Negro Journal of Religion* 3 (1937): 5, 12. Another of Austin's sermons, "Jesus' Idea of Royalty," was published in the *Negro Journal of Religion* 1 (1935): 8–9.

20. Lewis G. Jordan, *Negro Baptist History, U.S.A., 1750–1930* (Nashville, Tenn.: Sunday School Publishing Board, n.d.), 80.

21. Michael Wesley Harris, "The Advent of Gospel Blues in Black Old-Line Churches in Chicago, 1932–33, As Seen through the Life and Mind of Thomas Andrew Dorsey" (Ph.D. diss., Harvard University, 1982), 176. Harris is quoting from an interview that he conducted with Austin's son, the Reverend Junius C. Austin, Jr., on June 24, 1977.

22. See *Pilgrim Baptist Church Achievement Celebration*, cited above, and the church's commemorative column *Gold and Silver Anniversary Honoring Dr. J. C. Austin, 1901–1951* (Chicago: Sumar Press, n.d.), 5, 6.

23. Michael Wesley Harris, *The Rise of Gospel Blues: The Music of Thomas Andrew Dorsey in the Urban Church* (New York: Oxford University Press, 1992), 200, and passim. My

account of the role of music at Pilgrim is largely drawn from Harris's work. It should be noted that Harris is highly critical of what he views as the crass opportunism in Austin's efforts to adopt crowd-pleasing strategies, whether in his preaching or in his musical styles. He describes, for instance, Edward Boatner's disgust at Austin's decision to welcome Dorsey's music, and recounts Austin's declaration to Boatner that as long as he (Austin) was musical director, the gospel chorus would be acceptable only if it sat in the back of the church. "Only one who was driven by the anticipation of success," Harris concludes, would accept such an ultimatum. See 198 and 196–202.

24. Drake and Cayton, *Black Metropolis*, 427–28.

25. Miles Mark Fisher, "History of Olivet Baptist Church of Chicago" (Master's thesis, University of Chicago, 1922), especially 82–98; "Six Major Negro Churches," in Federal Writers Project Papers, Box 187, Illinois State Historical Library, Springfield. I am grateful to Roger D. Bridges for bringing this and other material concerning Black churches in Chicago to my attention.

26. Lacey Kirk Williams had pastored the largest Baptist churches in Texas and had served as president of the Baptist Missionary and Educational Convention in that state. He was brought to Olivet Church in the hope that he "would sustain relations between the Olivet Church and the white Baptists of Chicago" and would also "unite the Negro Baptists of Chicago," Fisher, "History of Olivet Baptist Church," 84.

27. Harris, "Advent of Gospel Blues," 190–91.

28. Junius C. Austin to Nannie H. Burroughs, September 11, 1929, in Nannie H. Burroughs Papers, Container 1, Library of Congress, Washington, D.C. The "other side" to whom Austin refers is undoubtedly the National Baptist Convention of America, the second largest Black Baptist denomination, formed in 1915.

29. T. C. and N. H. Burroughs to Junius C. Austin, September 24, 1929, Burroughs Papers, Letters Sent, Box 33, Library of Congress. The feisty Nannie Burroughs, who in 1903 had founded the National Training School for Girls and Women in Washington, D.C., was by this time already having her own troubles with Lacey K. Williams and the establishment leadership of the National Baptist Convention. See Evelyn Brooks Barnett, "Nannie Burroughs and the Education of Black Women," in *The Afro-American Woman: Struggles and Images*, ed. Sharon Harley and Rosalyn Terborg-Penn (Port Washington, N.Y.: Kennikat Press, 1978), 97–108. The problem had to do both with the jealousy of some men in the NBC of the power that Burroughs had acquired as one of the founders of the women's division of the convention and with the independent sources of revenue that she had developed among both Black and white Baptist women. The problem began as early as 1920, intensified in 1928 (see, for example, "Controversy Sidestepped by Williams," *Chicago Defender*, [February 25, 1928], part I, p. 2; and "Shall We Crucify a Woman?" by J. Pius Barbour, *Baptist Leader* 51, no. 21 [April 20, 1928], p. 1), and came to a head a

decade later when L. K. Williams took the extraordinary action of cutting off all NBC funds to the National Training School. Barnett, "Nannie Burroughs," 99.

30. See, for example, "Baptists Lead Drive to Solve Slaying," *Chicago Defender*, May 3, 1930, a copy of which, along with other clippings, press releases, and correspondence concerning the Pierson case, may be found in the Barnett Papers, CHS. Suspicion about L. K. Williams's involvement in Pierson's murder apparently lingered in the NBC, as is evident from a banner headline in the *Chicago Defender* more than a decade after the event: "[Adam Clayton] Powell Denies Naming L.K. Williams in Pierson Murder," *Chicago Defender*, December 7, 1940, 1. I am indebted to Matthew McMichael for tracking down, in the Indiana Commission on Public Records, the letter from the governor of Tennessee to the governor of Indiana refusing to extradite the Townsends to Indiana for trial. He also located numerous Indiana newspaper accounts of the murder and directed me to the Scott County, Indiana, Circuit Court records concerning the case. These records are found in "State of Indiana v. George Washington, alias William Moorehead," Scott Circuit Court, file nos. 2469 and 2471, available from the Clerk of Courts, Scottsburg, Indiana. The case was dropped in 1931, when Pierson's widow and children asked that it not be pursued further.

31. See, for example, *Chicago Defender*, August 30, 1930; *Baltimore Afro-American*, August 30, 1930; and *Pittsburgh Courier*, August 30, 1930.

32. *Pittsburgh Courier*, July 18, 1931, sec. 2, p. 10.

33. *Pittsburgh Courier*, June 27, 1931, sec. 3, p. 10.

34. *Philadelphia Afro-American*, September 20, 1941, 10. Another factor that undoubtedly affected the outcome of the NBC election was a visit by J. C. Austin to Father Divine's Peace Mission movement headquarters just prior to the election. Austin insisted that he only consulted Divine "as a student of people and religions. I watch every movement going on in America, whether close to my door or not. Whenever I see a man like Divine who is able to gather great groups about him, I investigate, because I want to see what it is he is offering the people, what it is he has that attracts, which fills some need of the masses." Austin's opponents, of course, had a field day with the episode, and the notorious Rev. Thomas Harten declared that if the Reverend Mr. Austin had been spending time in Father Divine's heavens and associating with the cult leader, he did not believe Austin to be a fit man to be elected president of the National Baptist Convention. *Philadelphia Afro-American*, September 6, 1941, 1, and September 13, 1941, 3. See also *Baltimore Afro-American*, September 6, 1941, 4; September 20, 1941, 8. I am grateful to Robert Weisbrot for calling my attention to this episode.

35. *Chicago Defender*, September 20, 1941, 2.

36. Broadside, "The Cooperative business, Professional and Labor League," n.d. (ca. 1926), with a photo of Rev. J. C. Austin in the center, Irene McCoy Gaines Papers, CHS.

37. Harold F. Gosnell, *Negro Politicians: The Rise of Negro Politics in Chicago* (Chicago: University of Chicago Press, 1935), 52.

38. Ibid., 60.

39. Allan H. Spear, *Black Chicago: The Making of a Negro Ghetto, 1890–1920* (Chicago: University of Chicago Press, 1967), 121–22.

40. Gosnell, *Negro Politicians*, 52.

41. Ibid., 62. Another useful source is Ralph J. Bunche's contemporaneous analysis of "The Thompson-Negro Alliance," *Opportunity: A Journal of Negro Life* 7 (1929): 78–80.

42. *Pittsburgh Courier*, July 4, 1931, eds. 1, 4.

43. Ibid., 6.

44. "The Non-Partisan Negro Conference, Held in Washington, D.C., December 2, 3, and 4, 1931," Mimeograph, 3 in Burroughs Papers, Box 315, Library of Congress. A copy of the meeting's agenda may be found in the Gaines Papers, CHS.

45. Andrew Buni, in his study of *Robert L. Vann of the Pittsburgh Courier: Politics and Black Journalism* (Pittsburgh: University of Pittsburgh Press, 1974), reports that Vann withdrew from the Non-Partisan League during the 1932 presidential election, accusing DePriest of attempting to make it a political arm of the Republican party (373, n. 135). Nancy J. Weiss, in *Farewell to the Party of Lincoln: Black Politics in the Age of FDR* (Princeton, N.J.: Princeton University Press, 1983), makes no mention of the Non-Partisan Negro Conference as a factor in the realignment of Black voting patterns. Weiss, unfortunately, does not deal with the Black church as a factor in the transformation of Black political affiliation, although she acknowledges the role of individual members of the clergy in that process.

    The stated goal of the Non-Partisan Negro Conference was not to shift Black voters wholesale into the Democratic party but rather to enable Blacks to stand apart from both parties and use their leverage as a swing vote to achieve political gains for the race. Evidence that Austin took this "balance-of-power" approach seriously is suggested by the fact that although he supported Democratic politicians in the 1940s, he took a leading role in supporting Dwight D. Eisenhower (to the surprise of many) in the 1952 and 1956 presidential campaigns. See Roi Ottley, "Negro Pastor Urges His Race to Back Ike," undated clipping, Barnett Papers, Box 386, CHS.

46. For a partial listing of Austin's membership in voluntary associations, see the brief biographical sketch in Joseph J. Boris, ed., *Who's Who in Colored America* (New York: Who's Who in Colored America Corp., 1927), 1: 7–8. Documents in the Irene McCory Gaines Papers, CHS, illustrate Austin's involvement with the Brotherhood of Sleeping Car Porters and the Chicago Scottsboro Defense Committee.

47. Archie L. Weaver to Frank M. Turner, December 17, 1931; Broadside, "The National Association for the Advancement of Colored People . . . Hear Robert W. Bagnell at Pilgrim Baptist Church" (n.p., n.d.); Form letter, A. C. MacNeal to

"Dear Reverend," December 2, 1935; Walter White to A. C. MacNeal, January 29, 1937; J. C. Austin to Walter White, February 1, 1937. All of these materials are in the NAACP Papers, Branch Files, Group 1, Series G, Boxes 50, 52, and 53, located in the Manuscript Division of the Library of Congress. I am grateful to Michael Homel for calling these and other papers concerning J. C. Austin to my attention.

48. Memorandum, Coordinator of Branches [E. Frederick Morrow] to National Office, November 14, 1939; see also Walter White to E. Frederick Morrow, November 16, 1939; E. Frederick Morrow to Walter White, November 22, 1939; and Memorandum, Mr. Morrow, Subject: Chicago Branch, December 20, 1939. All of these materials may be found in the NAACP Papers, Branch Files, Group 1, Series G, Box 54, Library of Congress.

49. Edward A. Freeman, *The Epoch of Negro Baptists and the Foreign Mission Board* (Kansas City, Kans.: Central Seminary Press, 1953), 160. See also J. H. Jackson, "A Voyage to West Africa and Some Reflections on Modern Missions," in *Proceedings of the Fifty-sixth Annual Session of the National Baptist Convention, September 9–14, 1936* (n.p.), 203.

50. Quoted in Freeman, *Epoch of Negro Baptists*, 269. Baptist missionary Gladys East (daughter of James E. East, Foreign Mission Board corresponding secretary, 1921–1934), who served in Liberia from 1944 until her retirement in 1976, vividly recalled the visit of the "Tall Pines" to West Africa in 1950. She remembered the delegation's visit as an extraordinary event in the history of Black Baptist missions in Africa. Personal interview, July 9, 1982.

51. J. C. Austin to Claud Barnet [sic], March 4, 1950, Barnett Papers, CHS; Associated Negro Press releases entitled "Chicago Welcomes Rev. Austin Back from African Mission," "Mayor Joins Throng at Pilgrim Reception" (dated April 5, 1950), and "Rev. J. C. Austin Reports on Baptist Ministers' Tour of West Africa: Finds Encouragement for Trading Program: Sees Readiness to Fight for Freedom" (dated April 12, 1950), all in Barnett Papers, CHS.

52. Martin Kilson, "Political Change in the Negro Ghetto, 1900–1940," in *Key Issues in the Afro-American Experience*, ed. Nathan I. Huggins, Martin Kilson, and Daniel M. Fox (New York: Harcourt Brace Jovanovich, 1971), 2: 167–92, especially 2: 179. My attention was drawn to this essay by Charles Branham's excellent article "Black Chicago: Accommodationist Politics before the Great Migration," *Ethnic Chicago*, ed. Melvin G. Holli and Peter D'A. Jones, rev. ed. (Grand Rapids, Mich.: William B. Eerdmans Publishing, 1984), 338–79.

53. Kilson, "Political Change in Negro Ghetto," 186.

54. Frederic H. H. Robb, ed., *1927 Intercollegian Wonder Book; or The Negro in Chicago 1779–1927* (Chicago: Washington Intercollegiate Club of Chicago, 1927), 167. This rare but marvelously informative history of Black Chicago is reprinted in Randall K. Burkett, Nancy H. Burkett, and Henry Louis Gates, Jr., eds., *Black Biographical Dictionaries 1790–1950* (Alexandria: Chadwyck-Healey, 1989).

SELECTED BIBLIOGRAPHY FOR FURTHER READING

Drake, St. Clair and Horace R. Cayton. *Black Metropolis: A Study of Negro Life in a Northern City*. New York: Harcourt, Brace, 1945.

Lincoln, C. Eric and Lawrence H. Mamiya. *The Black Church in the African American Experience*. Durham, NC: Duke University Press, 1990.

Luker, Ralph. *The Social Gospel in Black and White: American Racial Reform, 1885–1912*. Chapel Hill: University of North Carolina Press, 1991.

Paris, Peter. *The Social Teaching of the Black Churches*. Philadelphia: Fortress Press, 1985.

Wilmore, Gayraud. *Black Religion and Black Radicalism*. Maryknoll, NY: Orbis, 1983.

MARTIN LUTHER KING, JR., AND
THE AFRICAN-AMERICAN SOCIAL GOSPEL

16 ::

Clayborne Carson

:: Studies of Martin Luther King, Jr. have either focused on how his ideas were influenced by his studies in northern white institutions such as Crozer Theological Seminary and Boston University and his reading of white theologians and Mahatma Gandhi, or on his southern African-American religious roots. In the following essay, Clayborne Carson argues that King's stature as the leader of the Civil Rights movement and his appeal across racial lines was based on his unique ability to appropriate elements of many different traditions: white and black, religious and secular, elite and folk. ::

MARTIN LUTHER KING, JR., AND THE AFRICAN-AMERICAN SOCIAL GOSPEL

Clayborne Carson

:: **M**ost recent studies of Martin Luther King, Jr., emphasize the extent to which his ideas were rooted in African-American religious traditions. Departing from King's own autobiographical account and from earlier studies that stressed the importance of King's graduate studies at Crozer Theological Seminary and Boston University,[1] contemporary scholars have focused attention on King's African-American religious roots.[2] The Martin Luther King, Jr., Papers Project has contributed to this scholarly trend by documenting the King family's longstanding ties to Ebenezer Baptist Church and the social gospel ministries of his father and grandfather, both of whom were civil rights leaders as well as pastors.[3] The King project's research also suggests, however, that the current trend in scholarship may understate the extent to which King's African-American religious roots were inextricably intertwined with the European-American intellectual influences of his college years. The initial volumes of the project's fourteen-volume edition of King's papers have contributed to a new understanding of King's graduate school experiences, demonstrating that his academic writings, though flawed by serious instances of plagiarism, were often reliable expressions of his complex, evolving *Weltanschauung*.[4] Moreover, King's writings make clear that his roots in African-American religion did not necessarily separate him from European-American theological influences, because many of the black religious leaders who were his role models were themselves products of predominantly white seminaries and graduate schools. Rather than being torn between two mutually exclusive religious traditions, King's uniquely effective transracial leadership was based on his ability to combine elements of African-American and European-American religious traditions.

King was deeply influenced by his childhood immersion in African-American religious life, but his years at Crozer and Boston increased his ability to incorporate aspects of academic theology into his sermons and public speeches. His student papers demonstrate that he adopted European-American ideological ideas that ultimately reinforced rather than undermined the African-American social gospel tradition epitomized by his father and grandfather. Although King's advanced training in theology set him apart from most African-American clergymen, the documentary evidence regarding his formative years suggests that his graduate studies engendered an increased appreciation for his African-American religious roots. From childhood, King had been uncomfortable with the emotionalism and scriptural literalism that he associated with traditional Baptist liturgy, but he was also familiar with innovative, politically active, and intellectually sophisticated African-American clergymen who had themselves been influenced by European-American theological scholarship. These clergymen served as role models for King as he mined theological scholarship for nuggets of insight that could enrich his preaching. As he sought to resolve religious doubts that had initially prevented him from accepting his calling, King looked upon European-American theological ideas not as alternatives to traditional black Baptist beliefs but as necessary correctives to those beliefs.

Tracing the evolution of his religious beliefs in a sketch written at Crozer entitled "An Autobiography of Religious Development," King recalled that an initial sense of religious estrangement had unexpectedly and abruptly become apparent at a Sunday morning revival meeting he attended at about the age of seven. A guest evangelist from Virginia had come to talk about salvation and to seek recruits for the church. Having grown up in the church, King had never given much thought to joining it formally, but the emotion of the revival and the decision of his sister to step forward prompted an impulsive decision to accept conversion. He reflected, "I had never given this matter a thought, and even at the time of [my] baptism I was unaware of what was taking place." King admitted that he "joined the church not out of any dynamic conviction, but out of a childhood desire to keep up with my sister." In the same sketch, he wrote that, although he accepted the teachings of his Sunday school teachers until he was about twelve,

this uncritical attitude could not last long, for it was contrary to the very nature of my being. I had always been the questioning and precocious type. At
the age of 13 I shocked my Sunday School class by denying the bodily resurrection of Jesus. From the age of thirteen on doubts began to spring forth unre-
lentingly.[5]

King's recognition that he did not share some of the religious convictions of
other family members might have been emotionally devastating, but his inalien-
able sense of belonging to the church led him toward reconciliation rather than
continued rebellion. Although his convictions removed him from the kind of
fundamentalist faith that placed great importance on emotionalism and a conversion experience, he never considered abandoning his inherited faith. His early
doubts did not interfere with his intense involvement in church life, his love of
church music, or his fascination with the art of preaching. His father, Martin
Luther King, Sr., noted the way in which his son absorbed attitudes ("he loved
church . . . the feeling for ceremonies and ritual, the passionate love of Baptist
music") and skills ("a great speaker . . . and he sang, too, in a fine, clear voice")
that would prepare him for a preaching career.[6] Letters written to his parents in
his early adolescence reveal an intimate knowledge of the details of Baptist
church life: congregational governance, ward meetings, church finances, and
continual social events.[7]

Moreover, King was aware that the accomplishments of his father's generation of African-American religious leaders represented more than just emotional
folk preaching and scriptural literalism. Despite theological differences, King attributed his decision to enter the ministry to the influence of a father who "set
forth a noble example that I didn't [mind] following." King's father and grandfather were not only Baptist ministers but also pioneering exponents of a distinctively African-American version of social gospel Christianity. When King's
grandfather, the Reverend A. D. Williams, arrived in Atlanta in 1893, social
gospel activism was becoming increasingly common among both black and white
urban clergymen. After taking over the pastorate of Atlanta's Ebenezer Baptist
Church in March 1894, Williams built a large congregation through forceful
preaching that addressed the everyday concerns of poor and working-class residents. Baptist denominational practices encouraged ministers such as Williams to
retain the support of occasionally rebellious congregations through charismatic
leadership that extended beyond purely spiritual matters. Having arrived in
Atlanta on the eve of a major period of institutional development among African-
American Baptists, Williams joined two thousand other delegates and visitors

who met at Atlanta's Friendship Baptist Church in September 1895 to organize the National Baptist Convention, the largest black organization in the United States.

For the remainder of his life, Williams played a leading role in Baptist affairs, both at state and national levels. In addition, he took the lead in responding to W. E. B. Du Bois's call for civil rights activism by joining five hundred other black Georgians in February 1906 to form the Georgia Equal Rights League. In 1917, Williams became one of the founders of the Atlanta branch of the National Association for the Advancement of Colored People (NAACP). After becoming president of the local chapter in 1918, he mobilized newly enfranchised African-American women in a campaign to register black voters. He also led a successful drive to pressure white officials into providing improved educational facilities for black children. This effort resulted in the establishment of a black high school that Martin Luther King, Jr., later attended.

Martin Luther King, Sr., continued this tradition of social gospel activism after he married Williams's only daughter in 1926. Although his son would sometimes depict him as a conservative, King, Sr., identified himself as a social gospel preacher who believed that his ministry should be focused on the everyday needs of his congregation rather than otherworldly concerns. While a theology student at Morehouse College, King, Sr., had been exposed to the liberal theological ideas of C. D. Hubert, who headed the school's theology program. As the two ministers struggled to retain the loyalty of their congregations during the Great Depression, King recalled that Williams insisted, "Whosoever carries the word must make the word flesh." King explained that Williams used church funds to "make food available to the hungry and clothes to those without them. We kept children while mothers worked. The church bought and supplied medicines. Ebenezer tried to be an anchor as the storm rose."[8]

After taking over Ebenezer upon Williams's death in 1931, Martin Luther King, Sr., expanded the scope of his predecessor's politically engaged ministry. Early in 1935, he organized meetings to encourage blacks to register to vote and, despite resistance from more cautious clergymen and lay leaders, organized a march to City Hall. A year later he became chairman of the Committee on the Equalization of Teachers' Salaries, which was formed to protest against discriminatory policies that paid higher salaries to white teachers than to equally qualified blacks. In spite of receiving threatening hate letters, he played a leading role in the sustained struggle for pay equity.[9] King's firm insistence that the Christian church should participate in civil rights activities set him apart from politically conservative scriptural fundamentalists. In 1940, he revealed his commitment to social gospel Christianity in an address on "the true mission of the Church" delivered to the Atlanta Missionary Baptist Association:

> Quite often we say the church has no place in politics, forgetting the words of the Lord, "The spirit of the Lord is upon me, because he hath [anointed] me to preach the Gospel to the poor; he hath sent me to heal the broken-hearted, to preach deliverance to the captives, and the recovering of sight to the blind, to set at liberty them that are bruised."
>
> . . . God hasten the time when every minister will become a registered voter and a part of every movement for the betterment of our people. Again and again has it been said we cannot lead where we do not go, and we cannot teach what we do not know.
>
> As ministers a great responsibility rests upon us as leaders. We can not expect our people to register and become citizens until we as leaders set the standard.[10]

In addition to seeing his father as both a social activist and a scriptural conservative, King, Jr., was also aware of many other models of politically engaged religious leadership. He admired the Reverend William Holmes Borders, who had built Wheat Street Baptist Church into Atlanta's largest black church and who possessed the academic credentials that King's own father lacked. Although both ministers had struggled from poverty to graduate from Morehouse College, Borders had also obtained a divinity degree from Garrett Theological Seminary and a master's degree from Northwestern before returning to Atlanta, where he taught religion at Morehouse and became an outspoken preacher at Wheat Street. According to biographer Taylor Branch, King and his friends studied "Borders' mannerisms, his organizational style, and above all the high-toned sermons in which he aroused his congregation without merely repeating the homilies of eternal life."[11]

After entering Morehouse College at the age of fifteen, King was profoundly influenced by the example of the college's president, Dr. Benjamin Elijah Mays, a family friend who was the kind of dedicated, intellectually sophisticated religious leader that King wished to emulate. Selected in 1940 to succeed John Hope as head of Morehouse, Mays was the first Morehouse president with a Ph.D. Although not a "Morehouse man" himself, Mays had internalized the Morehouse tradition calling for students to use their skills on behalf of the black community. An outstanding debater during his own undergraduate years, Mays often used his Tuesday morning talks to the student body as occasions to express his commitment to the social gospel and to challenge Morehouse students to struggle against segregation rather than accommodate to it. By the time King entered college, Mays had returned from a trip to India as one of a growing number of African-American disciples of Mahatma Gandhi. King later described Mays as one of the "great influences" in his life.[12]

At Morehouse, King received his initial exposure to modern critical theology when he took a course on the Bible taught by another family acquaintance, Professor George D. Kelsey, a Morehouse graduate who had recently received his doctorate from Yale. In 1945, Kelsey had initiated an Annual Institute for the Training and Improvement of Baptist Ministers and had thereby gained the admiration of King, Sr., who described Kelsey as a teacher who "saw the pulpit as a place both for drama, in the old-fashioned, country Baptist sense, and for the articulation of philosophies that address the problems of society." Kelsey later remembered King, Jr., as an earnest student who took the subject matter of the course seriously. "I made it my business to present lectures on the most strenuous teaching of Jesus," Kelsey recalled. "It was precisely at this time that Martin's eyes lit up most and his face was graced with a smile."[13] Shortly after teaching King, Kelsey published an article arguing that "the problem of race is indeed America's greatest moral dilemma," giving King a phrase that he would use in his first book, *Stride toward Freedom* (1958).

In addition to Mays and Kelsey, King was also undoubtedly aware of many black religious leaders who combined academic erudition with a thorough grounding in African-American religious traditions. While at Crozer Seminary, King often debated theological and political issues with J. Pius Barbour, a family friend and Morehouse graduate, who had graduated from the seminary a decade before King's arrival. King was also familiar with the progressive ideas of Howard University president Mordecai Johnson, whose 1949 speech in Philadelphia recounting a trip to India stirred King's interest in Gandhian ideas. Howard Thurman, whose influential social gospel statement *Jesus and the Disinherited* appeared in 1949, was also a family friend of the Kings: he had attended Morehouse with King, Sr. When Thurman became Boston University's dean of the chapel, he developed a personal acquaintance with King, Jr., who was then attending the university.

Benefiting from this extensive exposure to proponents of African-American social gospel, King was able to perceive theological training as a means of reconciling his inclination to follow his father's calling with his desire for intellectual respectability. King's descriptions of his decision to enter the ministry reveal that he had accepted the social mission of the church even though he had not yet resolved his theological doubts. He realized that the Baptist religion he had absorbed during his youth had derived mainly from daily contact with church life rather than from theological reflection. Growing up in the church provided a substitute for orthodox theological convictions; born a Baptist, he never felt the need to affirm all the tenets of the denomination. In his "Autobiography of Religious Development," he explained: "Conversion for me was never an abrupt something. I have never experienced the so called 'crisis moment.' Religion has just been something that I grew up in. Conversion for me has been the gradual intaking of the noble ideals set forth in my family and my environment, and I must admit that this intaking has been largely unconscious."[14]

The consistency of King's basic religious and political convictions throughout his life suggest that his collegiate training was not a transformative experience but was rather a refinement of preexisting religious attitudes. Recognizing that a Ph.D. degree from a northern university would set him apart from most other Baptist ministers, he approached his graduate education with skepticism and perhaps even a touch of cynicism, self-consciously acquiring academic credentials that would add intellectual respectability to ingrained beliefs rooted in early religious experiences. King's rejection of scriptural literalism did not lead him away from the Baptist church but toward an increasing interest in liberal theology. His understanding that religious belief could be rooted in reason also enabled him to think more seriously about an idea he had previously rejected: becoming a minister.

The elder King had always wanted both of his sons to follow his career choice and eventually, perhaps, serve as pastors for the Ebenezer congregation. He listened to his wife's entreaties on the need for the children to make their own career choices, while hoping that his sons would make use of his connections among Baptists: "family ties, school and fraternal relationships, the so-called hometown connections that kept phones ringing and letters moving in consideration of help requested and granted, favors offered and accepted."[15] Despite being aware of their father's wishes, however, King, Jr., and his younger brother, A. D., were reluctant to conform to paternal expectations. The latter dropped out of Morehouse before finally deciding on a ministerial career, and the former spent his first three undergraduate years determined to become first a physician and then a lawyer—but not a minister like his father. Determined to assert his independence from his father and continuing to question aspects of his father's religious beliefs, King, Jr., nevertheless received a strong impetus toward becoming a preacher from his father's ever-present example.

A crucial period in King's deliberations about his career came during the summer of 1947, when he led religious services for his fellow student workers at a tobacco farm in Simsbury, Connecticut. Even before leaving Atlanta he had received his preaching license, and—more than he had during his 1944 stay in Simsbury—welcomed the opportunity to lead the weekly religious gatherings at the farm. After several weeks of deliberation, he telephoned his mother from Simsbury to tell her of his intention to become a minister. By the time he returned to Morehouse for his final year, he had pushed doubt out of his mind. His initial inclination to become a doctor or lawyer was overwhelmed by an "undying urge to serve God and humanity through the ministry." The decision was the culmination of his experiences. "My call to the ministry was neither dramatic nor spectacular," he later wrote in his application to seminary.

> It came neither by some miraculous vision nor by some blinding light experience on the road of life. Moreover, it was a response to an inner urge that gradually came upon me. This urge expressed itself in a desire to serve God and humanity, and the feeling that my talent and my commitment could best be expressed through the ministry. . . . During my senior year in college I finally decided to accept the challenge to enter the ministry. I came to see that God had placed a responsibility upon my shoulders and the more I tried to escape it the more frustrated I would become.[16]

Once the decision was made, King's friends recognized its inevitability, given his experiences, contacts, and abilities. Even at this early stage in his development as a preacher, his abilities as a pulpit orator were evident to those who heard him. Samuel DuBois Cook recalled that King delivered a "Senior Sermon" in the Morehouse Chapel a week before graduation. "He knew almost intuitively how to move an audience," Cook remembered. "He asserted that there are moral laws in the universe that we cannot violate with impunity, anymore than we can violate the physical laws of the university with impunity."[17] King resolved to become a minister, but he continued to reject the anti-intellectualism that he associated with fundamentalism. His subsequent critical study of biblical texts and religious practices was driven by a desire to strengthen the rationale for a decision he had already made. He applied to several seminaries known to be academically rigorous and hospitable to liberal religious views, including Andover Newton in Massachusetts, Union in New York, and Crozer in Pennsylvania.

King's graduate school education should be viewed within the context of his struggle to synthesize his father's Christian practices and his own theological skepticism. Seen from this perspective, King's experiences at Crozer and Boston constituted neither a pilgrimage toward the social gospel views of his Crozer professors nor a movement toward the personalism of those at Boston. Instead,

King eclectically drew upon the writings of academic theologians and he moved away from Christian liberalism toward a theological synthesis closer to aspects of his father's religious faith, particularly toward a conception of God as a source of support in times of personal need. Rather than becoming more liberal in college, he became increasingly skeptical of intellectualized conceptions of divinity. As King became increasingly aware of the limitations of liberal Christian thought, he acquired a renewed appreciation for his southern Baptist roots. His Crozer papers occasionally referred to his experiences in order to explain his theological preferences. He noted that his initial attraction to liberalism stemmed from its willingness to "answer new problems of cultural and social change," unlike its theological opponent, fundamentalism, which sought "to preserve the old faith in a changing milieu."[18] As he continued his studies, however, King found his initial attraction to liberal theology "going through a state of transition." His personal experience with "a vicious race problem" had made it "very difficult . . . to believe in the essential goodness of man"; on the other hand, he explained that "in noticing the gradual improvements of this same race problem I came to see some noble possibilities in human nature." While remaining wary of his father's conventional religious beliefs, King was becoming, he acknowledged, "a victim of eclecticism," seeking to "synthesize the best in liberal theology with the best in neo-orthodox theology."[19]

At Crozer, King was introduced to personalism, a philosophical school of thought that had developed in the late nineteenth century at Boston University and other American universities. After reviewing a text by Boston professor Edgar S. Brightman, a leading personalist theologian, King reported, in an essay for one of his classes, that he was "amazed to find that the conception of God is so complex and one about which opinions differ so widely." King conceded that he was still "quite confused as to which definition [of God] was the most adequate," but thought that Brightman's personalist theology held the greatest appeal.[20] Its emphasis on the reality of personal religious experience validated King's own religious experiences. King reaffirmed his belief that "every man, from the ordinary simplehearted believer to the philosopher intellectual giant, may find God through religious experience."[21] His reading of Brightman led him to discover his own spirituality:

> How I long now for that religious experience which Dr. Brightman so cogently speaks of throughout his book. It seems to be an experience, the lack of which life becomes dull and meaningless. As I reflect on the matter, however, I do remember moments that I have been awe awakened; there have been times

that I have been carried out of myself by something greater than myself and to that something I gave myself. Has this great something been God? Maybe after all I have been religious for a number of years, and am now only becoming aware of it.[22]

Brightman's explanation of religious experience convinced King that he could experience God's powerful presence in his own life without the benefit of a sudden religious conversion. Personalism validated the notion that experience rather than intellectual reflection should be the basis of religious belief. "It is through experience that we come to realize that some things are out of harmony with God's will," King wrote in another essay. "No theology is needed to tell us that love is the law of life and to disobey it means to suffer the consequences."[23] King's adoption of personalism as a theological orientation enabled him to reject abstract conceptions of God while continuing his search for cogency and intellectual sophistication.

By the time King entered Boston University, he was learning how to use his theological training to enrich his preaching and, in the process, return to his roots as a Baptist preacher. King's academic theological studies at Crozer had encouraged him to question many aspects of his religious heritage, but by his final year King had also become skeptical of many tenets of theological liberalism. The church of his parents and grandparents had imparted an understanding of God and of the purposes of Christian ministry that could not be displaced by theological sophistication. He later explained that his study of personalism at Crozer and Boston reinforced his beliefs rather than supplanted them. Personalism's "insistence that only personality—finite and infinite—is ultimately real strengthened me in two convictions: it gave me a metaphysical and philosophical grounding for the idea of a personal God, and it gave me a metaphysical basis for the dignity and worth of all human personality."[24]

At Boston, King expanded his criticism of theological liberalism by adopting many of the ideas of Reinhold Niebuhr. King applauded Niebuhr's rigorous analysis of "the fundamental weaknesses and inevitable sterility of the humanistic emphasis" of liberalism in the twentieth century.[25] He was also drawn to Niebuhr's economic and moral analysis of capitalism, such as the notion that modern industrial civilization was responsible for "appalling injustices," particularly the "concentration of power and resources in the hands of a relatively small wealthy class."[26] Injustices are inherent in human society, Niebuhr argued, because humans engaged in collective activity are essentially immoral, whereas individuals acting on their own possess a moral conscience. Niebuhr sought to resolve the tension between "moral man and immoral society" by reinterpreting the traditional Christian notion of *agape*, or divine love.[27] Agreeing with Niebuhr's analysis, King stated that *agape* may not be achievable in an immoral society but "remains a leaven in society, permeating the whole and giving texture and consistency to life."

King was particularly receptive to Niebuhr's criticism of love and justice as conceived in both liberal and orthodox theology. In orthodoxy, "individual perfection is too often made an end in itself," whereas liberalism "vainly seeks to overcome justice [through] purely moral and rational suasions." Liberalism, King wrote, "confuses the ideal itself with the realistic means which must be employed to coerce society into an approximation of that ideal." King agreed with Niebuhr's emphasis on making realistic moral choices and with his social analysis, but he believed that Niebuhr lacked an adequate explanation of how *agape* operates in human history: "He fails to see that the availability of the divine *Agape* is an essential [affirmation] of the Christian religion."[28]

Given the academic environment in which he attended graduate school, it is hardly surprising that King's theological writings did not explicitly draw upon the insights of African-American religion. Yet, although King's graduate school writings understated the degree to which his attitudes had been shaped by African-American religious writings, he was certainly aware of the publications of Kelsey and Mays and probably those of Thurman and Borders. Once accustomed to contrasting the religious emotionalism of his father's religion with the intellectual sophistication he saw in the writings of white academic theologians, King became aware during his graduate research that orthodox Christianity was not necessarily anti-intellectual.

Overall, King's theological development in seminary and graduate school reflected his lifelong tendency to incorporate the best elements of each alternative. As when choosing between capitalism and communism or between power politics and pacifism, King sought to synthesize alternative orientations: "An adequate understanding of man is found neither in the thesis of liberalism nor in the antithesis of neo-orthodoxy, but in a synthesis which reconciles the truths of both."[29] King described his graduate training as an attempt to bring together "the best in liberal theology with the best in neo-orthodox theology" in order to come to an understanding of man. His enormous respect for the writings of Reinhold Niebuhr derived from the pleasure he felt in finding a theological stance that synthesized faith and intellect. He probably heard echoes of his father's fundamentalism in Reinhold Niebuhr's neo-orthodoxy, which reaffirmed the limits of human perfectibility. Niebuhr provided an intellectual rationale for King's recognition of the limitations of liberal theology. As King wrote during these years, he had become "so enamored of the insights of liberalism that I almost fell into the trap of accepting uncritically everything it encompasses." After reading Niebuhr, King recalled becoming more aware of "the depths and strength of sin" and

> the complexity of man's social involvement and the glaring reality of collective evil. I realized that liberalism had been all too sentimental concerning human nature and that it leaned toward a false idealism. I also came to see that the superficial optimism of liberalism concerning human nature overlooked the fact that reason is darkened by sin. The more I thought about human nature, the more I saw how our tragic inclination for sin encourages us to rationalize our actions. Liberalism failed to show that reason by itself is little more than an instrument to justify man's defensive ways of thinking. Reason, devoid of the purifying power of faith, can never free itself from distortions and rationalizations. [30]

By the time he finished his course work, King had come to affirm some of the enduring values of his religious heritage, particularly conceptions of a divine goodness capable of acting in history. In one qualifying examination King declared that, despite modern society's moral relativism, God's judgment was final and eternal. "God has planted in the fiber of the universe certain eternal laws which forever confront every man. They are absolute and not relative. There is an eternal and absolute distinction between right and wrong." One indispensable answer to the theodicy question, King argued, was contained in the concept of the suffering servant, one of the "most noble" teachings of the Old Testament. "His suffering is not due to something that he has done, but it is *vicarious* and *redemptive.* Through his suffering knowledge of God is [spread] to the unbelieving Gentiles and those unbelievers seeing that this suffering servant is innocent will become conscious of their sins and repent and thereby be redeemed. The nation would be healed by his [wounds]." The death of Jesus Christ on the cross was the fulfillment of the prophecy of the suffering servant, but King argued that humanity should not wait on His saving grace. An individual's "faith and fellowship with God," King wrote, was the "ultimate solution to the problem of suffering."[31]

King's choice of a dissertation topic reflected an interest in the nature of God that derived both from his academic studies and from his preaching. In addition to writing several term papers on the topic, King wove the theme of theodicy into several sermons while at Boston, including one entitled "What Does It Mean to Believe in God?"[32] In his introduction to the dissertation King explained that the conception of God should be examined because of "the central place which it occupies in any religion" and because of "the ever present need to interpret and clarify the God-concept."[33]

By early 1953, when King enrolled in a course on dissertation writing at the beginning of his research, he was fairly certain about the conclusions he would reach in his dissertation. King recognized the limitations in the thinking of theologians Paul Tillich and Henry Nelson Wieman. "Both overstress one side of the divine life," he wrote, "while [minimizing] another basic aspect. Wieman [stresses] the goodness of God while minimizing his power. Tillich stresses the power of God while [minimizing] his goodness."[34] With his own beliefs still rooted in an African-American religious tradition that perceived God as a personal force interceding in history, King found Tillich's and Wieman's conceptions of divinity unworthy of worship. In the evaluative chapter, King expressed belief in a "living" God, not Tillich's "being-itself" or Wieman's "source of human good." "In God there is feeling and will, responsive to the deepest yearnings of the human heart; this God both evokes and answers prayer." Conceiving of such a God as a person was preferable to Tillich's and Wieman's use of abstract philosophical terms. "It would be better by far to admit that there are difficulties with an idea we know—such as personality—than to employ a term which is practically unknown to us in our experience." King concluded that Tillich and Wieman both set forth a God who is less than personal, despite their comments to the contrary suggesting that God was more than personal, unable to be defined by the concept of personality. "Both Tillich and Wieman reject the conception of a personal God, and with this goes a rejection of the rationality, goodness and love of God in the full sense of the words."[35]

Despite his disagreement with certain aspects of both men's conceptions of divinity, King appreciated their criticism of humanism. King approvingly noted that Tillich and Wieman both emphasized God's immanence, or "the primacy of God over everything else in the universe." "Such an emphasis," he argued, "sounds a much needed note in the face of a supernaturalism that finds nature so irrational that the order of creation can no longer be discerned in it, and history so meaningless that it all bears the 'minus sign' of alienation from God." In a characteristic effort to reconcile two positions that were in dialectical tension, King extracted what he considered positive aspects of their thought to create an eclectic synthesis. Echoing his preliminary analysis of their positions, King asserted that "both Tillich and Wieman are partially correct in what they affirm and partially wrong in what they deny. Wieman is right in emphasizing the goodness of God, but wrong in minimizing his power. Likewise Tillich is right in emphasizing the power of God, but wrong in minimizing his goodness."[36]

In the sermons King delivered while writing his dissertation, he expressed his conception of God using more vivid language than his stilted, derivative academic diction. He skillfully incorporated into his sermons those aspects of his theological training that affirmed his ties to the religion of his parents and grandparents. His father later affirmed that his son's roots in the African-American preaching tradition remained strong even after years of graduate study. "M. L. was still a son of the Baptist South, there'd never be any doubt about that."[37]

King's ability to blend these elements can be seen in his earliest known recorded sermon, "Rediscovering Lost Values."[38] King delivered the sermon to a large Baptist church in Detroit in late February 1954, just days after finishing his final comprehensive examination and a few weeks before the graduate school approved his dissertation outline. In the Detroit sermon, King told the familiar biblical story of Joseph and Mary, who realized, while walking to Nazareth, that they had left Jesus behind in Jerusalem. Just as Joseph and Mary had returned to rejoin Jesus, King advised, society should rediscover the precious values that had become lost in the rationalizations that guided behavior in the modern world. "If we are to go forward," he said, "if we are to make this a better world in which to live, we've got to go back. We've got to rediscover these precious values that we've left behind." Despite the many technological advances and material comforts of American society, King argued, humanity had lost the spiritual compass provided by a deep and abiding faith in God. "The real problem is that through our scientific genius we've made of the world a neighborhood, but through our moral and spiritual genius we've failed to make of it a brotherhood." King insisted that "*all* reality hinges on moral foundations," that "this is a moral universe, and . . . there are moral laws of the universe, just as abiding as the physical laws." Decrying ethical relativism—"Now, I'm not trying to use a big word here"— King expressed a belief in moral absolutes that evoked enthusiastic responses from the congregation.

> I'm here to say to you this morning that some things are right and some things are wrong. *(Yes)* Eternally so, absolutely so. It's *wrong* to hate. *Yes, That's right*, It always has been wrong and it always will be wrong! *(Amen)* It's wrong in America, it's wrong in Germany, it's wrong in Russia, it's wrong in China! *(Lord help him)* It was wrong in two thousand B.C., and it's wrong in nineteen-fifty-four A.D.! It always has been wrong, *(That's right)* and it always will be wrong! . . . Some things in this universe are absolute. The God of the universe has made it so.[39]

In King's view contemporary society had lost sight of this "mighty precious value," adopting instead "a pragmatic test for right and wrong." In the modern world, he asserted, most people believed that "it's all right to disobey the Ten Commandments, but just don't disobey the eleventh, Thou shall not get caught." The moral decay that King identified in modern culture could be recovered only by ethical living. "The thing that we need in the world today, is a group of men and women who will stand up for right and be opposed to wrong, wherever it is."[40]

King argued that making ethical decisions was impossible without rediscovering the precious value of faith in God. King charged that many people, including those who attended church every Sunday, had lost their faith in God. "We must remember that it's possible to affirm the existence of God with your lips and deny his existence with your life." Returning to the biblical parable, King asserted that "we had gone a whole day's journey, and then we came to see that we had unconsciously ushered God out of the universe." The materialism of American consumer culture had caused some to lose sight of God, and King cautioned that "automobiles and subways, televisions and radios, dollars and cents, can *never* be substitutes for God."[41]

King's sermon drew upon traditional African-American religious ideas, particularly the notion of God acting in human history. Alluding to a verse in Psalm 23 and to a familiar hymn, King concluded by affirming faith in the God "who walks with us through the valley of the shadow of death, and causes us to fear no evil," in the God "who has been our help in ages past, and our hope for years to come, and our shelter in the time of storm, and our eternal home."[42] King concluded with a rousing affirmation of God as an integral part of his life. "As a young man with most of my life ahead of me, I decided early to give my life to something eternal and absolute. Not to these little gods that are here today and gone tomorrow. But to God who is the same yesterday, today, and forever."[43]

Seen in the context of his preadult experiences, King's graduate school years enabled him to acquire academic credentials while retaining his basic religious beliefs. When he applied to Boston University's doctoral program, King had stressed his desire to enter the world of theological scholarship, stating that he was "desirous of teaching in a college or a school of religion."[44] At Crozer, King had initially been estranged from his roots, but by the time he entered Boston University he had rediscovered the liberating potential of his African-American Baptist heritage. Although he clearly wanted to base his religious beliefs on solid theological foundations, he left Boston as a preacher rather than as a scholar. Forging an eclectic synthesis from such diverse sources as personalism, theological liberalism, neo-orthodox theology, and the activist, Bible-centered religion of his heritage, King affirmed his abiding faith in a God who was both a comforting personal presence and a powerful spiritual force acting in history for righteousness. This faith would sustain him as the civil rights movement irreversibly transformed his life.

King's rapid rise to prominence resulted from his ability to combine the insights of European-American theological scholarship with those of African-American homiletics. Although his published descriptions of his "pilgrimage to non-violence" generally emphasized the impact of his academic training,[45] in more personal statements he acknowledged his black Baptist roots. "I am many things to many people," King acknowledged in 1965, "but in the quiet recesses of my heart, I am fundamentally a clergyman, a Baptist preacher. This is my being and my heritage for I am also the son of a Baptist preacher, the grandson of a Baptist preacher and the great-grandson of a Baptist preacher."[46] Rather than being torn between mutually exclusive cultural traditions, King's public, transracial ministry marked a convergence of theological scholarship and social gospel practice. Drawing upon a variety of intellectual and religious traditions to arouse and enlighten his listeners, King was profoundly affected by his experiences both as a preacher's son at Ebenezer and as a diligent student at Crozer Seminary and Boston University. King's theological education distinguished him from all but a few African-American preachers and temporarily separated him from his childhood environment, but theological studies ultimately led King to a deeper appreciation of traditional African-American conceptions of God as a source of support, especially in times of personal crisis. Later in his career as a movement leader, King would reflect that when he had "been battered by the storms of persecution," he had gained strength and determination from

> the reality of a personal God. True, I have always believe[d] in the personality of God. But in the past the idea of a personal God was little more than a metaphysical category that I found theologically and philosophically satisfying. Now it is a living reality that has been validated in the experience of everyday life. God has been profoundly real to me in recent years.[47]

NOTES

1. See, for example, Martin Luther King, Jr., *Stride toward Freedom: The Montgomery Story* (New York: Harper & Row, 1958), chapter 6; Kenneth L. Smith and Ira G. Zepp, Jr., *Search for the Beloved Community: The Thinking of Martin Luther King, Jr.* (Valley Forge, Pa.: Judson Press, 1974); and John J. Ansbro, *Martin Luther King, Jr.: The Making of a Mind* (Maryknoll, N.Y.: Orbis, 1982).

2. See, for example, James H. Cone, "Martin Luther King, Jr.: Black Theology—Black Church," *Theology Today* 40 (January 1984): 409–12; Lewis V. Baldwin, *There Is a Balm in Gilead: The Cultural Roots of Martin Luther King, Jr.* (Minneapolis: Fortress Press, 1991).

3. Clayborne Carson, Ralph E. Luker, and Penny A. Russell, eds., *The Papers of Martin Luther King, Jr.,* vol. 1, *Called to Serve, January 1929–June 1951* (Berkeley and Los Angeles: University of California Press, 1992).

4. See Clayborne Carson et al., "Martin Luther King, Jr., as Scholar: A Reexamination of His Theological Writings," *Journal of American History* 78 (June 1991): 93–105.

5. Martin Luther King, Jr., "Autobiography of Religious Development," in Carson et al., eds., *Papers of Martin Luther King, Jr.,* 1: 361. According to King's application to Crozer Theological Seminary, the date of his joining the church was May 1, 1936.

6. Martin Luther King, Sr., with Clayton Riley, *Daddy King: An Autobiography* (New York: William Morrow, 1980), 127.

7. See Carson et al., *Papers*, 1: 102–7.

8. Ibid., 89.

9. Ibid., 104.

10. Martin Luther King, Sr., "Moderator's Annual Address—1940," quoted in Carson et al., *Papers*, 1: 34. On the eve of the Montgomery bus boycott of 1955–56, King would use similar arguments in a speech to the Birmingham branch of the NAACP criticizing the apathy of church leaders on political issues. "'You must do more than pray and read the Bible,' to destroy segregation and second-class citizenship," the local newspaper reported him saying, "'you must do something about it.'" See "Apathy among Church Leaders Hit in Talk by Rev. M. L. King," *Birmingham World*, January 25, 1955. King would later deliver the speech, entitled "A Realistic Approach to Progress in Race Relations," on many occasions.

11. Taylor Branch, *Parting the Waters: America in the King Years, 1954–63* (New York: Simon and Schuster, 1988), 54, 64. See also James W. English, *The Prophet of Wheat Street* (Elgin, Ill.: David C. Cook, 1967).

12. King, Jr., *Stride toward Freedom*, 145.

13. Renee D. Turner, "Remembering the Young King," *Ebony*, January 1988. In this article Kelsey recalled that King took Kelsey's course "The Teachings of Jesus" in his sophomore year.

14. King, Jr., "Autobiography of Religious Development," *Papers*, 1: 361.

15. King, S., and Riley, *Daddy King*, 128.

16. Statement of Martin Luther King, Jr., August 7, 1959, written in response to a request by Joan Thatcher, publicity director of the Board of Education and Publication of the American Baptist Convention, Division of Christian Higher Education, July 30, 1959, Martin Luther King Collection, Mugar Library, Boston University; quoted in Mervyn Alonza Warren, "A Rhetorical Study of the Preaching of Dr. Martin Luther King, Jr., Pastor and Pulpit Orator" (Ph.D. dissertation, Michigan State

University, 1966), 35–36. While at Crozer, King wrote: "My call to the ministry was not a miraculous or supernatural something, on the contrary it was an inner urge calling me to serve humanity. I guess the influence of my father also had a great deal to do with my going in the ministry. This is not to say that he ever spoke to me in terms of being a minister, but that my admiration for him was the great moving factor; he set forth a noble example that I didn't min[d] following. Today I differ a great deal with my father theologically, but that admiration for a real father still remains." King, Jr., "Autobiography of Religious Development," *Papers*, 1: 363.

17. Samuel DeBois Cook, quoted in Turner, "Remembering the Young King," 42.

18. Martin Luther King, Jr., "The Sources of Fundamentalism and Liberalism Considered Historically and Psychologically," in Carson et al., *Papers of Martin Luther King, Jr.*, 1: 240.

19. Martin Luther King, Jr., "How Modern Christians Should Think of Man," in Carson et al. *Papers of Martin Luther King, Jr.*, 1: 274.

20. Martin Luther King, Jr., "A Conception and Impression of Religion Drawn from Dr. Brightman's Book Entitled *A Philosophy of Religion*," in Carson et al., *Papers of Martin Luther King, Jr.*, 1: 410–11.

21. Martin Luther King, Jr., "The Place of Reason and Experience in Finding God," in Carson et al. *Papers of Martin Luther King, Jr.*, 1: 234.

22. King, Jr., "Conception and Impression of Religion," *Papers*, 1: 415–16.

23. King, Jr., "Place of Reason and Experience," *Papers*, 1: 234.

24. King, Jr. *Stride toward Freedom*, 100.

25. Martin Luther King, Jr., "Reinhold Niebuhr," April 2, 1952, in Carson et al., *Papers of Martin Luther King, Jr.*, vol. 2 (forthcoming).

26. Martin Luther King, Jr., "Reinhold Niebuhr's Ethical Dualism," May 9, 1952, in Carson et al., *Papers of Martin Luther King, Jr.*, vol. 2 (forthcoming).

27. Reinhold Niebuhr, *Moral Man and Immoral Society* (New York: Scribner, 1933).

28. King, Jr., "Niebuhr's Ethical Dualism," *Papers*, vol. 2 (forthcoming).

29. Martin Luther King, Jr., *Strength to Love* (Philadelphia: Fortress Press, 1963), 149. In resolving the conflict between capitalism and Marxism, he wrote, "The Kingdom of God is neither the thesis of individual enterprise nor the antithesis of collective enterprise, but a synthesis which reconciles the truths of both."

30. King, Jr., "How Modern Christians," *Papers*, 1: 274. King later asserted that "Niebuhr's great contribution to contemporary theology is that he has refuted the false optimism characteristic of a great segment of Protestant liberalism, without falling into the anti-rationalism of the continental theologian Karl Barth, or the semi-fundamentalism of other dialectical theologians. Moreover, Niebuhr has extraordinary insight into human nature, especially the behavior of nations and social groups. He is keenly aware of the complexity of human motives and of the relations between morality and power. His theology is a persistent reminder of the reality of sin on every level of man's existence. These elements of Niebuhr's thinking helped

me to recognize the illusions of a superficial optimism concerning human nature and the dangers of a false idealism. While I still believed in man's potential for good, Niebuhr made me realize his potential for evil as well. Moreover, Niebuhr helped me to recognize the complexity of man's social involvement and the glaring reality of collective evil." King, Jr., *Stride toward Freedom*, 99.

31. Martin Luther King, Jr., Qualifying Examination Answers, Theology of the Bible, November 2, 1953, in Carson et al., *Papers of Martin Luther King, Jr.*, vol. 2 (forthcoming).
32. King gave this sermon at First United Baptist Church in Lowell, Massachusetts, on April 12, 1953.
33. Martin Luther King, Jr., "A Comparison of the Conceptions of God in the Thinking of Paul Tillich and Henry Nelson Wieman" (Ph.D. dissertation, Boston University, 1955), in Carson et al. *Papers of Martin Luther King, Jr.*, vol. 2 (forthcoming).
34. King, Notes for "A Comparison of the Conceptions of God and the Thinking of Paul Tillich and Henry Nelson Wieman," February 4–May 22, 1953, Martin Luther King Papers, Mugar Library, Boston University, Box 107, Folder 28.
35. Martin Luther King, Jr., "A Comparison of the Conceptions," in Carson et al., *Papers of Martin Luther King, Jr.*, vol 2 (forthcoming).
36. Ibid.
37. King, Sr., and Riley, *Daddy King*, 147.
38. A tape recording of the sermon at Detroit's Second Baptist Church on February 28, 1954, was preserved by the church's historical committee. The tape recording served as the basis for the transcription of "Rediscovering Lost Values" that appears in Carson et al., *Papers of Martin Luther King, Jr.*, vol 2 (forthcoming).
39. King, "Rediscovering Lost Values," *Papers*, vol. 2 (forthcoming). The congregation's responses, which are indicated in italics and parentheses, have been retained in this lengthy quotation, but omitted in other quotations from this sermon. They are preserved in the complete transcription.
40. Ibid.
41. Ibid.
42. King alluded to the hymn "Oh God, Our Help in Ages Past."
43. King, "Rediscovering Lost Values," in Carson et al., *Papers of Martin Luther King, Jr.*, vol. 2 (forthcoming).
44. Martin Luther King, Jr., "Fragment of Application to Boston University," in Carson et al. *Papers of Martin Luther King, Jr.*, 1: 390.
45. See, for example, King, Jr., *Stride toward Freedom*, chapter 6, and Martin Luther King, Jr., *Strength to Love* (Philadelphia: Fortress Press, 1963), chapter 15.
46. Martin Luther King, Jr., "The Un-Christian Christian," *Ebony* 20 (August 1965), 76.
47. King, Jr., *Strength to Love*, 155.

SELECTED BIBLIOGRAPHY FOR FURTHER READING

Branch, Taylor. *Parting the Waters: America in the King Years, 1954–1963*. New York: Simon and Schuster, 1988.

Findlay, James F. *Church People in the Struggle: The National Council of Churches and the Black Freedom Movement, 1950–1970*. New York: Oxford University Press, 1993.

Garrow, David. *Bearing the Cross: Martin Luther King, Jr., and the Southern Christian Leadership Conference*. New York: Morrow, 1986.

Kapur, Sudarshan. *Raising Up a Prophet: The African American Encounter with Gandhi*. Boston: Beacon Press, 1992.

Morris, Alden D. *The Origins of the Civil Rights Movement: Black Communities Organizing for Change*. New York: Free Press, 1984.

AFRICAN-AMERICAN RELIGIOUS CULTURE

VI::

Cheryl Townsend Gilkes

17 ::

:: Many African-American women gained personal and social power through their role as moral exemplars in their communities. Cheryl Townsend Gilkes explores the roles of church mothers as part of the "dual-sex" system prevalent in black churches. Through such roles, African-American women organized and led numerous church-based organizations by which they influenced their communities. ::

:: 17

THE ROLES OF CHURCH AND COMMUNITY MOTHERS

Ambivalent American Sexism or Fragmented African Familyhood?

Cheryl Townsend Gilkes

‥ **T**he slave's lament, "Sometimes I feel like a motherless child," was more than a mere commentary on the individual desolation and disorganization which accompanies the shock of enslavement a "long way from home"—the African Motherland. This melodious grieving also conveyed the slaves' loss of their West African political, religious, and family systems which attached importance, sometimes great importance, to the role of the Mothers as well as the Fathers of Civilization. Slaves came from social systems where men and women shared power in various ways, but most often through economic interdependence. The slaves correctly perceived their new life in the United States as a "war on African familyhood . . . those expressions and manifestations of individual/community/ national life and organization which emerge from the African world view of relationships between Man, Woman, and the Universe."[1] The slaves not only lost their homeland, they also lost a social system whose culture and social organization was guided by the obligations of kinship and whose policies grew out of these obligations.

Aspects of the black religious and political experience in the United States reflect elements of this ethic of "familyhood." In both sacred and secular community settings, there are powerful and respected older women addressed by the title, "Mother."[2] In secular settings, such mothers are often the heads of black women's organizations and hold positions of power and authority in more broadly based community and civil rights organizations. In sacred places, particularly the churches, they are occasionally pastors, sometimes evangelists, more often pastors' wives and widows, but most often leaders of organized church women (missionaries, deaconesses, mothers' boards, etc.). Regardless of their institutional offices, these women wield considerable authority in both sacred and secular settings. The members of the community call them "Mother" and their "children" are often religious and political leaders who owe their power and authority to the sponsorship of such women. The roles of these mothers represent an important yet unresearched aspect of the black experience that must be examined if the position of black women within the black community is ever to be fully understood.

At present, a movement dominated by white feminists is forcing rapid reorganization of traditional expectations based on gender. Black women's absence from or reluctant or ambivalent participation in this movement is overwhelmingly evident.[3] Although black women evince a clear understanding of their multifaceted exploitation by white Americans, male and female, they are ambivalent about aiming the same criticism at black institutions and black men.[4] The complicated response of black women to the women's liberation movement represents an unconscious and implicit understanding that black women's roles and status *within* the black community are *qualitatively* distinct although not independent from their roles and status within the dominant society. Black women, at various levels of consciousness, know that the feminist theories and critiques of American society do not entirely fit the facts of their existence.

Although the institutional arrangements of the dominant society are the source of the political-economic victimization of black people, white customs, traditions, and ideas do not fully explain the responses of black people to their victimization. Furthermore, not every aspect of black social organization and culture in this society should be seen merely as a response to victimization.[5] The cultural segregation which has accompanied racial oppression in America is remarkably similar to the indirect rule that has characterized colonialism everywhere. The concept of "internal colonialism"[6] is invaluable for understanding aspects of the behavior of black people in community and religious organizations. Additionally, the colonial model suggests that the history of black people *as Africans* is as relevant as their history in the United States for interpreting the black experience. Some cultural artifacts and symbols (music, language patterns, kinesics, and worship styles) have been explained only with some degree of reference to the African background.[7] Why not incorporate such references into histories and analyses of black womanhood within *relatively* autonomous social worlds?

Black women figure prominently in the sacred and secular affairs of black communities. Black women's church and community work represents more than mere support for male organizations aimed at social change. Black women community workers participate in the affairs of local, regional, and national black organizations. These women manage and administer large community and human services agencies and programs as well as serve on boards of many kinds. While at local and regional levels, they are likely to hold the same leadership positions as men, national leadership is available mainly through women's organizations.[8] Since much of the work involved in social change, group survival, and community politics takes place at the local level, black women's leadership is important. Black women's church work generally encompasses active membership in local churches, clubs, and religious auxiliaries, as well as teaching Sunday school. Depending upon the denomination or congregation, church work also includes founding churches, administering their affairs, and founding and maintaining national, state, and local auxiliaries of church women.[9] In a few but significant cases, church work also involves pastoring or, at least, "hav[ing] charge of a church in the absence of its Pastor."[10] Addressing such women as "mother" signifies the community's recognition of the importance of their various roles and length of service in the public institutions of Afro-American community life.

CHURCH AND COMMUNITY MOTHERS

The roles of church and community mothers represent impositions of familistic and pseudo-familistic ties upon social organizations and the process of social influence. These mothers serve effectively for a very long time and accumulate great prestige and in many cases very real authority. Not only are they role models, power brokers, and venerable elders, but the actuarial realities of black life are such that elderly black women provide the continuity necessary to promote unity in the face of ever-changing historical conditions. Such women are the senior members of diverse networks of community workers and provide a counterforce to the potential for fragmentation. In some religious settings, particularly the late-nineteenth- and early-twentieth-century Sanctified churches, these women provided continuity through the crises wrought by the deaths of charismatic local and national leaders. Their particular organizational roles and degree of power varied from one organization to another. Still their roles are part of a larger tradition of female leadership at various levels of community life. Finally, these women, bridges between the women's world and the world of men, exercise authority not only in an autonomously organized world of black women but also in areas dominated by black men.

Within northern black communities and independent black women's organizations, the power of these mothers is a reflection of black women's independence from male authority and economic support.[11] Within several black Pentecostal and Holiness denominations, regardless of the level of "formal" sexism, an ethic of female autonomy operates to enforce a reality of more or less shared power in a "dual-sex" political system, "a system in which "the major interest groups are defined and represented by sex."[12] When viewed with reference to aspects of West African social organization and culture, these diverse settings provide important insights into black women's access to authority. The positions these women hold are similar to those held by women in pre-Colonial West African societies, thus supporting the claim that Euro-American models of sexual oppression are *not* totally reproduced in the public affairs of Afro-American life. Any analysis of the position of black women within the black experience must take into account the admittedly unconscious persistence of African processes within social organizations based upon Euro-American organizational models.

The first part of this analysis reviews the relevant features of the West African background, revealing both a legacy of female leadership within the context of a dual-sex political system[13] and an ethic of "familyhood."[14] The several contemporary issues confronting community and church mothers are described with reference to their African parallels in order to highlight the contradictions and dilemmas which exist in the organization of gender-based roles in Afro-American life. Finally, these examples are critically examined in terms of their implications for the future role of black women in a changing society.

THE WEST AFRICAN LEGACY OF INDEPENDENT WOMANHOOD

West Africa was the source of the world view with which the newly enslaved Africans mediated and negotiated a harsh, shock-filled, and absurd new world.[15] In spite of violent and radical discontinuities, slavery reinforced certain aspects of black women's West African social and economic roles. Because "the social and cultural forces that have shaped Black women in America differed in subtle and sometimes sharp ways from those which molded white women," both the

African and American historical contexts are "keys in determining the character of Black women in America today" even though "it is difficult to assess how lasting the influence of African norms [has] been in the American setting."[16]

In Africa, the themes of female independence and self-reliance were reflected in the organization of economic, family, and political roles. "In numerous West African societies, women were persons in their own right with responsibilities and privileges not derived from husbands and fathers." Women controlled the marketplaces and this economic monopoly provided the women with "considerable mobility and leeway for autonomous action." As a result, African women achieved "considerable economic independence; in religious ceremonies, women were priests, even leaders of some cults. Women also maintained their own secret societies."[17]

From this independent economic base, women wielded considerable power in African societies which were patrilocal and patriarchal. According to Judith van Allen, women had their own political institutions through which they were able to "express their disapproval and secure their demands by collective public demonstrations, including ridicule, satirical singing and dancing, and group strikes."[18] This "dual-sex organization contrasts with the 'single-sex' system that obtains in most of the Western world, where political status-bearing roles are predominantly the preserve of men. In the single-sex system, women can achieve distinction and recognition only by taking on the roles of men in public life and performing them well."[19] In West African societies such as the Igbo of Eastern Nigeria, women's organizations like the *otu umuada* (organization of the daughters of a lineage) and the *otu inyemedi* (organization of the wives of a lineage) represented the women's collective interests in the problems of mutual aid, violations of domestic law, decisions concerning agricultural labor, and the social control of men.[20] Economic and political independence were acknowledged in women's title societies, membership in which was based on economic advantage. Such membership then led to even greater economic and political advantage, since leadership in women's political organizations was often based upon titles.[21] Such social organization is found throughout West Africa. The additional presence of age-grade organizations, such as the "*otu umu agbogho* ('groups of eligible girls'),"[22] meant that the African woman existed in a "society of women her own age. These women are called sisters, and the women her mother's age were called mothers." The role of mother was more important than the role of wife.[23] Developing against the background of this social context, Afro-American sex-role ideology sees women's work outside the home as important and legitimate.[24]

Within the context of the dual-sex political system, the African woman had recognized access to authority. The roles of *omu* (loosely translated "queen" but meaning "female king" or head of the women's world) and the *ilogo* (women's cabinet) represented roles of real power. The term "queen mother" comes down to us as the English translation of this role in various West African societies. However, these women were not wives of kings but rather, in the context of decision-making, the important contact points between the men's and the women's world.[25] The stability of women's power was guaranteed through the autonomy of a well-organized women's world. African women thus developed their own legacy of political leadership which included military campaigns against European colonialism as late as the early twentieth century.[26] Heroines of this legacy include Queen Hatshepsut whose trading skills renewed the wealth of Egypt, Queen Nzinga who insisted on her royal prerogatives when negotiating with the Portuguese and later led major military campaigns against them; and the Ashanti (Akan) Queen Mother Yaa Asantewaa who is remembered as "the woman who carried a gun and the sword of state into battle."[27] One African queen, Candace, led military campaigns of such ferocity that "all later queens have borne the same generic name," *Candaces*.[28] Geraldine Wilson was correct when she stated that "women of Africa had the care, love, protection, and institutional and societal support of men as they—the women—carried out major military, governmental, and family economic responsibilities."[29]

The independence of African women did not mean that their lives were cut off from the lives of men. Slave traders discovered that if they captured African men, "these black women are so loyal to their men that they would follow them even into hell. Yet many of these same women would seek death directly, by attacking [slave raiders] and [their] armed guards. These [women] of course were beaten and chained the same as the male slaves."[30] Throughout slavery, black women were expected to carry the same economic load as men and to continue to be the primary caretakers of children. They also had certain opportunities for ad hoc leadership in religious affairs and resistance activities within the slave community. The equality of political powerlessness and economic exploitation which characterized the slave experience set the stage for those aspects of contemporary black women's roles which contradict traditional European presumptions concerning patriarchy.[31] The public prestige and real power of certain elderly black women in community work diverged from dominant (white) cultural norms.

COMMUNITY MOTHERS: POWER THROUGH INDEPENDENCE

Mothers in community work have carried on the roles of elders in traditional West African societies where accumulated wisdom is power. They have occupied positions of leadership in women's organizations (*e.g.*, the National Association of Colored Women) and in local branches of national organizations (*e.g.*, the National Association for the Advancement of Colored People). They participated in the strategies that produced real changes for "the Race." Their successes over the years generated broad networks of appreciative community members who, in turn, became an increasingly valuable resource for confronting new community problems. The elders, reflecting on their successes and failures, offered advice, warnings, and cautions. The backing and encouragement of these elders were necessary for the mobilization of new movements and organizations and for the legitimation of new community workers. The blessing of the elders carried weight. Community mothers were living links to the heroes and heroines of earlier eras. They had met and worked with such women as Mary McLeod Bethune, Mary Church Terrell, Ida Wells Barnett, and Margaret Murray (Mrs. Booker T.) Washington. At public events like meetings and banquets, these elders recounted the victories which contributed to social change. They provided an important sense of the community's history and potential effectiveness. The women performed the *griot* or African storyteller role for the community just as the grandmothers in black families had been the keepers of the family records.[32] Community mothers are the guardians of community political traditions. Their ability to function as power brokers stemmed from their leadership within historical black women's movements and organizations.

In response to Jim Crow, oppressive work situations, and negative images and stereotypes, black women formed local and national organizations. The Colored Women's League and the National Federation of Afro-American Women were merged in 1896 to form the National Association of Colored Women.[33] During the Depression, black women led by Mary McLeod Bethune, organized the National Council of Negro Women.[34] Both organizations stressed the problems of "the Race" and the special problems of black women in the home and labor force.[35] In the late nineteenth century, these women insisted that their movement was a "women's movement" in that it was "a movement led by women." While many of their concerns were feminist, they insisted that their movement was designed not to exclude men but to develop women leaders. They focused on the economic, social, and political problems of the entire black community.[36] Club activities grew out of involvements in the suffrage movement, mother's clubs concerned with education and mutual aid, and the growth of the NAACP. The problem of household domestics represented a significant area of activity. In the early years of this century, some women cooperatively purchased clubhouses which currently house and administer a variety of grants and demonstration projects. Contemporary community mothers are direct descendants of the leaders of these women's organizations. Their movements grew out of their economic independence as professionals, businesswomen, and working wives. Community mothers' influence and power has reached beyond the black community and into the world of intergroup conflict. In one major city, when community members staging a sit-in in a public building were threatened with arrest, they sent a taxi to bring Mother Williams[37] to the sit-in. When she arrived and joined the sit-in, the police immediately called their superior and were ordered not to arrest the demonstrators. These elder community workers, "Mother" to most of the younger black politicians, agency heads, and activist ministers, were women who had very long careers working for social change. Mother Braxton, whose passing brought twelve hundred grateful community members, religious leaders, and state, local, and national politicians together for her funeral, stated:

> That [change] is what we look[ed] forward to in this generation I'm in, and I worked in. And of course now that the generation is moving out and a newer generation of younger women, like the age of my daughter and people like that, are coming in and taking up where we left off . . . and seeing that we did start a movement, it gives them an opportunity to work for real change— permanent change.[38]

These elders recognized that it was their movement, "led by women," that was the source of the skills and authority that made it possible for them not only to become symbolic leaders and role models, but also to exercise real power from a base of economic and political independence.

The dual-sex nature of community work networks is not immediately obvious to the outsider, but this characteristic becomes apparent when the worlds of church work and community work overlap. Many male community workers are ministers from the larger and more prominent denominations (Baptist, Congregational, African Methodist Episcopal, African Methodist Episcopal Zion, and United Methodist). While women community workers are also churchwomen, their community work networks are grounded in secular organizations and agencies. Although the community elders are also called mother within their churches, they do not have the same access to religious authority that they have to secular political power and influence, nor was their devotion to their churches always recognized in secular community folklore. Still there was a more liberal attitude towards women's preaching in those churches where community mothers' "children" were pastoring, and being the "first women to deliver the sermon at . . ." was an important part of their public biographies.

CHURCH MOTHERS: VARIETIES OF SHARED POWER

The situation of church mothers differs from that of community mothers. The paradoxes and ambivalence surrounding the appropriate roles of women in public life are more obvious within the churches. Within larger Baptist and Methodist denominations, women are organized under a system of relatively unyielding male authority. Baptist and Methodist Church Mothers tended to be influential and venerable elders. Within the Sanctified Churches, those Pentecostal and Holiness denominations which were founded and managed by black people and which have retained more of the traditional southern and African elements of black religious worship and liturgy, there is a broader range of attitudes and practices concerning the position of women. Church mothers are not only role models and venerable elders—according to some ministers, "women who are important for moral guidance within our congregations"—but also older, venerated, Spirit-filled women who hold considerable power within *nearly* autonomous and well-organized parallel women's worlds. Such women may be known as heroic co-workers of powerful elders, bishops, and church founders. Others may owe their prestige, and occasionally real power, to their roles as wives and widows of elders, bishops, pastors, and church founders. Some are community prayer band leaders or prayer warriors.[39] Most importantly, some church mothers are church founders, preachers, and congregational leaders with full authority within congregational and denominational structures. While women's roles range from symbolic role models to nearly-independent power brokers, all are called "Mother." Their various positions exhibit some vestige of the African concept of familyhood or the dual-sex organization of power in religious life.

One of the most powerful and well-organized groups of church mothers is the women's department of the Church of God in Christ (COGIC). From the time of Mother Lizzie Roberson, the COGIC recognized a parallel, but subordinate, women's authority structure. The writings of the founder and other former bishops of the Church advanced the beliefs that women should be led by women and that "neither is the man without the woman, neither the woman without the man . . ."[40] These beliefs led to the appointment of "overseers" or "organizers" of women's work, a system which evolved into a separate women's convention whose jurisdiction and officers parallel precisely the authority of the elders and bishops of the church.

The position of church mothers reflected an ideological and theological ambivalence on the part of the church. On the one hand, the COGIC recognized "that there [were] thousands of talented, Spirit-filled, dedicated and well-informed devout women capable of conducting the affairs of a church both administratively and spiritually."[41] Histories of the church placed Mother Roberson among the founders (in one case, "founding fathers") and mentioned numerous women missionaries, evangelists, national supervisors, and state supervisors. Historians paid particular attention to Mother Lillian Brooks Coffey, "As a woman of distinction [Mother Coffey] has a great influence in her chosen field as a religious worker, humanitarian, and dreamer . . . Like Lucretia Mott, she has combined her effective speech for [women's] suffrage [with her work] in the Church of God in Christ."[42]

On the other hand, according to some of these same bishops, "nowhere can we find a mandate to ordain women to be an Elder, Bishop or Pastor. Women may teach the gospel to others . . ., have charge of a church in the absence of its Pastor . . . without adopting the title of Elder, Reverend, Bishop, or Pastor." The entire tone of the official church manual's section, "Women in the Ministry,"[43] reflected the ambivalence of men who were aware that "the 'proper' place of women in the church is an age-old debate and from all appearances it seems that it perhaps will be an eternal one—for most mortals at least."[44]

The debate over women's proper place was confined largely to those areas where participation required that one be a pastor, elder, or bishop. In the area of higher education, the church imposed no restrictions; thus, half of the students at the Charles H. Mason Seminary are women. The evolution of Saints' University, COGIC's undergraduate institution in Lexington, Mississippi, was credited to Dr. Arenia C. Mallory, a protege of Mary McLeod Bethune.[45] Mallory started as a teacher in 1925, and in 1930 Bishop C. H. Mason appointed her president.[46] In 1975, while she was still president, the presiding Bishop appointed her Commissioner of Education. The resolution of the church's General Assembly stated that "many of the noted leaders of the Church of God in Christ owe a debt of gratitude to Dr. Arenia C. Mallory King for the great role she has played in grooming their lives for top leadership in the church . . ."[47] In 1975, she was the only black woman college president.[48]

arranging music for the Brunswick Recording Company, one of the top five record companies in the peak years of the industry (Dixon and Godrich 1970, 42; Godrich and Dixon 1982, 20; Dorsey 1961, 65).

While these instances of turning back to secular blues clearly compromised Dorsey's renewed religious dedication, they did not really amount to a rejection of his faith. They were, instead, desperate attempts at remaining financially solvent and at having a sense that he was still making progress as a songwriter/performer. But he wrote and recorded one other blues song in September 1928. This piece so clearly differed from any he had composed that one would have to conclude that Dorsey had all but abandoned his new religious growth. This piece was called "It's Tight Like That." A guitarist friend, Hudson Whitaker, wrote the lyrics, which were full of sexual innuendo. Together, Dorsey and Whitaker recorded this song as the team of Georgia Tom and Tampa Red. Not only did Dorsey seem to have departed significantly from his gospel blues but, as fate would have it, he was rewarded for doing so: his first royalty check, the highest amount in his career, was written for $2,400.19. By December, the song was so popular that he and Whitaker recorded two more versions of it. The two became so notorious for their cunningly erotic blues that they coined a word for the style (*hokum*) and went on to name their duo after it, the Famous Hokum Boys. By 1932, they would make over sixty recordings of Dorsey's songs, appropriately titled, for example, "Pat that Bread" and "Somebody's Been Using that Thing" (Dorsey 1961, 36–37; Dixon and Godrich 1970, 62–63; Godrich and Dixon 1982, 199–200, 224–25, 344, 352, 574, 683–84, 748).

Just as Dorsey was basking in this fame, the kind for which he had craved during most of his career, his gospel songs seemed to attract new attention as well. A young woman sang "If You See My Savior" during the August 23, 1930, morning session of the annual meeting of the National Baptist Convention in Chicago. It was a decided hit, with "every man, woman, and child . . . singing or humming the tune" (Dorsey 1961, 70; Harris 1976). This is the event that Dorsey marks as the beginning of his success as a gospel songwriter: "[I've] been in the music business ever since. . . . That was the big moment right there." Having sold over four thousand copies at the Convention, Dorsey certainly had reason to feel that he had reached the level of acceptance for which he had labored for two years (Dorsey 1961, 69–70; Harris 1976, 1977a).

This point also may be considered the final resolution of the inner conflicts that had dogged him since 1926. Even though he had decided to dedicate himself to a Christian life and his music talents to sacred music, Dorsey had to fight against the cultural obstinacy of the big churches and the economic draw of his old career. Dorsey had tried to keep his gospel music going in a small church; even that was little consolation: "I wasn't giving all my time to the church, see. I was kind of straddling the fence—making money out there on the outside, you know, in the band business and then going to church Sunday morning helping what I could do for them for they wasn't able to pay nothing. I could make money out there" (Harris 1976).

A resolution of the same sort was about to bring Chicago's major Black churches to a more inclusive worship ritual. At Ebenezer Baptist Church, where the European orientation of the worship music matched or exceeded that at Pilgrim and Olivet, the desire for a more traditional mode of worship was fueled by the call of its pastor, J. H. L. Smith, one Sunday morning in the fall of 1931, for a new group to sing the older music. As recalled by June Levell, the historian of the Ebenezer Gospel Chorus, the pastor declaimed, "I have a vision of a group singing the good old fashion songs that were born in the hearts of our forefathers down in the Southland. I want those songs that my old forefathers and mothers sing down in, way down in the Southland" (Harris 1977b).

Smith, who had assumed the Ebenezer pastorate in August of that year, had found his first months in one of the most acculturated of Chicago's Black old-line churches discomforting. Having arrived in Chicago from Birmingham, Alabama, Smith had a pronounced preference for the very Southern worship style that these Chicago old-line churches were dedicated virtually to eradicating. He was, moreover, greatly encouraged to call for such a drastic change because the congregation had been split over the sudden (and suspicious) departure of the previous pastor. Ebenezer, therefore, was demoralized; its worship, uninspiring.

Not even one so convinced of the appropriateness of the traditional African-American worship ritual as Smith could have anticipated the surge to affirm his call for the older music. On the second Sunday in January 1932, a chorus of over one hundred members made its debut at Ebenezer with Dorsey as pianist and Theodore Frye as director. At the root of this surprising development was more than Smith's call for down-home, musical therapy. Most of the one hundred choristers were recent migrants from the rural South. Since the beginning of World War I, their numbers had been growing steadily. Nowhere was this increase more evident than in the large, old-line churches. The new arrivals were drawn to the large churches because these institutions had social programs that included aid for settling in Chicago and for finding employment. To a great extent, however, the newcomers' presence had little effect on operations and virtually none on worship standards, since those churches served almost exclusively as the domains of Chicago's Black old settlers, residents, in many cases, for several generations. This group was most closely tied to the effort to guide the old-line churches into their mimicry of white Protestant worship norms. If this group had a visual and auditory locus in old-line churches, it was the choir. Thus the new migrants, large in number but weak in influence, sat passively, Sunday after Sunday, listening to their counterparts espouse the virtues of white middle-class culture through the Western European choral anthem:

> A lot of people here who remembered what singing was like down home, liked Smith, Lord, yes. The music the Senior Choir was singing was not what Reverend Smith nor the congregation was used to. And then them old songs that they had been used to hearing, like "This Rock I'm Standing On" or "By and By," see, the Senior Choir didn't sing them. They sang ooh, ah, ooh, way up high and [they sang] the anthems. (Harris 1977b)

What had seemed an inexorable movement toward alien religious norms was now about to be brought to a halt by Smith's deliberate parrying of the migrants' musical sentiments off those of the old settlers: "And when he came here, of course, he'd been used to that old time singing down there and he wanted the same thing at Ebenezer" (Harris 1977b). Thus, at Smith's initiative, migrants gained a literal voice in the Sunday morning worship hour and, through them, traditional African-American religious culture regained a place in old-line Protestantism.

This development is significant in that it represents the same resolution of a conflict between original and assimilated cultural experiences that Dorsey underwent. Dorsey's stumble back into down-home blues provided the correction for his earlier long slide into the commercial, Tin Pan Alley blues of his time of professional assimilation. Ebenezer's turn back to religious songs of the Southland likewise provided a counterforce to its long slide into religious assimilation. There is also a similarity to Dorsey's religious resolution: just as Dorsey experienced unrest by not being as sincere in his religious outlook as he felt he should, based on his mother's piety, so was Ebenezer deeply troubled by its attempt to separate Black Christianity from its cultural roots. In this instance the parallel situations are found in Dorsey's nervous breakdown and Ebenezer's demoralization at the loss of its preacher. In both cases, a spiritual rejuvenation was inextricably bound to music in a contextualized African-American setting.

The point is more than coincidental: it portrays a delicate symbiosis between Dorsey's life and the emergence of gospel blues—indeed, between Black culture, Dorsey as an archetype of that culture, and the middle-class Black church as an institutionalization of that culture. Dorsey as an African American and the church as African-American religion have complete histories only as subsets of African-American culture. From the perspective of this interdependency, Dorsey's role as the "father" of gospel blues was limited in the sense of his being able to lay claim to its genesis. There was an asymmetry of old and new cultures—manifested as rural Southern and urban Northern—in Black churches. Dorsey happened to be there with an urbanized version of the rural culture's music that was powerful enough to counter the Beethoven and Mozart of the Northern culture and that was authentic enough to give status to the former Southerners. Thus, Dorsey conceived of "gospel blues," but its purpose and ultimate shape were not his to determine.

If there is a cause—effect factor in this tripartite symbiosis of (1) secular and sacred, (2) lower class and middle class, and (3) rural Southern and urban Northern, it has to be the notion of duality and its pervasiveness not just in Dorsey's life but in African-American culture and religion. The similarities among exposure, conflict, and resolution between Dorsey's life and the church and the culture are traceable to the twoness that is central to the African-American experience.

REFERENCES CITED

This chapter draws on interviews the author conducted with Thomas A. Dorsey in 1976 and 1977 in Chicago.

Albertson, Chris. 1972. *Bessie*. New York: Stein and Day.

Atlanta City Directory. Listings for 1909–15.

Bradford, Perry. 1965. *Born with the Blues: Perry Bradford's Own Story: The True Story of the Pioneering Blues Singers and Musicians in the Early Days of Jazz*. New York: Oak Publications.

Chicago Defender. 1920, and 1924.

Dixon, Robert M. W., and John Godrich. 1970. *Recording the Blues*. New York: Stein and Day.

Dorsey, Thomas A. 1935. *Inspirational Thoughts*. Chicago: Thomas A. Dorsey.

———. 1941. *Songs with a Message: With My Ups and Downs*. Chicago: Thomas A. Dorsey.

———. ca. 1961. "The Thomas Andrew Dorsey Story: From Blues-Jazz to Gospel Song." Unpublished typescript, Dorsey collection.

Du Bois, William E. B. 1902. "The Work of Negro Women in Society." *The Spelman Messenger* (Feb.): 1–3.

———. [1903] 1961. *The Souls of Black Folk*. Reprint. Greenwich, CT: Fawcett Publications, Inc.

Godrich, John, and Robert M. W. Dixon, comp. 1982. *Blues and Gospel Records: 1902–1942*. London: Storyville Publications and Co.

Harris, Michael W. 1976, 1977a. Interviews with Thomas A. Dorsey, Chicago.

———. 1977b. Interview with June Levell, Chicago, Dec. 8.

Johnson, J. Rosamond, transc. 1930. *Utica Jubilee Singers Spirituals: As Sung at the Utica Normal and Industrial Institute of Mississippi*. Boston: Oliver Ditson Company.

Payne, Bishop Daniel E. [1891] 1968. *History of the African Methodist Episcopal Church*. Edited by C. S. Smith. Reprint. New York: Johnson Reprint Corporation.

Rust, Brian, comp. 1978. *Jazz Records: A–Z: 1897–1942*. 4th ed. 2 vols. New Rochelle, N.Y.: Arlington House.

Titon, Jeff T. *Early Downhome Blues: A Musical Analysis*. Urbana: University of Illinois Press.

Townsend, A. M., ed. 1924. *The Baptist Standard Hymnal with Responsive Readings: A New Book for All Services*. Nashville: Sunday School Publishing Board, National Baptist Convention, U.S.A.

Work, John. 1915. *Folk Songs of the American Negro*. Reprint. New York: Negro Universities Press, 1969.

SELECTED BIBLIOGRAPHY FOR FURTHER READING

Davis, Gerald L. *I got the Word in me and I can sing it, you know: A Study of the Performed African-American Sermon*. Philadelphia: University of Pennsylvania Press, 1985.

Harris, Michael W. *The Rise of Gospel Blues: The Music of Thomas Andrew Dorsey in the Urban Church*. New York: Oxford University Press, 1992.

Pipes, William H. *Say Amen, Brother!: Old-Time Negro Preaching, A Study in American Frustration*. Detroit: Wayne State University Press, 1992.

Spencer, Jon Michael. *Protest and Praise: Sacred Music of Black Religion*. Minneapolis: Fortress, 1990.

Titon, Jeff Todd, ed. *Give Me This Mountain: Life History and Selected Sermons of C.L. Franklin*. Urbana: University of Illinois Press, 1989.

:: An alternative folk medicine variously known as conjure, hodoo, or root doctoring has operated alongside Christianity in the folk culture of many Southern blacks and rural whites since the time of slavery. Long maligned, attacked, or ignored by both African Americans and European Americans, folk culture is beginning to attract the attention it deserves from scholars. Conjure and magic, argues Bruce Jackson, is an important alternative belief system and an integral part of African-American folk culture. ::

:: 19   THE OTHER KIND
OF DOCTOR

Conjure and Magic in
Black American Folk Medicine

Bruce Jackson

There is a remarkable account of conjure work in the *Narrative of the Life Adventures of Henry Bibb: An American Slave Written by Himself*, originally published in 1849. Bibb tells of slaves who adopted various techniques to avoid whippings. "The remedy is most generally some kind of bitter root; they are directed to chew it and spit towards their masters when they are angry with the slaves. At other times they prepare certain kind of powders, to sprinkle about their master's dwellings."[1] Bibb says he got into a scrape for slipping off one time. He expected to be flogged; so he went to a conjurer who gave him both a powder to sprinkle and a root to chew, and "for some cause I was let pass without being flogged that time."[2] The next week, encouraged by his apparent power over the master, Bibb stayed away most of the weekend and on his return talked back to the master. "He became so enraged at me for saucing him, that he grasped a handful of switches and punished me severely, in spite of all my roots and powders."[3] Bibb went to another conjure doctor who told him the first doctor was a quack; the second supplied him with a sneezing powder to sprinkle about the master's bed; it would, he said, turn feelings of anger to love. The only effect was the master and his wife both suffered violent sneezing fits. Bibb "was then convinced that running away was the most effectual way by which a slave could escape cruel punishment."[4]

His interest in flight was suspended for a while when he got interested in women. Even though he'd been ill-served by conjure doctors before, he once again turned to them for help. "One of these conjurers, for a small sum agreed to teach me to make any girl love me that I wished. After I had paid him, he told me to get a bull frog, and take a certain bone out of the frog, dry it, and when I got a chance I just step up to any girl whom I wished to love me, and scratch her somewhere on her naked skin with this bone, and she would be certain to love me, and would follow me in spite of herself, no matter who she might be engaged to, nor who she might be walking with."[5] One Sunday, Bibb saw a woman he liked walking with her lover. He "fetched her a tremendous rasp across her neck with this bone, which made her jump." It also made her rather angry. He went to still another conjure adviser, an old slave who told him to place a lock of his lady's hair in his shoes, an act which would "cause her to love me above all other persons." He was by that time interested in another girl, but she refused him the hair. "Believing that my success depended greatly upon this bunch of hair, I was bent on having a lock before I left that night let it cost what it might. As it was time for me to start home in order to get any sleep that night, I grasped hold of a lock of her hair, which caused her to screech, but I never let go until I had pulled it out. This of course made the girl mad with me and I accomplished nothing but gained her displeasure."[6]

To the modern reader, Bibb's experience must seem absurd on at least two major counts: how could he believe such devices would function? and after he saw they didn't help him, why didn't he learn from experience that the conjure doctor's advice was not only not helpful but sometimes downright dangerous to him?

We must change the logic a bit, shift the basic premises. What if we assume that events in this world are *causally* rather than *randomly* linked? What if we assume the world has a sense to it greater than accident and less than total divine plan? Then the only real problem is to find out how to influence the various operations. The *donnée* would be that the world *can* be influenced for good or ill, that both events and persons can be directed in significant ways. The various failures Bibb reports could then be viewed as resulting from incompetence on the part of the practitioners or some mistake on Bibb's part, but they do not themselves invalidate the theory, the process, the art.

The curious thing about the stuff so often referred to as "primitive" medicine or magic is that it is terrifically logical. It assumes the operation of the universe is causal, not gratuitous. The educated executive in New York may attribute his fall down a flight of steps to bad luck, his missing a plane to uncommon traffic congestion, but the so-called primitive would ask why he—rather than someone else—had the mass of cars in his way that afternoon and why he should have missed that top step he had always found in the past. The "logical" answer is that something caused it to happen.

A. B. Ellis, writing of Gold Coast folklore, said:

> To the uncivilized man there are no such deaths as those we term natural or accidental. All deaths are attributed directly to the actions of men or to the invisible powers. If a man be shot or his skull be fractured by another man, the cause of death appears to the uncivilized man obvious. Such and such an injury has been inflicted by So-and-so, and experience, either personal or derived, has shown him that death results from such injuries. But should a man be drowned, be crushed by a falling tree in the forest, or be killed by lightning, such an occurrence would not be considered an accident; and a man who met his death in one of these modes would be believed to have perished through the deliberate act of a malignant being. And such, to us, accidental deaths, prove to the uncivilized man both the existence and the malignancy of these beings. A man is drowned. Who has killed him? So-and-so, a local spirit of the sea or a river has dragged him down. . . .
>
> Thus far for violence and sudden deaths; but the same belief is held with regard to deaths which are really due to disease or old age. These are likewise attributed to the action of the invisible powers directly, or to witchcraft, that is to say, to the indirect action of the same powers; for it is from them that wizards and witches obtain assistance and mysterious knowledge.[7]

An extraordinary amount of folk culture is devoted to ways of dealing with what highly literate groups like to consider luck. If there are potent beings in the universe, they can do well or ill; if they exist, they can probably be influenced; if they can be influenced for good, they can be influenced for ill; if someone has caused an evil influence, perhaps someone else can cause a good one, or at least undo the evil. The world of folk magic and medicine, as many commentators have noted, assumes a total coherence in the operation of the world.

What has been assumed to be learned fatalism among lower-class American blacks in the seventeenth, eighteenth, and nineteenth centuries wasn't fatalism at all: most *knew* quite well that whatever happened was *caused*. Some things were beyond their power of influence. That didn't mean it was beyond anyone's influence—only theirs, in that place at that time.[8]

If the magic didn't work, it meant either that it was done imperfectly or that someone else was working something stronger. It is curious that a high degree of learning is directed away from the "logical" and toward the gratuitous. But the random and gratuitous are far harder to accept and live with, far more fearful exactly because one cannot cope with them.[9]

In a recent article on folk medicine, Don Yoder writes:

> Of folk medicine there are essentially two varieties, two branches: (1) natural folk medicine, and (2) magico-religious folk medicine. The first of these represents one of man's earliest reactions to this natural environment, and involves the seeking of cures for his ills in the herbs, plants, minerals, and animal substances of nature. Natural medicine, which is sometimes called "rational" folk medicine, and sometimes "herbal" folk medicine because of the predominance of herbs in its material medica, is shared with primitive cultures, and in some cases some of is many effective cures have made their way into scientific medicine. The second branch of folk medicine is the magico-religious variety, sometimes called "occult" folk medicine, which attempts to use charms, holy words, and holy actions to cure disease. This type commonly involves a complicated, prescientific world view.[10]

The important difference between the two kinds of folk medicine is that the first assumes a direct cause and effect between application of some substance to some somatic problem while the other attempts to influence some agent other than the doctor or patient or subject. The first is quite close to what we usually consider proper medical practice; the second is closer to what we consider religious manipulation.

In Old World black culture, the two were often combined. The medicine man or voodun in Africa or Haiti would not only cure with herbs but would also act as intermediary with various divinities in the manipulation of a variety of situations. What is curious about the American situation is that the second aspect survived, but it survived without the theological framework upon which it was based. George J. McCall, for example, reports:

> "Hoodoo" represents the syncretistic blend of Christian and Nigritic religious traditions in the United States, corresponding to *vodun* ("voo-doo") and *obeah* in Haiti, *shango* in Trinidad, *candomble* and *macumbo* in Brazil, *santeria* in Cuba, and *cumina* in Jamaica. In twentieth-century hoodoo, however, Catholic elements are less prominent than in the other variants, and Nigritic collective rituals have largely disappeared. Instead, hoodoo has been assimilated to the bewildering variety of store-front spiritualist churches in its truly religious aspect, leaving a heavy residue of sorcery and fetishism as the remaining native elements.

As with sorcery among other peoples, the major foci of hoodoo sorcery lie in the realms of health, love, economic success, and interpersonal power. In all these cases, hoodoo doctors—after careful spiritual "reading" of the client— prescribe courses of action (which always include some hoodoo ritual) and gladly sell him the charms, potions, and amulets the ritual requires.[11]

At its most fully developed, as in Haiti and nineteenth-century New Orleans, voodoo is a system which explains the world; it has various deities assigned a variety of tasks, deities who may be supplicated or motivated in various ways. The voodoo doctors are trained in such manipulation. But rootwork, the more common form found in the rest of the United States, is only technique; much of the work done by root doctors and conjure men has to do with common folk remedies and with good luck (or bad luck for others) charmers. The voodoo doctors sometimes engaged in simple medical work, but they originally did such work through the agency of a powerful outsider, a god.

The function of the voodoo doctor in the Haitian and Louisiana traditions is close enough to the function of African medicine man that we may cite John S. Mbiti's long description of the medicine man's work:

First and foremost, medicine-men are concerned with sickness, disease and misfortune. In African societies these are generally believed to be caused by the ill-will or ill-action of one person against another, normally through the agency of witchcraft and magic. The medicine-man has therefore to discover the cause of the sickness, find out who the criminal is, diagnose the nature of the disease, apply the right treatment and supply a means of preventing the misfortune from occurring again. This is the process that medicine-men follow in dealing with illness and misfortune: it is partly psychological and partly physical. Thus, the medicine-man applied both physical and "spiritual" (or psychological) treatment, which assures the sufferer that all is and will be well. The medicine-man is in effect both doctor and pastor to the sick person. His medicines are made from plants, herbs, powders, bones, seeds, roots, juices, leaves, liquids, minerals, charcoal and the like; and in dealing with a patient, he may apply massages, needles or thorns, and he may bleed the patient; he may jump over the patient, he may use incantations and ventriloquism, and he may ask the patient to perform various things like sacrificing a chicken or goat, observing some taboos or avoiding certain foods and persons—all these are in addition to giving the patient physical medicines. In African villages, disease and misfortune are religious experiences, and it requires a religious approach to deal with them. The medicine-men are aware of this, and make attempts to meet the need in a religious (or quasi-religious) manner—whether or not that turns out to be genuine or false or a mixture of both. . . .

On the whole, the medicine-man gives much time and personal attention to the patient, which enables him to penetrate deep into the psychological state of the patient. Even if it is explained to a patient that he has malaria because a mosquito carrying malaria parasites has stung him he will still want to know why that mosquito stung him and not another person. The only answer which people find satisfactory to that question is that someone has "caused" (or "sent") the mosquito to sting a particular individual, by means of magical manipulations. Suffering, misfortune, disease and accident, all are "caused" mystically, as far as African peoples are concerned. To combat the misfortune or ailment the cause must also be found, and either counteracted, uprooted or punished. This is where the value of the traditional medicine-man comes into the picture.[12]

The most complex and highly structured voodoo work in this country apparently occurred in and around New Orleans because both the black and white populations there had strong ties with Haiti. One of the most interesting descriptions of that scene is offered by Zora Neale Hurston. In the second half of *Mules and Men*, she describes how, while doing research as a Columbia graduate student, she was several times initiated as a voodoo doctor. She offers formulas for various influences: "Concerning Sudden Death," "To Rent a House," "For Bad Work," "Court Scrapes," "To Kill and Harm," "Running Feet," "To Make a Man Come Home," "To Make People Love You," "To Break Up a Love Affair";[13] and she quotes some "Prescriptions of Root Doctors."[14]

The tradition she describes is essentially Caribbean and African; it operates with the claimed mediation of deities and through the application of chemicals, and some of the practitioners claim temporary apotheosis as the source of their power. Luke Turner, descendant of famed voudooienne Marie Leveau, gives Hurston a long description of Levau's work and says, "Marie Leveau is not a woman when she answer one who ask. She is a god, yes. What ever she say, it will come so."[15]

Turner described in some detail Leveau's method of affixing a curse:

She set the altar for the curse with black candles that have been dressed in vinegar. She would write the name of the person to be cursed on the candle with a needle. Then she place fifteen cents in the lap of Death upon the altar to pay the spirit to obey her orders. Then she place her hands flat upon the table and say the curse-prayer.

"To the Man God: O great One, I have been sorely tried by my enemies, and have been blasphemed and lied against. My good thoughts and my honest actions have been turned to bad actions and dishonest ideas. My home has been disrespected, my children have been cursed and ill-treated. My dear ones have been backbitten and their virtue questioned. O Man God, I beg this that I ask for my enemies shall come to pass:

"That the South wind shall scorch their bodies and make them wither and shall not be tempered to them. That the North Wind shall freeze their blood and numb their muscles and that it shall not be tempered to them."

There follows a catalog of bodily afflictions and diseases and infirmities that make the plagues of Exodus seem a mild sentence in comparison.[16]

It is difficult to estimate the actual spread of voodoo worship in Louisiana in the nineteenth century, but the practice was extensive enough to get wide contemporary coverage in popular magazines in other parts of the country. George Washington Cable, for example, told the urban readers of *Century Magazine* in April 1886 of the potency of voodoo worship:

Whatever the quantity of Voodoo *worship* left in Louisiana, its superstitions are many and are everywhere. Its charms are resorted to by the malicious, the jealous, the revengeful, or the avaricious, or held in terror, not by the timorous only, but by the strong, the courageous, the desperate. To find under his mattress an acorn hollowed out, stuffed with the hair of some dead person, pierced with four holes on four sides, and two small chicken feathers drawn through them so as to cross inside the acorn; or to discover on his door-sill at daybreak a little box containing a dough or waxen heart stuck full of pins; or to hear that his avowed foe or rival has been pouring cheap champagne in the four corners of Congo Square at midnight, when there was no moon, will strike more abject fear into the heart of many a stalwart negro or melancholy quadroon than to face a leveled revolver. And it is not only the colored man that holds to these practices and fears. Many a white Creole gives them full credence.[17]

But outside of the curious situation in southern Louisiana, black folk medicine on the mainland United States has in general lacked an overarching theory or any coherent organization of deities. Much of what Hurston's doctors do is simply the uttering of folk superstitions, many of which are common to European traditions. ("If you kill and step backwards over the body, they will never catch you. . . . If you are murdered or commit suicide, you are dead before your time comes. God is not ready for you, and so your soul must prowl about until your time comes. . . . Bury the victim with his hat on and the murderer will never get away . . .")[18] Her root doctor prescriptions cover common diseases—bladder trouble, rheumatism, swelling, blindness, lockjaw, upset stomach, loss of mind, poisons. Though some of the salves for swelling might work well enough, it is hard to see how some of the treatments for gonorrhea ("parch egg shells and drink the tea" or "fifty cents iodide potash to one quart sarsaparilla; take three teaspoons three times a day in water") or for syphilis ("ashes of one good cigar, fifteen cents worth of blue ointment; mix and put on the sores" or "get the heart of a rotten log and powder it fine; tie it up in a muslin cloth; wash the sores with good castile soap and powder them with the wood dust")[19] would help sufferers much. (Of course, the techniques of medical doctors at the time weren't any better for treating those diseases.)

Although there was—and still is in some rural areas—much belief in the efficacy of various magical practices and the potency of folk doctors and the existence of certain supernatural beings, that body of belief does not form a system so much as a great mass of techniques varying widely from place to place; and just about everywhere in this country, it is the technological, rather than the theological, aspect which is operative.

The most spectacular collection of black folk medicine is Dr. Harry M. Hyatt's *Hoodoo—Conjuration—Witchcraft—Rootwork*.[20] The first four volumes of this projected five-volume work consist of almost thirty-eight hundred pages of interviews with hoodoo doctors and thousands of samples of techniques for various situations and afflictions. The fifth volume, an index being done under the direction of Wayland D. Hand, should make this enormous mass of rare data more easily accessible and approachable. At present, it is pretty much like wandering in a cataloged but unindexed archive, where we have the names and titles of performers but can only sense the holding by experiencing the entire collection. Dr. Hyatt is quite aware of his collection's value and limitations. "Though *Hoodoo* is full of magic rites and cures," he wrote me recently,

> always I sought the professional operator, the *doctor*, his appearance, personal mannerisms, origin of his power, possible descent from a predecessor, activities, beliefs, methods and the atmosphere surrounding him. The latter also means a study of his clients. As you can see, *Hoodoo* is an archive, not a logical presentation of material or a *Golden Bough* trying to prove a theory; but a picture of living people, talking, demonstrating rites in front of you, 1600 of us, asking study by the scholar.

The literature on black folk medicine and magic, on conjure and such, is quite extensive.[21] In the nineteenth century, long before F. J. Child began his monumental library work at Harvard, gifted amateurs were already hard at work in the field collecting Negro folk tales (Joel Chandler Harris's first Remus book was published in 1880)[22] and folk song (Thomas Wentworth Higginson's influential article "Negro Spirituals" was published in *The Atlantic Monthly* in June 1867, and the first book-length collection of black American songs, *Slave Songs of the United States* was published in the same year.)[23] There were numerous articles about black superstition, magic, and medicine in the third quarter of the nineteenth century,[24] and when the American Folklore Society was organized in the late 1880s, its founders set forth as one of its areas of special concern the folklore of the Negro.

But there is another reason why there is so much material on black folk medical and magical practices and customs: there was in fact a great deal of such material around. There were few other sources of power available to the slaves and ex-slaves; there was no justice in the courts for them and no regular source of financially reasonable medical aid from the white doctors in town. Because of custom and the policy of the controlling class, those practices among the folk survived long after they had become moribund in other groups. It is still difficult to know how much of that nineteenth-century material was African survival and how much was European material translated into black idiom and style. Just as with spirituals, there remains something of both. But those things remained because they were necessary, because more sophisticated devices of control were absent. I think John Dollard expresses this as well as anyone else:

> There is another means of accommodating to life when it is not arranged according to one's wishes. This is the use of magic. Of course, one can think of magical practices among the Negroes as lagging culture patterns, which they are, but one can also think of them as forms of action in reference to current social life. Magic accepts the *status quo*, it takes the place of political activity, agitation, organization, solidarity, or any real moves to change status. It is interesting and harmless from the standpoint of the caste system and it probably has great private value for those who practice it. . . . Magic, in brief, is a control gesture, a comfort to the individual, an accommodation attitude to helplessness. There is no doubt that magic is actively believed in and practiced in Southern-town and country.[25]

I think it is clear that one of the reasons many of these practices have become rarer in the past three decades is that those lacks Dollard notes have become real-

ities: there has been considerable "political activity, agitation, organization, solidarity, [and other] real moves to change status." But the remembrance of such
time is still with us. Mrs. Janie Hunter told Guy and Dancie Carawan in the early
1960s:

> We didn't go to no doctor. My daddy used to cook medicine—herbs medi-
> cine: seamuckle, pine top, lison molasses, shoemaker root, ground moss,
> peachtree leave, big-root, bloodroot, read oak bark, terrywuk.
>
> And you hear about children have worm? We get something call jimsey
> weed. You put it in a cloth and beat it. And when you done beat it, you squeeze
> the juice out of it, and you put four, five drop of turpentine in it, give children
> that to drink. You give a dose of castor oil behind 'em. You don't have to take
> 'em to no doctor. . . .
>
> All this from old people time when they hardly been any doctor. People
> couldn't afford doctor, so they have to have and guess. Those old people dead
> out now, but they worked their own remedy and their own remedy come out
> good.[26]

But it wasn't just for medical problems that people visited the folk doctors.
Social affairs were just as much in their domain. There are many reports similar
to the story told by Henry Bibb about people visiting hoodoo or conjure doctors
to try to get help in managing the difficulties of simply getting on in the world.
John Dollard wasn't the first observer to understand how such belief compensated for a sense of impotence or for a lack of other kinds of organization. Leonora
Herron and Alice M. Bacon, writing in the *Southern Workman* in 1895, said:

> Overt and natural means of obtaining justice being forbidden the Negro, was
> it surprising that, brought up in ignorance, and trained in superstition, he
> should invoke secret and supernatural powers to redress his wrongs and afford
> him vengeance on those of his follows whom envy, jealousy or anger prompt
> him to injure?
>
> The agent of this vengeance was usually the Conjure Doctor. This individual
> might be a man or a woman, white or colored, but was found in every large
> Negro community, where though held in fear and horror, his supernatural
> powers were still implicitly believed in. The source of these powers is but ill
> defined.[27]

As the source of power some of their informants cite the devil; some God;
some, education. Basically, they say, "The conjure doctor's business was of two
kinds: to conjure, or 'trick,' a person, and to cure persons already 'conjured.'"[28]

The conjure doctor is simply a library of folk beliefs and techniques in the areas of contagious and homeopathic magic. Many people know of these matters and can cite a limited number of cures or techniques, but he is the man (or woman) one goes to for the best technique for a specific situation. He is known by various names, but his functions are relatively constant. Richard Dorson describes categories of such operators when he discusses the term *two-head*: "Although 'two-head' designates any person with esoteric gifts, the Southern Negro speaks of three separate kinds. The hoodoo doctor diagnoses and treats diseases caused by hoodoo evil. The fortuneteller, like renowned Aunt Caroline Dye of Newport, Arkansas, prophesies the future, and locates lost persons and property. The healer cures natural ailments that baffle doctors through his secret arts. Some of the most graphic stories told by Negroes involve these two-header practitioners."[29]

Dorson is no doubt correct that there are three separate kinds of practitioners in this area, but the boundaries dividing them are sometimes rather amorphous. Most of the reports in this century suggest that the practitioners assume a variety of functions which seem to depend as much on neighborhood needs as on professional divisions of labor.

Carl Carmer, for example, describes an Alabama conjure woman whose name is Seven Sisters. "It's a spirit in me that tells," she told Carmer, "a spirit from the Lord Jesus Christ. Used to be old voodoo woman lived next to my mammy's cabin. She tol' me how to trick. She say her mammy in Africa teached her. But she was a bad ol' woman—a voodoo conjure woman. I tricks in the name o' the Lord."[30] She offers recipes and techniques for various conjure acts. One will "keep your wife from flirting around; take a persimmon sprout about six inches long and bury it under the doorstep while her flirting spell is on." Other cures have to do with getting good crops, inflicting revenge on an enemy, knowing when you've been tricked by another conjurer, or curing warts. You can get a girl to sleep with you if you "steal something dirty from being next to her skin—a string from her drawers, moisture from under her right arm, best of all a menstruation cloth—stick nine pins in it and bury it under the eaves of the house" or "take hair from her head, make it into a ball, sew it up, and wear it under your right arm."[31] Norman Whitten, reporting on such practices in North Carolina, found a similar combination of activity. The conjurer, he said, "is the professional diviner, curer, agent finder, and general controller of the occult arts. Local synonyms for the conjurer are "'root doctor,' 'herb doctor,' 'herb man,' 'underworld man,' 'conjure man,' and 'goofuhdus man.' [This last is probably *gooferdust man*, referring to the graveyard dust such doctors sometimes use.] The principal function and role of the conjurer is to deal with and control the occult. This he does for a fee."[32] And Loudell F. Snow, reporting on a voodoo practitioner in Tucson, Arizona, says her informant will treat any sort of disorder: "I don't turn down nothin'," the practitioner said to Snow, "I don't care what's wrong with 'em, I just have confidence. I tell you what. I believe in God. I believe God can do anything and everything. That is a high power, faith and the belief. I never lose faith, I never doubt myself. I know there's nothin' I can do *without* him, and I feel like He's with me at all times."[33]

This last is in many ways close to the white Fundamentalist preacher who sometimes also assumes the power of healing; she is clearly a long way from the complex theological framework of the African slaves and New Orleans devotees of Haitian voodoo of the last century. It would be difficult to separate which of her techniques derive from European and white American tradition and which derive from African and black American tradition. Clearly some significant melding has occurred, and many old contexts have disappeared. I don't think this informant is anomalous; although there are remnants of those older traditions still around, one would now be hard put to duplicate the monumental fieldwork of Hyatt or the important collection of Puckett.

But it isn't completely dead. Although these practices are not much in evidence in modern American cities (and the majority of America's population— white and black—lives in urban centers now), there are occasional reports that suggest some of the old power is still there, that it still influences behavior in significant ways. Though fewer people may be involved in the various levels of practice than in previous years (as is the case with most rural folk traditions brought to the city), many still take them with as much seriousness as ever, with deadly seriousness. Both the folk remedies and the techniques for control still surface as significant elements in certain communities. Consider the following item, an Associated Press dispatch datelined Miami, February 12, 1974:

COURT REFUSES TO APPOINT VOODOO DOCTOR

The court was bedeviled when a defense lawyer asked to have the defendant examined by a voodoo doctor or an exorcist.

"What's a voodoo doctor?" Circuit Court Judge Dan Satin asked at a hearing Monday.

"One who by training has learned about the powers of voodoo," replied defense lawyer David Cerf.

Mr. Cerf pointed out that the defendant, Harvey Lee Outler, has been determined component for the murder of his common law wife but the evaluating doctor said Outler believed he was under a curse.

Mr. Cerf said Outler, 36, believed that Mable Young, 31, had put a curse on him. Police say Outler shot Mrs. Young with a pistol April 13.

"Your honor, a voodoo curse is just as deadly as a threat with a gun," Mr. Cerf said.

Judge Satin said: "I respect any man's rights. But if you think I'm going to appoint a voodoo doctor, you've got another think coming."

Mr. Cerf's motion was denied.

NOTES

1. In Gilbert Osofsky, ed., *Puttin' On Ole Massa: The Slave Narratives of Henry Bibb, William Wells Brown, and Solomon Northup* (New York: Harper and Row, 1969), p. 70.

2. Ibid., p. 70.

3. Ibid., p. 71

4. Ibid.

5. Ibid., p. 73

6. Ibid.

7. A. B. Ellis, *The Tshi-Speaking Peoples of the Gold Coasts of West Africa: Their Religion, Manners, Customs, Laws, Languages, Etc.* (London: Chapman and Hall, 1887), p. 13.

8. See, for example, Norman E. Whitten, Jr., "Contemporary Patterns of Malign Occultism Among Negroes in North Carolina," *Journal of American Folklore*, 75 (1962), 311–325; reprinted in Alan Dundes, ed., *Mother Wit from the Laughing Barrel* (Englewood Cliffs, N.J.: Prentice-Hall, 1973), pp. 402–418. Whitten notes: "Everything has its antithesis. For instance, for every disease there is an antidote if man can only find it" (p. 413). See also Ruth Bass, "Mojo," in *Scribner's Magazine*, 87 (1930), 83–90, reprinted in Dundes, *op. cit.*, pp. 380–387. Bass writes: "So far as I have been able to discover, there seems to be a trick for every kind of occupation and desire in life. To the swamp Negroes nothing is inanimate, incapable of being tricked. I have heard a swamp Negress talking about her pot because it was slow about boiling. She begged it to boil, pointed out the advantages of boiling over not boiling, and when it remained obstinate she resorted to a trick which consisted of rubbing her belly. The pot promptly cooked faster" (p. 383).

9. The story of Job, which is one of the most popular stories in the Old Testament, is of course an attempt to deal with exactly this problem: it suggests the Lord acts in ways which are not for man to question. The problematic nature of the solution put forth in Job is attested to by the fact that it is the most frequently analyzed book of the Old Testament.

10. Don Yoder, "Folk Medicine," in *Folklore and Folklife: An Introduction*, ed. Richard M. Dorson (Chicago: University of Chicago Press, 1972), p. 192.

11. George J. McCall, "Symbiosis: The Case of Hoodoo and the Numbers Racket," in Dundes, *op. cit.*, p. 420.

12. John S. Mbiti, *African Religions and Philosophy* (Garden City, N.Y.: Doubleday Anchor, 1970), pp. 221–22.

13. Zora Neal Hurston, *Mules and Men* (New York and Evanston, Ill.: Perennial Library, 1970), pp. 332–335.

14. Ibid., pp. 340–343.

15. Ibid., p. 243.

16. Ibid., pp. 245–246.

17. George Washington Cable, "Creole Slave Songs," *Century Magazine*, 11 (April, 1886); reprinted in *The Negro and His Folklore in Nineteenth Century Periodicals*, ed. Bruce Jackson (Austin: University of Texas Press and the American Folklore Society, 1967), pp. 237–238.

18. Hurston, *op. cit.*, p. 332.

19. Ibid., pp. 340–341.

20. Harry M. Hyatt, *Hoodoo—Conjuration—Witchcraft—Rootwork*, 4 vols. (Hannibal, Mo.: Memoirs of the Alma Egan Hyatt Foundation, 1970–1975).

21. See, for example, quoted material and reference in Dundes, *op. cit.*; Jackson, *op. cit.*; Richard M. Dorson, *American Negro Folktales* (New York: Fawcett, 1967); Newbell Niles Puckett, *Folk Beliefs of the Southern Negro* (Chapel Hill: University of North Carolina Press, 1926); Georgia Writers' project of the Works Project Administration, *Drums and Shadows* (Athens: University of Georgia Press, 1940); Robert Tallant, *Voodoo in New Orleans* (New York: Macmillan, 1946).

22. Joel Chandler Harris, *Uncle Remus: His Songs and His Sayings* (New York: D. Appleton, 1880).

23. *Slave Songs of the United States*, ed. William Francis Allen, Charles Pickard Ware, Lucy McKim Garrison (New York, 1867; reprint ed., New York: Peter Smith, 1951).

24. See Jackson, *op. cit.*, p. 134 ff.

25. John Dollard, *Caste and Class in a Southern Town* (Garden City, N.Y.: Doubleday Anchor, 1957), p. 265.

26. Guy and Candie Carawan, *Ain't You Got a Right to the Tree of Life?* (New York: Simon and Schuster, 1966), p. 45. The photograph on the opposite page (p. 44) shows an old woman (who may not be Mrs. Hunter, since the photos and interviews were arranged separately) sitting in a wooden chair before an old iron stove. The walls beyond her are papered with pages of newspapers. It may be that the newspapers serve because nothing else is at hand—but anyone from that area knows full well that *hants* (spirits, ghosts, demons), who sometimes possess people at night, are compulsive counters, and grains of salt or pages of a newspaper will serve as adequate protection because it takes so long to count the grains or letters that dawn comes before the hants can do any harm. I am reminded of a visit to the Massachusetts Hospital for the Criminally Insane at Bridgewater about ten years

ago. A guard tried to prove to me how batty one particular old black inmate was. He called the man over and asked him about the devils in his room at night. The man said there weren't any devils in his room; "The devils in your army, not mine." That seemed rational enough a position. The guard urged the man to tell me how he kept the devils out, and the man said it wasn't devils he kept out.

"Is it hants?" I asked.

He said it was hants and looked at the guard, who at that point was starting to look oddly at me.

"Tell him what you do," the guard said, "about the newspapers."

"You put newspapers on the floor to keep them out?" I asked.

"That's right."

"Where are you from? South Carolina? Georgia?"

He named a coastal town in northern Florida.

I asked the guard just what it was about the man that was supposed to be so batty. He scowled and asked, "How'd you know where he was from?"

"Because of the hants." I pointed out that no southern doctor would consider that sort of superstition adequate grounds for incarceration. "Lots of the old people there used to do that." The guard, obviously no student of folklore, looked at me as if I were as batty as the inmate and walked way, shaking his head.

27. Leonora Herron and Alice M. Bacon, "Conjuring and Conjure Doctors," in Dundes, *op. cit.*, p. 360. (Originally in *Southern Workman*, 24)

28. Ibid.

29. Dorson, *op. cit.*, p. 187.

30. Carl Carmer, *Stars Fell on Alabama* (1934; reprint ed., New York: Hill and Wang, 1961), p. 218.

31. Ibid.

32. Whiteen, *op. cit.*, p. 409.

33. Loudell F. Snow, "'I was Born Just Exactly With the Gift': An Interview with a Voodoo Practitioner," *Journal of American Folklore*, 86 (1973), 277–278.

SELECTED BIBLIOGRAPHY FOR FURTHER READING

Baer, Hans A. *The Black Spiritual Movement: A Religious Response to Racism.* Knoxville: University of Tennessee Press, 1984.

Hurston, Zora Neale. *Mules and Men.* New York: Harper & Row, 1970.

Murphy, Joseph. *Working the Spirit: Ceremonies of the African Diaspora.* Boston: Beacon Press, 1993.

Puckett, Newbell Niles. *Folk Beliefs of the Southern Negro.* Chapel Hill: University of North Carolina Press, 1926.

Snow, Loudell F. *Walkin' over Medicine: Traditional Health Practices in African-American Life.* San Francisco: HarperCollins, 1993.

:: Scholars may disagree to what degree the traditional gods of Africa died in African-American folk culture, but it is increasingly clear that the gods are returning through the influx of immigrants to North American cities such as New York, Montreal, and Miami from the Caribbean and South America where African religions survived to a greater degree than in the United States, in various traditions such as Santeria, Candomble, and Vodun. Karen Brown has been a pioneer in examining Vodun in Haiti and its growing presence in the United States. ::

SYSTEMATIC REMEMBERING, SYSTEMATIC FORGETTING

Ogou in Haiti

Karen McCarthy Brown

:: Ogou is a central figure in Haitian religion. While little known in some areas of rural Haiti, in others he is one of the most important spirits[1] of African origin who are venerated in the Vodou religious system. In cities he has a more prominent role, so that in Port-au-Prince, where no temple neglects him entirely, Ogou frequently is the major spirit of priests and priestesses. Among Haitians who migrate to New York City, those who have Ogou as their *mèt tet*, "master of the head," may well be in the majority.[2]

Ogou in Haiti has his roots in the Gu or the Ogun of the Dahomean or Yoruba peoples, who (along with the Kongo peoples) seem to have contributed the largest concentrations of slaves to Haiti and consequently to have had the strongest influence on its culture. However, he is not simply a reproduction of these African deities. Certainly the Old World played a strong role. Large numbers of slaves were young men whose activities in the African homeland were often centered on the military, hunting, or ironworking—the areas where Ogun was a major patron (Barnes 1980:3, 17, 19–30, and personal communication). It was only natural, then, that this preponderant sector of the incoming population should bring ideas of Gu/Ogun to the New World. In Haiti, however, hunting and smithing were no longer crucial to everyday life, while the soldier took on new guises and added significance. Thus the Haitian Ogou became important to men, and women, of all ages. He also came into contact with Roman

Catholicism, the religion of the slaveholders. Indeed, the Catholic saints penetrated the whole world of Vodou—its visual representations, where chromolithographs of the saints came to be used as images for Afro-Haitian spirits, and its naming system, where saint names and Afro-Haitian spirit names came to be used interchangeably. Also central to the development of the Haitian Ogou were several centuries of political and military upheaval, a historical legacy which transformed the African religious cosmos.

It is important to emphasize that any understanding of the centrality of Ogou in present-day urban Haitian Vodou must include an understanding of the history and of the social and political structures of Haiti. Astide has written that the slave diaspora had the effect of separating "the world of symbols, collective representations, and values from the world of social structures and their morphological bases" (1978: 155). In his view, the process by which African religious systems moved into the New World consisted of a search for appropriate social structural "niches" in which symbolic representations could survive.[3] In some cases, such as the match between Ogou and the military in Haiti, such niches were found. In others they were not. When they were found, the fit between cultural image and social structure was never perfect, and therefore the process by which the two came together was one of continuous negotiation, so that, over time, both were changed by virtue of their interaction.

The point I wish to stress about the continuation of African religions in the New World is that elements which are retained as a legacy from the past are subject to systematic and continuous redefinition and restructuring, and that out of this process new cultural forms emerge. The current Haitian Ogou is one such form.

I begin by placing Ogou in relation to the two major pantheons of urban Vodou. I then turn to analyze his various manifestations, mainly through sacred songs. This discussion focuses on military power and its transformations in a variety of political and social contexts. Finally, I will place the Ogou in relation to another group of spirits, the Gède, who occupy a parallel but clearly contrasting place in Vodou cosmology. I conclude that the emphasis given to Ogou in contemporary Haitian Vodou can be attributed to the fact that he is able to mediate between two diametrically opposed forces in Haitian life. These forces, represented by the two major urban pantheons, have gone through many incarnations in the course of Haitian history, but they are perhaps most succinctly named by pairs of contrasting terms such as insiders/outsiders, family members/foreigners, slaves/slaveholders, oppressed/oppressors.

THE RADA AND THE PETRO SPIRITS

The Vodou spirits, or *Iwa* as the Haitians call them, were once divided into several *nanchon*, "nations"—Rada, Petro, Kongo, Nago, Ibo, and so on. In most cases, their names clearly indicate their African origins. This pattern is still used in some rural parts of Haiti. However, in and around Port-au-Prince, Haiti's major urban center, two pantheons, the Rada and the Petro, have emerged as dominant, largely by observing the other nations into themselves.

The Rada and the Petro groups express contrasting views of the world. One way of capturing this difference would be to say that the Rada pantheon articulates the ethos of insiders and family members, as opposed to the Petro pantheon, which describes that of outsiders and foreigners.[4] One of the most significant changes to take place in African religions as a result of the slave experience was what I call the socialization of the cosmos. For example, natural powers such as those of storm, drought, and disease paled before social powers such as those of the slaveholder. This caused a massive refocusing of the explanatory energies of the African religious systems. This characterization of Rada and Petro as respectively insiders and outsiders is thus in keeping with the general character of African religions in the New World.

The Rada spirits, whose name comes from the town of Allada in ancient Dahomey, are known as *Iwa rasin*, "root *Iwa*," or by a more general title, *Iwa Gine*, "African *Iwa*." The Rada are associated with the right hand, with the downward direction, and therefore directly with *Gine*, "Africa," a spiritual home for ancestors and spirits which the Haitians locate in the water under the earth. Hence the Rada pantheon connects the Haitians directly to their African homeland. Indeed, the names and characteristics of most of the spirits grouped in this pantheon have African counterparts.

The Rada *Iwa* are intimate spirits who surround one with their protection on a day-to-day basis. Their protective power is of a noncoercive sort and is said to reside mainly in their spiritual knowledge. For example, they are often said to "know leaves," which means they are familiar with herbal healing. Their protective role is further articulated in the fact that they are socially familiar beings who are well-known and trusted. They are the elders of the family and therefore they are sometimes experienced as stern and austere; their fundamental benevolence, however, is never doubted. If a sacrifice is promised to a Rada *Iwa* and there is not enough money this year, the spirit can be convinced to wait until next year. The Rada *Iwa* thus represent one existential option. Their way of being-in-the-world is defined by family. The central consciousness of this mode of being is group consciousness and its highest value is the preservation of the group.

The origins of the Petro pantheon, and specifically the name itself, are obscure. Some writers have suggested the name can be traced to an eponymous hero, Dom Pedro, who was a Spanish Vodou priest, but there seems to belittle historical evidence for this theory.[5] More promising is the suggestion that while few of the specific Petro spirit names indicate Kongo origins, the general ambiance of the group does (Thompson 1983: 179–80).

The powers and symbols of the Petro *lwa* stand in marked contrast to those of the Rada group. They are associated with the left hand, with the upward direction, and with leaping flames and heat. In personality, the Petro *lwa* are fierce, severe, and uncompromising. Promises to them must be kept and services rendered with care. One does not break or even bend the rules when dealing with the Petro *lwa*. The ritual vocabulary of the Petro spirits is that of the slaveholders. These *lwa* are served with fire, small explosions of gunpowder, cracking whips, and shrieking police whistles. Some have argued that the Petro spirits represent an expression of rage against enslavement,[6] or an attempt to imitate the slavemasters. I prefer to state it another way: The Petro *lwa* represent an effort to expropriate the power of slaveholding and its contemporary transmutations—oppression, prejudice, economic discrimination—and to use that power against itself.

The Petro *lwa* are the outsiders. Like stereotypic "strangers," the Petro *lwa* tend to look alike and act alike. When they possess their followers, they have personalities that are much less distinguishable from one another than the Rada *lwa*. For example, it is said of the Petro *lwa* that "if you feed one, you feed them all." In spite of this tendency to blend together, the Petro *lwa* are highly individualistic in their mode of being. Likewise, those who seek them out can do so for partisan, even individualistic, purposes. Furthermore, money, notorious for its ability to create social distance, is an area of life where the Petro *lwa* are thought to be particularly effective. The Petro *lwa* thus represent another existential option, a way of being-in-the-world which puts stress on the use of coercive power and the pursuit of self-interest. Because these traits are considered by the Haitians to be too dangerous to become central in the conduct of life, the Petro *lwa* are never given so much emphasis as to displace the Rada *lwa*.

Vodou priests and priestesses in Haiti and in New York are careful to keep their service to the spirits balanced in favor of the right hand, the Rada *lwa*. Yet none is so foolish as to cut himself or herself off completely from the power of the Petro *lwa*.

In urban Vodou, the Ogou are recognized by all to be Nago spirits. This name is the ancient Dahomean title for the Ketu Yoruba (Thompson 1983:17). Nevertheless, these days it is felt that the Ogou should also be classified according to the binary system set up by the Rada and Petro pantheons. The difficulty Haitians currently have in agreeing on how this is to be done points to Ogou's mediating role between the pantheons.

The Rada spirits are associated with water, the Petro with fire. From this perspective, Ogou appears to be clearly Petro. Ogou has a fiery nature: bonfires are lit for him; those who serve him wear red; those who are possessed by him act aggressively. He is also said to fear water, the wisdom of this being captured in the Haitian proverb *Tizo difè di li fou men li pa janm fè nan cheman dlo*, "A firebrand, say it's crazy, but it will never get in the way of water." This otherwise neat picture is complicated by the existence of one Ogou—there are many—who is a water-dwelling spirit. This is Ogou Balendyo, escort of the Rada sea spirit, Agwe. Ogou Balendyo, who also can be identified with Ogou Batala (from the Yoruba Obatala), is known for his herbal knowledge, another Rada domain. For these reasons and because Ogou is clearly a root *lwa* with strong ties to the African homeland, some informants confidently state that the Ogou are Rada spirits. Métraux, who worked in the Port-au-Prince area in the late 1940s, just as confidently assigned at least one of the Ogou (Ogou Yamson) to the Petro pantheon (1972:89). And a Vodou priestess in New York claims that all Ogou are *en dèz o*, "in two waters"; by this she means that the Ogou can manifest themselves equally well in either the Rada or the Petro mode. From this we must conclude that Ogou's ambivalence in relation to the dominant Rada/Petro classification system is a significant dimension of his character.

Ogou's mediating role is further illustrated by the libations offered to the various groups of Vodou spirits. As we might expect, the central element in libations for the Rada *lwa* is water; for the Petro it is fire. Ogou is given libations of rum (fiery water), which are poured on the ground and set on fire, or, mimicking rain, sprayed upward through the air in a fine mist.

The significance of the opposition between Rada and Petro emerges clearly in the ritual rule that the two pantheons cannot be allowed to touch or mix. This principle is articulated in various ways within the Vodou system, including temple architecture, where Rada and Petro altars must be kept separate. Urban Vodou *ounjo*, "temples," consist of a large central space for ritual activities, and *dyevo*, small side-rooms where altars, offerings, and ritual clothing are kept. The number of *dyevo* varies with the financial resources of the temple. Usually the two pantheons are given separate altar rooms; however, even in *ounfo*, where only one side-room is available, the Rada and Petro altars are separated by a partition such as a curtain or they are set at right angles to one another. In one temple outside Port-au-Prince where there are several *dyevo*, the separation is further reinforced by the location of an Ogou altar room in between the Rada and Petro chambers.

Ogou's mediating role finds further expression in ritual sequence. Large drumming and dancing ceremonies, of the sort that are common in urban Vodou, begin with an invocation of the Rada spirits in the order of their importance. A similar set of invocations for the Petro spirits follows. The transition from Rada to Petro cannot be accomplished without a shift in the ritual action. Sometimes this is accomplished by a short socializing break in which people eat, drink, and talk with their neighbors. At other times, Ogou will be called between the two pantheons, if only perfunctorily. In each of these examples, we have seen that Ogou mediates between two opposed ways of being represented by the Rada and the Petro pantheons, allowing movement from one to the other.

The urgent work of the various Ogou is to negotiate the social opposition represented in the two major pantheons. The Rada spirits delineate and reinforce familial bonds. They are treated as family and, in turn, treat their devotees with the indulgence and nurturing accorded to family members. The Petro *lwa*, by contrast, embody the individualism, effectively, and power of foreigners. Petro spirits are not indulgent; they operate according to hard and fast rules that allow no exceptions. The Ogou model a way of being in the world that mediates between family members and foreigners, insiders and outsiders, the home and the larger world outside of it. They are intimate like the Rada spirits, yet powerful like the Petro. But Ogou power, in contrast to that of the Petro spirits, cannot be managed by faithful adherence to rule and principle. Ogou's power is rooted in feeling, specifically in rage, and so it is subject to all the complexities of emotion. As one Haitian put it: "Ogou loves to give people gifts even when he is very angry; he will reward at the same time as he punishes."

The center of Vodou worship, regardless of the classification of the spirits being addressed, is possession-performance. Singing and dancing are said to entice the spirits to possess a devotee. The *lwa* is then said to ride the person like a horse. Once possessed, the *chwal*, "horse," is treated exactly as if he or she were the spirit. Acts of obeisance are performed, gifts are proffered, and the spirit in turn gives advice to individuals and general admonitions to the community. The possession-performance of Ogou, like that of other *lwa*, has certain ritual constants around which the individual *chwal* can improvise. One such constant comes at the beginning of the ceremonial possession, when Ogou does a ritual

dance with his sword. First he attacks the imaginary enemy: he rushes wildly about the temple clanging the sword on door frames and brandishing it in the air. Then he threatens the immediate community: with smaller gestures, he brings the sword's point threateningly close to the bodies of those standing nearby. Finally he turns the sword on himself: lodging the point in his solar plexus, he poses. This performance is to body language what proverbs are to spoken language. In one elegant series of motions, it conveys the message that the same power which liberates also corrupts and inevitably turns on itself.

This exploration of the constructive and destructive uses of power is central to the character of each of the many different Ogou. In the following discussion we will be looking at several of the Ogou through one or more of their songs. It is not possible here to look at the entire range of Ogou symbolism; therefore, a word of caution is necessary. Rather than seeing one Ogou as illustrating a positive use of power and another a negative one, it is more accurate to see each as spinning out another version of the paradox of power expressed in a simple series of movements with the ritual sword.

THE POWER OF OGOU: AGAINST HIS ENEMIES

Militant imagery is the perfect vehicle to handle the complex social negotiation which is the work of Ogou. Soldiers are given powers beyond those of the ordinary citizen. Ideally they use them to defend the group. Political and military emblems are conspicuously displayed in most Vodou temples. The Haitian coat of arms, with its palm tree, flags, and cannons, appears alongside images of the spirits in temple wall paintings and many temples decorate their ceilings with strings of tiny paper Haitian flags. Until the Duvalier regime fell in February of 1986, pictures of the ruling family often appeared along with the flags. It would be easy to see this as simply politically expedient, but it is not. The political and military imagery penetrates to the heart of Vodou symbolic language about the Ogou. The Ogou are soldiers (Ogou Feray, Sin Jak Majè, Ogou Badagri) or politicians (Ogou Panama, Achade Bokò, Ogou Chango). The military-political complex has provided the primary niche for Ogou in Haiti. It is partly Ogou who, over time, made the Haitian experience of these institutions manageable, and it has been the particular historical configuration of these institutions that, in part, gave life and definition to Ogou.

Sin Jak Majè (St. Jacques Majeur) is the senior Ogou. In ceremonies, he is saluted before all other Ogou. Haitians use the Catholic chromolithograph of Santiago, astride his horse crushing the enemy underfoot, to represent Sin Jak.

One of the songs used to greet Sin Jak Majè has this refrain: *Sin Jak Majè/Gason lagèou ye,* "Sin Jak Majè/You're a warrior."

Ogou Feray is head of all the soldier Ogou. An especially popular song for him is this one:

1   Seremoni Feray yo premye klas-o
2   Feray Layman, ki chita sou pè-a,
3   l'ap tire kanon. (Repeat)
4   Sa l'a di. Sa l'a fè avek zanfan la-vo.
5   Sa l'a di. Sa l'a fè avek timoun la-vo.

1   Ceremonies for Feray are first class.
2   Feray the Magnet, who sits on the altar,
3   he's firing the canon. (Repeat)
4   That is what he will say. That is what he will do with his children.
5   That is what he will say. That is what he will do with his little ones.

The language of songs for the *lwa* is cryptic and multivalent. It is never possible to do a full translation or exhaustive exegesis of them. The word *seremont*, for instance, can refer to healing work done in the name of Feray; to magical work similarly performed (and by implication almost any action done in a Feray manner); to a dancing and drumming feast held for Feray; or to a military parade, a ritual version of which is performed for Ogou. *Seremoni* also refuse to the vèvè, abstract drawings which are executed on the floor of Vodou temples to call up the spirits from Africa. The vèvè for Ogou Feray is an abstraction of the Haitian coat of arms. So the reference in this song to the "first class" *seremoni* for Feray can be taken as an allusion to Haiti itself. Such chauvinism is understandable among a people who pride themselves on having carried out a successful slave revolution and founding the first independent Black republic in the Western Hemisphere.

It should also be said that Vodou military images always include, at some level, a reference to military culture heroes. One is Toussaint L'Ouverture, a brilliant military strategist and canny statesman who emerged as the leader of the revolution soon after it began in 1791. He was considered a saint in his time, and contemporary Haitians continue to venerate him. Subsequent soldier-kings of Haiti have sought to legitimize their rule by imitating Toussaint. Awestruck, unquestioning respect is one layer (among many) in the Haitian attitude toward soldiers, human and divine.

The title Feray the Magnet connects this Ogou to magical and healing powers. Magnets are valued for their ability to find lost objects, particularly pins and needles dropped on the ground. Because of these properties, magnets are often included in healing charms and lucky talismans. Feray Layman is therefore a magician-soldier "who sits on the altar" gathering the lost to himself and waging war in their name. A vodou altar is the repository of the history of a people. In addition to images of spirits, it contains earthenware pots called *govi* in which reside the protective spirits of the ancestors. In this song, Ogou Feray is thus ensconced at the head of a vast battalion of spirits and ancestors, firing his cannon and launching a revolution on behalf of all his "children." The reference here is clearly to those who follow and serve him, for the Ogou have no children of their own. Through this multivocal symbolism, contemporary Ogou worship in Haiti shows itself to be a fecund marriage of experiences such as the slave revolution with memories of the African Ogun, warrior and forger of weapons. Added to this portrait, through a cryptic reference to Ogou's power to gather in the lost, is a hint at his nurturing or protective side.

The protective power of Ogou is revealed more explicitly in the following verse form, a song in which he is called upon to guard the people against police harassment.

1   Aye, Aye.
2   Lapolis a rete mwen.
3   Jij a pa kondane mwen.

1   Aye, Aye.
2   The police will arrest me.
3   The judge won't condemn me.

Arrest, often arbitrary, is a frequent fact of life in Haiti: "The police will arrest me"; however, Ogou's protection will suffice in the end: "The judge won't condemn me." Echoes of Ogou's ability to protect those who act in his name could be heard from many sources during the demonstrations and acts of civil disobedience that preceded Haiti's recent change of government. For example, a fisherman in the northern town of Gonavaïes, a center for anti-Duvalier protest, said he was able to stand up to the police only because of special protection given him by Ogou.

The Ogou operate in extreme social situations—in difficult, trying, perilous times—and so the strength they exhibit in themselves and call forth in their devotèès is the strength of someone pushed to the limit. The Ogou call on one another and their followers to tap their deepest reserves of energy, as the next song indicates:

1   Ogou Badagri, sa ou ap fè la?
2   Ou sèviye, ou met envèye.
3   M-ta dòmi, Feray, m-envi dòmi-o.
4   M-ta dòmi, Feray, m-pase dòmi-o.
5   Se Nan lagè mwen ye!
6   Ou met m-envèye, o Feray o.
7   Gason lagè mwen ye!
8   Yo met m-envèye.

1   Ogou Badagri, what are you doing?
2   You are on guard duty, you must wake up.
3   I would sleep, Feray, I need to sleep.
4   I would sleep, Feray, I am beyond sleep.
5   I am in the war!
6   You must wake me, oh Feray oh.
7   I am a soldier!
8   They must wake me.

In this song Ogou Feray, in his role as leader of all Ogou who are soldiers, calls out to Ogou Badagri, who threatens to fall asleep at his guard post. Badagri responds that he knows it is a situation of war, and even though he badly needs sleep, he is first and foremost a soldier and will stay at his post. The song's message is two-pronged. It first makes a realistic assessment of the situation: This is a situation of war and people are taxed beyond reason. In the second part of the message, it indicates people are up to the challenge. In the New World, in slavery, in the revolution and in the chaotic times that followed it, in the modern experience of political oppression, and for some, as we shall see, in the ghetto life of New York, war becomes the metaphor for life itself.

Ogou is a protective weapon for those who serve him. To wage war daily requires constant watchfulness and herculean energy. It is possible because Ogou taps the deepest source of human energy: anger, the final defiant refusal to admit defeat. Ogou's anger empowers those who serve him, as this song for Ogou Achade illustrates:

1   Baton pase nan men mwen,
2   Achade pou ehè raje mwade mwen. (Repeat)
3   Achade, ki jen m-ap fè sa-ye?
4   Achade, ki jen pou-m fè sa-ye?

1   The club passes into my hand,
2   Achade, for the mad dog bites me. (Repeat)
3   Achade, how am I going to do that?
4   Achade, how am I going to be able to do that?

The same theme is echoed in a song for Ogou Feray which contains the line *Jou m-en ko'è enryè pa sa jèmwen*, "The day I am angry nothing will happen to me." In situations of oppression, then, to touch one's anger is to reclaim one's power, position, and dignity in the world. This is the psychological maneuver at the heart of Ogou's message.

When Ogou is very angry, he can *chante pwen*, "sing a point song." The point song is another weapon against life's trials. *Pwen* means point, the point of a story, a comment, a complex human situation, as in, "Do you get the point?" In short, *pwen* is the condensation of a thing, its pith. When it is a spirit's power that is condensed, it becomes a talisman. Within vodou, *pwen* refers to an object or a series of words or actions designed to focus the power of a particular *lwa* and thus enable a person to use that power by internalizing it. *Pwen* can be sung, swallowed, put under the skin, worn around the neck, or performed over a person. Thus, when Ogou sings a point song, at the same time that he is sending a pithy communication to his enemies he is also providing his followers with a talisman to use when they are angry. One of Ogou's point songs begins this way:

1   Ankò m-kay mèt-ye.
2   Bef mouri nan mem mwen.

1   I am still the master of the house.
2   The bull dies by my hand.

This song evokes an image of rural Haiti where the father is both head of the household and head priest, controlling the family's access to the spirits by presiding over their sacrifices. As a point song, it provides a clear and poignant way of reminding those who cross Ogou that he is in charge, while assuring those who serve him that his power will prevail.

THE POWER OF OGOU: AGAINST HIS FOLLOWERS

The anger of Ogou vacillates. It is directed outward toward the enemy, but can quickly turn toward his own people when they fail him. Ogou's discipline is severe. To serve Ogou is to be in an army where control of the self makes possible control of the enemy. Ogou's anger and his attacks on his wayward followers are key elements in the possession-performance of Ogou. When the ceremony is large enough and the space sufficient, rituals for Ogou include a kind of military parade, with flags and swordbearer. After several revolutions around the sacred center pole of the temple, the sword bearer suddenly reverses directions and stages a mock attack on his own retinue. Ogou may even discipline his own *chwal*, "horse," the very person possessed by him. The following is a report of a conversation with a *manbo*, a Vodou priestess who lives in New York, where she has served the spirits for twenty-five years.

> Manbo: When Ogou Feray is really mad, he takes his sword and he (gesture) breaks his own head.
>
> Author: Why do you think he would do something like that?
>
> Manbo: If you do something to make Ogou Feray angry, when he rides you, you suffer. If he is really mad at his *chwal*, when he leaves you have the pain to show for it.

The tendency of Ogou's anger to turn on his own people is captured in another song.

1 Ogou o.
2 Yo di ou ap sonde chwal mwen.
3 Jou me-en kolè m-a vante pwen mwen.
4 Ogou o.
5 Yo di ou ap sonde pwen mwen.
6 Jou m-en kolè enryè pa sa fè mwen.
7 M-di Feray, vre, ou Nago Feray.
8 M-di Feray, ou Nago Feray

1 Ogou oh.
2 They say you are testing my horse.
3 The day I'm angry, I will boast about my point.
4 Ogou oh.
5 They say you are testing my point.
6 The day I'm angry nothing will happen to me.
7 I say Feray, truly, you are Nago Feray.
8 I say Feray, you are Nago Feray.

In Vodou songs, as in biblical psalms, the spirit is sometimes the speaker and sometimes the one spoken to. In this song, there is an intentional ambiguity about who is speaking. Thus the song communicates simultaneously that Ogou tests those who serve him and gives them protection, a *pwen*, in their time of trial.

Taken a step further, and it often is, Ogou's anger ceases to be about anything as rational as discipline. It becomes blind rage, which, lacking access to the real enemy, destroys whatever is at hand. This is the anger of a child throwing a tem-per tantrum. One song sung to Ogou with an unusually gay lilting melody cap-tures both aspects of his rage.

1   Ki ki li ki o-ewa.
2   Papa Ogou tou piti kon sa.
3   Papa Ogou enrarè!

1   Cock a-doodle do.
2   Papa Ogou all little children are like that.
3   Papa Ogou enraged!

The song can be read as a caution to Ogou: "Don't be so angry with your follow-ers; all 'children' are that way." Equally, it can be heard as saying, "Ogou throws a tantrum, just like all children."

The vacillation of Ogou's anger, its tendency to switch targets from his ene-mies to his followers, has historical precedent. This is a facet of his character which is present in the Yoruba tradition,[7] which the slaves no doubt brought to the Island of Hispaniola. It has been amply reinforced by experiences Haitians have had with their own soldiers and politicians. Time and agains the Haitians have experienced their leaders turning on them. They are deeply ambivalent about their own military and political history, and that is why Ogou, who moves between constructive and destructive uses of power, has been a natural vehicle for making their history comprehensible.

Three chapters from Haitian history illustrate this point. Jean-Jacques Dessalines was the first Haitian head of state. He gained a place in history by striking the final blow for Haitian independence in 1804. He restored order and brought the economy out of chaos. He also gave the Haitians their revenge by slaughtering all of the whites who remained after the defeat of the French. But he then warned Haitians who resisted his rule of law that they would "merit the fate of ungrateful people" (Leyburn, 1966:33). Dessalines built a large army and then began a practice, imitated since, of using it for domestic control. The economic order brought by Dessalines was based on forced labor, and, for the great major-ity, liberty came to be indistinguishable from slavery. Dessalines outlawed the use of the whip on plantations, but he said nothing when a local vine was used in its place. Laborers, Dessalines said, could "be controlled only by fear of punishment and even death" (Leyburn 1966:41). In spite of this record, some Haitians argue that Dessalines is the most revered of all Haitian heroes. In his own time there were those who felt otherwise. Dessalines was assassinated near Port-au-Prince in 1806.

A second Haitian leader, Guillaume Sam, took office in 1915. Less than a year after his election, and as a result of his execution of 168 political prisoners, Sam was set on by his own people and torn limb from limb. The United States government used this incident as an excuse to invade the country and to deploy its marines to occupy Haiti for nineteen years.

When the third figure, François (Papa Doc) Duvalier, was elected president in 1957, he called on the U.S. Marines to train his army. Like the others, Duvalier used force in pursuit of power.[8] On the one hand, he enjoyed the support of large sectors of the public. He used Vodou networks as a power base and spoke appreciatively of the folk culture of the Haitian people. His popularity was thus built in part on an appeal to Black pride. On the other hand, he established the *tonton makout*, a civilian militia, which exercised an unrestrained brutality toward those who questioned Duvalier's rule. The arrogance, efficiency, and power of the American marines added one more layer of experience to the imagery of Ogou. The Black pride mixed with brutality of the *tonton makout* added another.

Haitians have summed up this aspect of their historical legacy in the following song to Ogou:

1   Sin Jak pa la.
2   Se chè ki la.

1   Sin Jak is not there.
2   It's a dog who's there.[9]

While a previous song (page 445 above) has told us that it is Ogou who puts the club in our hands to deal with mad dogs, this one suggests that the mad dog could be none other than Ogou himself.

The moral, that power is easily abused and that leaders tend to destroy their own people, is stated most succinctly in the spirit known as Ogou Panama. Ogou Panama takes his name from a story told about Florvil Hippolyte, president of Haiti from 1889 to 1896. There were rumblings of political dissent from Jacmel in the South of Haiti, and Hippolyte, it is said, set out on a punitive journey in which he vowed to wipe out the entire town of Jacmel, leaving only one man and one woman to repopulate the area. As he mounted his horse to leave Port-au-Prince, Hippolyte's fashionable Panama hat fell off. The president's son took this as a bad omen and pleaded with him not to go. Hippolyte persisted. He was not yet out of the capital when he fell unconscious from his horse. Shortly thereafter he died. The falling Panama hat not only provided the Haitians with a jaunty refrain for secular songs of political satire (Courlander 1960:150–52), it also provided within Vodou a succinct and appropriately indirect reminder of the dangers of the misuse of political power. One of the songs for Ogou Panama has this refrain:

1   M-di Panama ye,

2   Papa Ogou se neg Panama ye.

3   O Panama ye,

4   Neg Nago se neg Panama ye.

1   I say Panama,

2   Papa Ogou is a Panama man.

3   Oh Panama,

4   The Nago man is a panama man.

THE POWER OF OGOU: AGAINST HIMSELF

Ogou's anger comes full circle and ultimately is directed against himself. This is the dimension of Ogou's character that reveals itself in the final movement of his ritual sword dance, when he points the weapon at his own body.

Hints of this self-destructive potential are found in Ogou Chango. A brief explanation of the history of this figure is necessary. In Yoruba contexts, Sango is the deity of lightning and thunder. As king, Sango indulged himself in an arrogant display of power, inadvertently calling down lightning on his own palace and killing his wives and children. In despair he hung himself (Pemberton 1977:20). Likewise, in Yoruba mythology Ogun inadvertently killed his own townspeople and, in despair, committed suicide by falling on his sword (Barnes 1980:28). Sango and Ogun, who are quite distinct among the Yoruba, have merged in Haiti.[10] Although Vodou mythology contains no stories about the suicide of Ogou Chango, the "point" of such stories is preserved in his character, as the following song indicates:

1   Kapten Chango, Achade Bokò ye.

2   O Kapten Chango, Achade Bokò ye.

3   Achade li ki ye.
4   Kapten Kenmbe, li pa kon lage-ou
5   Kapten Chango, Achade Bokò ye.

1   Kapten Chango, Achade Bokò is.
2   Oh Kapten Chango, Achade Bokò is.
3   Achade is who he is.
4   Kapten holds you, he won't let you go.
5   Kapten Chango, Achade Bokò is.

This song connects Chango to Achade, an Ogou who appears separately in other contexts. Achade is a *bokò*, a "sorcerer," and this adds yet another facet to the complex mix of powers which are executed by the Ogou. The powers of the sorcerer, like those of the soldier and politician, are assertive, aggressive ones that are appropriately in confrontational situations. The arena of their action is an eminently social one in which people are divided into two camps: friends/enemies, insiders/outsiders. The inclusion of a sorcerer spirit in the pantheon of the Ogou suggests a situation in which power is unevenly distributed, for sorcery is the weapon of the underdog. Haitians are wary of sorcery. While its effectiveness is accepted, it must be carried out with absolutely correct intentions or it will come back and destroy the one who unleased its power. The "work of the left hand" is to be avoided because one can easily become trapped in an escalating debt to the powers it calls upon. Finally the only way to pay that debt is with one's own life. The highly ambiguous line in this song, "Kapten holds you, he won't let you go," may speak of care and comfort on the surface, but its sinister meaning lies just below.

Yamson[11] exhibits another dimension of Ogou's penchant for self-destructiveness. Consider the next song:

1   Ogou Yamson sa kap pase?
2   M-ape mande Papa Ogou ki kote ou ye.
3   Lè nou bezwen ou, Ogou Yamson,
4   Nou pa bezwen ou saka tafya.
5   M-ape mande Papa Ogou ki kote ou ye.
6   Kote gildyev ou-a, saka-tafya?
7   Yo ap mande Papa Ogou ki kote ou ye, Ogou Yamson.
8   Lèyo bezwen ou, Ogou Yamson.
9   Yo pa bezwen ou saka tafya.

1 Ogou Yamson, what's happening?
2 I'm asking Papa Ogou where you are.
3 When we need you, Ogou Yamson,
4 We don't need you guzzling rum.
5 I'm asking Papa Ogou where you are.
6 Where is your rum-making apparatus, drunkard?
7 They are asking Papa Ogou where you are, Ogou Yamson.
8 When they need you, Ogou Yamson.
9 They don't need you guzzling rum.

In this song, self-destruction takes the form of degradation.

The degradation of Agèou Hantò,[12] another of the Ogou, comes not through liquor but through other forms of social disintegration, lying and begging.

1 Agèou, ou, o.
2 Agèou, ou hantò!
3 Agèou, ou neg Dahome.
4 Ou mande charite.
5 Ou fè di-set an,
6 T-ap manje youn sèl epi de mai.

1 Agèou, you, oh,
2 Agèou, you liar!
3 Agèou, you Dahomey man.
4 You beg for alms.
5 You passed seventeen years,
6 Eating only one ear of corn.

The direct point of this song speaks of the shame of hunger and the exaggerated stories beggars sometimes tell to move those capable of acts of charity, but the indirect point speaks of the breakdown of the family as the cause of Agèou's plight. In Haiti beggars are reminders not only of the failure of a particular individual to support himself or herself, but also, and more to the point, of the failure of a family to take care of its own. Many times Haitians giving alms will inquire first about the family situation of the beggar and then express more outrage at the absent or irresponsible relatives than at the immediate manifestations of the beggar's destitute condition. The large number of beggars in Port-au-Prince today is a direct reflection of the fracturing of the sustaining family structure that occurs as more and more people are forced to the cities by the soil erosion, drought, and political corruption that are wasting the Haitian countryside.

A poignant song for Ogou Achade captures at once the isolation of the urban migrant cut off from family support, and, reaching back in history, that of the slave cut off from ancestral roots in Africa.

1   Achade o,
2   M-pa genyen mama isit ki pou pale pou mwen.
3   Achade o, zami move o.
4   m-pa genyen fanmi isit ki pou pale pou mwen.

1   Achade oh,
2   I have no mother here who can speak for me.
3   Achade oh, friends are no good.
4   I have no family here who can speak for me.

The songs of Ogou suggest that power is isolating. While the Ogou are said to marry and have lovers from both the Rada and Petro pantheons, they have no children of their own. This biographical detail adds further to our understanding of their power. Theirs is a solitary, individual power, not the collective power of close-knit groups, not the power of the united family. It is true that the solider is charged with the defense of his people, yet face-to-face with the enemy, he stands alone. Similarly, the politician is isolated in office; the sorcerer works apart and late at night; the city-dweller fends for himself or herself in the world of work; and the immigrant is thrown on his or her own resources. Loneliness is the other side of power.

The loneliness of those who seize Ogou power is thus another form of self-destruction or self-wounding. This kind of chosen isolation causes deep psychic wounds, wounds not easily seen or healed, as is recognized in a song to Sin Jak Majè:

1   Sin Jak o Majè,
2   M-blese, m-pa we san mwen.

1   Sin Jak oh Majè
2   I'm wounded but I don't see my blood.

Broken families, lost pride, loneliness, alcoholism, indigency, anger without a clear object—these are the wounds of the oppressed and the underside of the self-assertiveness of the Ogou. The following song, which speaks collectively of the Ogou as the Nago *nanchon*, makes this point well. It suggests that while railing against one's fate may not bring success and surely will not bring peace, it provides, quite simply, the last line of defense against suffering. Short of God's miraculous intervention, Ogou-like defiance is the most effective response to hardship. Ogou's tendency to keep fighting in the face of overwhelming odds is thus seen as both an endearing trait and a character flaw.

1   Tout nanchon genyen defo pa-yo.

2   Se pa Nago-a kap pase mizè. (Repeat)

3   Mwen di ye, rele l-a ye.

4   Mwen di ye, rele l-a ye.

5   Kote defans sa-yo? Neg Nago genyen.

6   L-a rele Bondye.

1   All peoples have their flaws.

2   The Nagos don't know how to suffer.

3   I say it is, cry out it will be.

4   I say he is, cry out he will be.

5   Where is their defense? The Nago man has it.

6   He will call on God.

OGOU OF THE HAITIAN DIASPORA

Haiti is the poorest country in the Western Hemisphere and one of the poorest in the world. The average annual income has been estimated at $260. When this is adjusted to take into account the considerable wealth of the elite, it appears that most people in Haiti get by on less than $100 a year. Eighty percent of the people are illiterate and unemployment in Port-au-Prince hovers around fifty percent.[13] Political repression, poverty, and the diseases associated with malnutrition, including a high rate of infant mortality, are everyday facts of life. Most wealth is controlled by less than ten percent of the population, and the power of this elite group is highly visible and oppressive. Tourism, an important part of the Haitian economy until tourists stopped coming because of the political and social unrest following Duvalier's departure, reinforced the perceived gap between the haves and have-nots of the world. Haiti's moment of glory lies in the past, when her armies and revolutionary heroes stood up to the French and won their independence.

For many Haitians, hope for the future means leaving Haiti. More than a million people, from a total population of 5.5 million have left the island for the urban centers of North America, principally Montreal, New York, and Miami. Haitians have migrated on and off to the United States since the slave revolution began in 1791, but the present community in greater New York, estimated at 400,000, has been built largely since the late 1950s after François Duvalier came to power. Here the Haitian experience of being on the wrong side of the power balance takes new forms: ghettoization, with all of its attendant problems; racism and degradation at social service agencies; and exploitation on the job market. Those who migrate illegally live in constant fear of being found out and deported. They often work for less than the minimum wage at jobs that are exhausting, and even dangerous. Only a small percentage live with hope for a significantly better future.

Ogou plays a prominent role in the religious life of New York's Haitians. At a small ceremony in Crown Heights, Brooklyn in 1975, some twenty people crowded into the tiny room of a priestess who was carrying out a "headwashing" ritual. The young woman for whom the ceremony was being performed could not find a job and she was plagued by severe and frequent headaches. Her problem was diagnosed as spiritual. She needed to "baptize Ogou in her head" and the headwashing was the first step. When Ogou came to the woman, she had trouble stabilizing the possession. Young and inexperienced devotees sometimes have difficulty making the transition into a trance state. The struggle of this woman was violent and prolonged. When Ogou was finally and firmly in control, a live rooster was brought in. The spirit himself is expected to sacrifice the animal offered to him, but this small and flustered horse of Ogu could not wring its neck. Ogou's anger emerged and, uncharacteristically, it mixed with tears. In this state, Ogou's horse bit through the neck of the chicken.

This was not the only time I have seen Ogou cry in New York. At a much larger and more elaborate ceremony in 1980, Ogou possessed another woman —a strong, no-nonsense person for whom tears in any context would be uncharacteristic. During the course of the possession-performance, the Ogou, in this case Agèeou Hantò, spoke with a woman who had lost her oldest child a few months before. The ten-year-old boy was sent back to Haiti to live with family and he died there after being beaten for misconduct. The tears rolled down Agèou's face and the faces of many who listened as he said "You know if I could have helped him, I would have helped him."

The tearful despair of these New York Ogou is a facet of the spirit's character that is difficult to imagine being acted out in Haiti. Perhaps a new dimension of the Haitian Ogou is emerging in the North American setting. Will he one day strut and attack, wave his sword about threatening those near him, turn the point of the weapon against himself, pose defiantly, and then collapse in tears? At the end of the temper tantrum is the exhausted, teary child. It could be said that the majority of Haitian people have always been oppressed, but only in the exile communities do they experience being a minority people on the wrong side of a gross power imbalance. This situation may be bringing out something new in Ogou. Tears could never replace Ogou's aggression, but it may be that immigrant life in New York has revealed another dimension of his anger.

Ogou's way of being-in-the-world provides a cognitive map for Haitians who take up the challenges of contemporary life, whether in Haiti or in New York. As we have seen, Ogou delineates both the possibilities and the potential hazards of doing battle in the modern urban world. This much the Haitian Ogou shares with his contemporary Nigerian counterpart. However, the Haitian Ogou has not taken up the challenge of interpreting modern technology, as he has in Nigeria. To the extent that this latter role has developed at all in Haiti, a country that has experienced much less of modern technology than Nigeria, it has accrued to a different group of spirits, the Gède.

OGOU AND GÈDE

The only other group of spirits that functions in the ritual process as the Ogou do, that is, as mediators between the Rada and Petro pantheons, is the Gède. A Gède possession occurring between the Rada and Petro segments of a ceremony makes a transition possible between these two otherwise antithetical modes. To the extent that ritual process mirrors life process, the Gède and the Ogou can be seen to represent the two major options that the Vodou system provides for handling situations of transition or change.[14]

The Haitian Gède is quite similar to the Dahomean trickster figure Legba and, in some of his aspects, to the Yoruba trickster Eshu (Elegbara), Legba has survived in Haiti but as a venerable old man who has sloughed off his sexuality and, along with it, his tricksterism. For a people so brutally cut off from their ancestral roots, tricksterism may have been unbearable in the spirit responsible for communication between humans and their protective spirits. Legba's tricksterism and his sexuality appear to have been taken on by the Gède. Gède is simultaneously the spirit of the dead, protector of small children, guardian of human sexuality, and irrepressible social satirist. The Gède are licensed to beg, to steal, to tell dirty jokes, and to engage in various other forms of antisocial behavior.

The Gède appear to be the most open and growing group of spirits. Spongelike, they soak up new roles that appear on the social horizon, many of them having to do with newly introduced professions and technologies. Among the Gède are an automobile mechanic, a dentist, a doctor, and a Protestant missionary. The Gède, the Haitians say, are not a *nanchon* but a *fanmi*, "family." The significance of this will emerge shortly.

As mediators between the opposing forces of Rada and Petro, family members and foreigners, the Ogou and the Gède represent two options for survival in the modern world—a world in which the interaction between insiders and outsiders is increasingly intense, dangerous, and complex. We have seen the option represented by the Ogou. They wage war in the modern world; they face challenges head-on. The devotee of Ogou leaves a starving family to make a living in the city, and ideally to send money home. The Ogou devotee leaves Haiti for New York to do battle with the welfare system and the business world. It is Ogou power that enables the individual to face the isolation inevitably involved in making these moves. It is the distilled wisdom of Ogou's complex personality that keeps an individual from going mad when faced, for example, with the wrenching choice of making progress in the new life or sending money to the family back in Haiti.

The Gède are quite different. Their mediating power comes from a different way of being-in-the-world. The Gède triumph over suffering through humor. Thus a raucous Gède laugh can emerge from a devotee who only an instant before was possessed by a somber, awesome Rada *lwa*. The same quick transition between moods occurs in the marketplace, in the home, and on the job. A tense situation is instantly flipped on its back by a sudden laugh, a quick joke, or a bit of clowning. This is not the confrontational power of Ogou; this is the power of redefinition. And, it always depends on the cooperation of the group.

The Gède are *fanmi*, "family," *par excellence*. As spirits of death and sexuality, they connect Haitians to their macro-family extending backward through time to the ancestors and forward in time to descendants yet unborn. They are the spirits to whom one can bring the smallest of life's problems. They are gossips who process neighborhood events and invoke in-group norms. Their powers are distilled homely wisdom and satiric humor that dissipate fear and level pretense.

Here lies the complementary centrality of Ogou and Gède. Life presents many problems, not the least of which are oppression, deprivation, and isolation. The social cul-de-sac represented by situations of extreme oppression does not necessarily lead to surrender. There are two possible human responses: rage or humor, Ogou power or Gède power.

SUMMARY AND CONCLUSION

For slaves in the New World, social conflict pushed issues that were traditionally emphasized in African religious systems into the background. The powers of nature paled in relation to the powers that some human beings exercised over others. The religious heritage of the African homeland shifted and blended in response to a need for emphasis on social problems. In Haiti Ogou emerged as central and important because he was effective in this perilous social negotiation.

Ogou's importance in urban Haitian Vodou is clearly demonstrated in his mediating role between the Rada and Petro pantheons. His position as a mediator is reinforced when we compare the Ogou to the parallel, but contrasting, Gède. The opposition between Rada and Petro is seen as an opposition between different ways of being-in-the-world. Familial modes of action appropriate to in-group situations are opposed to the partisan and coercive ways of the foreigner or outsider. Orgou's personality and his mode of action, imagery, song, and possession-performance provide a model for negotiating between these otherwise irreconcilable ways of being.

In Haiti, Ogou's central theme is power. Ogou the revolutionary hero frees his people and puts weapons in their hands for self-protection. He intervenes on their behalf before the civil authorities. He gathers his followers to him like precious lost objects. But he also exacts strict discipline and punishes those who tire or waver. Sometimes his anger turns to blind rage, irrationally attacking those close to him or even himself. His penchant for self-destruction is acted out in sorcery, alcoholism, and indigency. Ogou thus articulates the possibilities and the dangers of power as it is found in contemporary life. He shows the way to self-assertion and self-respect necessary for success in the modern world. Yet each of his manifestations keeps the negative side of claiming power clearly in view.

Ogou in Haiti provides an accurate description of the social conditions of an oppressed people. In psychological terms, he presents an almost clinical diagnosis of what happens when people internalize anger. However, it would be naive to assume that the Vodou spirits simply mirror the Haitian people. All religions have a moral dimension that makes the transformation of human lives possible (Brown 1987). The transformative potential of Haitian Vodou does not reside in the capacity of the spirits to model morally appropriate behavior, but rather in their capacity to keep the full range of possibilities latent in any way of being-in-the-world before the eyes of the believers. The assumption is that people will choose a right way to behave (there may be many right ways) in a given situation when they have sufficient insight into that situation. Haitian military history yields rich moral lessons when filtered through Ogou. The metaphoric extension of military power to civil power, and beyond to all situations of willfulness and assertion, allows Ogou to give guidance in many troublesome areas of life.

Just as Ogou has interpreted the history and social structure of the Haitian people, so have those realities shaped him. The hunting and iron-smithing connections of the Old World Ogun have not survived in Haiti, because these occupations are no longer central to Haitian life.[15] Neither has the Haitian Ogou taken up the challenge of dealing with modern technology. The central conflict in Haitian life is social conflict. The defining imagery of the Haitian Ogou is military imagery. The Haitian Ogou's anger, alternately turning outward toward the enemy and inward toward his own people and even himself, has parallels in the African Ogun. However, these Ogou traits have been reshaped through interaction with Haitian history. Ogou therefore has new personae (Ogou Panama) and new dimensions of character (in New York, Ogou cries).

Any attempt to account for the changes that African religious systems underwent in the New World must be sensitive to the complex interactions between memory and the material conditions of life in that new place. Through the Middle Passage, into the life of slavery and on into the life of minority peoples, African culture searched for niches in the New World order. Some aspects of African culture found these niches; others did not and were forgotten; those that did were changed in the process. The point is to see these remembering and forgettings, as well as the apparently new creations, as systematic. African religions did not survive in happenstance fragments in the New World. They blended, shifted, and took on new forms in response to new social conditions, and they continue to do so today.

NOTES

1. Haitians refer to the Vodou *lwa* (a Fon word) as *sin yo*, "the saints," and as *espri yo*, "the spirits," but never as gods or divinities. God, Bondye, is the one and only god and the *lwa* are his servants or messengers. I respect this distinction and follow their language in this paper.

2. Every Vodou initiate has a *mèt tet*, "master of the head." This is the Vodou spirit with whom that person is most closely related. To some extent, there is a mirroring between the personality of the spirit and that of the devotee.

3. "Niche" is the term Bastide uses to describe those parts of the New World social structure that were receptive to African cultural interpretations.

4. This particular formulation of the contrast between the Rada and Petro pantheons is my own. See my Ph.D. dissertation (1976:80–112) for a more detailed analysis of this point. Such precise and abstract language is not characteristic of the way Vodou is discussed among Haitians.

5. The earliest reference to this theory of the origin of the Petro name occurs in Lous Elie Moreau de Saint-Méry 1797–98: v.1, pp. 210–11. Moreau de Saint-Méry is questioned on this point, however, by Alfred Métraux (1972:38–39).

6. Maya Deren believes that the origins of Petro worship are found in "rage against the evil fate which the African suffered . . . to protest against it" (1970:62).

7. "There are stories of Ogun's intoxication with the taste of blood in battle. Such is his thirst that on occasion he kills his own followers as well as the enemy." See Pemberton 1977:17.

   It is interesting that Pemberton, who uses the structural method of analysis in this article, also found Ogun to be a mediating figure between two major groups of Yoruba deities. He describes the opposition between these two groups as that between life and death, or culture and nature.

8. "The readiness of Duvalieristes to use force probably exceeds that of any Haitian government in more than a century." Sidney W. Mintz, "Introduction to the Second Edition" of Leyburn 1966: xvi.

9. Dogs are not sacrificed in urban Haitian Vodou, but the dog is a traditional sacrifice among the Yoruba for Ogun. See Barnes 1980:39 and Pemberton 1977. Pemberton quotes an *oriki*, "praise name," for Sango which states: "The dog stays in the house of its master/but it does not know his intentions" (pp. 19–20).

10. The appropriateness of a union between Ogun and Sango is instinctively understood by the contemporary Yoruba poet Wole Soyinka. Their coming together, he says, would be "the ideal fusion . . . to preserve the original uniqueness and yet absorb another essence" (1967:86).

11. The name of the spirit Ogou Yamson is possibly derived from that of Oya Yansan, who among the Yoruba was a consort of both Ogun and Sango. However, the Vodou Ogou Yamson is male; there are no female Ogou in Haiti.

12. Agèou Hantò is an Ogou whose relationship to a Cuban spirit is instructive. In Cuban Santeria, Agaju is associated with the fire of dormant volcanoes. This fire connection provides one link to the Haitian Ogou. Another can be seen in the relation between the drought imagery in the song for Agèou Hantò (seventeen years and only one ear of corn to eat) and the barren and blighted landscape around volcanoes. Such a correspondence between Cuban and Haitian imagery could suggest an original African source for this spirit's connection to dry, uninhabitable terrain. Another name for the Cuban Agaju is Agaju Solo, the solitary one. In keeping with the strong social emphasis of Haitian Vodou, the image of natural desolation and solitude has been replaced with a social one. Agèou's solitary state arises from social ostracism; he is a beggar. Personal communication, Judith Gleason.

13. Such figures from Haiti are not precise since there are no accurate census data. However, most people who know the country would agree about the general accuracy of these figures taken from an article by Gilbert Lewthwaite in *The Baltimore Sun*, November 1981.

14. The link between Ogou and Gède is expressed in many places in the Vodou system. One such place is the initiation ritual. Each person is initiated "on the point" of their *mèt tet*, their major or controlling spirit. This means, among other things, that initiates literally lie down on the emblem of that spirit. When a person's *mèt tet* is a Gède, special measures have to be taken because the death and sexuality connections of the Gède forbid their presence in the initiation chamber. In those cases, it is Ogou who stands in for Gède.

Furthermore, in the chromolithograph of Santiago that is used for Sin Jak Majè, the knight behind Santiago is commonly understood to be Gède. His full armor, including helmet and visor, is said to make him resemble a skeleton.

15. While it is true that the iron-smithing connections largely have been lost to Ogou in Haiti, they survive in details of Ogou symbolism such as the name of Ogou Feray (*feraille*), "scrap iron," and the Nago shrine that is maintained at most urban Vodou temples. This shrine is a simple clearing on the earth near the temple entrance where bonfires are lit for Ogou. The fire is built around an iron rod thrust into the earth. Métraux notes that this rod is called Ogou's forge (1972:109).

REFERENCES CITED

Barnes, Sandra T. 1980. *Ogun: An Old God for a New Age*, Philadelphia: ISHI.

Bastide, Roger. 1978. *The African Religions of Brazil: Toward a Sociology of the Interpenetration of Civilizations*, Baltimore: The Johns Hopkins University Press.

Brown, Karen McCarthy. 1976. "The *Vèvè* of Haitian Vodou: A Structural Analysis of Visual Imagery," Ph.D. dissertation, Temple University.

————. 1987. "Alourdes: A Case Study of Moral Leadership in Haitian Vodou," in *Saints and Virtues*, John S. Hawley (ed.), Berkeley: University of California Press.

Courlander, Harold. 1960. *The Drum and the Hoe: Life and Lore of the Haitian People*, Berkeley: University of California Press.

Deren, Maya. 1970. *Divine Horsemen: The Voodoo Gods of Haiti*, New York: Delta.

Leyburn, James G. 1966. *The Haitian People*, with an introduction by Sidney W. Mintz, New Haven: Yale University Press.

Métraux, Alfred. 1972. *Voodoo in Haiti*, New York: Schocken.

Moreau de Saint-Méry, Louie Elie. 1797–98. *Déscription topographique, physique, civile, politique et historique de la partie française de l'isle de Saint-Dominique*, 2 vols., Philadelphia.

Pemberton, John III. 1977. "A Cluster of Sacred Symbols: Orisa Worship Among the Igbomina Yoruba of Ila-Orangun," *History of Religions*, vol. 17, no. 1, pp. 1–28.

Soyinka, Wole. 1967. *Indanre and Other Poems*, London: Methuen.

Thompson, Robert Farris. 1983. *Flash of the Spirit: African and Afro-American Art and Philosophy*, New York: Random House.

SELECTED BIBLIOGRAPHY FOR FURTHER READING

Barnes, Sandra T., ed. *Africa's Ogun: Old World and New*. Bloomington: Indiana University Press, 1989.

Brandon, George. *Santeria from Africa to the New World: The Dead Sell Memories*. Bloomington: Indiana University Press, 1993.

Brown, Karen. *Mama Lola: A Vodou Priestess in Brooklyn*. Berkeley: University of California Press, 1991.

Murphy, Joseph. *Santeria: African Spirits in America*. Boston: Beacon Press, 1992.

Simpson, George E. *Black Religions in the New World*. New York: Columbia University Press, 1978.

PERMISSIONS::

Permission to reprint selections from the following sources is gratefully acknowledged:

1. David W. Wills: From *Religion and Intellectual Life* 5 (1987): 30–41.

2. Charles H. Long: From *History of Religion* 11 (1971): 54–66.

3. Sidney W. Mintz and Richard Price: From *The Birth of African-American Culture: An Anthropological Perspective* (Boston: Beacon Press, 1992), 7–22, 81–84.

4. Lawrence W. Levine: From *Anonymous Americans: Explorations in Nineteenth-Century Social History,* ed. Tamara K. Hareven (Englewood Cliffs, NJ: Prentice-Hall, 1971), 99–130.

5. Albert J. Raboteau: From *The Evangelical Tradition in America,* ed. Leonard I. Sweet (Macon, GA: Mercer University Press, 1984), 181–97.

6. Vincent Harding: From *The Making of Black America,* ed. August Meier and Elliot Rudwick, vol. 1 (New York: Athenaeum, 1969), 179–97.

7. Will B. Gravely: From *The Journal of Religious Thought* 41 (1984): 58–73.

8. Carol V. R. George: From *Antislavery Reconsidered: New Perspectives on the Abolitionists*, eds. Lewis Perry and Michael Fellman (Baton Rouge: Louisiana State University Press, 1979), 75–95.

9. William H. Becker: From *Journal of the American Academy of Religion* 40 (1972): 316–33.

10. Evelyn Brooks Higginbotham: From *Righteous Discontent: The Black Women's Movement in the Black Baptist Church, 1880–1920* (Cambridge, Mass.: Harvard University Press, 1993), 1–18.

11. Timothy E. Fulop: From *Harvard Theological Review* 84 (1991): 75–99.

12. Hans A. Baer and Merrill Singer: From *Anthropological Quarterly* 54 (1981): 1–14.

13. C. Eric Lincoln: From *The Muslim Community in North America*, eds. E.H. Waugh, B. Abu-Laban and R. Qureshi (Edmonton: University of Alberta Press, 1983), 215–33.

14. Iain MacRobert: From *Pentecost, Mission and Ecumenism: Essays on Intercultural Theology*, ed. Jan A.B. Jongeneel (New York: Peter Lang, 1992), 73–84.

15. Randall K. Burkett: From *African-American Christianity: Essays in History,*

ed. Paul E. Johnson (Berkeley: University of California Press, 1994), 134–58.

16. Clayborne Carson: From *African-American Christianity: Essays in History*, ed. Paul E. Johnson (Berkeley: University of California Press, 1994), 159–77.

17. Cheryl Townsend Gilkes: From *Journal of Feminist Studies in Religion* 2 (1986): 41–59.

18. Michael W. Harris: From *We'll Understand It Better By and By: Pioneering African American Gospel Composers,* ed. Bernice Johnson Reagon (Washington DC: Smithsonian Institution Press, 1992), 165–82.

19. Bruce Jackson: From *American Folk Medicine: A Symposium,* ed. Wayland D. Hand (Berkeley: University of California Press, 1976), 259–72.

20. Karen McCarthy Brown: From *Africa's Ogun: Old World and New*, ed. Sandra Barnes (Bloomington: Indiana University Press, 1989), 65–89.

HANS A. BAER is Professor of Anthropology at the University of Arkansas in Little Rock. He is the author of *The Black Spiritual Movement: A Religious Response to Racism* (1984), and co-author with Merrill Singer of *African-American Religion in the Twentieth Century: Varieties of Protest and Accommodation* (1992).

WILLIAM H. BECKER is Professor of Religion at Bucknell University, and has published several articles in the fields of African-American religion and theology.

KAREN MCCARTHY BROWN is Professor of the Sociology and Anthropology of Religion in the Graduate and Theological Schools of Drew University. She is the author of *Mama Lola: A Vodou Priestess in Brooklyn* (1991).

RANDALL K. BURKETT is Associate Director of the W. E. B. Du Bois Institute for Afro-American Research at Harvard University, is the author of *Garveyism as a Religious Movement* (1978), the editor of *Black Redemption: Churchmen Speak for the Garvey Movement* (1978), and has also co-edited, with Nancy H. Burkett and Henry Louis Gates, Jr., *Black Biography, 1790–1950: A Cumulative Index* (1991) and *Black Biographical Dictionaries, 1790–1950* (1991).

CLAYBORNE CARSON is Professor of History at Stanford University, and Editor and Director of the Martin Luther King, Jr. Papers Project. He is the author of *In Struggle: SNCC and the Black Awakening of the 1960s* (1981).

TIMOTHY E. FULOP is Assistant Dean of Faculty and Lecturer in the History of Christianity at Columbia Theological Seminary in Decatur, Georgia. He has published articles in African-American religious history, Reformation studies, and American evangelicalism, and is currently at work on a study of popular religion and primitivism in early national New England.

CAROL V. R. GEORGE is Professor of History at Hobart and William Smith Colleges in Geneva, New York. She is the author of *Segregated Sabbaths: Richard Allen and the Rise of Independent Black Churches, 1760–1840* (1973) and *God's Salesman: Norman Vincent Peale and the Power of Positive Thinking* (1993).

CHERYL TOWNSEND GILKES is Associate Professor of African-American Studies and Sociology at Colby College and an ordained Baptist minister. Her articles on religion and African-American women have appeared in numerous anthologies and scholarly journals.

WILL B. GRAVELY is Professor of Religious Studies at the University of Denver. He is the author of *Gilbert Haven, Methodist Abolitionist* (1973) and of many journal articles examining African-American religion, abolitionism, and Methodism. Professor Gravely is completing an interpretive study of the 1947 lynching of Willie Earle, the last lynching in South Carolina.

VINCENT HARDING is Professor of Religion and Social Transformation at the Iliff School of Theology in Denver and the author of numerous works, including *There is a River* (1981) and *Hope and History* (1990). Professor Harding was the first director of the Martin Luther King, Jr., Memorial Center, a founder of the Institute of the Black World, and senior academic advisor to the prize-winning PBS series "Eyes on the Prize."

MICHAEL W. HARRIS is Associate Professor of History and African American World Studies at the University of Iowa. He is the author of *The Rise of Gospel Blues: The Music of Thomas Andrew Dorsey in the Urban Church* (1992).

EVELYN BROOKS HIGGINBOTHAM is Professor of Afro-American Studies and African American Religious History at Harvard University. She is the author of *Righteous Discontent: The Women's Movement in the Black Baptist Church, 1880–1920* (1993) and numerous essays on race, history, and feminist theory.

BRUCE JACKSON is Distinguished Professor of English at the State University of New York at Buffalo. He has written numerous books on American folklore, including *"Wake up Dead Man": Afro-American Worksongs of Texas Prisons* (1972), *Fieldwork* (1987), and *Disorderly Conduct* (1992).

LAWRENCE W. LEVINE is Professor of History at the University of California, Berkeley. He is the author of *Defender of the Faith: William Jennings Bryan: The Last Decade, 1915–1925* (1965) and *Highbrow-Lowbrow: The Emergence of Cultural Hierarchy in America* (1990).

C. ERIC LINCOLN is Professor of Religion and Culture at Duke University, and author of numerous books, including *The Black Muslims in America* (1961), *The Black Church Since Frazier* (1974) and *Race, Religion and the Continuing American Dilemma* (1984). He is the editor of the C. Eric Lincoln Series in Black Religion, and co-editor, with Lawrence H. Mamiya, of *The Black Church in the African American Experience* (1990).

CHARLES H. LONG is Professor of Religion and Director of the Center for Black Studies at the University of California, Santa Barbara. He is the author of numerous works on the history of religions, including *Alpha: The Myths of Creation* (1963) and *Significations: Signs, Symbols, and Images in the Interpretation of Religion* (1986).

IAIN MACROBERT is Principal Lecturer at Sandwell College in England. He is the author of *The Black Roots and White Racism of Early Pentecostalism in the USA* (1988) and a contributor to *Religion, State and Society in Modern Britain* (1990).

SIDNEY W. MINTZ is the William L. Straus, Jr., Professor of Anthropology at the Johns Hopkins University. He is the author of *Worker in the Cane: A Puerto Rican Life History* (1974), *Caribbean Transformations* (1974), and *Sweetness and Power: The Place of Sugar in Modern History* (1986).

RICHARD PRICE has taught at Yale, Johns Hopkins, Stanford, and Princeton Universities and now lives in Martinique, where he continues his study of Afro-Caribbean historical consciousness. His books include *First-Time: The Historical Vision of an Afro-American People* (1983), and *Alabi's World* (1990).

ALBERT J. RABOTEAU is the Henry W. Putnam Professor of Religion at Princeton University. He is the author of *Slave Religion: The "Invisible Institution" in the Antebellum South* (1978) and *Fire in the Bones* (1995). With David W. Wills, he is co-director of "Afro-American Religion: A Documentary History Project," which will produce a multi-volume collection of primary sources.

MERRILL SINGER is the Research Director of the Hispanic Health Council in Hartford, Connecticut. He has written about the Black Hebrews of Israel, and has numerous publications in the fields of medical anthropology, and the anthropology and sociology of African American and Hispanic religions. He co-authored, with Hans A. Baer, *African-American Religion in the Twentieth Century: Varieties of Protest and Accommodation* (1992).

DAVID W. WILLS is Professor of Religion at Amherst College. He has edited, with Richard Newman, *Black Apostles at Home and Abroad: Afro-Americans and the Christian Mission from the Revolution to Reconstruction* (1982) and published several articles on African American religious history. With Albert J. Raboteau, he is co-director of "Afro-American Religion: A Documentary History Project," which will produce a multi-volume collection of primary sources.